NAVIGATING SYSTEM 7
Understanding the Macintosh Operating System

JAN L. HARRINGTON

MIS: PRESS

A Subsidiary of
Henry Holt and Co., Inc.

Copyright ©1994 MIS:Press

All rights reserved. Reproduction or use of editorial or pictorial content in any manner is prohibited without express permission. No patent liability is assumed with respect to the use of the information contained herein. While every precaution has been taken in the preparation of this book, the publisher assumes no responsibility for errors or omissions. Neither is any liability assumed for damages resulting from the use of the information contained herein.

Throughout this book, trademarked names are used. Rather than put a trademark symbol after every occurrence of a trademarked name, we used the names in an editorial fashion only, and to the benefit of the trademark owner, with no intention of infringement of the trademark. Where such designations appear in this book, they have been printed with initial caps.

First Edition—1994

ISBN 1-55828-305-6

Printed in the United States of America.

10 9 8 7 6 5 4 3 2 1

MIS:Press books are available at special discounts for bulk purchases for sales promotions, premiums, fund-raising, or educational use. Special editions or book excerpts can also be created to specification.

For details contact: Special Sales Director
MIS:Press
a subsidiary of Henry Holt and Company, Inc.
115 West 18th Street
New York, New York 10011

CONTENTS

PREFACE XI

What You Need to Know Before You Begin xii
The Disk xii
Acknowledgments xiii

CHAPTER 1: OPERATING SYSTEM BASICS 1

A Brief History of Operating Systems 2
Modern Microcomputer Operating Systems 3
    Managing the User Interface 4
    Managing Memory 5
    Managing Processes 6
    Managing External Storage 7
    Managing I/O 7
    System Administration 8

CHAPTER 2: A TOUR AROUND THE OPERATING SYSTEM 11

What You Need to Run System 7 11
System 7's Versions 12
    The Hardware Updates 13
    System 7 Pro 14
Inside the ROM 14
At First Look at System Startup 15
Required System Files and Folders 16
Optional System Files and Folders 18
    Opening Control Panels 23

Installation Hints: The "Clean" Install 26
The System 7 Finder 29
Making the Interface Easier to Use: Easy Access 32
Making the Interface Easier to See: CloseView 33
Getting Help 35
Making the Interface Easier for Novices: At Ease 37

CHAPTER 3: CONFIGURING YOUR SYSTEM 41

The General Controls 42
    Setting and Displaying the Date and Time 42
    The Alarm Clock 44
    Choosing a Blinking Rate 46
    Changing the Desktop Pattern 46
Setting Date and Time Formats 48
Monitors 51
The Startup Screen 52
Sound 53
Keyboard 55
Mouse 55
Numbers 56
Color 57
The Scrapbook 57
The Chooser and Printer Device Drivers 58
The Map 60
Screen Shots 62
Customizing Your Macintosh with QuicKeys 63
Securing Your Macintosh 66
    Securing the Macintosh Against Unauthorized Access 66
    Virus Protection 72
Protecting Your Screen 74

CHAPTER 4: DISKS, FOLDERS, AND FILES 77

The User's View 77
    Volumes and Disk Partitioning 79
    Unmounting Versus Ejecting Volumes 80
    Choosing the Startup Volume 81

File Organization and File Systems	82
Looking at Disk Contents	84
Getting File and Folder Info	90
Notes on Copying, Moving, and Deleting Files and Folders	92
Notes on Renaming Disks, Files, and Folders	94
Managing Disk Contents with Labels and Aliases	96
Locating Files and Folders	100
Changing Icons	102
The Operating System's View	105
Disk Formatting	105
Logical Disk Organization	107
The Desktop File	112
Disk Fragmentation	114
Making Invisible Files Visible	115
Disk and File Compression	117
File Compression	117
Disk Compression	119
Disk Backup	120

CHAPTER 5: APPLICATIONS AND PROCESS MANAGEMENT ... 123

Understanding Multitasking	123
Preemptive Multitasking	124
Cooperative Multitasking	126
Launching Applications	127
Opening and Saving Documents	130
Switching Applications	133
Background Printing	134
How Background Printing Works	134
Turning on Background Printing	135
Managing the Print Queue	136
PrintMonitor Memory Problems	139
Process Problems: Crashes and Hangs	140
Crashes and the 68040 Caches	143

CHAPTER 6: MEMORY ... 145

Introducing Macintosh Memory	145

Measuring Memory 146
  The Relationship between Memory and the System Bus 148
  Memory Allocation 150
Operating System Memory Management Schemes 156
  Memory Fragmentation 157
Managing Memory Use 158
  Viewing Memory Use 159
  Setting Application Memory Size 159
  The Memory Control Panel 162
  Working with 32-Bit Addressing 162
Virtual Memory 164
  How Virtual Memory Works 164
  The Pros and Cons of Virtual Memory 166
  Virtual Memory and Specific Macintosh Models 166
  Using Virtual Memory 167
The Disk Cache 168
  How a Disk Cache Works 168
  Disk Cache Size 169
  Using the System 7 Disk Cache 169
RAM Disks 170
  Using the System 7 RAM Disk 171
  RAM Disks for Macintoshes that Don't Support
    the System 7 RAM Disk 172

CHAPTER 7: FONTS 175

Typographic Terminology 175
Types of Macintosh Fonts 176
  Bitmapped Fonts 176
  PostScript Fonts 178
  TrueType Fonts 183
Obtaining Fonts 185
Installing and Removing Fonts 186
  Installing Bitmapped and TrueType fonts 186
  Installing PostScript Printer Fonts 186
  Removing Fonts Under System 7.0 187
  Removing Fonts Under System 7.1 188
Creating Font Suitcases 188

Organizing Fonts with Suitcase 189
Cleaning up the Font Menu 191

CHAPTER 8: INIT MANAGEMENT 195

Types of Add-On Programs 195
    System Extensions 196
    Control Panels 196
    Desk Accessories 197
    FKEYs 198
INITs: To Use or Not To Use? 198
Loading INITs 199
INIT Conflicts 200
    Using Extensions Manager 202
    Commercial INIT Managers 205
Choosing INITs 208

CHAPTER 9: PUBLISH AND SUBSCRIBE 211

How Publish and Subscribe Works 211
Publishing Parts of a Document 212
Subscribing to Published Editions 214
    Handling Subscriber/Edition Links 216
Handling Edition Containers 217

CHAPTER 10: NETWORKS AND FILE SHARING 219

Macintosh-Friendly Networks 219
    Hardware versus Software 220
    AppleTalk Network Configuration 220
    Ethernet Network Configurations 222
    Connecting Networks: Zones 224
System 7 Networking Capabilities 226
Preparing a Macintosh for File Sharing 227
    Naming the Macintosh 227
    Turning on File Sharing 228
    Creating Users and User Groups 229
    Setting Volume Permissions 232

Accessing Remote Volumes 233
    Mounting Remote Volumes 234
    Unmounting Remote Volumes 237
Program Linking 237
    Turning on Program Linking 238
    Enabling Linking for an Application 238
    Enabling Users to Link 239
Stopping File Sharing 239
Stopping Program Linking 241
Seeing Who's Connected 241
Logging onto an AppleShare Server 242
Exchanging and Sharing Files with MS DOS PCs 244
    What You Can Share 244
    Working with MS DOS Floppy disks 245
    Translating MS DOS Files 251

CHAPTER 11: SYSTEM 7 PRO: INSTALLATION, QUICKTIME, AND APPLESCRIPT 253

System 7 Pro Installation 254
QuickTime 255
AppleScript 255
    What Gets Installed 256
    Apple Events 256
    Determining Which Applications Support Apple Events 258
    Recording Scripts 258
    Saving a Script 260
    Running a Script 261
    Writing Scripts 262

CHAPTER 12: SYSTEM 7 PRO: POWERTALK SETUP AND CONFIGURATION 267

What Gets Installed 267
Setting Up PowerTalk 269
    Before You Begin 270
    Beginning PowerTalk Setup 270
    Finishing Setup for a PowerShare Server 271
    Finishing Setup for a Peer-to-Peer Environment 274
Controlling PowerTalk Access 275

Unlocking the PowerTalk Key Chain 277
Locking the PowerTalk Key Chain 277
Changing Your PowerTalk Access Code 278
PowerTalk Services 278
Adding Other Services 280
Removing Services 281
Working with Information Cards and Catalogs 282
Catalogs and PowerTalk Addresses 282
Creating User Information Cards 284
Creating Group Information Cards 292
Creating and Using Personal Catalogs 293
Using an AppleTalk Catalog 295
PowerShare Catalog Notes 296
Searching Catalogs 296

CHAPTER 13: SYSTEM 7 PRO: SENDING AND RECEIVING MESSAGES WITH POWERTALK 299

Sending Items: Finder Objects 299
Sending Items: Letters and the Apple Mailer 300
Introducing the Mailer 301
Changing the Sender 302
Choosing Recipients 303
Entering a Subject 307
Adding Enclosures 307
Sending the Letter 308
Saving and Using Letterheads 309
AppleMail Print Options 312
The Mailer and Application Programs 313
Using the Mailbox 314
Working with the Out Tray 317
Working with the In Tray 318
Using Tags to Filter Mail 319
Assigning Tags 320
Removing Tags 321
Filtering Mail with Tags 321
Maintaining the Tag List 322
The Mailer and Incoming Mail 322
Replying to Mail 323

    Forwarding Mail 324
Using PowerTalk Off-line 325
Setting Up for Guest Users 326
Customizing PowerTalk with PowerRules 327
Document Security 331
    PowerTalk Encryption 332
    Signing a Message 334
    Validating a Received Message 336
    Getting an Approved Signer 338
    Maintaining an Approved Signer 343

APPENDIX A: PRODUCT LIST 347

GLOSSARY 353

INDEX 365

PREFACE

No—wait—stop—don't put this book down! It isn't just another System 7 book! Sure, it will tell you how to do all sorts of useful and neat things with the Macintosh operating system, and it's full of loads of nifty tricks and tips. But it will also tell you about how operating systems work and what things you should expect an operating system to do. You'll learn about things like virtual memory, caching, networking, and multitasking. If you don't understand what any of these terms mean, don't worry; when you finish reading this book, you will. And you'll know how each of those features work, what impact they have on your system's performance, and how to decide whether they're appropriate for you.

In addition, this book looks at some of the problems and limitations of System 7 and how to solve them. You'll be introduced to some utility programs that can smooth out System 7 use. You'll also become familiar with a variety of add-on programs that fill in the gaps in System 7's capabilities. These programs are discussed throughout the book at points where their functions are most needed. However, you will also find an entire chapter that looks at the issue of INITs (programs that load into memory when you start your computer): how to choose them and how to manage conflicts between them.

Chapters 1 through 10 of this book are based on System 7.1. If you haven't installed the 7.1 upgrade, then you may find that some of your files are in different locations from those described in this book. (This is particularly true for fonts.) In most other instances, the book applies to both 7.0 and 7.1.

Chapters 11 through 13 look at System 7 Pro, a new release of System 7 that adds significant new functions to the operating system, including support for AppleScript (a scripting system for customizing and automating the way you interact with your Macintosh) and PowerTalk (the first portion of a group of Apple software that provides collaboration services, in this instance bringing electronic mail to the Macintosh Desktop).

What You Need to Know Before You Begin

This book is for people who are currently working with System 7 and for people who are getting ready to upgrade from System 6. It assumes that you have some basic familiarity with your Macintosh. You should be able to identify major hardware components (for example, CPU, RAM, monitor, disk drive).

You should also have been exposed to the Macintosh operating system, although not necessarily System 7. You should know how to:

- work with menus and windows
- use folders
- work with application programs such as a word processor or spreadsheet
- open, save, and print documents

The Disk

The disk that comes with this book contains the Extension Manager, a utility licensed from Apple that helps take care of INIT conflicts. It also includes a collection of freeware and shareware utilities that will enhance your use of System 7. I've tested each of these utilities under System 7.1 to be sure they run without a problem, although there is certainly no guarantee that they won't conflict with any INITs you have on your machine that I don't have on mine.

ACKNOWLEDGMENTS

A lot of people helped make this book a reality. (Although it would be fruitless to try to keep this even as short as a speech at a TV, music, or movie award ceremony, I'll try to be brief.) I'd like to thank all the following wonderful folks:

The people at MIS:Press who were with the book from start to finish:

- Steve Berkowitz, publisher
- Cary Sullivan, the editor who shepherded this project through
- Erika Putre, editorial assistant
- Joanne Kelman, who did the wonderful design and layout

The people at many software companies who provided copies of their products for discussion in this book:

- Nancy Morrison at Apple Computer for System 7 Pro
- Julie A. Boudreaux, formerly of Fifth Generation Sytems, for Suitcase
- Phillus Gaye of Fifth Generation Systems for AutoDoubler
- Sue Nail of CE Software for QuicKeys
- Dodie Bump of ColorAge Inc. for Freedom of Press Classic
- Lynn Halloran of Now Software for Now Up-to-Date and Now Utilities
- Debbie Deguitis at Connectix for Maxima
- Bonnie Orsini at DataViz for MacLinkPlus/Translators
- A whole bunch of people at Beyond, Inc. for PowerRules

The shareware software developers whose programs appear on the disk that accompanies this book:

- Rick Christianson (OneClick!)
- B. Kevin Hardman (Symbionts)
- Greg Kearney (Move to Apple 2.0)

- John A. Schlack (Attributes)
- Keith Turner (CatFinder)

And all the other folks who helped:

- Gene Steinberg for the Memory control panel screen shot
- Trudy Edelson at Farallon who supplied the photos of network connectors
- Kurt Stammberger and George Parsons at RSA for information on PowerTalk security and getting me the approved signer file on very short notice

JLH

CHAPTER 1
Operating System Basics

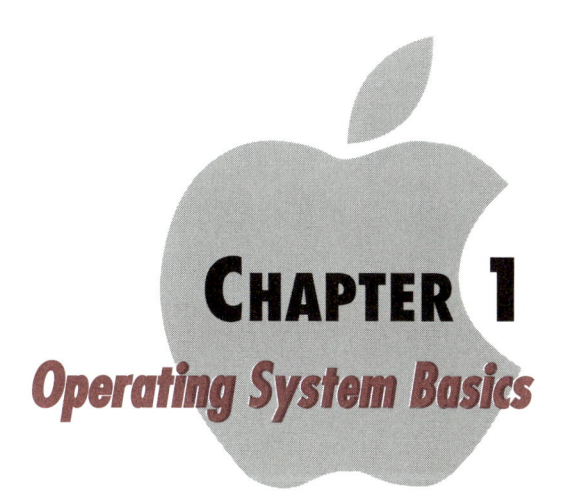

An *operating system* is a group of programs that manage a computer. As simple as that definition might sound, most people who have worked with a computer know that an operating system performs a wide range of tasks, many of which are hidden from the user's view. A Macintosh user's view of the Macintosh operating system is the Finder, the program that handles the Desktop. However, there's a lot more to it than just the Finder. Throughout this book you'll learn about the full range of the Macintosh operating system's capabilities, from the Finder to memory management.

> **BY THE WAY!** The Macintosh operating system doesn't have an official name. Because the operating system has no name, when the Macintosh first appeared in 1984 many people thought the computer didn't have an operating system at all!

This first chapter introduces you to a bit of operating system history and to the functions found in most of today's operating systems. This will give you a framework into which you can place all the things that the Macintosh operating system does for your computer. It will also give you an appreciation for the complex tasks facing an operating system, and help you understand why operating systems are sometimes fragile (in other words, why they crash).

NAVIGATING SYSTEM 7: Understanding The Macintosh Operating System

> **BY THE WAY!** An operating system is part of a larger group of software known as *system software*. System software also includes *utility programs (utilities)*—stand-alone programs that add functions to an operating system—and software such as assemblers and compilers that are used to translate computer programs into executable form.

A Brief History of Operating Systems

The very first computers had no operating systems. The computer operator loaded a program into the computer, pressed a "Go" button, and waited for the computer to run the program (see Figure 1.1). No other programs could be loaded until the currently running program finished. This meant that the computer sat idle while the operator removed the output of one program and loaded another. Given the cost and limited availability of early computers, this was extremely wasteful.

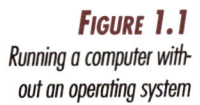

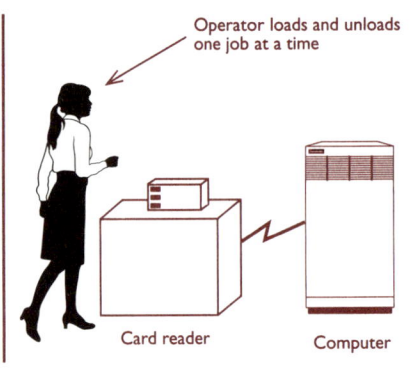

FIGURE 1.1
Running a computer without an operating system

The first operating systems were created to get rid of the wasted time between programs. Known as a *serial-batch operating system*, this type of operating system took programs off of a magnetic tape. Although programs still ran one at a time, the operating system loaded a new program as soon as the previous program had finished, eliminating the operator tear-down and set-up time. Programs were loaded onto the tape off-line, usually by a punch-card reader that transferred the contents of cards onto tape without any processing. The only time an operator was required was to change tapes and to remove output from the printer and card punch machine (see Figure 1.2).

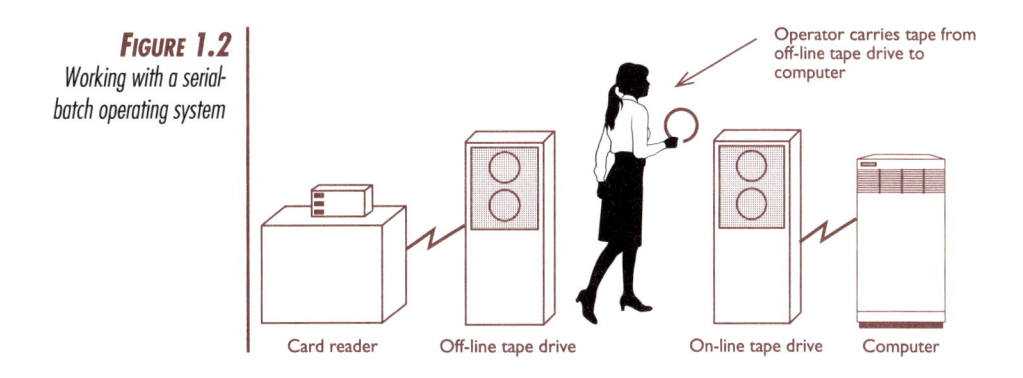

FIGURE 1.2
Working with a serial-batch operating system

Operator carries tape from off-line tape drive to computer

Card reader | Off-line tape drive | On-line tape drive | Computer

Serial-batch operating systems eliminated the time between programs, but a computer was still wasting time waiting for input and output. For example, if a program needed to print some output, the computer had to wait for the relatively slow printer to finish before it proceeded. Because CPU time was the most expensive resource in an entire computer system, operating system designers were looking for some way to take advantage of idle time that occurred when the computer was waiting for a slow I/O device.

The solution to the problem was a technique for running more than one program at a time. Although only one program could use the CPU at any instant, when a program had to wait for I/O it would give up control of the CPU to another program, which could then execute for a time. This CPU sharing technique is used by most of today's operating systems, including the Macintosh operating system. Originally called *multiprogramming* or *time sharing*, it is now more commonly known as *multitasking*.

MODERN MICROCOMPUTER OPERATING SYSTEMS

There are six basic functions provided by today's operating systems:

- interaction with the user (the user interface),
- allocation and management of main memory (memory management),
- management of program execution (process management),
- management of external storage,

- management of input and output, and
- system administration.

Typically, the core functions are organized into a *kernel* (see Figure 1.3). The kernel provides basic input and output, process management, and memory management functions. In most operating systems, the kernel is always present in RAM, where it can execute as quickly as possible. The remaining parts of the operating system are swapped in and out of main memory as needed so they don't take up RAM when they aren't in use. This provides a good trade-off between performance and the amount of memory used by the operating system.

FIGURE 1.3
The organization of an operating system

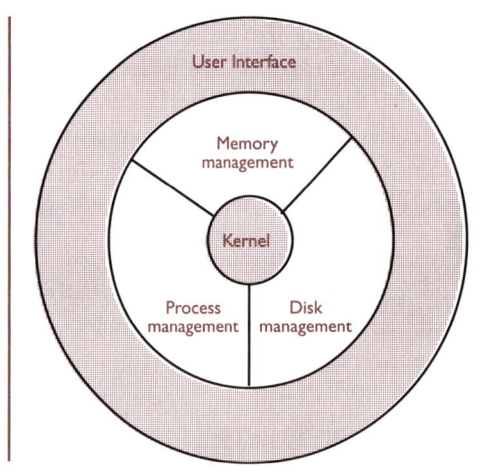

Although you find in-depth discussions of operating system functions throughout this book, the remainder of this chapter provides a general overview to get you started.

MANAGING THE USER INTERFACE

A *user interface* is whatever mechanism an operating system uses to accept input from a user and to respond to the user. Some operating systems, such as MS DOS, and UNIX, are *command-driven*: The user types command words that are sent to the operating system for processing. This type of user interface is often known as a *command interpreter* because it must break the command into its component parts, interpret what each part means, and then perform the required action.

Some pioneering work at Xerox PARC, however, suggested that there was another way for an operating system to interact with a user. Users would choose commands from a menu of choices and manipulate icons and windows with a pointing device (a mouse). This type of *menu-driven* user interface provided the underlying concepts for the Macintosh operating system's Finder.

The way in which a user interacts with command-driven and menu-driven user interfaces is fundamentally different (typing commands versus pointing and clicking with a device such as a mouse). However, the difference extends beyond what the user sees and does to the way in which the operating system programs are written.

Command-driven operating systems wait for the user to type a command; nothing happens until the user presses the **Enter** key to transmit a command. A menu-driven operating system, however, can't simply sit idly by and wait for a command to be sent to it. Instead, it must continually check to see if something has happened.

Anything that happens in the Macintosh environment is known as an *event*. The operating system continually checks possible sources of events (for example, disk drives, the mouse, and the keyboard) to determine if something has occurred. Whenever an event occurs (for example, inserting a floppy disk into a floppy drive, pressing down the mouse button, or pressing a key on the keyboard), the operating system records the event. If the event is something that the operating system handles, it performs the appropriate action. For example, if a user working with the Finder moves the mouse to the menu bar and presses the mouse button, the operating system drops down the menu so the user can see its options. If the event should be handled by an application program or a utility, then the event is placed in the *event queue*, a waiting list of events, so that the appropriate program can handle it. An operating system that responds to events in its environment rather than waiting for a command is said to be *event-driven*.

MANAGING MEMORY

An operating system must allocate and protect blocks of RAM. As you will see in Chapter 6, the Macintosh must use part of its RAM to hold some of the operating system as well as any application programs you might be running. Each one of those programs must be isolated in its own section of RAM. If one program were to invade the space of another, it would destroy the program whose block it invaded. The operating system must therefore keep track of where every program is located and make sure that no program escapes its boundaries. It must also allocate RAM as new programs are launched.

An operating system can also extend the physical memory installed in a computer by providing *virtual memory*. A virtual memory scheme uses space on a hard disk to simulate extra RAM. You will find details about System 7's virtual memory in Chapter 6.

Managing Processes

A *process*, or *task*, is the operating system word for a program of any type that is being executed by a computer. As you read earlier in this chapter, early operating systems (including MS DOS) could handle only one application process at a time. However, current operating systems such as the Macintosh operating system can have more than one program executing at the same time.

> **BY THE WAY!** Although the terms "process" and "task" are used more or less interchangeably, *multiprocessing* is not the same as *multitasking*. Multiprocessing refers to having more than one CPU in the same computer. It is then possible to do multitasking with each of the computer's CPUs. Multiprocessing is rare on the desktop, but typical of mainframes and supercomputers.

Even if an operating system supports multitasking, a CPU can still only do one thing at a time. That means that the operating system must have some way of deciding which process has control of the CPU at any given time; it must also have a way to switch between running processes. As processes are swapped in and out of the CPU, they must be frozen in their current state so that they can pick up exactly where they left off the next time they have control of the CPU. The operating system must manage this as well.

There are at least two types of multitasking—*preemptive* and *cooperative*. Some people believe that the cooperative multitasking used by the Macintosh operating system isn't true multitasking. You will find details about both types of multitasking and the reasons why people don't think cooperative multitasking is really multitasking in Chapter 5.

Many operating systems provide a way for running processes to communicate with one another (*interprocess communication*). The Macintosh operating system provides two types of interprocess communication. The first, known as *publish and subscribe*, lets a portion of a document (a *published edition*) be placed within another document (the document *subscribes* to the published edition). When the source document from which the edition was published is updated, any subscribers to that edition are updated as well. Although the operating system manages publish and subscribe, application programs must also be written specifically to provide publish and subscribe capabilities. (You will find more about publish and subscribe in Chapter 9.)

Many Macintosh applications are now also being written to respond to *Apple Events*. An Apple Event is a special type of event that is handled by a program written in *AppleScript*, a programming language designed specifically to intercept and process Apple Events. An AppleScript program can automate actions a user performs when working with a program and can transfer messages between programs that are running at the same time. Working with AppleScript requires application programs that respond to Apple Events as well as a means to write and execute scripts.

The most recent version of the Finder (part of System 7 Pro) can respond to Apple Events. You will find an introduction to Apple Events and AppleScript in Chapter 11.

MANAGING EXTERNAL STORAGE

An operating system is responsible for keeping track of files on external storage, regardless of whether that storage is disk or tape, magnetic or optical. As you will learn in Chapter 4, the Macintosh operating system maintains a set of data structures that organize files and folders, making it possible for you to store, retrieve, and organize files.

MANAGING I/O

In addition to organizing files on external storage, an operating system manages the transfer of data from the outside world to the computer and from the computer to the outside world. This involves transferring data to and from external storage, transferring data to printers and monitors, and receiving data from mice, keyboards, and other input devices.

The translation between the computer and an I/O device is handled by a special piece of software known as a *device driver*. Typically, there is one device driver for each I/O device. Device drivers and other special system extensions are covered in Chapter 7.

Many operating systems provide support for networking, a special type of I/O that involves telecommunications lines. Every Macintosh has AppleTalk built onto its motherboard; some Quadras and Centrises also come with Ethernet. System 7 supports *peer-to-peer networking* using either AppleTalk or Ethernet. With the addition of the PowerTalk capabilities of System 7 Pro, the Macintosh operating system also provides electronic mail. (You will learn more about System 7's networking capabilities in Chapters 10, 12, and 13.)

SYSTEM ADMINISTRATION

System administration, which sits apart from most other operating system functions, covers a wide variety of activities, including system security, user control, and accounting. System security involves protecting data stored on a computer or that travels over a network. The Macintosh operating system provides few security features for a stand-alone computer; security must be implemented through an add-on program. (System security is covered at the end of Chapter 3.)

Operating systems can be classified as *multi-user* or *single-user*. A multi-user operating system such as UNIX supports more than one user at a time. Because each user is running at least one process, a multi-user operating system must have multitasking capabilities. A single-user operating system (for example, the Macintosh operating system or MS DOS) allows only one user. It may or may not have multitasking capabilities.

Multi-user operating systems provide a way to control who can log on and use the computer. As a single-user operating system, the Macintosh operating system doesn't need this type of user control. Whoever is sitting at the keyboard has access to any part of the Macintosh environment that isn't protected by an add-on security program.

However, when files are shared over a network, it is important to control who has access to shared data. This type of user control is provided through the Macintosh operating system's file sharing capabilities. (User control during file sharing is discussed in Chapter 10; PowerTalk security is covered in Chapter 13.)

> **BY THE WAY!** Although the Macintosh isn't a multi-user operating system, many applications have been written to function as multi-user programs running on top of the Macintosh's networking facilities. Such programs usually provide their own user control with a combination of user names and passwords.

Most multi-user operating systems have some way of keeping track of when users are logged on to the system as well as the programs they run. Originally, this information was used to charge users for the amount of CPU time they used. Today, users rarely pay for computer use in this way. Accounting information is therefore primarily used to provide statistics on system use that can be used to fine-tune the system to increase performance. Because the Macintosh operating system isn't designed as a multi-user operating system, it doesn't provide system accounting functions.

CHAPTER 2
A Tour Around the Operating System

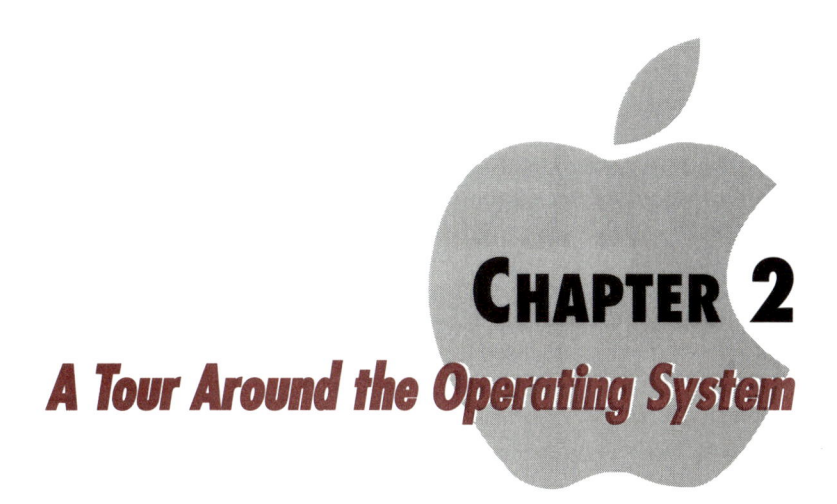

As you read in Chapter 1, an operating system is a collection of programs that manage a computer. The programs that make up the Macintosh operating system are found in two places: the Macintosh ROM and inside the System folder on a startup disk. This chapter takes a brief look at where the Macintosh operating system keeps all its parts, those that are required to run the computer and those that add useful functions.

WHAT YOU NEED TO RUN SYSTEM 7

Every Macintosh from the Macintosh Plus on theoretically can run System 7. However, System 7 requires a lot of RAM, which presents some significant problems when trying to run it on a Macintosh with a 68000 microprocessor (for example, the Plus, SE, or Classic). The 68000 computers are limited to 4Mb of RAM; System 7 usually takes up more than 2Mb, leaving very little room for application programs.

To run System 7 effectively, you generally need at least 8Mb RAM. If you have a 68000 Macintosh and want to use System 7, consider upgrading your computer with a CPU accelerator card, many of which support RAM up to 16Mb. Accelerator boards for 68000 Macs generally use 68030 microprocessors and therefore bring significant increases in processing speed along with the possibility of installing enough RAM to make good use of System 7.

System 7's Versions

There are three versions of System 7 in wide distribution today: 7.0, 7.0.1, and 7.1. The release of 7.0 was heralded by a tidal wave of publicity; everybody knew it was coming. Many people upgraded to 7.0 or 7.0.1 by downloading software from on-line services such as CompuServe or America Online. The upgrade was also sold through retail outlets. User groups were licensed to distribute it.

However, the release of 7.1 was kept relatively quiet. Initially, it wasn't available in retail stores; it hasn't been licensed to user groups nor is it available on on-line services. The only way to get it is to order it directly from Apple or purchase it from a retail store.

Should you bother to get 7.1? Probably. It has some new features that make working with the operating system a bit easier. In particular, it has a different way of handling fonts from previous releases that appears to be cleaner and more efficient.

System 7.1 is available in versions tailored for many languages. Current language versions can be found in Table 2.1. The version that you receive when you buy System 7.1 is generally determined by the country in which you make the purchase. In most cases when using a non-English version of the operating system, you should be certain that you are purchasing application programs that have been specifically tailored for other languages.

TABLE 2.1
Language versions available for System 7.1

Arabic	French	Polish
British	German	Romanian
Bulgarian	Greek	Russian
Canadian, French	Hebrew	Spanish
Catalan	Hungarian	Swedish
Chinese	Icelandic	Swiss, French
Croatian	Italian	Swiss, German
Czech	Japanese	Thai
Danish	Korean (Hangul)	Turkish
Dutch	Norwegian	U.S.
Finnish	Persian	

The mass-market Macintosh models—the Performas—come with a specially tailored version of System 7: 7.0P or 7.1P. Although basically the same as 7.0 and 7.1, the Performa operating systems contain some features that make them easier to use. For example, they include At Ease, a Finder shell that hides many Finder capabilities from a novice user. (At Ease is discussed at the end of this chapter.)

The Hardware Updates

In addition to the three System 7 versions, there are two hardware updates. Hardware System Update 1.0 is intended for System 7.0 and 7.0.1; Hardware System Update 2.0 is intended for System 7.1. The updates, which should not be used with the Performa versions of System 7, fix problems with specific Macintosh models, including the following:

- For the LC, LC II, IIsi, IIvx, IIvi, Classic II, Quadra 900, and Quadra 950, fix problems with high-speed modems.
- For the LC, LC II, IIsi, IIvx, IIvi, Classic II, Quadra 900, and Quadra 950, increase the accuracy of the system clock.
- For the IIsi, IIci, IIvx, IIvi, Quadra 700, and Quadra 950, fix the problem with ejecting a floppy disk when the computer is shut down.
- For the IIsi, IIci, IIvx, IIvi, Centrises, Quadras, PowerBooks, and PowerBook Duos, fix some possible problems with both floppy and hard disk drives.
- For the Color Classic, update the system enabler so that you can add the Apple IIe board to that computer.
- For the Centrises and Quadras, fix possible problems with color on the Apple Basic Color monitor.
- For the Centrises and Quadras, fix display problems when scrolling on the Macintosh 16-inch Color Display.
- For the PowerBook 160, 165c, and 180, update the system enabler to let these models work with 12-inch monitors.
- For all Macintoshes, update system software to provide better sound.
- For all Macintoshes, add system software that lets you connect the Apple Adjustable Keyboard without installing special keyboard software.

- For all Macintoshes, update the Memory control panel to fix problems with large RAM disks. (The Memory control panel and RAM disks are discussed in Chapter 6.)

The updates also include new versions of Apple HD SC Setup (a utility for formatting hard disks) and Apple Disk First Aid (a utility for repairing damaged disks), as well as a system extension that lets you format disks in IBM low-density format (720K).

The Hardware System Updates can be downloaded from on-line information services or from Macintosh dealers. Should you make the effort to get an update and install it? In most cases, the updates will generally increase operating system performance as well as fix the previously mentioned problems. The updates are therefore generally worth installing.

SYSTEM 7 PRO

Apple has released a set of System 7 extensions and a new version of the Finder as a bundle called System 7 Pro. Sold as a separate product, System 7 Pro provides support for PowerTalk (electronic mail capabilities), AppleScript (add-on programs that customize and enhance operating system operation), and the multimedia extension, QuickTime. System 7 Pro's capabilities are covered in Chapters 11, 12, and 13.

INSIDE THE ROM

The Macintosh ROM, like the ROM in most other desktop computers, contains just enough of the operating system to start the computer when the power is first turned on. During the startup cycle, the Macintosh performs a series of diagnostics, checking the RAM, ROM, and other integrated circuits on the computer's *logic board* (the main circuit board). Assuming that the computer passes the diagnostic tests, then the Macintosh begins searching disk drives for a System folder. The ROM's part in the boot process is finished once it locates the disk-based portion of the operating system (stored in the System folder).

> **BY THE WAY!** Some microcomputers, such as the Apple II+ and early IBM PCs, had their entire operating systems in ROM. This meant that you could boot and use the computer without an attached disk drive. Programs could either be loaded from a cassette tape drive or typed in the BASIC programming language. The major drawback to placing an entire operating system in ROM is that an operating system upgrade requires a ROM change.

The rest of the Macintosh ROM contains programs that support the Macintosh user interface. System software and application programs use the ROM routines to

- Draw and manage elements of the user interface such as windows, menus, dialog boxes, and alerts.
- Draw, fill, size, move, and otherwise manipulate graphics objects (QuickDraw).
- Manage text (TextEdit).
- Handle networking (Communications Toolbox).
- Manage RAM and virtual memory (Memory Manager).
- Manage external storage (Standard File Package, File Manager).
- Manage input and output (Print Manager).
- Store and retrieve data from a network database (Data Access Manager).
- Work with sound (Sound Manager).
- Support multitasking (Process Manager).
- Provide interapplication communication (PPC ToolBox, Edition Manager).

As a user, you don't interact directly with the contents of the Macintosh's ROM. Instead, you use programs that use the contents of the ROM.

AT FIRST LOOK AT SYSTEM STARTUP

When you power up your Macintosh, the ROM looks for a System folder on a disk. The disk can be a floppy disk, a hard disk, a removable hard disk or optical cartridge, or a CD-ROM. The Macintosh checks disks in the following order:

- First internal floppy drive,
- Second internal floppy drive (if present),
- Serial hard disk (Macintosh 128K, 512K, 512Ke, Plus, and SE only), then
- SCSI devices, beginning with the highest SCSI address (unless a specific SCSI address has been designated as the startup drive).

As the Macintosh checks disks, it ejects any piece of removable media it encounters that doesn't contain a System folder. If it checks all disks and still can't find the files it needs, it displays a floppy disk icon with a flashing question mark.

> **BY THE WAY!** When it comes to looking for operating system files, the Macintosh operating system is much friendlier than command-driven operating systems such as MS DOS. MS DOS also checks its floppy drives first. If a floppy without system files is inserted in a floppy drive when the computer is booted, the operating system simply reports an error and asks the user what to do; it doesn't go on to check the computer's hard disk.

REQUIRED SYSTEM FILES AND FOLDERS

Much of what we store in a System folder actually isn't required to boot the Macintosh. In fact, the minimum contents of a System folder include only two files: System and Finder.

The Finder is responsible for managing the Macintosh desktop. It also handles file and process management. The Finder provides a means for you to communicate with the operating system through its menus, windows, and control panels. It is an executable program that is launched at the end of the boot process and remains running as long as the computer is running.

> **BY THE WAY!** Under special circumstances, the Finder can be replaced with another program that runs when booting is finished. In that case, the only required operating system file is the System file. The disk used as a startup disk must be modified to indicate the name of the program other than the Finder that is to be run. You will see exactly where this is stored on disk in Chapter 3.

CHAPTER 2: A Tour Around the Operating System

> **FLASH BACK:** Prior to System 7, the portion of the operating system that remained running to handle multitasking was a separate program known as MultiFinder. Using MultiFinder was optional. If MultiFinder wasn't running, launching an application program stopped the Finder and replaced it with the application program. Quitting the application program launched the Finder again. In System 7, MultiFinder's capabilities have been merged into the Finder.

The System file is a holding area for several parts of the operating system, including the following:

- **ROM patches:** Because ROM can't be changed, the Macintosh operating system stores programs that replace portions of ROM in the System file (*patches*). When a program needs to use the ROM routine for which a patch exists, the patch is loaded into RAM so the program can access it.

- **Resource:** A *resource* is static data used by the operating system to create the Macintosh user interface. For example, a window resource contains information about the type of window, its initial size and position on the screen, and characteristics such as whether it has scroll bars, a close box, and/or a zoom box. A number of resources, such as sounds and keyboard layouts, can be present in the System file.

> **BY THE WAY!** Application programs can override the resources in the System file by including their own resource definitions. That is how application programs produce custom features such as special cursors.

> **FLASH BACK:** Prior to System 7, fonts and desk accessories were installed in the System file as resources. Under 7.0, desk accessories migrated to individual files inside designated folders in the System folder; fonts and sounds remained in the System file. With 7.1, however, fonts have also migrated to their own folder.

- **Additional operating system routines:** The System file can act as a repository for operating system routines that aren't present in the ROM.

FLASH BACK: Prior to System 7, operating system extensions were always stored within the System file. System 7, however, keeps many extensions in separate files and a separate folder within the System folder.

OPTIONAL SYSTEM FILES AND FOLDERS

Beyond the System file and the Finder, everything else in the System folder is optional. Nonetheless, to create an environment that is usable for day-to-day work, the Macintosh operating system is enhanced by a variety of extensions and resources. A typical System 7 installation includes the following files and folders:

- **Apple Menu Items folder:** The Apple Menu Items folder (Figure 2.1) contains programs such as desk accessories whose name should appear under the menu (see Figure 2.2). The folder can contain the actual program files or *aliases* for those files. (Using aliases is discussed in detail in Chapter 3.)

    If the item placed in the Apple Menu Items folder is a program, choosing its name from the menu executes the program. On the other hand, if the item placed in the Apple Menu Items folder is a folder, choosing its name from the menu opens the folder's window on the desktop.

Figure 2.1 An Apple Menu Items folder

FIGURE 2.2
The Apple menu produced by the folder in Figure 2.1

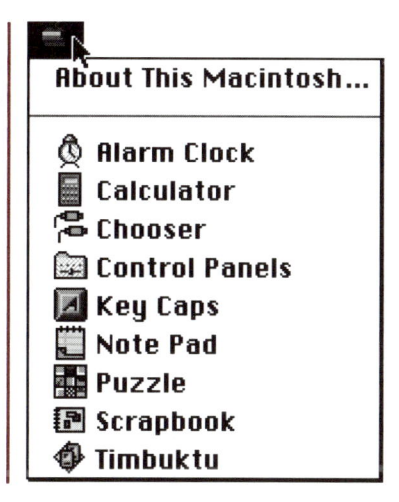

```
About This Macintosh...

  Alarm Clock
  Calculator
  Chooser
  Control Panels
  Key Caps
  Note Pad
  Puzzle
  Scrapbook
  Timbuktu
```

⚡FLASH BACK

For all intents and purposes, desk accessories don't exist under System 7. Desk accessories (for example, the calculator or puzzle) that installed as resources in the System file under earlier versions of the operating system exist as separate programs under System 7. They appear in the menu only because they have been placed in the Apple Menu Items folder. (With System 7, *any* program or folder can appear in the menu, not just those that were formerly considered desk accessories.) Also keep in mind that because MultiFinder is a permanent part of System 7, there is no need to handle desk accessories differently from any other program, whereas under earlier versions of the operating system, there was no way to ensure that MultiFinder would be present. Desk accessories therefore had to be executed differently from other programs so that they could run while an application program was running.

♦ **Clipboard file:** The Clipboard file contains the contents of the most recent cut or copy operation. You can see its contents by double-clicking on the file icon. For example, the Clipboard file in Figure 2.3 reflects the screen shot taken to produce Figure 2.2.

FIGURE 2.3
Looking at the contents of the Clipboard file

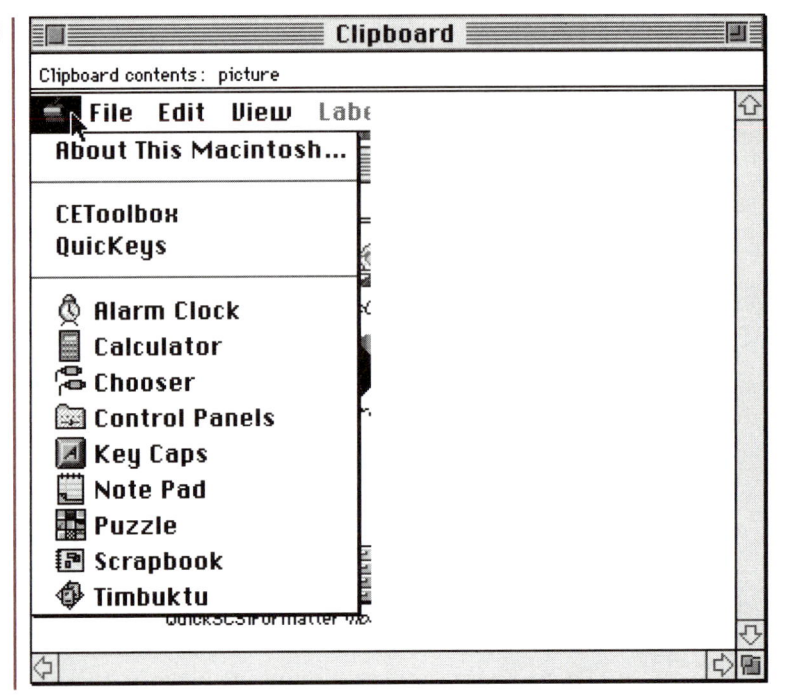

- **Control Panels folder:** Control panels, also known as *CDEVs*, are small programs most commonly used to configure the Macintosh environment. For example, the Memory control panel turns on and off virtual memory, 32-bit addressing, and disk caching; the Monitors control panel sets the number of colors or shades of gray displayed on all attached monitors.

- **Extensions folder:** Operating system extensions are placed in the Extension folder. Extensions include downloadable PostScript fonts, the PrintMonitor application that manages background printing, and a variety of patches to the operating system. Extensions include *System Enablers*, operating system patches that provide support for new Macintosh models. The introduction of enablers means that a new release of the operating system isn't required every time a new Macintosh model appears. Those Macintoshes that require enablers and the enablers that should be used with each specific model can be found in Table 2.2.

Table 2.2
Macintosh system enablers

Macintosh model	Current Enabler	Version	Old Enabler
IIvi, IIvx	001	1.0.1	
PowerBook 160, 180	131	1.0	111 v1.0.2
PowerBook Duo 210, 230	201	1.0.1	
LC III	003	1.0	
Centris 610, 650, Quadra 800	040	1.0	
PowerBook 165c	131	1.0	121 v1.0
Color Classic	401	1.0.5	
PowerBook 180c	131	1.0	
Performa 600	304	1.0.1	
Performa 450	308	1.0	
Performa 250	332	1.0	

Most operating system extensions (including portions of some control panels) must be kept in RAM while the computer is running. They are therefore loaded into memory at system startup *before* the Finder is executed. Files loaded in this way are known as *INITs*.

BY THE WAY! Successful loading of INITs can present a significant challenge. You'll learn more about INIT conflicts in Chapter 8.

- **Fonts folder:** The Fonts folder contains the bitmaps (screen versions) of fonts. Fonts can be stored in individual files but are more commonly grouped together into *font suitcases*. The Macintosh operating system places an arbitrary limit of 128 font suitcases in the Fonts folder. As you can see in Figure 2.4, double-clicking on a font suitcase opens a window that displays all the fonts stored inside; double-clicking on a font file opens a window that displays a sample of the font's bitmap.

FIGURE 2.4
The Fonts folder

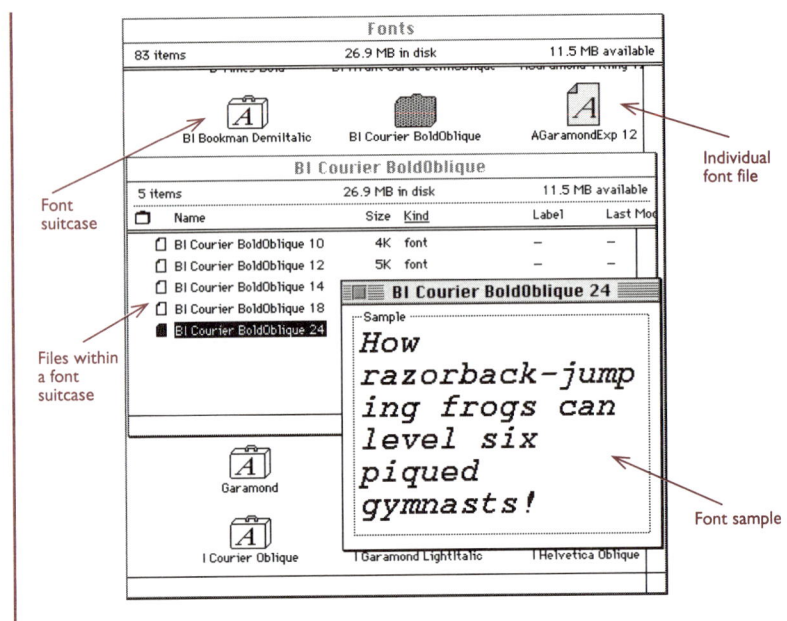

Prior to System 7, fonts had to be installed into the System file using an application called Font/DA mover. With System 7, all you have to do is drag the font suitcase or file over the System folder's icon. The Macintosh operating system places the fonts in the correct location for you, regardless of whether you are using 7.0 or 7.1.

- **Note Pad file:** The Note Pad file (Figure 2.5) stores the contents of the Macintosh's note page (an eight-page pad on which you can enter text).

- **Preferences folder:** The Preferences folder is used by many application programs to store files that contain default settings used whenever a new document is created.

- **PrintMonitor Documents:** The PrintMonitor Documents folder is used to store files that are waiting to be printed. Once printed, files are deleted from this folder.

- **Startup Items:** The Startup Items folder holds files other than control panels and extensions that should be executed or loaded into RAM at system startup. It is not uncommon for this folder to be empty.

FIGURE 2.5
The Note Pad

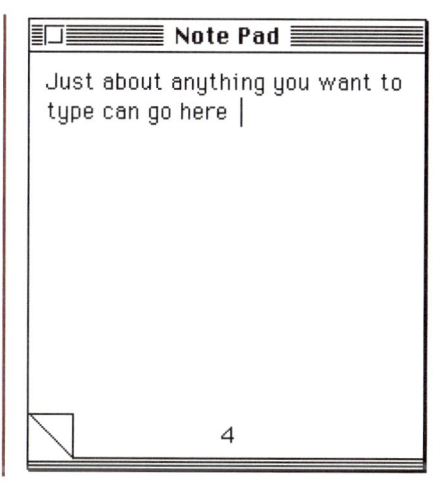

```
┌─────── Note Pad ═══════┐
│ Just about anything you want to
│ type can go here |
│
│
│
│
│
│         4
└────────────────────────┘
```

OPENING CONTROL PANELS

Many system extensions, particularly those that configure hardware or software, have been implemented as control panels. To make it easy to gain access to all installed control panels, an *alias* for the Control Panels folder is placed in the Menu folder. (An alias is a pointer to the location of a file or folder; you will find out more about aliases in Chapter 4.) (You can also get the Control Panels folder by opening the System folder. However, using the menu is a bit easier.)

Choosing Control Panels from the menu opens the window of the Control Panels folder (for example, see Figure 2.6). At this point, you can double-click on the control panel with which you want to work to open its window.

ADD-ON USEFUL

The System 7 menu is an improvement over System 6. However, it is somewhat limited in functionality and can be awkward to use (particularly for gaining access to control panels). One way to enhance the menu is to add a utility, such as NowMenus or HAM, that turns it into a hierarchical menu.

Both NowMenus and HAM can turn the contents of a folder into a menu. For example, notice in Figure 2.7 that the contents of the Control Panels folder appear as a menu. That means that you can open a control panel by choosing its name from a menu rather than going to the Control Panels folder and double-clicking on a control panel icon.

24 NAVIGATING SYSTEM 7: Understanding The Macintosh Operating System

FIGURE 2.6
The Control Panels folder

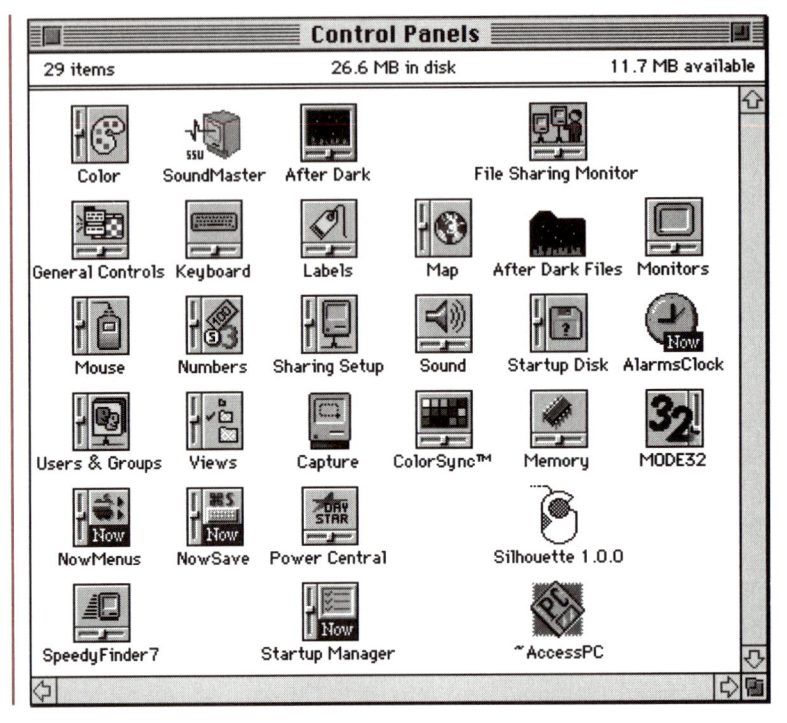

FIGURE 2.7
The hierarchical menus produced by NowMenus or HAM

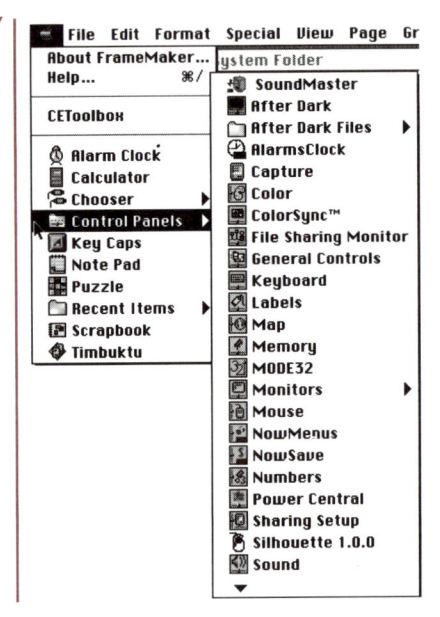

NowMenus (Figure 2.8) lets you choose which items appear in the menu. In addition, it provides a folder called Recent Items that acts as the top of the hierarchical menu containing your most recently used applications and files. The theory behind this is that the applications and documents used most recently are those most likely to be used again in the near future.

FIGURE 2.8
The NowMenus control panel

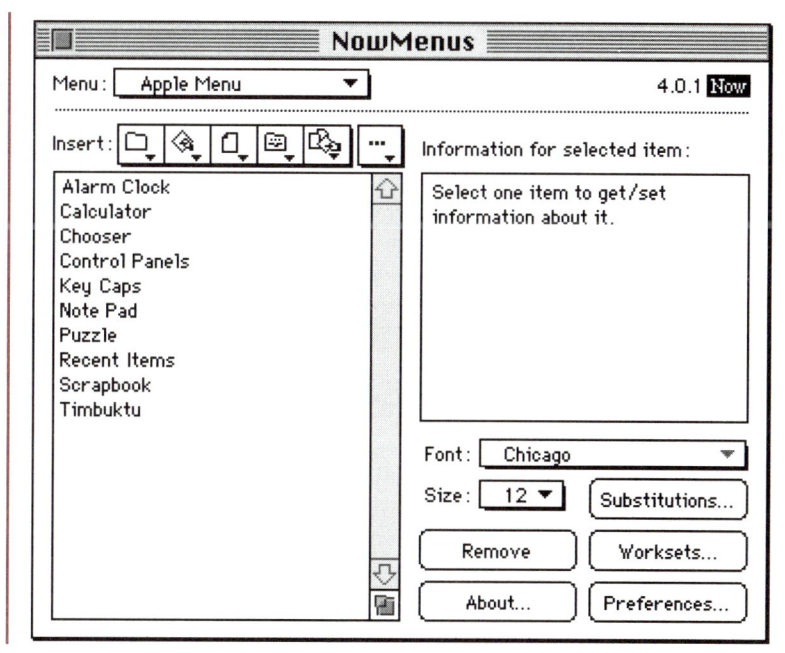

NowMenus can provide menus of recently used items at either the very left or very right of the menu bar. It also can produce a pop-up menu on the Desktop and assign hot keys to application menu items.

HAM (for Hierarchical Apple Menu) was originally intended as a part of System 7. When Apple decided not to include it in the system software, they returned the product to its developer, who released it as a commercial product. Like Now Menus, HAM (Figure 2.9) can create hierarchical menus out of the contents of folders.

HAM also lets you create sets of applications and documents called HAMlets. Once you create a HAMlet, its contents can be opened automatically when you start up your Macintosh.

Figure 2.9
The HAM control panel

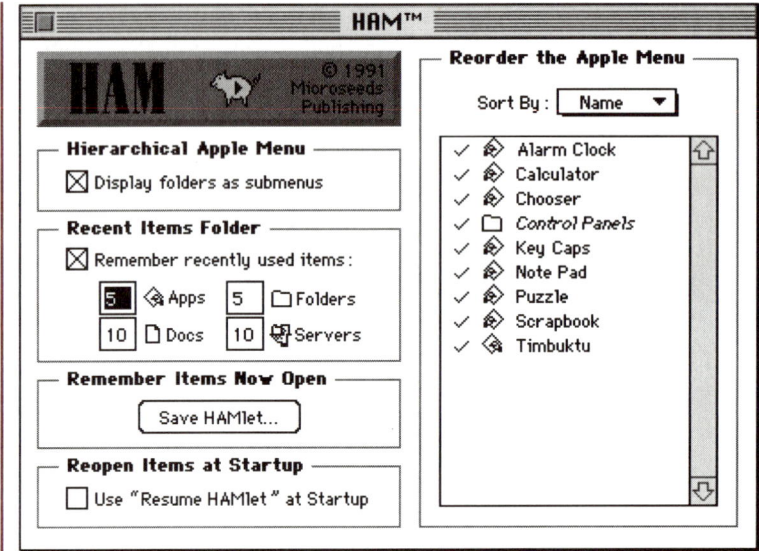

Installation Hints: The "Clean" Install

The Apple Installer program can make it easy to get system software onto your hard disk. Unfortunately, in many cases you won't get a successful installation. In particular, you may experience problems going from 7.0 to 7.1 or from either 7.0 or 7.1 to 7 Pro. Problems can be so serious that your Macintosh won't boot from the files copied onto your hard disk by the Installer.

The solution is something known as a *clean install.* It means that you create a completely new System folder, without trying to update an existing one. Although it is theoretically possible to perform a clean install by simply renaming your existing System folder and then installing a new one on the same disk volume, it doesn't always work. (Sometimes moving the Finder out of the System folder helps, but not always....) The safest way is to delete your current System folder entirely. A clean install can be time consuming, but it's usually worth the effort.

To perform a clean install, do the following:

1. Boot your computer with the Disk Tools disk. (This is essential; you won't be able to complete this process if the System folder on your normal startup disk is the current System folder.)

2. Make a copy of the entire System folder. (Although you won't be keeping all of it, it's easier this way.) You can place it on another partition on your hard drive or on removable media. For simplicity's sake, we'll call this the "old System folder."

> **BY THE WAY!**
>
> It is rather difficult to do a clean install if you don't have a hard or optical disk volume other than your startup volume. This is because the Installer is far smarter than it probably should be and can find an old System folder on the disk volume selected for installation of the new system software, regardless of what you name the old System folder or where you hide it. You've got to get rid of the old System folder completely by deleting it. If you only have one hard disk and don't have any removable mass storage (for example, a SyQuest or optical drive), then you can make the process much easier if you partition your hard drive. One partition can be relatively small (enough to hold your System folder and space to spool printer files). However, without at least two partitions, your only alternative for a clean install is to back up your old System folder to floppy disks, a process that is tedious at best.

3. If you place the old System folder on removable media that is used by a disk drive that requires an INIT, copy that INIT to the System folder on the Disk Tools disk. (You may need to unlock the Disk Tools disk first!) Devices that require such INITs include many SyQuest and optical drives. (This makes it possible to access your saved copy after the clean install or if something should go wrong with the installation.)

4. Delete the System folder from your normal startup disk. Be sure to empty the trash so that you can reclaim the disk space occupied.

5. Shut down the Macintosh.

6. Boot the computer with the Install disk. The Macintosh runs the Installer program.

> **BY THE WAY!**
>
> If you're feeling adventurous and a bit lazy, just eject the Disk Tools disk and insert the Install disk. (Pay no attention if the Macintosh asks for the Disk Tools disk.).Then, hit the reset button on the programmer's switch or press the key combination that resets your Mac.

7. Install the new system software on your normal startup disk (the one from which you just deleted a System folder). This becomes your "new System folder."

8. Quit the Installer. The Macintosh asks if you want to Restart or Shutdown.

9. Restart the Macintosh. This time, the computer boots from the new System folder.

10. If you need an INIT to access the drive used to store the old System folder, copy that INIT from the Disk Tools disk into your new System folder. Restart the Macintosh. After this restart, you should have access to the old System folder without needing the Disk Tools disk.

11. Copy third-party control panels and system extensions (including downloadable PostScript fonts) from the old System folder to the new System folder.

12. Move all fonts except the TrueType fonts already installed in the Fonts folder. The way in which you do this depends on the version of your old System.

    ▸ System 6 (any version): Use the Font/DA Mover (version 4.1 or later) to create font suitcases of all fonts you want to keep. Drag those suitcases to the new System folder. (For details on using Font/DA Mover to make font suitcases, see Chapter 7.)

    ▸ System 7.0: Open the old System folder and double-click on the System file. Drag the fonts (suitcases or individual font files) to the new System folder.

    ▸ System 7.1: Open the old System folder and open the Fonts folder. Drag the fonts (suitcases or individual font files) to the new System folder.

13. Move anything else you want to keep from the old System folder to the new System folder.

BY THE WAY! If you are upgrading from any version of System 6 and have some System 6-style desk accessories you want to use, they need some special handling before they are ready for use under System 7. Details can be found in Chapter 8.

---

14. Restart your Macintosh one more time. If all is well, you should boot normally and have access to everything you need.

Once you're convinced that your new system software installation is working properly, it's up to you whether you want to keep the old System folder as a backup. At the very least, you want to be sure to back up your new System folder!

THE SYSTEM 7 FINDER

If you are upgrading from System 6, you will discover that there some subtle differences between the System 6 and System 7 Finder. Although the differences may take a bit of getting used to, they do make working with the Finder easier.

The first noticeable difference is in the menu bar. As you can see in Figure 2.10, there are two menus at the right edge. The rightmost menu is known as the *Application menu*. Unlike System 6, System 7 doesn't place the names of running applications at the bottom of the menu. They are instead placed in the Application menu, as in Figure 2.11. The application with which you are working at the time you pull down the menu has a check mark next to its name and icon; the icon also appears in the menu bar as the Application menu's name. In this particular example, the Finder is the current application. (You will find more about using the Application menu in Chapter 5.)

FIGURE 2.10
The System 7 Finder menu bar

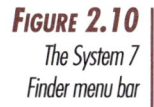

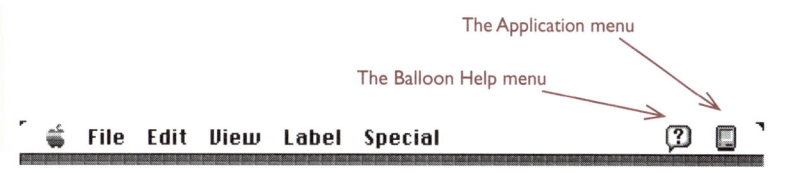

FIGURE 2.11
The System 7 Finder's Application menu

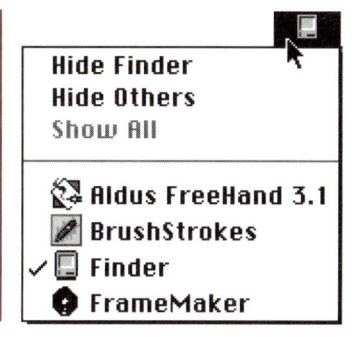

The *Balloon Help* menu, or simply *Help menu*, provides support for users who are learning to use Macintosh applications. It is discussed in depth later in this chapter. (See the section "Getting Help.")

The Labels menu (Figure 2.12) is new to System 7. A *label* is actually a category into which you can place a file or a folder. If you have a color monitor, then a label is also associated with a color that is applied to the icon of any object placed in that category. (Using labels in discussed in Chapter 4.)

FIGURE 2.12
The System 7 Finder's Labels menu

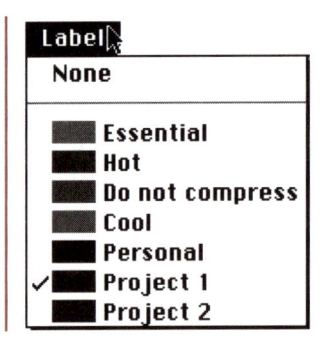

```
Label
None

▇ Essential
▇ Hot
▇ Do not compress
▇ Cool
▇ Personal
✓ ▇ Project 1
▇ Project 2
```

The remaining System 7 Finder menus are similar to the System 6 Finder menus, although there are some new commands and some of the old commands have been rearranged. The File menu in Figure 2.13, for example, is missing the Eject, Print Directory, and Get Privileges commands found in the System 6 Finder's File menu. However, there are three completely new commands: Print Window (replaces the Print Directory command), Sharing (used in System 7 networking), and Make Alias (used to ease access to files). Commands for access to System 7's improved file finding features have also been placed in the File menu. (Details on using aliases and finding files can be found in Chapter 4; System 7 networking is discussed in Chapter 10.)

The Edit and View menus are essentially unchanged from System 6 (see Figure 2.14). Notice, however, that the View menu has an additional option to let you group files and/or folders by label.

The System 7 Finder's Special menu (Figure 2.15) contains the Eject Disk command that was part of the File menu in System 6. It is missing, however, the System 6 Set Startup command. Under System 6, this command was used to indicate an application that should be launched at system startup. This capability is provided under System 7 by placing items in the Startup Items folder within the System folder. In this way you can designate as many items as you want to be launched at system startup, rather than being limited to one application as you were under System 6.

FIGURE 2.13
The System 7 Finder's File menu

File
- New Folder ⌘N
- Open ⌘O
- Print ⌘P
- Close Window ⌘W
- Get Info ⌘I
- Sharing...
- Duplicate ⌘D
- Make Alias ⌘M
- Put Away ⌘Y
- Find... ⌘F
- Find Again ⌘G
- Page Setup...
- Print Window...

New command used in System 7 networking

New command to ease access to files

Easy access to improved file finding features

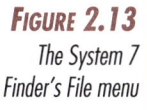

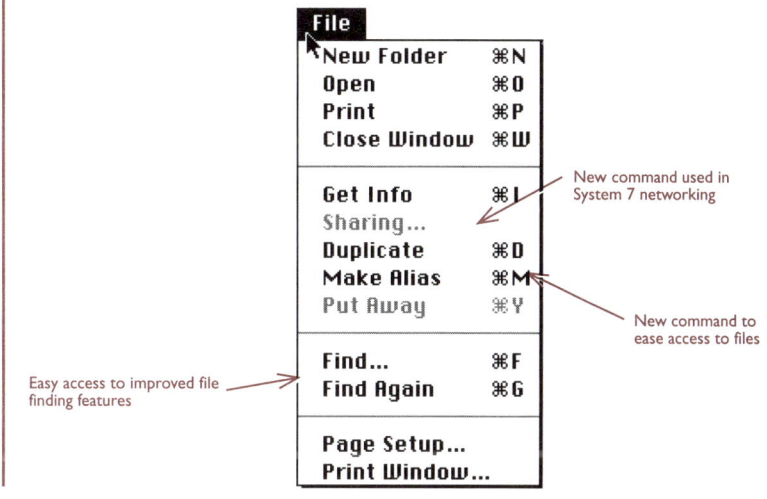

FIGURE 2.14
The System 7 Finder's Edit and View menus

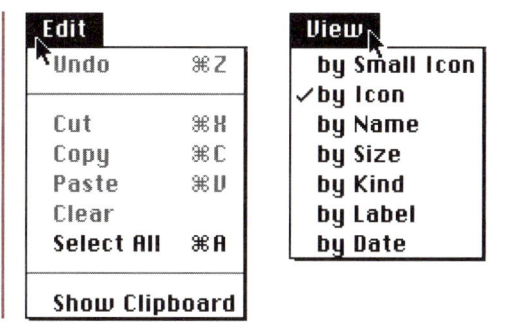

Edit
- Undo ⌘Z
- Cut ⌘X
- Copy ⌘C
- Paste ⌘V
- Clear
- Select All ⌘A
- Show Clipboard

View
- by Small Icon
- ✓by Icon
- by Name
- by Size
- by Kind
- by Label
- by Date

FIGURE 2.15
The System 7 Finder's Special menu

Special
- Clean Up Window
- Empty Trash
- Eject Disk ⌘E
- Erase Disk...
- Restart
- Shut Down

Making the Interface Easier to Use: Easy Access

As intuitive as the Macintosh user interface can be, it can present a problem to a user who doesn't have full mobility in both hands. The Macintosh operating system therefore includes a system extension called Easy Access that makes it easier to use the keyboard and mouse. Easy Access also can simplify making small mouse movements.

Easy Access is installed in the Extensions folder when you install System 7. It is therefore loaded into RAM when you boot your computer. If you don't want to use it, remove it from the System folder and reboot.

Easy Access is actually made up of two programs, Sticky Keys and Mouse Keys. Sticky Keys makes it possible to simulate pressing multiple keys at once. For example, to type an uppercase letter, you press the Shift key and a character key at the same time. With Sticky Keys, you press the Shift key and then press the character key. In other words, you can produce the uppercase letter one key at a time rather than both at once. Mouse Keys, on the other hand, lets you use the number keys on the numeric keypad to substitute for the mouse.

To turn on Sticky Keys, press the Shift key five times in succession. Be sure not to move the mouse. You will see a small icon at the far right of the menu bar indicating that Sticky Keys is on (see Figure 2.16a). To turn off Sticky Keys, press the Shift key five times in succession again.

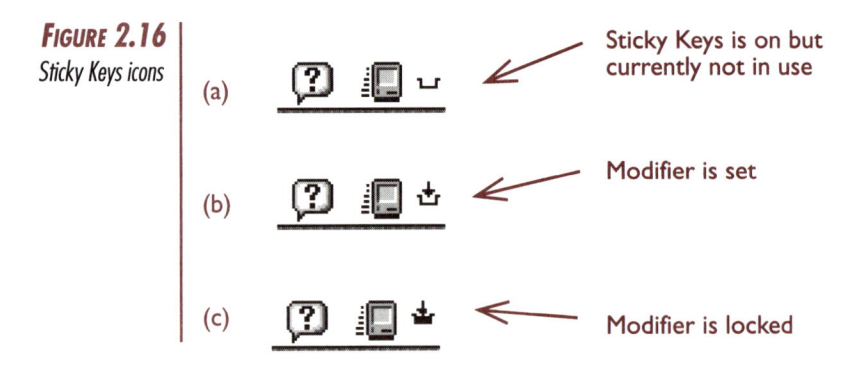

Figure 2.16
Sticky Keys icons

(a) — Sticky Keys is on but currently not in use

(b) — Modifier is set

(c) — Modifier is locked

When you want to use a key combination that includes a modifier key (**Shift**, **Option**, ⌘, or **Control**), press the modifier key alone. The Sticky Keys icon changes as in Figure 2.16b, indicating that the modifier key is "set." Press the key that should be modified. For example, to perform a Copy with the ⌘-C combination, first press the ⌘ key to set it and then press the **c** key. Keys that require two modifiers work in the same way. For example, to display the degree symbol (°), first press **Shift**, followed by **Option**, followed by **8**.

If you're going to be using the same modifier for a series of keystrokes, you can "lock" the modifier. To do so, press the modifier key twice before pressing any other key. As you can see in Figure 2.16c, the Sticky Keys icon darkens to indicate the lock.

Mouse Keys lets you use the numeric keypad instead of the mouse to move the mouse pointer. To turn on Mouse Keys, press ⌘-**Shift-Clear**. (The **Clear** key is at the top left of the numeric keypad.) When Mouse Keys is engaged, the keys in the numeric keypad move the mouse pointer as in Figure 2.17. The **5** key at the center of the keypad acts as the mouse button. Pressing it once is the same as clicking the mouse button; pressing it twice is the same as double-clicking the mouse button. To lock the mouse button so you can drag something, press the **0** key; press the decimal point key to release the mouse button. When you are finished working with Mouse Keys, press ⌘-**Shift-Clear** once more to turn it off.

FIGURE 2.17
Mouse Keys movements

MAKING THE INTERFACE EASIER TO SEE: CLOSEVIEW

CloseView, a system extension developed by Berkeley Systems, is included with System 7 to help visually impaired users. When engaged, it magnifies a portion of the screen to make it easier to see. CloseView installs as a control panel (see Figure 2.18).

34 NAVIGATING SYSTEM 7: Understanding The Macintosh Operating System

FIGURE 2.18
The CloseView control panel

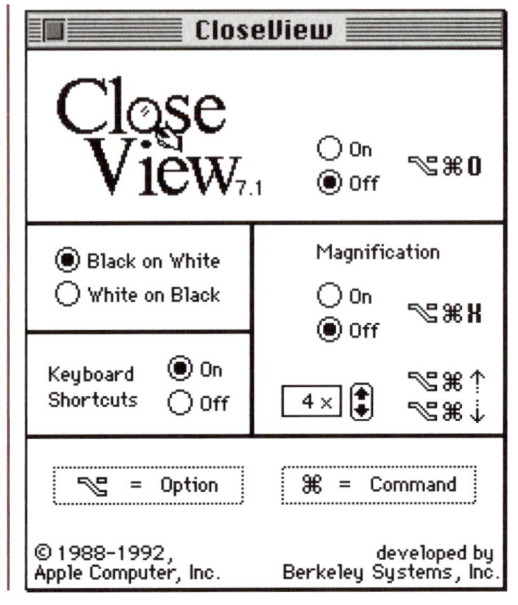

To activate CloseView, click the **On** button. When CloseView is on, but magnification off (as it is in Figure 2.18), the area that will be magnified is indicated by a rectangle with a heavy border (the "frame" in Figure 2.19). The rectangles follows the mouse pointer as you move it about the startup monitor; the rectangle and magnification, if it is turned on, disappear when the mouse pointer moves to any other monitor.

FIGURE 2.19
The CloseView magnification rectangle

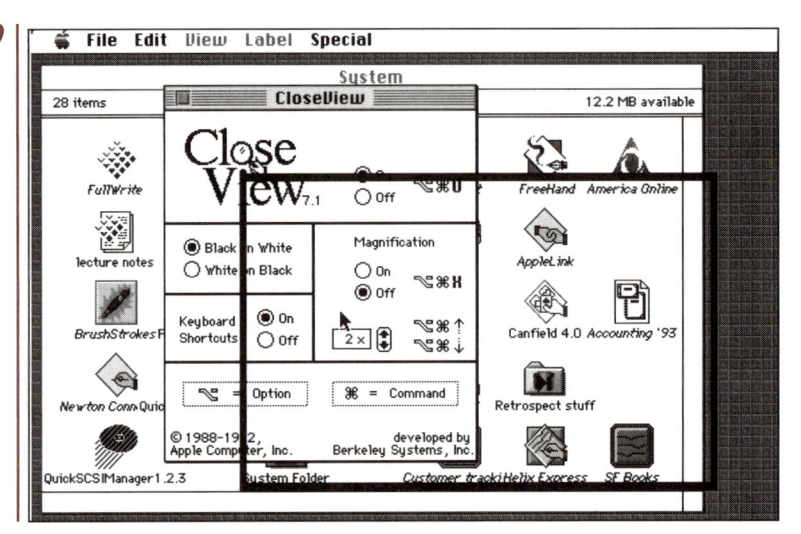

Magnification can be turned on with the control panel or with the key combination **Option**-⌘-**x**. The degree of magnification is controlled through the control panel or with the keyboard (**Option**-⌘-↑ increases magnification; **Option**-⌘-↓ decreases magnification).

Getting Help

One of the things Apple software designers were trying to do with System 7 was to make it easy for new users to get help with using the operating system and application software. To that end, they included a Help menu on the menu bar and implemented a feature known as **balloon help**. As you can see in Figure 2.20, the menu name is a rectangular balloon containing a question mark.

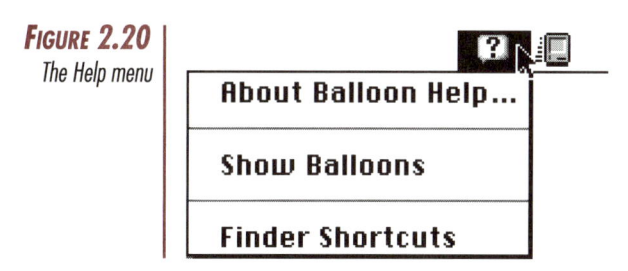

Figure 2.20
The Help menu

> About Balloon Help...
> Show Balloons
> Finder Shortcuts

Choosing the Show Balloons option turns on balloon help. (The Show Balloons option then changes to Hide Balloons so that you can turn it off.) When balloon help is on, moving the mouse pointer over an object on the Desktop produces a cartoon-like balloon that contains some help text about the object. For example, when the mouse pointer moves over an application, the balloon provides a very general definition of an application program (see Figure 2.21).

The Macintosh operating system provides balloons for most Finder objects. However, support for balloon help in application programs is the responsibility of the programmer. It therefore varies from one program to another whether balloon help is available.

To be honest, balloon help is useful while you are learning to work with software, but displaying the balloons slows down software performance. Once you're familiar with a piece of software, the balloons can also become more annoying or helpful. When that occurs, simply turn them off.

FIGURE 2.21
A help balloon

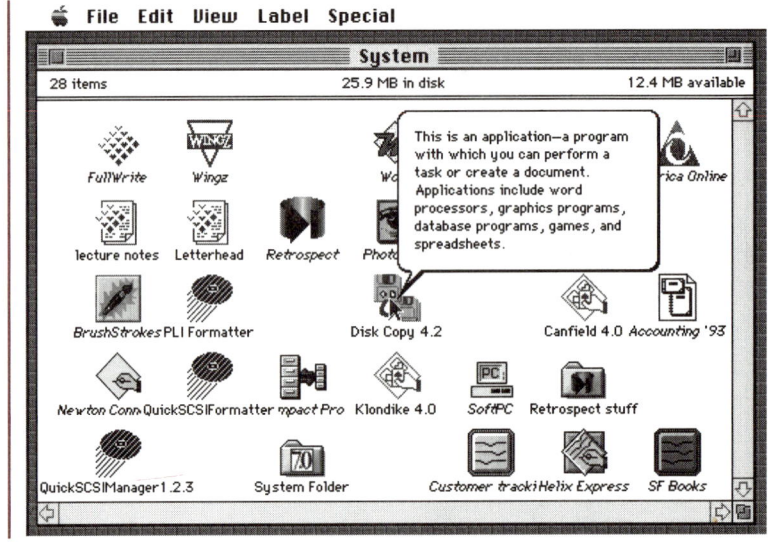

The **Finder Shortcuts** option in the Help menu produces a series of windows that describe keyboard shortcuts for many Finder menu options. For example, Figure 2.22 displays the keyboard shortcuts for working with Finder windows.

FIGURE 2.22
A help screen for Finder Shortcuts

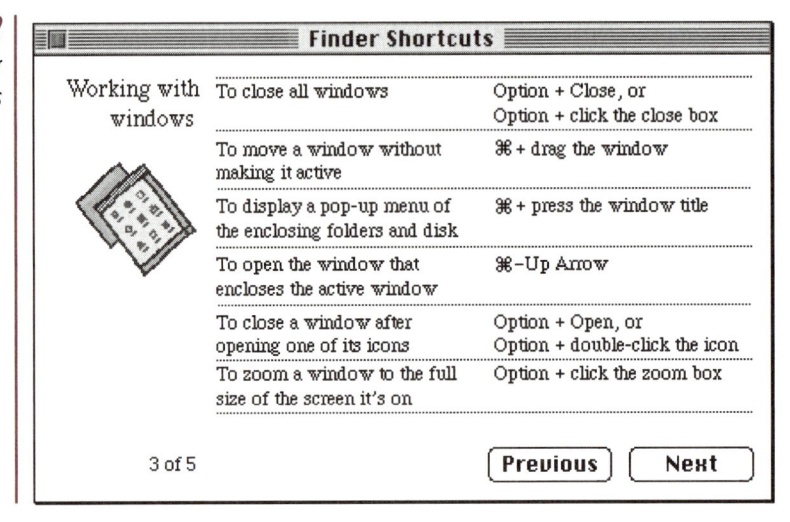

USEFUL ADD-ON

If you want to get rid of the Help menu entirely, you can do so with SpeedyFinder 7, a shareware program by Victor Tan that provides all sorts of useful System 7 additions. To get rid of the Help menu, choose Menu options from the SpeedyFinder 7 control panel and check the Hide Balloon Help Menu box (see Figure 2.23).

Figure 2.23
Using SpeedyFinder 7 to hide the Balloon Help menu

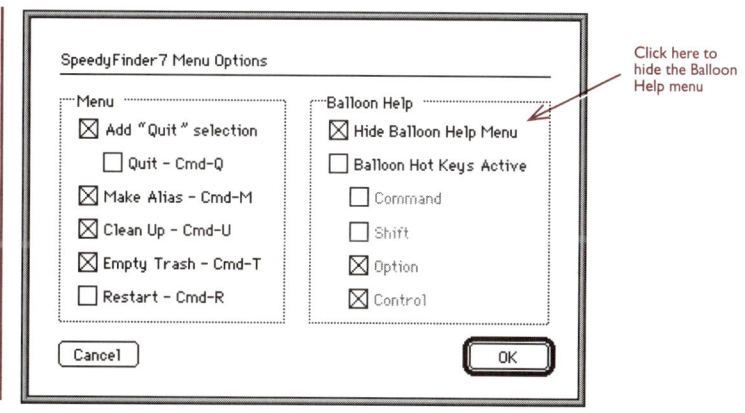

Making the Interface Easier for Novices: At Ease

As intuitive as the Finder may be for knowledgeable users, there is a group of users for whom the Finder is either too complex or inappropriate. Apple therefore provides a Finder extension, At Ease, that isolates such users from the Finder. At Ease is sold as a stand-alone product.

As you can see in Figure 2.24, At Ease provides a subset of the full Finder's menus as well as two large file folders on the desktop. The Applications folder contains icons for the applications to which a user should have access; the Documents folder, which the user displays by clicking on the folder's name, contains icons for the documents to which a user should have access.

At Ease installs as a control panel (Figure 2.25). The first step in setting up an At Ease environment is to choose applications and documents to appear on the At Ease folder (see Figure 2.26). Then, decide whether new documents should be added to the Documents folder or stored on a floppy disk (see Figure 2.27).

FIGURE 2.25
The At Ease control panel

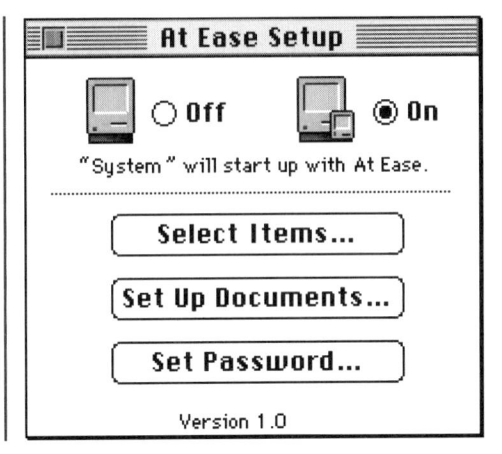

FIGURE 2.26
Adding applications and existing documents to the At Ease folders

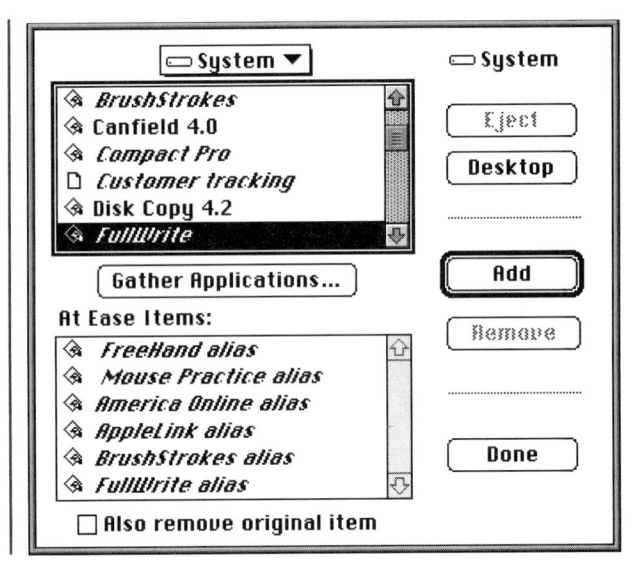

Installing At Ease adds an option to the bottom of the File menu: Go to Finder. The final step in configuring At Ease is therefore to install a password for full Finder access (see Figure 2.28). The password will also be required when the user wants to open a document that isn't part of the At Ease desktop.

WARNING: Be very careful when removing At Ease from your system. Be sure to turn it off before deleting files. Otherwise, you may find that you can't boot your Macintosh.

CHAPTER 2: A Tour Around the Operating System **39**

FIGURE 2.27
Deciding what to do with new documents

> **Set Up Documents**
>
> When saving new documents:
> ☒ Add a button to At Ease
> ☐ Require a floppy disk
>
> [Cancel]   [OK]

FIGURE 2.28
Setting an At Ease password

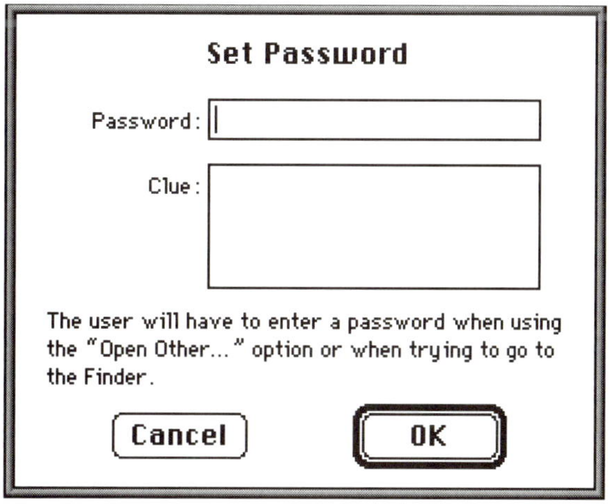

> **Set Password**
>
> Password: [   ]
>
> Clue: [   ]
>
> The user will have to enter a password when using the "Open Other..." option or when trying to go to the Finder.
>
> [Cancel]   [OK]

CHAPTER 3
Configuring Your System

Many of the characteristics of your Macintosh environment—for example, the date, time, keyboard repeat rate, number styles, and sounds—are set through a collection of control panels. This chapter looks at those control panels that handle general system configuration. You will read about control panels that handle specific functions (for example, memory and networking) later in this book.

> Prior to System 7, Control Panels was a single desk accessory with a scrolling list of icons that functioned as switches to select the specific control panel with which you would work. System 7 separates the control panels, making it easier to find and access them. System 7 control panels can also be accessed just like any other application (by double-clicking on an icon), something that wasn't possible previously.

Under System 7, control panels are *modeless dialog boxes*. That means that they can be moved around the screen like a document window. They also can be left on the desktop when you switch to work with another program. In fact, control panel windows don't go away unless you explicitly dismiss them, either by clicking on a close box or an **OK** button. (The method used to close a control panel window depends on the specific control panel.)

THE GENERAL CONTROLS

The General Controls control panel handles miscellaneous system configurations such as the current date and time. As you can see in Figure 3.1, it also sets the background desktop pattern and the rate of insertion point and menu blinking.

FIGURE 3.1
The General Controls control panel

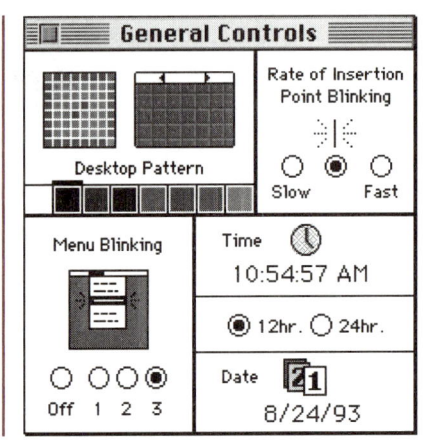

SETTING AND DISPLAYING THE DATE AND TIME

Keeping the correct date and time is vital to the operation of a Macintosh because the Macintosh operating system marks files and folders with the date and time they are created and the last date and time they were modified. You should therefore set the date and time when you first get your Macintosh and adjust it as needed for the change between daylight savings time and standard time.

> **BY THE WAY!** The Macintosh remembers the date and time even when you turn off the computer because the date and time are stored in *parameter RAM* (PRAM), special RAM whose contents is maintained by the Macintosh's battery. If your computer begins to have trouble keeping time, your battery probably needs replacing.

To set the date:

1. Click on the part of the date you want to change (either the month, date, or year). As you can see in Figure 3.2, up and down arrows appear at the far right of the control panel.

FIGURE 3.2
Changing the month

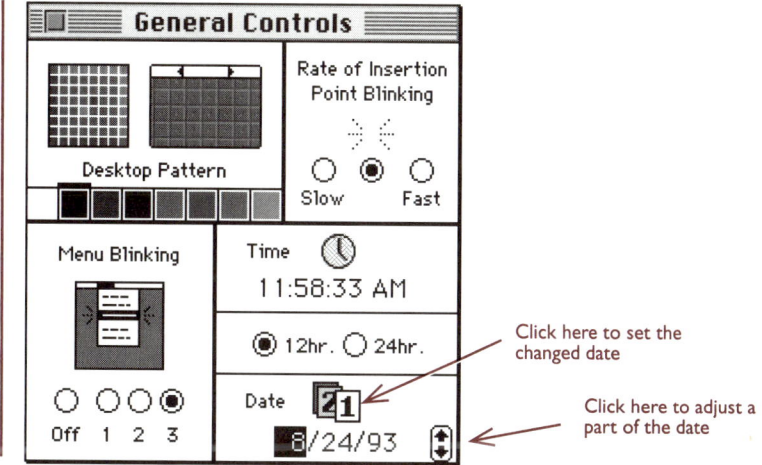

    2. Click either the up arrow or the down arrow to adjust the part of the date.

    3. Repeat steps 1 and 2 for each part of the date that needs changing.

    4. Click the calendar page icon above the date to set the changed date. (If you don't click the calendar page icon, the date reverts to its original setting when you close the General Controls window.)

Use the 12hr/24hr radio buttons to indicate whether the clock will keep 12-hour time (AM/PM times, commonly used in the U.S. and Canada) or 24-hour time (commonly used in Europe). This setting affects the operating system's alarm clock (discussed shortly).

To set the time:

    1. Click on a part of the time to be changed (either the hour, minute, seconds, or AM/PM indicator). Up and down arrows appear at the right of the time.

    2. Click either the up arrow or the down arrow to adjust the part of the time.

    3. Repeat steps 1 and 2 for each part of the time that needs changing.

    4. Click the clock face above the time to set the changed time. (If you don't click the clock face, the time reverts to its original setting when you close the General Controls window.)

The Alarm Clock

The Macintosh operating system provides a clock that you can place anywhere on your desktop. To display the alarm clock, choose Alarm Clock from the menu. A small modeless dialog box appears (see Figure 3.3). The Macintosh operating system updates the alarm clock to keep it current as long as it is open on the desktop.

Figure 3.3
The Macintosh operating system clock

`1:27:36 PM`

You can use the operating system's alarm clock to set the date and time as well as trigger an alarm at a specific date and time. To set the alarm:

1. Click on the key at the right of the small alarm clock window to drop down the rest of the dialog box (see Figure 3.4).

Figure 3.4
The expanded operating system alarm clock

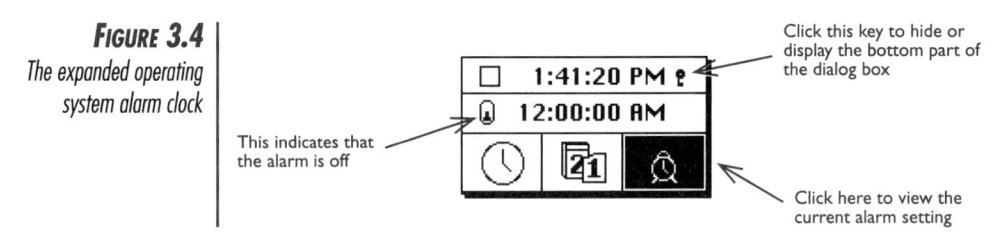

- 1:41:20 PM
- 12:00:00 AM
- This indicates that the alarm is off
- Click this key to hide or display the bottom part of the dialog box
- Click here to view the current alarm setting

2. Click on the alarm clock switch at the bottom right of the dialog box. Notice in Figure 3.4 that the button at the left of the alarm time is at the bottom. This indicates that the alarm is off.

3. Click the part of the time you want to change. Up and down arrows appear (see Figure 3.5).

Figure 3.5
Setting the alarm

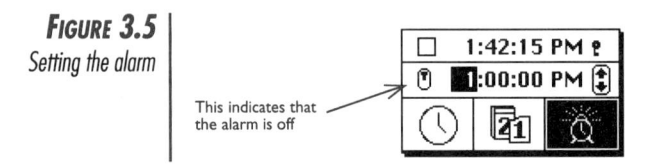

- 1:42:15 PM
- 1:00:00 PM
- This indicates that the alarm is off

4. Click an up or down arrow until the part of the time is set.

5. Repeat steps 3 and 4 until the alarm is set to the time you want.
6. Click the button at the left of the alarm time to set the alarm, as in Figure 3.5.
7. Close the alarm clock dialog box.

When the Macintosh's clock matches the alarm time, the Macintosh beeps the computer's speaker and flashes an alarm clock in the menu bar, just to the left of the menu. This icon continues flashing until you open the alarm clock and turn off the alarm by clicking on the button at the left.

The clock face switch at the bottom left of the alarm clock dialog box lets you set the system time; the calendar switch in the middle lets you set the system date. Setting the date and time from the alarm clock dialog box works just like setting it from the General Controls control panel.

USEFUL ADD-ON

The Macintosh operating system's alarm clock is somewhat limited. It can easily be hidden behind other windows and can only handle a single alarm setting that is within the next 24 hours. There are, however, a number of third party clocks that you can add to your system. Reminder (part of the Now Up-to-Date package), for example, places a clock in the menu bar (see Figure 3.6). Having the clock in the menu bar means that it will never be hidden by other windows.

FIGURE 3.6
The Reminder clock in the menu bar

Tue 2:07:19 PM

Reminder installs as a control panel (see Figure 3.7). Notice that you can configure the style with which the clock is displayed as well as which portion of the day and time actually appear in the menu bar. Reminder handles multiple alarm settings over a wide range of time, including settings that repeat at intervals (for example, weekly or monthly).

FIGURE 3.7
The Reminder control panel

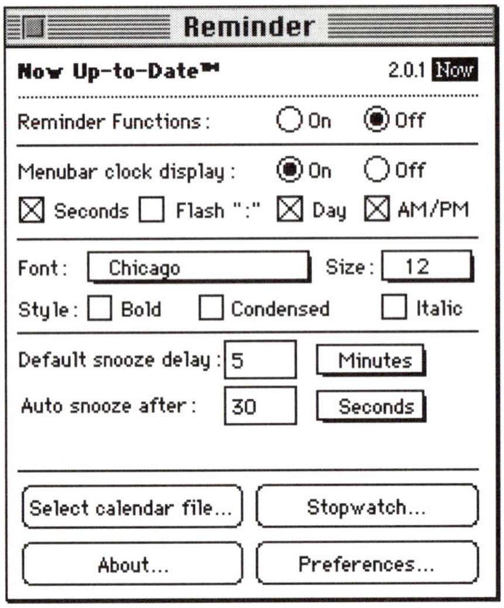

Choosing a Blinking Rate

The Macintosh user interface makes judicious use of blinking. (Too much blinking is hard on the eyes.) When you choose an option from a menu, the selected option blinks briefly before the menu closes; when you are entering text into a document, a straight-line insertion point blinks to show you where the next character will appear. The rate at which each of these blinks occurs is set in the General Controls control panel.

If you look at Figure 3.8, you can see that menu blinking can be turned off entirely or set to one of three relative settings (1 through 3). Blinking the insertion point cannot be turned off. However, it can be set to one of three relative settings (Slow through Fast).

Changing the Desktop Pattern

The desktop pattern is the background pattern on which the Finder's windows appear. Unless you change it, the pattern is a light gray. However, light gray can be very boring. The Macintosh operating system therefore provides several alternative patterns as well as a way to edit patterns.

To change the desktop pattern, use the tiny arrows in the menu bar of the small desktop at the top left of the General Controls control panel (see Figure 3.9).

Clicking on the arrows cycles through the built-in patterns. Each time you click one of the arrows, the desktop pattern actually changes; you don't need to wait until you close the control panel.

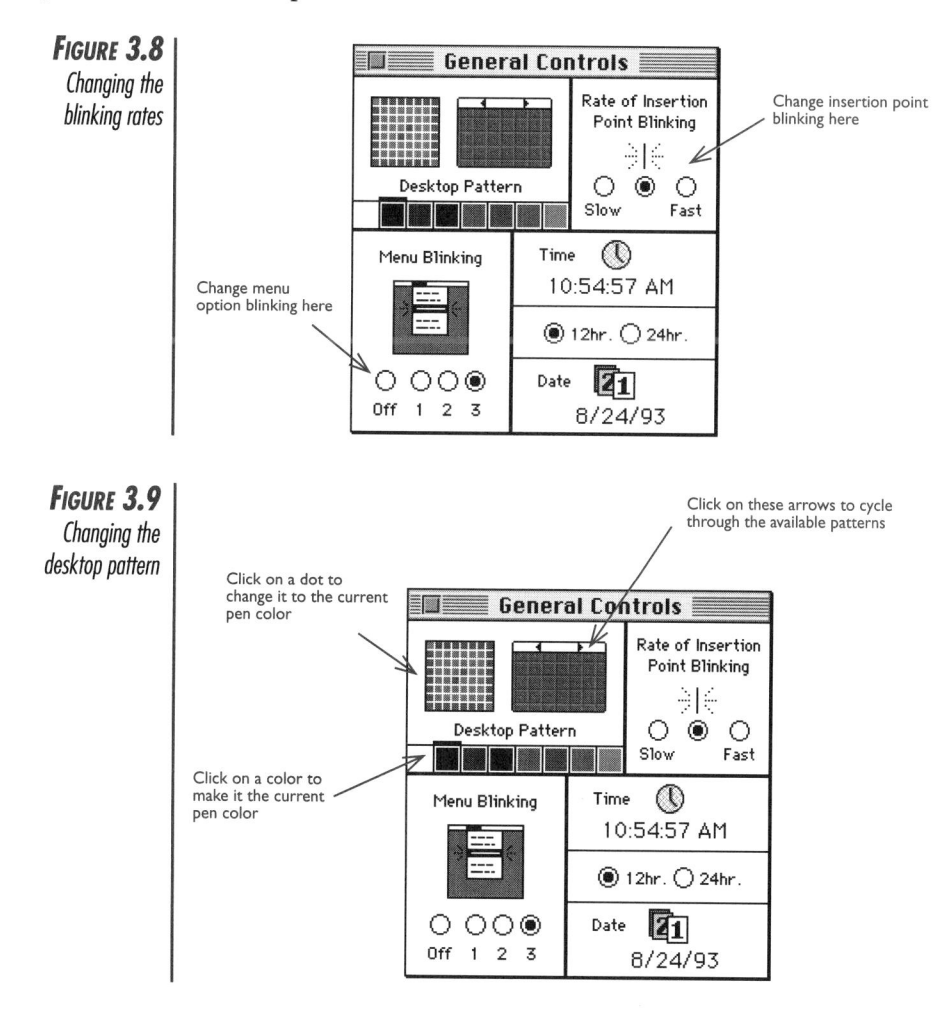

FIGURE 3.8
Changing the blinking rates

FIGURE 3.9
Changing the desktop pattern

A magnified view of the desktop pattern appears at the far left of the control panel. In it you can see the individual dots that make up the pattern. Below the miniature desktop and the magnified view is a palette of the colors or shades of gray used in the pattern. To edit the pattern:

1. Click on a color in the palette to make it the current pen color.

2. Click on a dot in the magnified view of the pattern to change its color to the current pen color.

3. Repeat steps 1 and 2 for every dot in the pattern you want to change.

> **USEFUL ADD-ON** If you aren't happy with any of the Desktop patterns supplied with System 7, consider a program that lets you add other patterns. One of the most popular is Before Dark, a shareware utility (Figure 3.10). There are hundreds of free Desktop patterns available through user groups and on-line services that can be installed with Before Dark.

FIGURE 3.10
Using Before Dark to install custom Desktop patterns

SETTING DATE AND TIME FORMATS

As illogical as it might seem, the date and time formats used for display in Finder windows aren't set in the General Controls control panel, but in a separate control panel called Date & Time (Figure 3.11). The two buttons at the bottom of the control panel's window give you access to dialog boxes in which formats are set.

Assuming that you are using the U.S. version of the operating system, date formats include most of the standard formats used in the U.S. (see Figure 3.12). Time formats (Figure 3.13) include either a 12- or 24-hour clock and the representation to be used for noon and midnight.

FIGURE 3.11
The Date & Time control panel for System 7.0 and 7.1

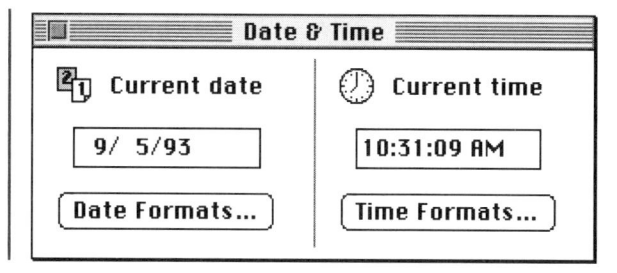

FIGURE 3.12
Setting the date format for the U.S. version of System 7

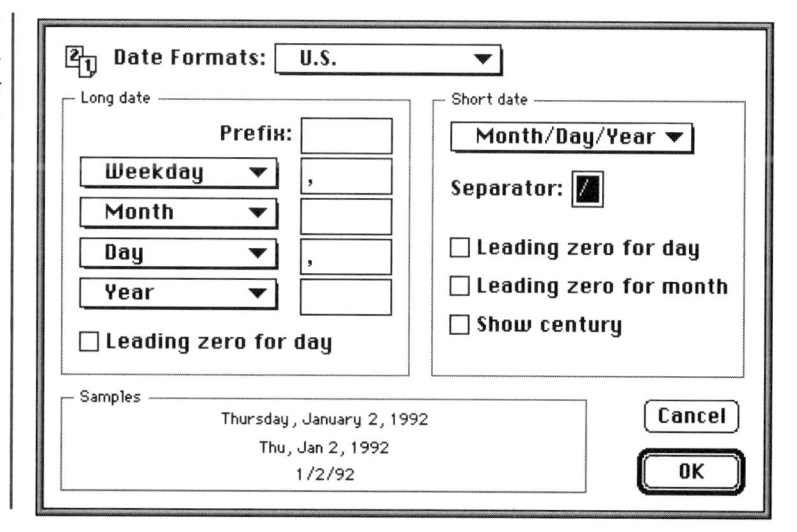

FIGURE 3.13
Setting the time format for the U.S. version of System 7

50 NAVIGATING SYSTEM 7: Understanding The Macintosh Operating System

If you are working with System 7 Pro, the Date & Time control panel has two additional settings (see Figure 3.14). Clicking the Set Time Zone button displays a list of cities throughout the world (Figure 3.15). To set the time zone in which your Macintosh is located, highlight a city in your time zone and click the **OK** button or press **Enter**. If your location uses daylight savings time, click the "Daylight Savings Time" check box. The Macintosh will then automatically adjust the system clock to account for seasonal time changes.

FIGURE 3.14
The Date & Time control panel for System 7 Pro

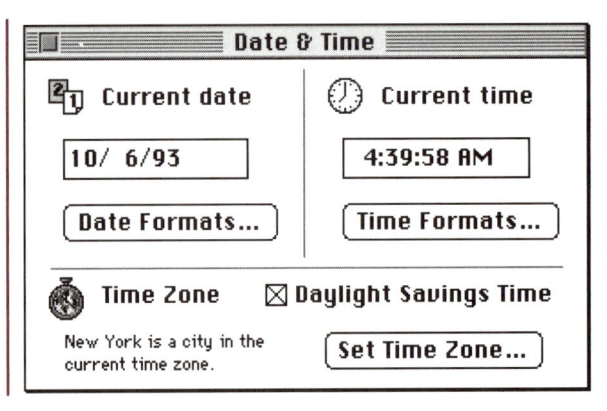

> **BY THE WAY!**
> If you are going to use System 7 Pro's electronic mail capabilities, then be sure to set the time zone and indicate whether your location uses daylight savings time. This is essential for the correct time stamping of mail transmissions.

FIGURE 3.15
Setting the time zone

CHAPTER 3: Configuring Your System   **51**

> **FLASH BACK** Prior to System 7, there was no choice of date and time formats; Finder windows used a standard, nonmodifiable format. This may account for the Date & Time control panel being separate from the General Controls, which were all part of System 6.

MONITORS

One of the most elegant features of the Macintosh is its ability to support more than one monitor and to manipulate the images on those monitors as a single Desktop. Monitor configuration is handled by the Monitors control panel (Figure 3.16). The bottom of the control panel contains a rectangle for each monitor connected to the Macintosh. The size of those rectangles is relative to the size of the monitor. In Figure 3.16, for example, monitor 1 is a 13-inch monitor; monitor 2 is a 20-inch monitor.

FIGURE 3.16
The Monitors control panel

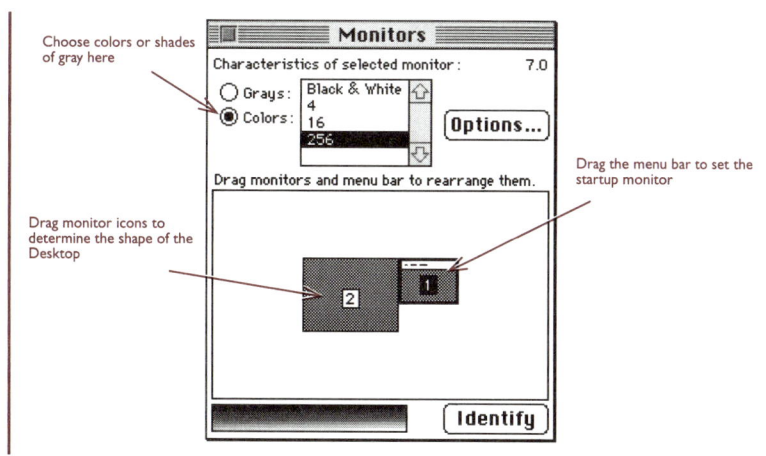

The position of the monitor rectangles relative to one another determines the shape of the Desktop. (This is completely independent of the physical position of the monitors.) To change the shape of the Desktop, click on the monitor rectangle you want to move and then drag it into its new position. Any changes made won't take effect until you restart the Macintosh.

The monitor rectangle that contains the menu bar determines the *startup monitor*. The startup monitor displays the menu bar; the icons for disks known to the

Macintosh appear along its right edge. To change the startup monitor, drag the menu bar from its current location to the monitor rectangle that should be the new startup monitor. This change also won't take effect until you restart the Macintosh.

The top portion of the Monitors control panel determines how many colors or shades of gray are displayed on each monitor. The maximum number of colors and shades of gray are determined by the type of Macintosh and the type of video circuitry installed. For example, a Macintosh with a 68000 microprocessor (for example, the Plus, SE, or Classic) supports only black and white monitors, although a video expansion board might be added to provide a second, larger monitor. Other Macintoshes support varying levels of grays or colors.

To set the number of grays or colors to be displayed on a monitor, click the monitor's rectangle in the bottom portion of the Monitors control panel; a black border appears around the rectangle, as it does around monitor 1 in Figure 3.16. The options in the top portion of the window reflect the selected monitor. (In this particular example, the monitor is connected to a Macintosh that supports color and has video circuitry for supporting 256 colors or shades of gray.)

Click the **Grays** radio button to work in black-and-white or grayscale; click the **Colors** button to work in color. Choose the number of colors or grays from the scrolling list of options. These changes take effect immediately, without having to close the control panel or restart the Macintosh.

The Startup Screen

When you start up your Macintosh, you see the default startup screen: a "Welcome to Macintosh" message on a gray background. If you find this a bit boring, there's an easy way to change it. Any bitmapped graphic file that is placed in the System folder with the name "StartupScreen" will be used instead of the default. In fact, many graphics programs actually give you the option of saving the document as a startup screen.

You can have as many startup screen files as you want. However, only one can be in the System folder at any time. (This only makes sense, because if you try to move a second file into any folder with the same name as a file already in the folder, you can either replace the existing file or abort the move operation.)

SOUND

When it comes to making noise, the Macintosh is a very accomplished computer. It has a special integrated circuit (the *Apple Sound Chip*, or ASC) that takes care of producing sounds through the Macintosh's internal speaker; it can also send those sounds to an external speaker if one happens to be attached.

The sound that you hear when an alert box appears on the screen (a *system beep*) is determined by the Sound control panel (Figure 3.17). The scrolling list at the right of the control panel displays all the sounds installed in the System file. To hear a sound, double-click on its name. To select a system beep sound, click on the sound name to highlight it.

FIGURE 3.17

The Sound control panel for System 7.0 and 7.1

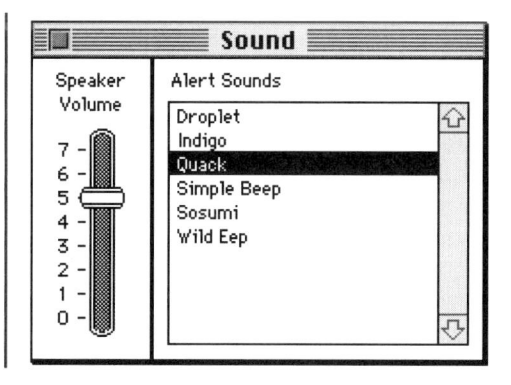

The slider at the left of the Sound control panel determines the volume at which sounds are played. Drag the slide up to increase volume; drag it down to decrease it. If you move the slider to 0, then you will hear no system beep when an alert appears. Instead, the menu bar will flash. This can be particularly useful if you are using your Macintosh in a situation where you don't want to disturb people around you (for example, on an airplane).

If you are using System 7 Pro, you will find that the Sound control panel has been enhanced to provide better support for Macintoshes with sound recording capabilities (see Figure 3.18). Notice that the pull-down menu above the slider lets a Macintosh that can record add sounds through its microphone. (If your Macintosh can't record, choosing Sound In simply displays an alert saying that you can't record.)

FIGURE 3.18
The Sound control panel for System 7 Pro

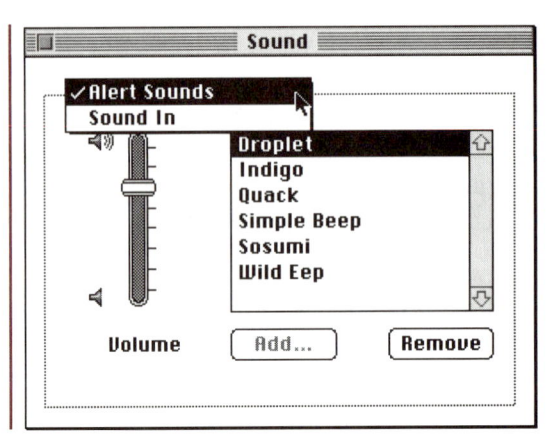

If you enjoy having a Macintosh that makes lots of sounds, consider using SoundMaster, a shareware control panel device that provides significantly more functionality than the Sound control panel. SoundMaster (Figure 3.19) lets you assign sounds to various events. For example, in Figure 3.19 the sound "He's dead, Jim" is assigned to a bad disk event.

FIGURE 3.19
The SoundMaster control panel

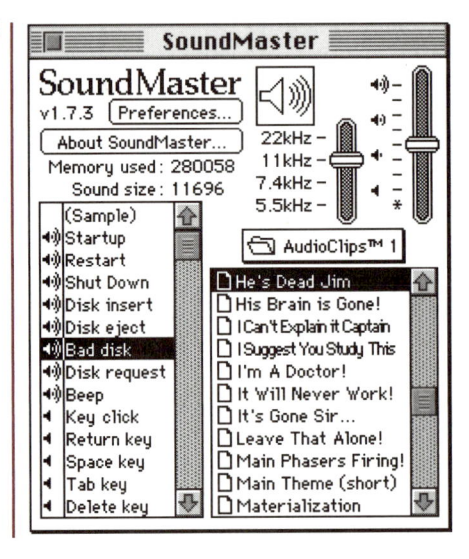

SoundMaster also lets you adjust the speed and volume of each individual sound. Sound files can be stored anywhere; they don't need to be part of the System file. Where do you get sound files? Some, like the Star Trek sounds in Figure 3.19, are commercial software. Many others are freeware or shareware, available from user groups and on-line services.

Keyboard

The Keyboard control panel (Figure 3.20) takes care of the key repeat rate and the keyboard layout. As you know, if you hold down a key for more than an instant, the character produced by that key repeats. The top half of the Keyboard control panel configures how fast duplicate characters are produced (the radio buttons **Slow** to **Fast**) and how long the Macintosh waits before it starts repeating (the radio buttons **Off** and **Long** to **Short**).

Figure 3.20
The Keyboard control panel

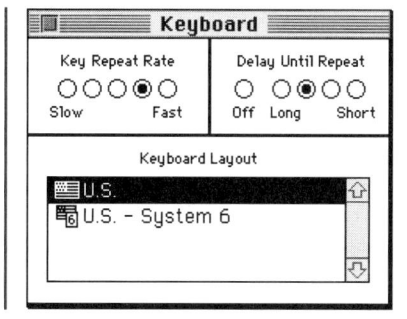

The bottom half of the control panel determines the way in which characters are mapped to the keyboard. The U.S. version of the Macintosh operating system includes a standard QWERTY keyboard layout. However, you can install and use alternative keyboard layouts, including the Dvorak layout. (Keep in mind that when you change to a different keyboard layout, the labels on the tops of your keys don't change!)

Mouse

The Mouse control panel (Figure 3.21) determines the speed at which the mouse pointer moves in response to mouse movement and how close together two clicks must be to be considered a double-click. In terms of mouse tracking speed, the general rule is the larger your Desktop, the faster the mouse tracking should be. This means that small mouse movements will generate relatively larger movements in the mouse pointer, making it easier to get the mouse pointer from one edge of the Desktop to the other. The double-click speed is usually a matter of personal preference; experiment with all three settings to see which you prefer.

FIGURE 3.21
The Mouse control panel

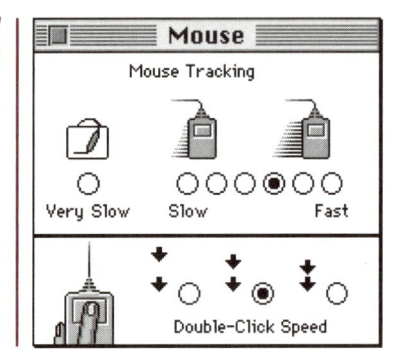

NUMBERS

The Numbers control panel (Figure 3.22) determines the default number display format. You can choose the character to be used as a decimal point (a period, a comma, or a space) and the character to be used to separate each group of three whole number digits (a comma, a period, a space, a single straight quote, or no separator). In addition, you can use it to set the currency symbol and to indicate whether the currency symbol should come before or after a number.

FIGURE 3.22
The Numbers control panel

COLOR

The Color control panel (Figure 3.23) determines default text highlighting and window border colors. The colors set in this control panel affect Finder windows. They also appear in some application windows if the application doesn't override Finder settings with its own colors.

FIGURE 3.23
The Color control panel

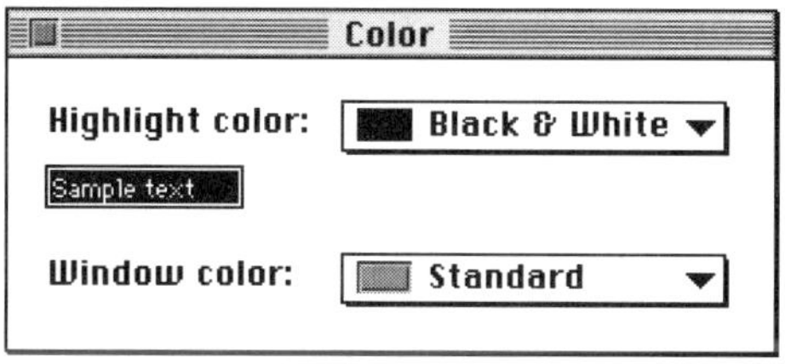

THE SCRAPBOOK

One feature of the Macintosh operating system that has been present since 1984 is the Scrapbook, a permanent holding area for text and graphics. The contents of the Scrapbook are maintained in a single file in the System folder. Because the Scrapbook file grows as you add items, it is most commonly used for small items that are used frequently, such as a logo or return address.

To gain access to the Scrapbook, choose Scrapbook from the menu. When the Scrapbook window appears, use the **Paste** command to place an item in the Scrapbook. If you need to use an image in the Scrapbook, **Copy** it to the Clipboard. To remove an item complete, **Cut** it out of the Scrapbook.

The Scrapbook can accept text (including word processor formatting codes) and bitmapped and QuickDraw graphics, such as the PICT image in Figure 3.24. However, if you want to place a PostScript graphic (for example, an Aldus Freehand or Adobe Illustrator image) in the Scrapbook, you need to transform it into a QuickDraw graphic plus embedded PostScript code. To do so, select the PostScript graphic. Then, hold down the **Option** key and select **Copy** from the Edit menu. Keep the **Option** key pressed until you see the message "Converting the Clipboard." When you use a converted graphic of this type, you will see a bitmap on the screen. However, when the graphic is printed, the embedded PostScript code will be used to print the original image.

FIGURE 3.24
A PICT graphic in the Scrapbook

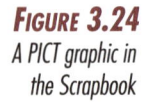

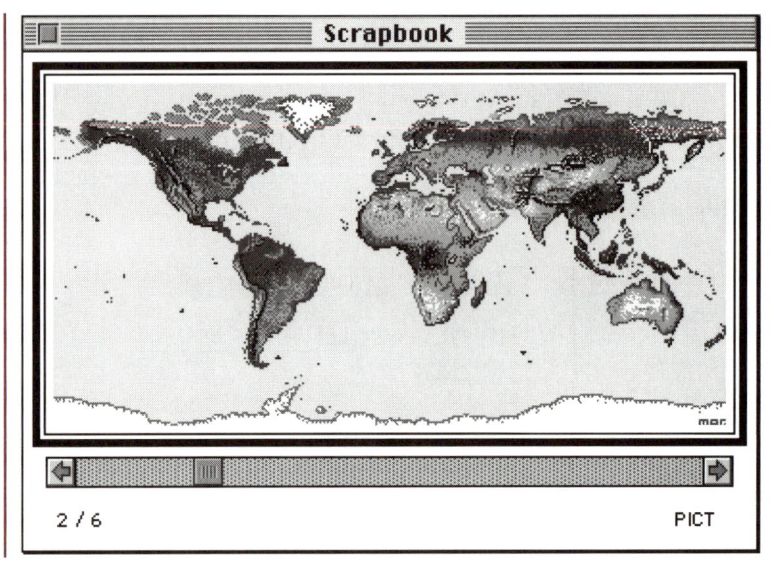

THE CHOOSER AND PRINTER DEVICE DRIVERS

The Chooser is a special control panel that lets you select the printer you want to use. (The Chooser is also used in System 7 file sharing. You will read about this in Chapter 10.) Once you select a printer using the Chooser, you don't need to change it unless you want to use a different printer.

To select a printer, choose Chooser from the menu. The Chooser window appears (Figure 3.25). The left of the window contains a scrolling list of types of hardware devices that the Chooser can recognize. In Figure 3.25, for example, all the icons except AppleShare and Autographix represent types of printers.

To be completely accurate, each icon in the Chooser represents a device driver. As you will remember, a device driver is a piece of software that acts as a translator between the Macintosh operating system and a piece of hardware such as printer, disk drive, or scanner. The same device driver can often be used with more than one manufacturer's printer. This is particularly true for laser printers. For example, the QMS laser printer listed at the right of Figure 3.25 uses Apple's LaserWriter driver. To find out exactly what driver to use with your printer, consult the documentation that came with your printer.

FIGURE 3.25
The Chooser

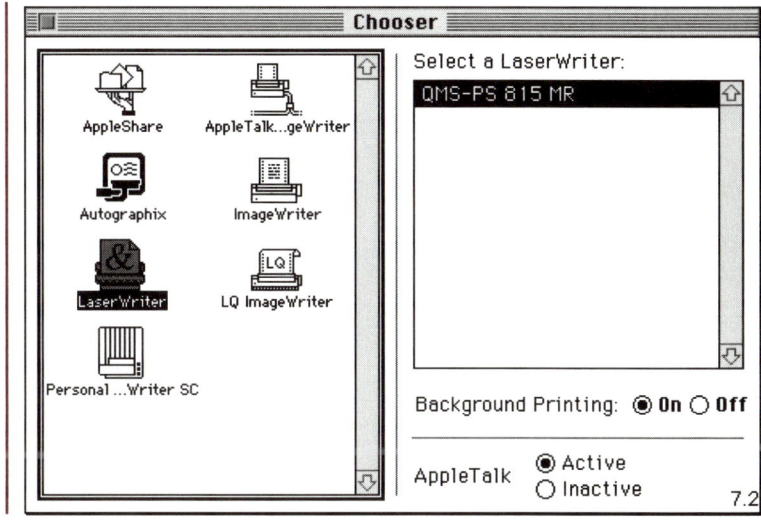

To select a printer driver, do the following:

1. If the printer is connected through an AppleTalk network, make sure that the **AppleTalk Active** radio button is highlighted.

2. Click on the printer driver's icon.

3. If the printer is connected through an AppleTalk network, a list of available printers that can use the selected printer driver appears at the right of the Chooser window, as in Figure 3.25. (A printer must be turned on and warmed up before it will appear in the list.) Click on the name of the printer you want to use.

4. If the printer is connected directly to a serial port, icons for the printer and modem ports appear at the right of the Chooser window (see Figure 3.26). Click the icon that represents the correct port. Note that if AppleTalk is active, it will be using the Printer port. Therefore, only the modem port will be available for a direct-connected printer.

5. Close the Chooser window. If you have changed printer drivers, you will see the alert in Figure 3.27.

6. Click **OK** to dismiss the alert.

FIGURE 3.26
Choosing a port for a printer connected directly to a serial port

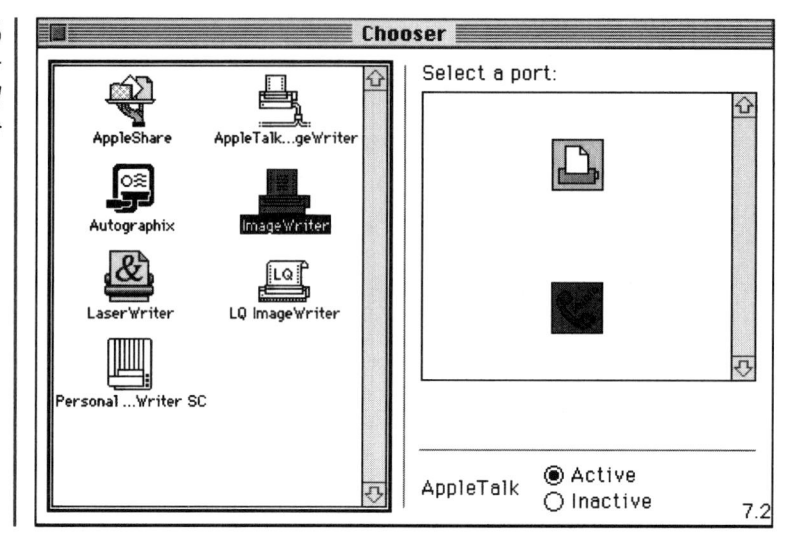

The alert in Figure 3.27 appears because different types of printers have different printing areas. In particular, a laser printer can't print on the outer .25-inch of a page, while other printers can print closer to the edge. Therefore, if you change printers while documents are open, you should do what the alert suggests: Choose **Page Setup** from the File menu of each running application. You don't need to make any changes in the Page Setup dialog box; simply click **OK**. This sets the correct print area for the selected printer driver.

FIGURE 3.27
A warning that changing the printer changes the printing area

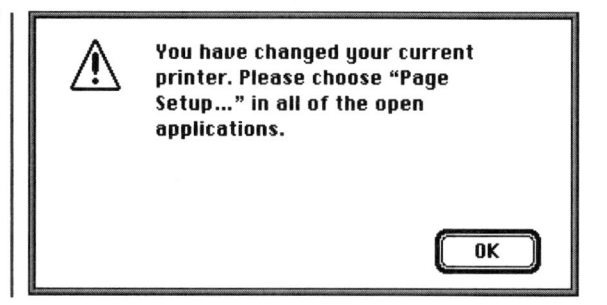

The Map

The Macintosh operating system provides a control panel that is a mystery to many people because they can't figure out what to do with it: the Map.

Theoretically, it might be useful if you were traveling and wanted to figure out how far it was from where you were to anyplace else. Other uses are more or less up to your imagination.

The Map control panel (Figure 3.28) provides a scrolling black-and-white map of the world. It has a number of pre-installed locations whose longitude, latitude, and time zone you can find. To locate a city, do the following:

1. Type the city's name in the text entry box below the **Add City** and **Remove City** buttons. (Actually, you don't have to type the entire name, just enough so the Map can tell it from other cities in its database.)

2. Click the **Find** button. The map display scrolls to show you the portion of the world in which the city is located. The city's location flashes.

3. To make the city's time zone your local time zone, click the **Set** button. This readjusts the Macintosh's clock to the new time zone.

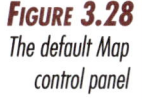

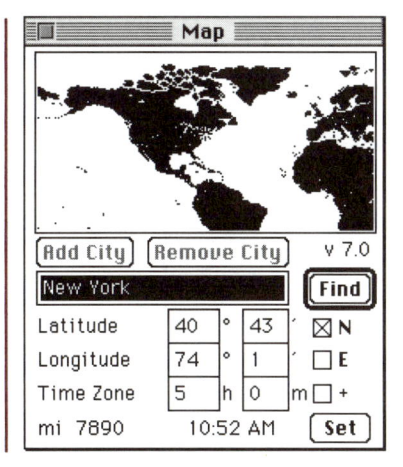

Figure 3.28
The default Map control panel

The mileage at the bottom left of the Map control panel is the distance between "where you were" (defined as the next to the last city you accessed with the Map control panel) and "where you are" (defined as the last city you accessed with the Map control panel).

To see all the cities currently in the Map control panel's database, hold down the **Option** key and click the **Find** button. Each time you do this, the Map control panel displays the "next" city, in alphabetical order, in its database.

You can also add cities of your own. First, enter a name for the city. If you know the city's latitude and longitude, enter them in the appropriate boxes in the control panel and click the **Add City** button. If you don't know the latitude and longitude, click the mouse button on the map itself to locate the city and then click the **Add City** button. To scroll the map to bring another portion of the planet into view, hold down the mouse button and drag to one edge of the map.

If you have a color monitor and you think the black-and-white map is boring, try pasting in the color map from the Scrapbook (the map seen in Figure 3.24). The Map is then a bit more esthetically pleasing (Figure 3.29). Notice also in Figure 3.29 the mark in the middle of the ocean. This is a "city" known as the Middle of Nowhere.

FIGURE 3.29
The Map control panel enhanced with the color map from the Scrapbook

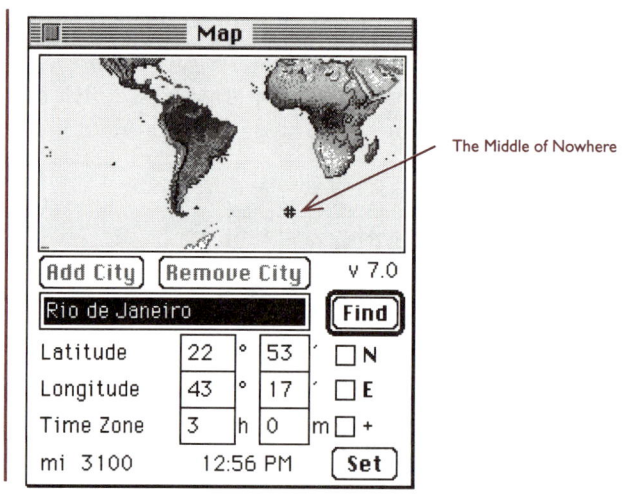

SCREEN SHOTS

One of the most fascinating features of the very first version of the Macintosh operating system was its ability to take a *screen shot*. A screen shot, also known as a *screen capture*, is a bitmappped image of all or part of the Macintosh screen.

> **FLASHBACK**
> When the Apple ImageWriter was the most typical Macintosh printer, the Macintosh operating system could print a screen shot directly to the ImageWriter. That capability is no longer part of the Macintosh operating system.

CHAPTER 3: Configuring Your System   **63**

The Macintosh operating system can perform a screen capture. To take a screen shot, press **Shift**-⌘-**3**. The operating system creates a file on your startup volume in PICT format. The file contains a bitmapped image of your entire Desktop (all monitors). You can then edit the image with any bitmapped graphics program that can open a PICT file.

USEFUL ADD-ON

Although the Macintosh operating system's screen capture capability works, it isn't very flexible. It can't capture menus when they are pulled down. It also can't capture any screen conditions that require pressing the **Shift**, **Option**, **Control**, or ⌘ key. Therefore, if you need more powerful screen capture capabilities, consider a third-party screen shot utility such as Capture.

Capture (Figure 3.30), which installs as a control panel, can be triggered by any key combination, including the function keys on the extended keyboard. You can capture the entire desktop, just the startup screen, or a portion of a screen that you select by dragging a rectangle around it. The screen capture can occur immediately after you trigger it or after some delay you specify. In addition, the target of the screen shot can be the Clipboard, the Scrapbook, a PICT file, or a TIFF file.

Figure 3.30
The Capture control panel

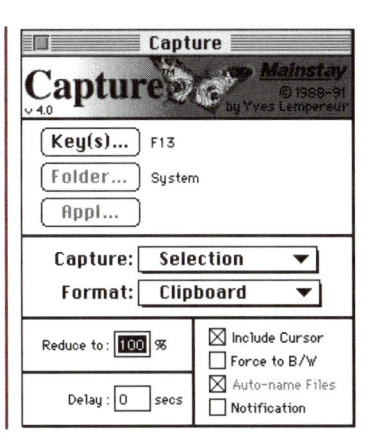

Customizing Your Macintosh with QuicKeys

Like any operating system, the Macintosh operating system includes commands and capabilities that the designers believe will be useful to the majority of users. Even though their design decisions are based on a lot of input from users, there will always be some way of working with the operating system or an application program that operating system designers haven't anticipated. You may want keyboard equivalents for commands that are only accessible through menus or you may want to use a single key sequence to invoke a series of actions that you perform repeatedly. Creating keyboard commands for just about anything you can do with the Macintosh is probably the ultimate form of customization.

Probably the most widely used software for creating customized keyboard commands is QuicKeys, a program that creates *keyboard macros*. The term "macro" comes from assembly language programming, where a short sequence of program statements are given a name. The name is then used in the program wherever the associated program statements should occur. When the program is assembled to turn it into executable form, the program statements associated with the macro name are substituted for the name. The macro simply makes it easier for a programmer because a short name can be used instead of repeating the same program statements over and over.

Keyboard macros associate a key sequence with one or more actions. For example, you might choose to have the sequence Option-N insert your name and address into a document you are preparing. When you press **Option-N**, the actions that you have associated with the key sequence are substituted for the keys pressed.

QuicKeys installs as several system extensions, adding three items to the Apple menu. Basic QuicKeys functions are available through the QuicKeys hierarchical menu (see Figure 3.31). The QuicKeys menu option in the submenu invokes the macro editor, which makes it easy to associate keystrokes with macros. In Figure 3.32, you can see the Universal Keyset, a group of macros that, among other things, adds support for keys on the extended keyboard, bringing those capabilities to applications that ordinarily do not support them.

The power of QuicKeys lies in its ability to create macros that consist of sequences of actions. Sequences can be created by recording actions as you perform them or by explicitly specifying actions using QuicKeys's sequence editor. Although certainly not as full-featured as general-purpose programming languages, the QuicKeys macro language does have essential programming language elements: the ability to execute actions one after each other, to repeat actions, and to make choices between actions based on a variety of conditions.

CHAPTER 3: Configuring Your System   **65**

FIGURE 3.31
Working with QuicKeys

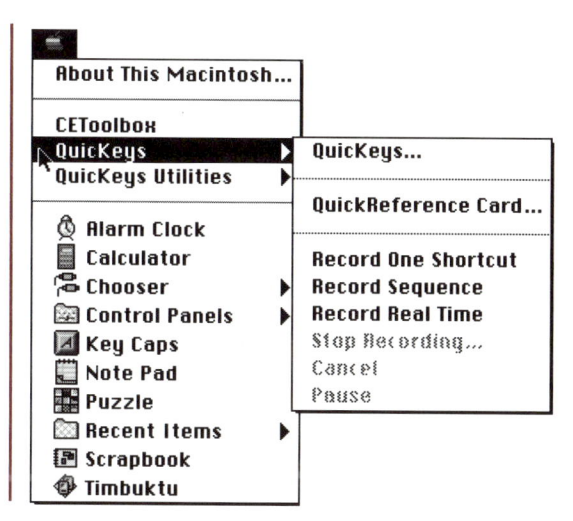

```
About This Macintosh...

CEToolbox
QuicKeys           ▶    QuicKeys...
QuicKeys Utilities ▶    ─────────────────
                        QuickReference Card...
🕐 Alarm Clock          ─────────────────
📱 Calculator           Record One Shortcut
📠 Chooser          ▶   Record Sequence
📇 Control Panels   ▶   Record Real Time
🔑 Key Caps             Stop Recording...
📓 Note Pad             Cancel
🧩 Puzzle               Pause
📁 Recent Items     ▶
📘 Scrapbook
🍵 Timbuktu
```

FIGURE 3.32
The QuicKeys macro editor

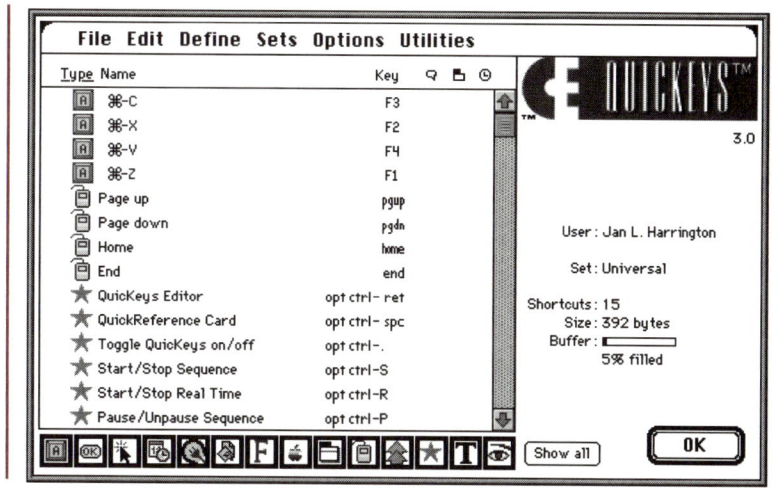

```
File  Edit  Define  Sets  Options  Utilities

Type Name                          Key      🔍 📁 🕐        ┌──────────┐
 A   ⌘-C                           F3                       │ QUICKEYS™│
 A   ⌘-X                           F2                       │          │
 A   ⌘-V                           F4                       │      3.0 │
 A   ⌘-Z                           F1
 📋  Page up                       pgup
 📋  Page down                     pgdn
 📋  Home                          home      User: Jan L. Harrington
 📋  End                           end
 ★   QuicKeys Editor               opt ctrl- ret    Set: Universal
 ★   QuickReference Card           opt ctrl- spc    Shortcuts: 15
 ★   Toggle QuicKeys on/off        opt ctrl-.         Size: 392 bytes
 ★   Start/Stop Sequence           opt ctrl-S         Buffer: ▓
 ★   Start/Stop Real Time          opt ctrl-R              5% filled
 ★   Pause/Unpause Sequence        opt ctrl-P

 [icons row]                        [Show all]      [  OK  ]
```

> **BY THE WAY!**
>
> If you happen to have one of the Macintoshes that supports PlainTalk speech recognition (for example, the Centris 660av or the Quadra 840av), you can use QuicKeys to create sequences of commands that can be triggered by voice commands. This is probably the best way to add functionality to the Macintosh's speech recognition capabilities.

Securing Your Macintosh

System security is a broad category of functions that relate to protecting the data stored on a computer. Threats to security can come from several sources, including people who actively attempt to access data they have no right to see, viruses, damage to monitors from screen burn-in, and damage to files that occurs when storage media are damaged. Other than the security provided through its file sharing capabilities, the Macintosh operating system has no security features. You must therefore add them through a combination of safety-oriented procedures and third-party software.

> **BY THE WAY!** The best hedge against data damage that results from damage to storage media is a good backup scheme. System backup is discussed in depth in Chapter 4.

Securing the Macintosh Against Unauthorized Access

A multi-user operating system handles security by requiring each user to have a user name/password combination that he or she must enter to gain access to the computer. Because the Macintosh was never designed to be multi-user, it doesn't support "users" for access to a single computer. Security must therefore be provided by add-on software.

> **BY THE WAY!** As you will see in Chapter 10, the Macintosh operating system does support "users" for access to disk volumes across a network.

There are three levels of protection you can apply to your Macintosh with third-party security software:

- **Desktop:** Desktop security prevents users from viewing the Desktop without entering a user name and password.

- **Volume:** Volume security prevents users from gaining access to a disk volume without entering a user name and password.

◆ **File:** File security can be applied by preventing users from gaining access to a file without entering a user name and password or by encrypting the file so that its contents appear meaningless without decrypting.

Which level of protection you select and how you implement it depends, of course, on your particular situation.

There are a number of third-party security products available. The rest of this section looks at products from two companies that take a different approach: FileGuard (an all-in-one program from ASD Software) and CryptoMatic, NightWatch II, and FolderBolt (a suite of products from KentnMarsh).

FileGuard

FileGuard, which installs as a system extension, provides the three levels of protection described in the preceding section. The Desktop, volumes, and folders are protected by user name/password combinations. File protection is provided through encryption.

Once FileGuard is loaded into main memory at system startup, a Protection menu appears to the right of all other menus in the menu bar. The menu is also accessible from the FileGuard program, which behaves like a control panel but isn't automatically placed in the Control Panels folder. (It is installed in the Extensions folder and must remain there for FileGuard to work properly.)

The first step in setting up a protection scheme is to create users and enter initial passwords for them (Figure 3.33). FileGuard imposes some rules on the construction of passwords: They must be at least three characters long and include at least one letter and one number. This type of password format helps ensure that a password, while easy to remember, is also hard to guess.

Figure 3.33
Defining a new user for FileGuard security

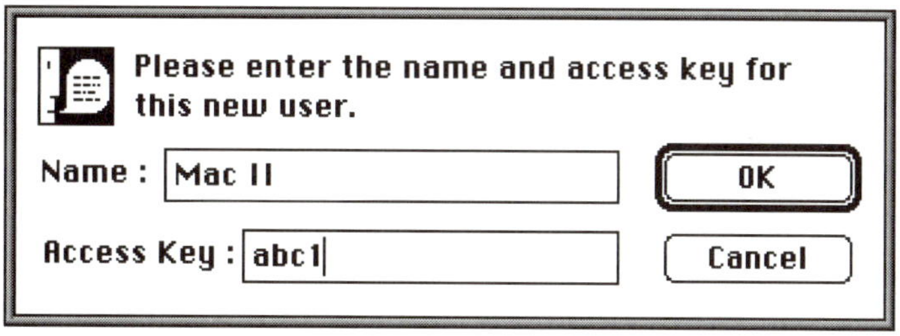

Once a user is created, you define access privileges for that user. Notice in Figure 3.34 that, by default, a new user has no access to anything. (Every square in the grid at the lower left of the dialog box has an X in it). By clicking in a square, the system administrator gives access rights to the user. Users can also be assigned to one or more groups, making it easy to give similar access privileges to multiple users without needing to configure each user individually.

FIGURE 3.34
Setting user access privileges

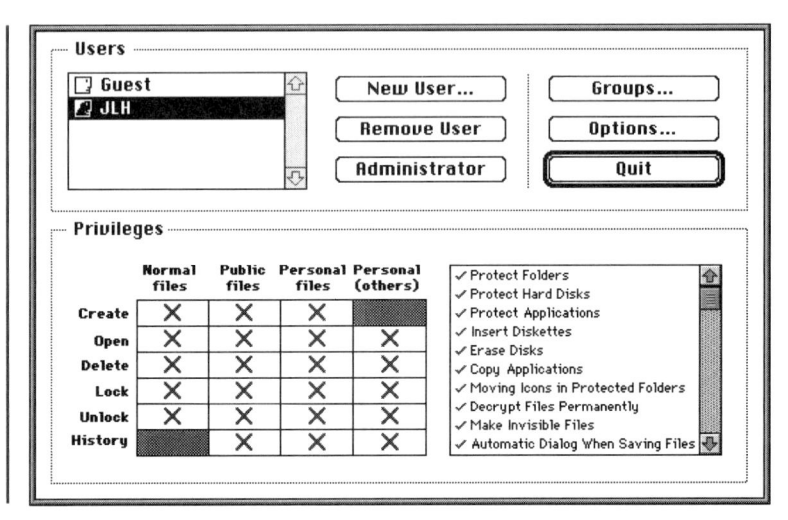

	Normal files	Public files	Personal files	Personal (others)
Create	X	X	X	
Open	X	X	X	X
Delete	X	X	X	X
Lock	X	X	X	X
Unlock	X	X	X	X
History		X	X	X

Users: Guest, JLH — New User..., Remove User, Administrator, Groups..., Options..., Quit

Privileges checklist:
- Protect Folders
- Protect Hard Disks
- Protect Applications
- Insert Diskettes
- Erase Disks
- Copy Applications
- Moving Icons in Protected Folders
- Decrypt Files Permanently
- Make Invisible Files
- Automatic Dialog When Saving Files

As soon as one user has been defined, a user name and password are required to access the Macintosh. When a user "logs off" at the end of a session, FileGuard blanks the screens of all attached monitors. The Desktop won't reappear until someone enters a recognized user name/password combination.

FileGuard keeps a record of all successful log-ons and unsuccessful log-on attempts. This user log can not only be useful for keeping statistics on system use, but can be instrumental in identifying someone who is illegally trying to break into a system.

Volume, folder, and file protection are added explicitly to existing objects. For example, the dialog box in Figure 3.35 is used to select a file and then either encrypt, decrypt, or view an access history. In addition, each time a file is saved for the first time, FileGuard asks the user if the file should be encrypted.

BY THE WAY! FileGuard also can be used to configure copy-protected floppy disks and demo disks that expire after a program is launched a specified number of times or after some time limit is exceeded.

CryptoMatic, NightWatch II, and FolderBolt

The suite of Kent•Marsh programs—CryptoMatic, NightWatch II, and FolderBolt—together provide a similar set of features as FileGuard. CryptoMatic, which handles file protection, supports several methods of file encryption (see Figure 3.36). "Code keys" provide password protection. An encrypted file can be made self-decrypting. That means that the file can be transmitted to another person, perhaps over data communications lines, and then decrypted without the CryptoMatic program. In addition, CryptoMatic can erase the space on a disk occupied by a deleted file. (Normally, deleting a file merely marks the space occupied by the file as available for reuse; the contents of a deleted file aren't destroyed until the space is reused by another file.)

Figure 3.36
Setting CryptoMatic encryption preferences

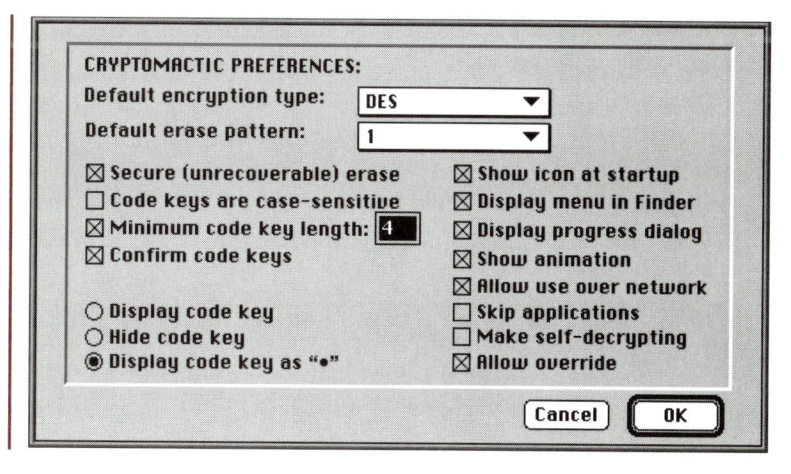

BY THE WAY! One of the encryption methods used by CryptoMatic—the Data Encryption Standard (DES)—is considered a "munition" by the U.S. Government. It can't be exported outside the United States or Canada. Versions of CryptoMatic for export therefore have a less effective, but not politically sensitive, form of encryption. This legal problem with the export of encryption algorithms affects all security software.

NightWatch II provides security at the disk level. It can be used to lock individual disk volumes, including removable media, and to control who can start up the Macintosh. The NightWatch II application (Figure 3.37), which must be installed on each disk being protected, applies and removes locks, provides access to the log of disk activity, and controls access to the user database. Each user has a pass-

70 NAVIGATING SYSTEM 7: Understanding The Macintosh Operating System

word that he or she must enter to gain access to the locked disk. Associated with a user is a set of configuration parameters that determine such things as the length and expiration date of the password (Figure 3.38).

FIGURE 3.37
The NightWatch II application

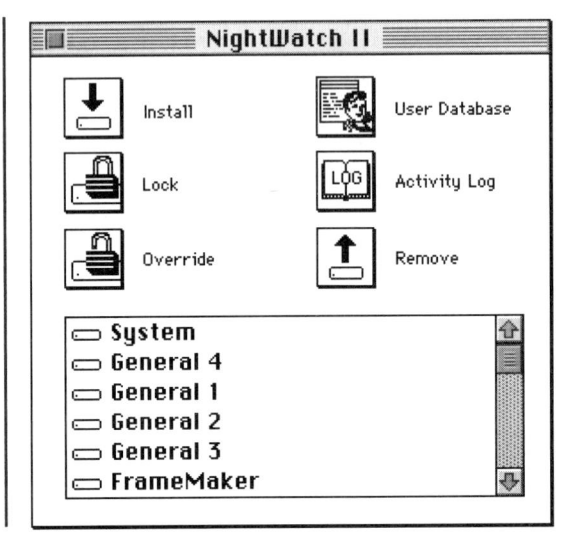

FIGURE 3.38
Creating a new user for NightWatch II security

NightWatch II protects system startup in one of three ways:

CHAPTER 3: Configuring Your System **71**

- A "diskless" installation means that a user only needs to enter an authorized user name and password.

- A "token disk" installation means that a user must supply both a user name/password pair and a floppy disk with a user database that contains the user name/password entered.

- A "key disk" installation means that no user name/password pair is required but the user must have a floppy disk with a user database on it.

The type of installation can be different for each disk volume used by a Macintosh.

FolderBolt provides folder-level protection. Any folder on any disk volume can be protected by a password and given as one of three types of file status (Figure 3.39):

- Completely locked (no access at all without the password),

- Read-only (viewing permitted, but no modification or deletion without the password), and

- Drop-box (writing permitted, but no viewing or deletion without the password).

FIGURE 3.39
Protecting a folder with FolderBolt

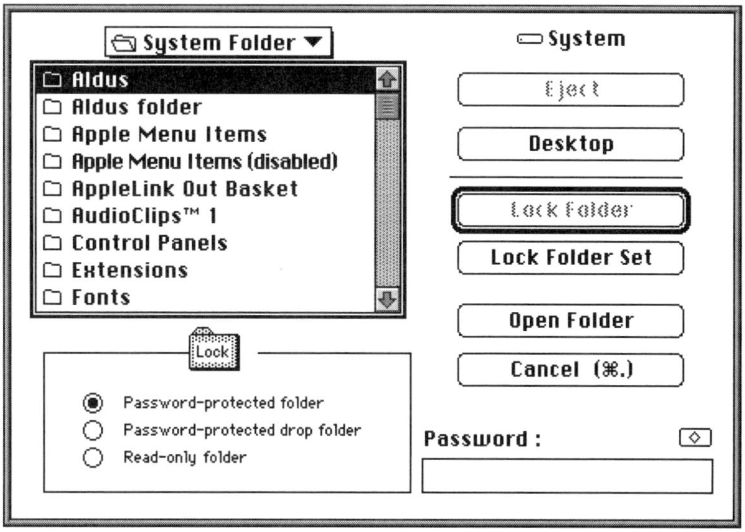

Virus Protection

A *virus* is a malicious, destructive program that, at the very least, disrupts ordinary data processing. More commonly, a virus modifies or destroys files. Viruses infect a computer system when a virus-infected file is introduced to the system. Usually just copying the infected file onto a disk used by a computer is enough to infect a new system.

The destructive activities of a virus are activated through a variety of mechanisms. If the infected file is an application program, launching the application can trigger the virus. Some viruses trigger themselves when a specific date or time arrives. For example, there is a group of viruses that activate whenever a Friday the 13th occurs. Others are triggered simply by the presence of the infected file.

There are several ways to protect your system from viruses. Prevention, although not always possible, is better than having to attempt a cure. The first step in virus prevention is to pay special attention to where you get your software:

- Commercial software: Most commercial software is virus free. However, there have been cases where viruses have crept into mass-duplicated commercial software. You should therefore not assume that all commercial software is safe.

- Online services and user groups: Now that threats from viruses are well known, commercial on-line services such as CompuServe and America Online as well as the larger Macintosh user groups pay special attention to the software in their libraries. They carefully check files submitted to the libraries to make sure they are virus free. Although there is always a chance that a virus will get through, software downloaded from reputable, commercial on-line services or obtained from large user groups such as BMUG (Berkeley Macintosh Users Group) or the Boston Computer Society's Macintosh User Group are as safe from viruses as any software can be.

- Other sources: Software you get from clients, friends, small bulletin board systems, and small user groups is the most likely source of a virus. Such software often isn't subject to the careful scrutiny paid to commercial software or software distributed by commercial on-line services and large user groups.

The second step in virus prevention is taking care when you download or install software:

- Before installing commercial software, lock the floppy disks on which the software is shipped. This prevents any viruses that might already be on your system from infecting the installation disks.

- Download software from bulletin boards and information services to floppy disk rather than to your hard disk. Run a virus detection program on the downloaded files before copying them to your hard disk. This will help prevent viruses from infecting your hard disk.

- Run virus detection software regularly to find out if any known viruses have crept into your system.

Virus detection software is primarily effective for identifying and removing *known* viruses. Some are commercial products (for example, Virex and Symantec Anti-Virus (SAM)); others, like Disinfectant, are free and available from on-line services and user groups. Disinfectant (Figure 3.40) can run as an application; alternatively, you can install the Disinfectant INIT so that checking for viruses occurs every time you start up your Macintosh. As new viruses appear, Disinfectant is upgraded to detect and remove them.

FIGURE 3.40
Using Disinfectant to scan for viruses

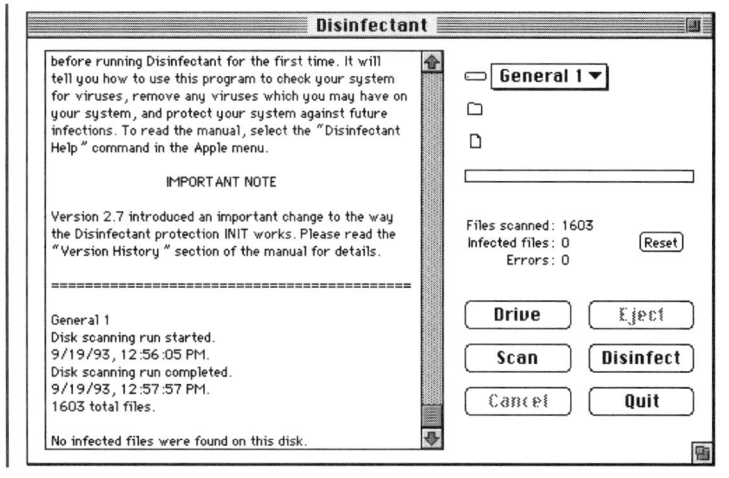

Keep in mind that there is an ever-escalating battle between the people who write viruses and the people who write virus detection software. As soon as a new virus appears, developers of virus detection software modify the program to handle the new virus. Once the virus developers realize that their virus has been neutralized, they create a new virus that current software can't handle. Given that virus developers take pleasure in destroying other computer users' data and that there is no effective way to prevent them from continuing their malicious activities, there is ultimately no way to ever be completely protected against all viruses. However, you should take some of the reasonable precautions discussed in this section to protect your Macintosh from most viruses.

Warning: Many of the "installer" programs that come with commercial software are incompatible with virus checkers. In fact, most installation instructions tell you to disable any virus detection programs before beginning the installation process. The irony of this, of course, is that there's always a chance that installing the commercial software could introduce a virus to the very computer whose virus detection you just disabled so that you could install the software.

Protecting Your Screen

Most monitors in use today stay brightly lit unless you either turn off the power or use a dial to turn down the brightness. If left at normal settings for long periods of time, the image on a monitor's screen may "burn in," leaving a faint, but permanent image on the screen. To avoid burn in, you can run a program known as a *screen saver*. A screen saver is loaded into RAM at system startup and takes over after a specified period of inactivity. It usually blanks the screen and then displays some pattern of moving images. Because the images move, they won't burn into the monitor.

> **BY THE WAY!** New "green" monitors that automatically reduce brightness and power consumption during periods of inactivity are beginning to appear on the market. Such monitors make screen savers unnecessary. However, many screen savers are just plain fun.

There have been many screen saver programs over the years, both shareware and commercial. One of the most popular is the commercial product After Dark. The After Dark engine (Figure 3.41) can run a variety of screen saver modules, including scenes from the original Star Trek television series and, most recently, Disney cartoons. Contests for After Dark module programming have also produced some whimsical displays such as the Lawnmower Man, who drives a riding mower across the screen, tirelessly mowing an endlessly growing field of grass and flowers.

Should you use a screen saver? Unless you have a monitor that automatically dims its screen, a screen saver is usually warranted.

FIGURE 3.41
The After Dark

CHAPTER 4
Disks, Folders, and Files

As you have read, one of the major functions of an operating system is storing, organizing, and retrieving files on external storage. The Macintosh operating system handles all types of disk-based media—floppy disks, hard disks, hard disk cartridges, optical cartridges, and CD-ROMs—in the same way. In this chapter, you will discover how a user of the Macintosh operating system views disk organization and how the operating system keeps track of what is stored on a disk.

The Finder is responsible for presenting you with the logical organization of the files you've stored on a disk. However, the way in which the operating system stores and keeps track of disk contents is very different. This chapter therefore first looks at the user's view of a disk's contents and then turns to how the Macintosh operating system actually organizes disk storage. It also looks at disk maintenance activities such as defragmentation and backup.

THE USER'S VIEW

A user's first view of the Macintosh operating system is the Desktop. It contains icons for the objects in the computing environment that can be manipulated in some way. The Desktop in Figure 4.1 is typical of many System 7 Desktops today. It has all the basic elements supplied by the Finder but also has been enhanced with some add-on programs that fill in gaps in the Finder's capabilities.

78 NAVIGATING SYSTEM 7: Understanding The Macintosh Operating System

The Finder's default Desktop provides the menu bar across the top of the startup monitor. It also displays a tiny Macintosh icon at the far right, indicating that the Finder is the program with which you are working. (The clock in Figure 4.1 is supplied by an add-on program.) The rest of the Desktop is reserved for disk storage of many kinds.

The open window in Figure 4.1 is named System because it is the startup disk. (The choice of System as the name of the startup disk is completely arbitrary; you can name disks more or less anything you want.) The open window displays the contents of the disk. Many of the icons in that window are custom icons, supplied either by an application program or by a Finder add-on program. (You will learn an easy way to install custom icons of your choice later in this chapter.) File or folder names that appear in italics are *aliases*, pointers to the actual location of files or folders. (Aliases are discussed in depth later in this chapter.)

This Desktop also has icons for a number of disks. All disk icons are custom icons, supplied by the user, the drive manufacturer, or an add-on program. For example, the DD and HD that appear on the floppy disk icons are produced by an add-on program. There are disks inserted into two floppy drives (a 1.4Mb SuperDrive and an 800K drive), a CD-ROM inserted into a CD-ROM drive, a cartridge inserted into a SyQuest cartridge hard drive, and seven icons representing the Macintosh's two hard disks. Each of these disks is said to be *mounted* because the disk inserted in the drive is recognized by the Macintosh operating system and has its icon displayed on the Desktop.

FIGURE 4.1
A System 7 desktop

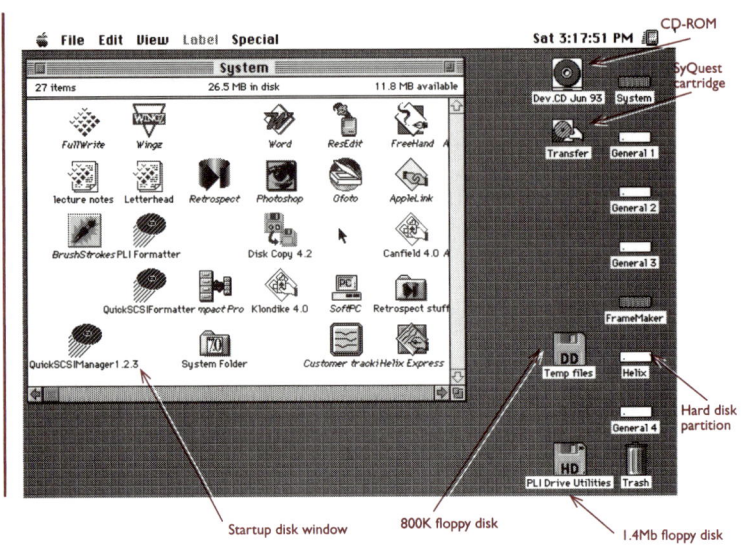

The Macintosh can also store and retrieve data on tape. However, in most cases tapes cannot be mounted on the desktop; access to tape contents must be managed by application software. The major exception is the DeskTape software from Optima Technology. DeskTape maintains a tape directory on disk that appears to the user like a disk directory. When you choose a file on tape with which you want to work, DeskTape fast forwards or rewinds the tape to the start of the correct file. DeskTape ships with Optima's digital audio tape (DAT) drives. It can also be purchased as stand-alone software for use with the DDS and SCSI-2 DAT mechanisms from Hewlett-Packard, Sony, WangDAT, Wangtek, and Archive as well as 150 and 600Mb Teac drives, Exabyte 8mm tape drives, and several other SCSI-2 tape drives.

VOLUMES AND DISK PARTITIONING

It's not a contradiction that there are seven icons for just two hard disks in Figure 4.1. This is because the large hard disk has been divided into sections known as *partitions*. In this example, there are six partitions (General 1, General 2, General 3, FrameMaker, Helix, General 4). Each partition is mounted on the Macintosh Desktop as if it were a separate physical disk. Because a disk icon on the Desktop doesn't necessarily represent a physical disk, it is known as a *volume*. A volume appears to the user as a separate disk, complete with its own files and folder hierarchy.

There are several good reasons to partition a large hard disk:

- It is easier to organize a disk when there are fewer files and folders on the disk.
- The data structures that the operating system uses to keep track of what files are stored on a disk and how they are organized take up space. As you will learn later in this chapter, those data structures can occupy significantly more space than necessary on large volumes.
- When there are many files on a disk, disk windows open slowly.
- The maximum volume size is 2Gb, regardless of the total capacity of the disk. Therefore, hard disks of more than 2Gb must be partitioned.

How big should partitions be? That depends on several factors:

- In most cases, your startup volume should be relatively small and used only to hold the System folder and other temporary files used by the operating system. This reduces the size of the data structures the operating system must use to keep track of files on the partition and also speeds up access to files on the disk. For example, in Figure 4.1 the startup volume resides on the Macintosh's internal 40Mb drive. That is enough room to store a loaded System folder (almost 25Mb), aliases for commonly used programs and files, and small, essential utilities, yet still have space for temporary storage of print files.

- Generally keep partitions under 200Mb. As you will see later in this chapter, the larger a partition gets, the greater the potential for wasted space.

- Consider the size of your backup media. If you are backing up to 150Mb tapes, then 150Mb partitions make a lot of sense. If you are backing up to 88Mb SyQuest cartridges, then make your partitions a multiple of 88Mb. This prevents you from wasting space on your backup media.

Unmounting Versus Ejecting Volumes

Throughout a typical workday, volumes are repeatedly mounted and removed from the Macintosh Desktop. This is particularly true for removable media such as floppy disks and CD-ROMs. However, simply ejecting a disk from its drive isn't the same as unmounting it.

When you eject a disk using the Special menu's Eject Disk command, the disk is ejected from the disk drive, but its icon remains on the Desktop and the volume's file system remains mounted. However, if you drag a volume's icon to the trash can, the volume is unmounted; the Macintosh operating system forgets all about it. In the case of removable media, unmounting also ejects the disk. In the case of a fixed hard disk, unmounting makes the volume inaccessible. To gain access to it again you will either have to reboot the computer or use a disk utility to mount it again.

If you are certain you won't be needing a removable volume again in the immediate future, then go ahead and unmount it by dragging its icon to the trash. Every mounted file system takes up RAM that could be used for other things; unmounting the volume therefore saves a little bit of memory.

There are, however, situations in which you might want to keep a removable volume's file system mounted. For example, assume that you have a single 44Mb SyQuest cartridge hard drive. You need to make a copy of a cartridge but don't have 44Mb free on your hard disk. The solution is to mount the original and then eject it. Then mount the cartridge onto which you will be copying. Drag the original's icon onto the copy's icon. The Macintosh will then prompt you to swap disks as necessary.

CHAPTER 4: Disks, Folders, and Files **81**

BY THE WAY! There's no question that the number of disk swaps needed to copy one 44Mb cartridge to another would be enough to make you want to throw the Macintosh across the room. A better solution would be to use yet another 44Mb cartridge to store files from your hard disk so you can delete them and make enough space on that disk to act as temporary storage for the cartridge copying.

CHOOSING THE STARTUP VOLUME

To choose the volume on which the Macintosh operating system will look first for a System folder, use the Startup Disk control panel (Figure 4.2). An icon appears for each mounted volume. To choose the disk from which you want to boot, click on any volume on that disk; it doesn't necessarily have to be the partition containing the System folder.

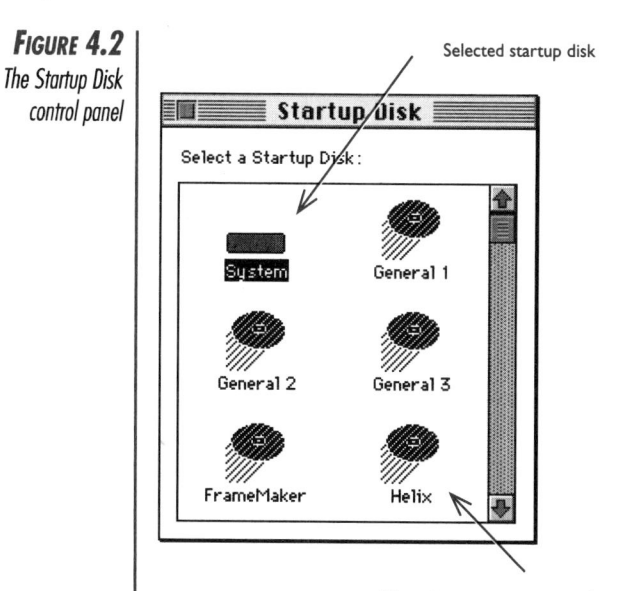

FIGURE 4.2
The Startup Disk control panel

Why can't you choose a specific partition on a hard drive from which to boot? It might be nice to have a System folder on more than one partition, each with a different system configuration. Unfortunately, if you are working with the Macintosh operating system's Startup Disk control panel, you can't do it.

The Startup Disk control panel only saves the SCSI ID of the startup device, not the name of the startup volume. Therefore, only one partition on a disk should have a System folder. To keep multiple System folders on different volumes on the same device (something you really shouldn't do), you will need to use some other formatting utility, such as the formatting software that came with the drive, to select a specific partition as the startup disk.

Although the Macintosh can boot from just about any type of disk storage, there is an advantage to using the device with SCSI ID 0 as the startup disk: The Macintosh will wait for the device to reach operating speed. (It generally takes a hard disk between 30 seconds and a minute to warm up enough to spin at full speed.) If a device other than that at SCSI ID 0 is used as the startup disk and the device isn't ready when the operating system is looking for a System folder, the operating system displays the floppy disk icon with the flashing question mark, indicating that it can't find a System folder.

BY THE WAY! Although the device with SCSI ID 0 is most commonly the primary internal hard disk, it needn't be. If a Macintosh doesn't have an internal hard disk, SCSI ID 0 can be assigned to an external hard disk.

FILE ORGANIZATION AND FILE SYSTEMS

As you know, the Macintosh operating system lets the user view the organization of files on a disk volume as a hierarchy. Files are grouped by placing them in folders (in operating system terms, *directories*). Folders can also contain other folders, building a tree-structure with theoretically no limits to how deep folders can be nested.

Each volume has its own, distinct hierarchy of folders. In operating system terms, such a hierarchy is known as a *file system*; the Macintosh operating system calls its implementation the *Hierarchical File System* (HFS). Mounting a volume on the Desktop in essence mounts the volume's file system. Understanding that each volume represents a separate file system is important because an operating system behaves somewhat differently when you are moving files within a single file system or between two file systems. (Moving and copying files is discussed later in this chapter.)

> **FLASH BACK**
>
> Although folders have always been a part of the Macintosh operating system, in early releases (prior to the 800K drive) folders were nothing more than a visual device. There was no true directory hierarchy; all files were at the top level of the disk (the *Macintosh File System* (MFS)). This was not only confusing, but made choosing a file from an Open File dialog box rather tedious.

The hierarchy of folders through which the operating system must travel to reach a given file or folder is known as the object's *pathname*. Although the Macintosh operating system rarely requires you to specify a complete pathname, you will see them displayed in a variety of places. Macintosh pathnames are constructed by placing a colon between each folder name in the hierarchy. (This is why the colon is the only character you can't use in a Macintosh file or folder name.) For example, assume a file named "Letter to John" is stored in a folder named "Correspondence" which in turn is stored in a folder named "Word processing," all of which are on a disk volume named "External hard disk." The pathname of the "Letter to John" file is:

    External hard disk:Word processing:Correspondence:Letter to John

To see a window's pathname (the sequence of folders in which it is nested) in a pop-up menu, move the mouse pointer over the name of the window. Then hold down ⌘ and press the mouse button (for example, see Figure 4.3).

FIGURE 4.3
A window's pathname

Looking at Disk Contents

When the Macintosh operating system debuted in 1984, there was one way to look at the contents of a disk: icons. Considering that the only storage device was a 400K floppy, icons were just fine. Today's hard disks, however, can easily store thousands of files in one partition and it's not unusual to have a single folder containing more than a hundred files. That being the case, looking at icons can be clumsy and confusing (even if the icons are pretty).

To make it easier to work with large capacity disks, System 6 introduced list views; they have been enhanced in System 7. In their most basic form, list views present a tiny generic icon for each file or folder along with the name, size, type, label (if any), and date of last modification (for example, see Figure 4.4). Notice that the column heading "Name" is underlined, indicating that the files and folders are arranged alphabetically by name.

Figure 4.4
A default list view

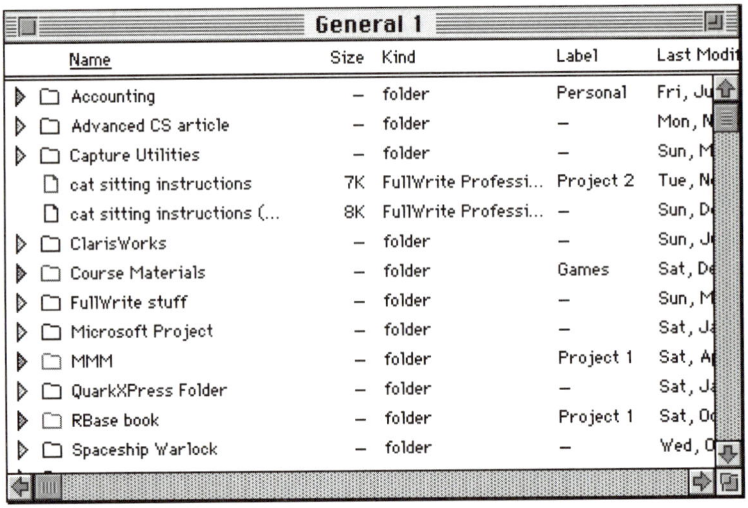

Name	Size	Kind	Label	Last Modif
▷ ☐ Accounting	—	folder	Personal	Fri, Ju
▷ ☐ Advanced CS article	—	folder	—	Mon, N
▷ ☐ Capture Utilities	—	folder	—	Sun, M
☐ cat sitting instructions	7K	FullWrite Professi…	Project 2	Tue, N
☐ cat sitting instructions (…	8K	FullWrite Professi…	—	Sun, D
▷ ☐ ClarisWorks	—	folder	—	Sun, J
▷ ☐ Course Materials	—	folder	Games	Sat, De
▷ ☐ FullWrite stuff	—	folder	—	Sun, M
▷ ☐ Microsoft Project	—	folder	—	Sat, Ja
▷ ☐ MMM	—	folder	Project 1	Sat, A
▷ ☐ QuarkXPress Folder	—	folder	—	Sat, Ja
▷ ☐ RBase book	—	folder	Project 1	Sat, Oc
▷ ☐ Spaceship Warlock	—	folder	—	Wed, 0

There are two ways to change the ordering. You can choose the order from the Finder's View menu (Figure 4.5) or you can click on a column header at the top of a list view. For example, clicking on the Kind header in Figure 4.5 produces the listing in Figure 4.6. The same result, of course, can be obtained by choosing "by Kind" from the View menu.

FIGURE 4.5
The Finder's View menu

```
View
  by Small Icon
✓ by Icon
  by Name
  by Size
  by Kind
  by Label
  by Date
```

FIGURE 4.6
A list window ordered by type of file or folder

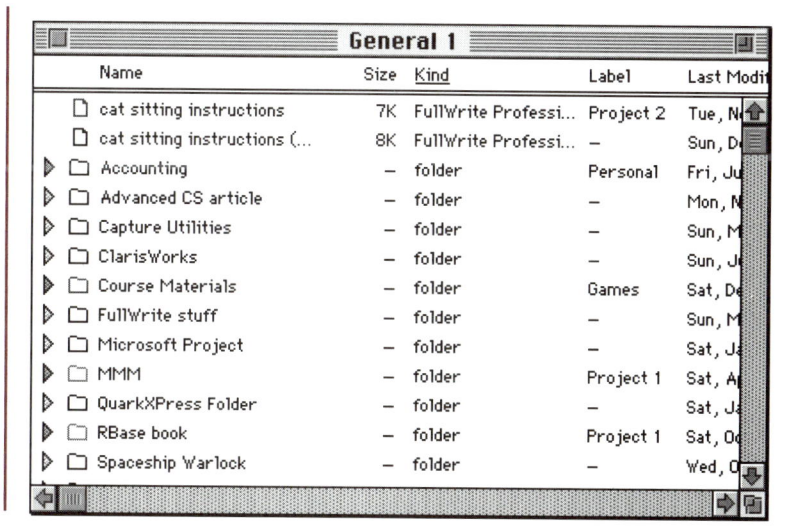

Name	Size	Kind	Label	Last Modi
🗋 cat sitting instructions	7K	FullWrite Professi...	Project 2	Tue, N
🗋 cat sitting instructions (...	8K	FullWrite Professi...	—	Sun, D
▷ 📁 Accounting	—	folder	Personal	Fri, Ju
▷ 📁 Advanced CS article	—	folder	—	Mon, N
▷ 📁 Capture Utilities	—	folder	—	Sun, M
▷ 📁 ClarisWorks	—	folder	—	Sun, J
▷ 📁 Course Materials	—	folder	Games	Sat, D
▷ 📁 FullWrite stuff	—	folder	—	Sun, M
▷ 📁 Microsoft Project	—	folder	—	Sat, J
▷ 📁 MMM	—	folder	Project 1	Sat, A
▷ 📁 QuarkXPress Folder	—	folder	—	Sat, J
▷ 📁 RBase book	—	folder	Project 1	Sat, O
▷ 📁 Spaceship Warlock	—	folder	—	Wed, O

Notice in Figure 4.5 that there are actually two icon views: "by Icon" and "by Small Icon." The "by Icon" option refers to the full-sized icons that have been with the Macintosh operating system from the beginning. Small icons retain as much of the icon as possible without taking up quite so much room (for example, as in Figure 4.7).

The Views Control Panel

System 7 provides control over exactly what appears in list and icon views with the Views control panel (Figure 4.8). The pop-up menu at the very top lets you choose the font you want to use in all disk windows. The second section of the control panel applies to both types of icon view.

FIGURE 4.7
The small icon view

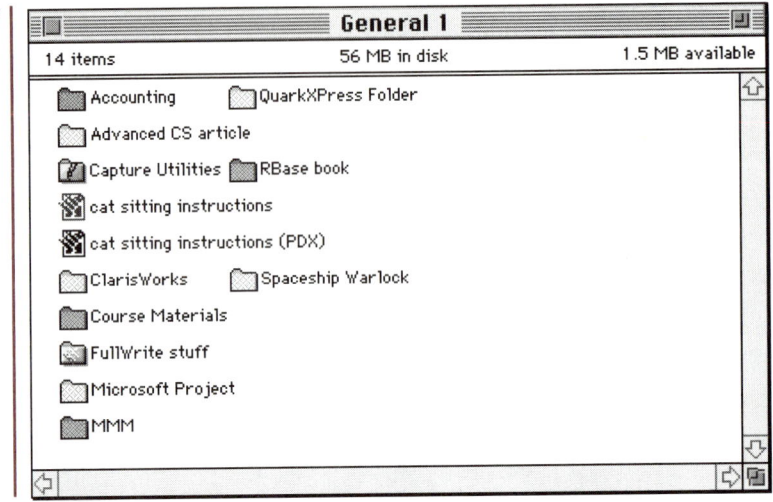

FIGURE 4.8
The Views control panel

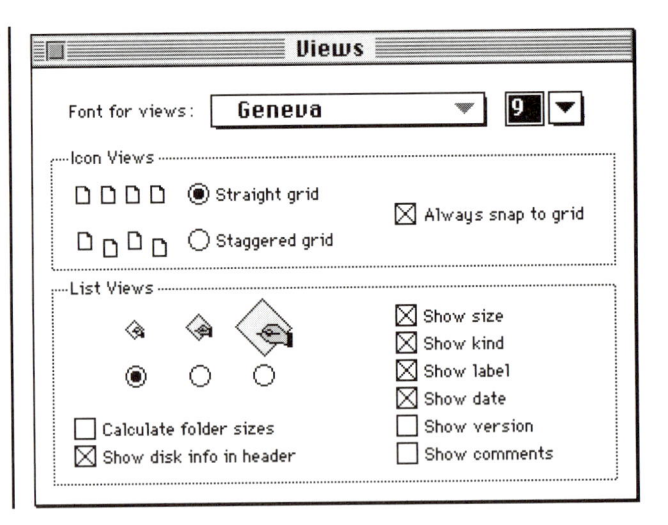

When looking at files and folders in an icon view, the Macintosh operating system maintains an invisible grid. If the "Always snap to grid" box is checked, whenever you move a file or folder, its final placement will automatically be aligned with the grid. This tends to keep the window neater. The grid can be straight, as it is in the icon view example you have seen, or it can be staggered. The advantage of a staggered grid is that long file or folder names aren't as likely to be hidden by the names of objects next to them. However, a staggered grid takes up more room, displaying fewer files/folders in the same space.

If you aren't snapping icons to the grid, icon views can quickly become messy. Icons can be too close (icons and names overlap) or too far apart (icons are hard to find). When that occurs, you can "clean up" the window with the Finder's Special menu's "Clean Up" option. Clean Up works in the following ways:

- Selecting the menu option without pressing any modifier keys aligns all icons with the grid.

- Selecting the menu option holding the **Option** key aligns all icons with the grid and sorts them according to the criteria in the last used list view. For example, if the last list view was by kind, icons will be sorted by type.

- Selecting the menu option holding down the **Shift** key aligns only selected icons with the grid.

To reverse the current "snap to grid" setting, hold down ⌘ when dragging an icon.

List views are controlled by the bottom half of the View control panel. Notice in Figure 4.8 that you can control the size of icons as well as the columns that appear in the list. Showing larger icons may be attractive, but keep in mind that they slow down scrolling of windows. In fact, using the smallest, generic icons is the fastest. This is of particular importance when you have hundreds of files/folders within a single folder.

The "Calculate folder sizes" box determines whether the Macintosh operating system figures out and displays the size of folders. Although it's often handy to know this, there is a big drawback to doing so. It takes the Macintosh time to figure out folder sizes each time you boot the computer or make a change to the contents of a folder. (Folder sizes aren't stored anywhere.) In most cases, the Macintosh operating system can compute folder sizes in the background while you get on with other work. However, if you are viewing by size, the operating system can't figure out how to organize windows until all folder sizes have been computed. This can seriously slow down the time it takes to boot the computer. In general, you will get better performance when you don't show folder sizes.

On the other hand, it's very useful to know how much space is left on a disk. To display that information, check the "Show disk info in header" box in the Views control panel. The Macintosh operating system then adds another header line to each window using a list view (for example, see Figure 4.9). Displaying disk info doesn't seem to cause any noticeable performance problems.

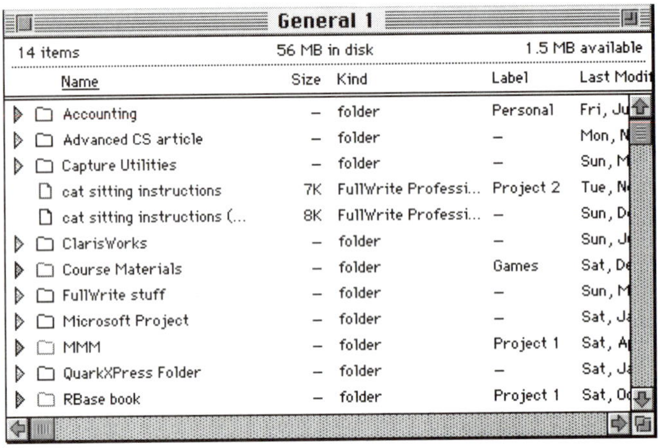

FIGURE 4.9
Displaying disk info in a window header

Name	Size	Kind	Label	Last Modi[fied]
▷ ☐ Accounting	—	folder	Personal	Fri, Ju
▷ ☐ Advanced CS article	—	folder	—	Mon, N
▷ ☐ Capture Utilities	—	folder	—	Sun, M
☐ cat sitting instructions	7K	FullWrite Professi...	Project 2	Tue, N
☐ cat sitting instructions (...	8K	FullWrite Professi...	—	Sun, D
▷ ☐ ClarisWorks	—	folder	—	Sun, J
▷ ☐ Course Materials	—	folder	Games	Sat, D
▷ ☐ FullWrite stuff	—	folder	—	Sun, M
▷ ☐ Microsoft Project	—	folder	—	Sat, J
▷ ☐ MMM	—	folder	Project 1	Sat, A
▷ ☐ QuarkXPress Folder	—	folder	—	Sat, J
▷ ☐ RBase book	—	folder	Project 1	Sat, O

Window header: General 1 — 14 items — 56 MB in disk — 1.5 MB available

There is one problem with list views of which you should be aware. The Finder doesn't automatically update all open disk windows when you save a file from within an application. In other words, the modification date and/or size of a file with which you are currently working won't necessarily be correct in a Finder window. This can cause a problem if you're viewing by date because the most recently modified version of a file won't necessarily be at the top of the window's list. The window will, however, be updated if you close the window and reopen it.

Viewing Folder Contents

Prior to System 7, the only way you could see the contents of a folder was to open its window. System 7, however, lets you expand the hierarchy of a volume by clicking on the small triangle found at the very left of each folder icon. (You can also expand a folder by selecting the folder and then pressing ⌘-→.) When the triangle is pointing to the right, the contents of the folder are hidden. Click on the triangle and it makes a 90° turn, exposing the contents of the folder, as in Figure 4.10. Expanding list views in this way can prevent your Desktop from being cluttered with lots of open windows and can provide faster access to files nested far down in the hierarchy. However, if you leave folders expanded, you will slow down window scrolling and updating.

The following keyboard shortcuts can make it easier to expand and collapse list view hierarchies:

- To collapse the contents of a single folder, select the folder and press ⌘-←.

- To expand the entire hierarchy nested within a folder (rather than just one level down), select the folder and press ⌘-**Option**-→.

- To collapse the entire hierarchy nested within a folder (rather than just one level down), select the folder and press ⌘-**Option**-←.

BY THE WAY!
If you want to keep your Desktop from getting too crowded with open windows, hold down the **Option** key when you double-click on a folder to open it; the window containing the folder will close as the folder's window opens. If you want to see the window in which an open folder is contained, press ⌘-↑.

FIGURE 4.10
A listing window with expanded folders

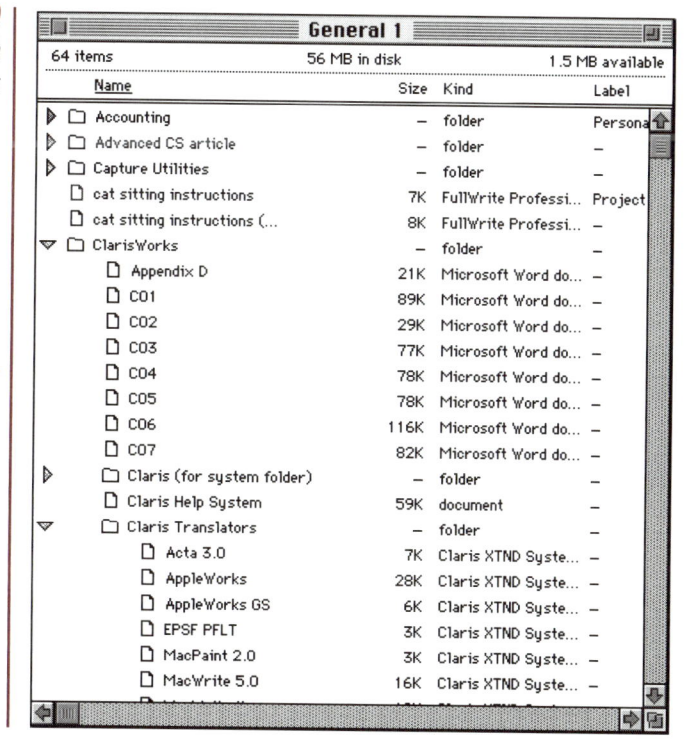

Name	Size	Kind	Label
▷ 📁 Accounting	—	folder	Persona
▷ 📁 Advanced CS article	—	folder	—
▷ 📁 Capture Utilities	—	folder	—
📄 cat sitting instructions	7K	FullWrite Professi...	Project
📄 cat sitting instructions (...	8K	FullWrite Professi...	—
▽ 📁 ClarisWorks	—	folder	—
📄 Appendix D	21K	Microsoft Word do...	—
📄 C01	89K	Microsoft Word do...	—
📄 C02	29K	Microsoft Word do...	—
📄 C03	77K	Microsoft Word do...	—
📄 C04	78K	Microsoft Word do...	—
📄 C05	78K	Microsoft Word do...	—
📄 C06	116K	Microsoft Word do...	—
📄 C07	82K	Microsoft Word do...	—
▷ 📁 Claris (for system folder)	—	folder	—
📄 Claris Help System	59K	document	—
▽ 📁 Claris Translators	—	folder	—
📄 Acta 3.0	7K	Claris XTND Syste...	—
📄 AppleWorks	28K	Claris XTND Syste...	—
📄 AppleWorks GS	6K	Claris XTND Syste...	—
📄 EPSF PFLT	3K	Claris XTND Syste...	—
📄 MacPaint 2.0	3K	Claris XTND Syste...	—
📄 MacWrite 5.0	16K	Claris XTND Syste...	—

Window title: General 1 — 64 items, 56 MB in disk, 1.5 MB available

USEFUL ADD-ON
One of the big problems people run into is keeping tracking of what files are stored on which disk. This is especially true if you have a lot of removable media such as floppy disks or SyQuest cartridges. A solution is to use a disk catalog program that maintains catalogs of the contents of your disks on your hard disk.

The shareware program CatFinder (included on the disk that comes with this book) is an easy-to-use disk cataloger. As you can see in

Figure 4.11, its interface looks much like the Finder's list views. The major advantage to such a catalog is that directories are available for disk volumes that currently aren't mounted on the Desktop.

FIGURE 4.11
A CatFinder disk catalog

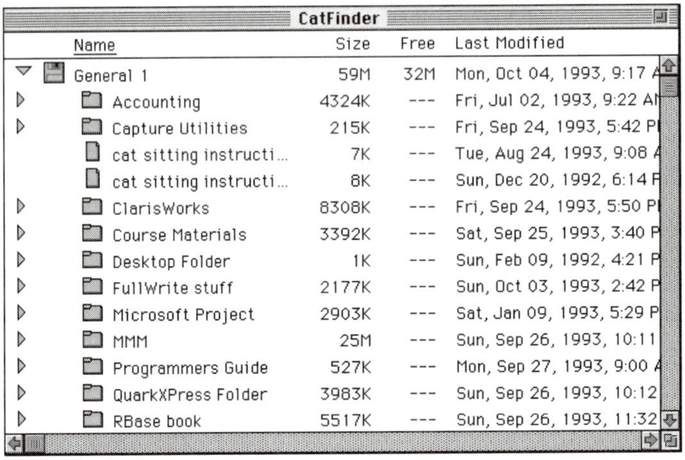

Name	Size	Free	Last Modified
▽ 📁 General 1	59M	32M	Mon, Oct 04, 1993, 9:17 A
▷ 📁 Accounting	4324K	---	Fri, Jul 02, 1993, 9:22 A
▷ 📁 Capture Utilities	215K	---	Fri, Sep 24, 1993, 5:42 P
📄 cat sitting instructi…	7K	---	Tue, Aug 24, 1993, 9:08 A
📄 cat sitting instructi…	8K	---	Sun, Dec 20, 1992, 6:14 P
▷ 📁 ClarisWorks	8308K	---	Fri, Sep 24, 1993, 5:50 P
▷ 📁 Course Materials	3392K	---	Sat, Sep 25, 1993, 3:40 P
▷ 📁 Desktop Folder	1K	---	Sun, Feb 09, 1992, 4:21 P
▷ 📁 FullWrite stuff	2177K	---	Sun, Oct 03, 1993, 2:42 P
▷ 📁 Microsoft Project	2903K	---	Sat, Jan 09, 1993, 5:29 P
▷ 📁 MMM	25M	---	Sun, Sep 26, 1993, 10:11
▷ 📁 Programmers Guide	527K	---	Mon, Sep 27, 1993, 9:00 A
▷ 📁 QuarkXPress Folder	3983K	---	Sun, Sep 26, 1993, 10:12
▷ 📁 RBase book	5517K	---	Sun, Sep 26, 1993, 11:32

You can use CatFinder to launch programs and open documents, just as you do the Finder. (CatFinder uses Apple Events to communicate with the operating system; you'll learn more about Apple Events in Chapter 11.) If the disk volume isn't mounted, CatFinder asks you to insert the needed disk.

GETTING FILE AND FOLDER INFO

Given that displaying folder sizes slows down booting and window updating, how can you find out how much space is occupied by a folder? The Get Info window is the solution. To display it, highlight the folder and press ⌘-I. (You can also choose **Get Info** from the Finder's File menu.)

What you see depends on the type of object. For example, Figure 4.12 contains the Get Info window for a folder. It shows the folder's size, how many items it contains, its pathname, the date and time it was created, and the date and time of last modification.

You can enter any comments you'd like in the Comments box at the bottom of the window. File and folder comments are stored in a pair of invisible files known collectively as the Desktop file. As you will learn at the end of this chapter, the Desktop file can become a problem as it grows, unnecessarily chewing up disk space. In general, avoid comments unless you really need them.

FIGURE 4.12
The Get Info window for a folder

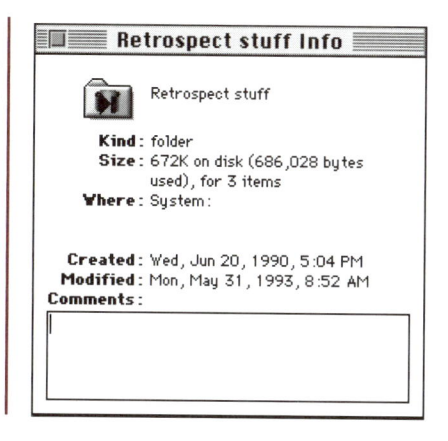

The Get Info window for a document file is similar (see Figure 4.13). Checking the "Locked" box in the lower left corner prevents the file from being modified or deleted. The "Stationary pad" box in the lower right corner turns the file into a template. When the file is opened, the application program creates a copy of the file named "untitled" rather than giving you the original to work with. This means that you don't run the risk of accidentally modifying a template that you want to use repeatedly.

The Get Info box for an application program (Figure 4.14) not only contains descriptive information about the file, but is used to specify the amount of memory to be used when the application is run. (You will learn more about this in Chapter 5.)

FIGURE 4.13
The Get Info window for a document file

FIGURE 4.14
The Get Info window for an application program

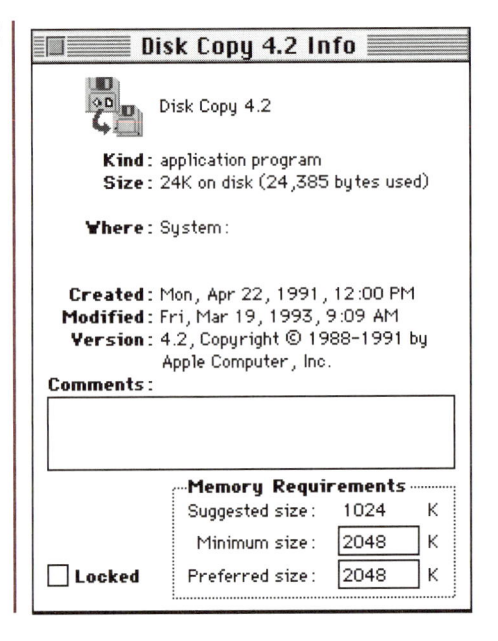

```
┌─────────────────────────────────────┐
│ ▤▤▤▤▤ Disk Copy 4.2 Info ▤▤▤▤▤     │
│                                     │
│     ▦   Disk Copy 4.2               │
│                                     │
│      Kind: application program      │
│      Size: 24K on disk (24,385      │
│            bytes used)              │
│                                     │
│     Where: System:                  │
│                                     │
│   Created: Mon, Apr 22, 1991, 12:00 PM │
│  Modified: Fri, Mar 19, 1993, 9:09 AM  │
│   Version: 4.2, Copyright © 1988-1991 by│
│            Apple Computer, Inc.     │
│  Comments:                          │
│   ┌─────────────────────────────┐   │
│   │                             │   │
│   └─────────────────────────────┘   │
│         ┌─Memory Requirements──┐    │
│         │ Suggested size: 1024 K│   │
│         │ Minimum size:   2048 K│   │
│  ☐ Locked│ Preferred size: 2048 K│   │
│         └───────────────────────┘   │
└─────────────────────────────────────┘
```

> **BY THE WAY!**
> Aliases and the trash can also have Get Info windows. They are discussed later in this chapter.

NOTES ON COPYING, MOVING, AND DELETING FILES AND FOLDERS

The Macintosh operating system seems to make copying and moving files and folders very intuitive: You simply drag the file or folder wherever you want it to go. However, what happens when you drag something from one place to another depends on whether the destination is in the same file system (volume) as the source.

If you drag a file or folder from one file system to another, the object you dragged is copied. To perform a move operation rather than a copy, you must delete the original once the copy is complete. However, if you drag a file or folder to a new location within the same file system, the object is moved rather than copied. To make a copy of an object within the same file system, hold down the **Option** key while dragging the file or folder to its new location.

CHAPTER 4: Disks, Folders, and Files **93**

USEFUL ADD-ON
CopyDoubler (see Figure 4.15) can significantly speed up copying (twice as fast) and deleting files (up to 10 times as fast). After installation at system startup, it operates transparently. CopyDoubler copies only changed files, which makes it particularly suitable for quick backups. It also can be configured to erase the disk space occupied by deleted files. Doing so makes it impossible to recover a deleted file, something that may be desirable for security purposes.

FIGURE 4.15
The CopyDoubler control panel

The trash can has always been the Macintosh metaphor for deleting files and folders. (As you read earlier, it is also used to unmount disk volumes.) Under System 7, objects remain in the trash until you empty it explicitly with the Special menu's **Empty Trash** command.

FLASHBACK
Prior to System 7, the trash can was emptied automatically whenever an application was launched. That meant that anything in the trash can wasn't "safe," as it is in System 7.

By default, the Macintosh operating system warms you every time you ask to empty the trash (Figure 4.16). This warning can become very annoying. To turn it off, open the trash can's Get Info box (Figure 4.17) and remove the check from the "Warn before emptying" box.

FIGURE 4.16
The trash warning

> ⚠ The Trash contains 1 item. It uses 21K of disk space. Are you sure you want to permanently remove it?
>
> [Cancel] [**OK**]

FIGURE 4.17
The trash can's Get Info window

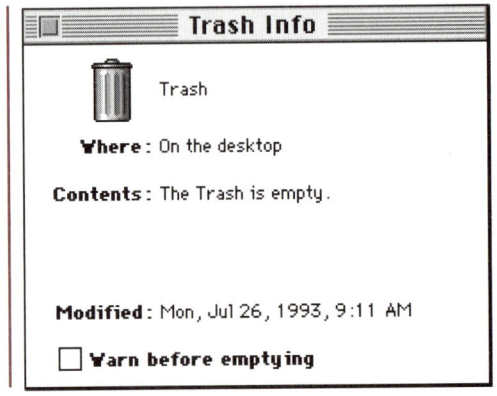

> **Trash Info**
>
> 🗑 Trash
>
> **Where:** On the desktop
>
> **Contents:** The Trash is empty.
>
> **Modified:** Mon, Jul 26, 1993, 9:11 AM
>
> ☐ Warn before emptying

If you would prefer to see the empty trash warning for most deletions, you can turn it off selectively by holding down the **Option** key when you drag an item to the trash. Using the **Option** key when trashing a file or folder also lets you delete locked files.

NOTES ON RENAMING DISKS, FILES, AND FOLDERS

Renaming a disk, file, or folder under System 7 is similar to renaming a file under earlier versions of the Macintosh operating system:

1. Click on the disk, file, or folder's *name* (not its icon). After a short delay, the entire name is highlighted and surrounded by a box, as in Figure 4.18.

FIGURE 4.18
A highlighted file name ready to be modified

> 💾 Disk Copy 4.2

2. To replace the entire name, type a new name.

3. To replace only a few characters, use the mouse pointer to highlight the characters you want to change and type the replacement characters. You can also click the mouse pointer anywhere in the name to place the insertion point. Use the "delete" key to remove characters to the left of the insertion point; use the → and ← keys to move the insertion point.

A word is in order here about the delay between clicking on a disk, file, or folder's name and the highlighting of that name for modification. Apple apparently introduced that delay with System 7 because users were accidentally modifying names when they only meant to highlight a disk, file, or folder so that it could be moved. Unfortunately, the Macintosh operating system doesn't provide any way to change or remove the delay.

USEFUL ADD-ON: One of the easiest ways to remove the renaming delay is with SpeedyFinder 7 (shareware by Victor Tan). Open the Speed Options dialog box (Figure 4.19) and click the No Rename Delay box.

FIGURE 4.19
SpeedyFinder 7's speed options

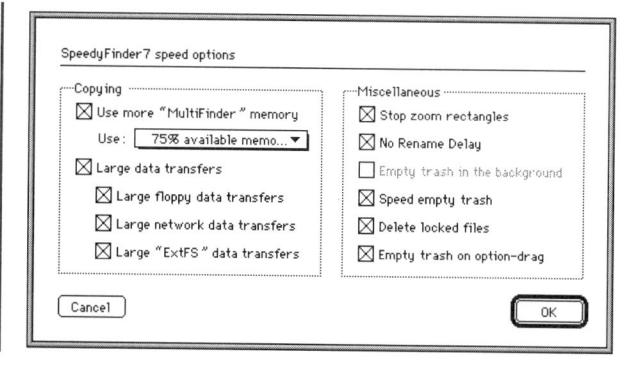

USEFUL ADD-ON: You can make a number of file management tasks easier with DeskTop Valet, a freeware application by Michael Love. You can get the most benefit out of Desktop Valet by placing copies of it throughout your Macintosh. Each Desktop Valet icon can be configured to do one thing: Move a file from its current location to the folder containing the Desktop Valet, delete a file, "shred" a file (make it unrecoverable after deleting), or create an alias of a file (see Figure 4.20). (Aliases are discussed in the next section of this chapter.)

FIGURE 4.20
Configuring a Desktop Valet

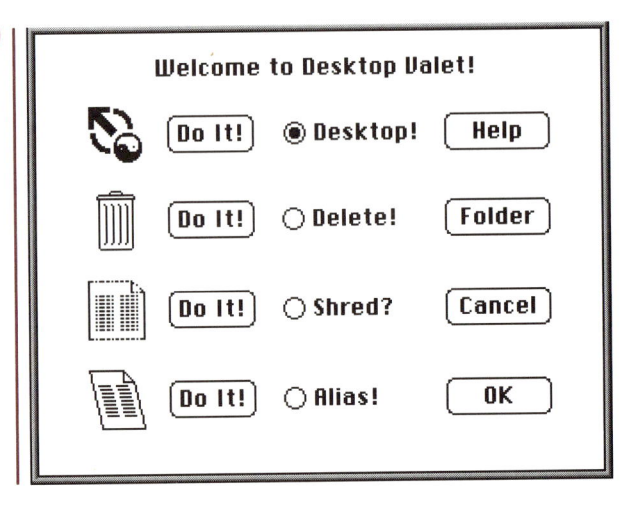

[Dialog box: "Welcome to Desktop Valet!" with Do It! buttons for Desktop!, Delete!, Shred?, and Alias! options, plus Help, Folder, Cancel, and OK buttons]

To configure a Desktop Valet, double-click on the application icon and then choose the function you want the Valet to perform. Then give it some meaningful name. To use it, drag the file you want the Valet to affect on top of the Valet's icon.

Managing Disk Contents with Labels and Aliases

System 7 introduced two useful ways to manage disk contents: labels and aliases. As you will see, labels are a useful organization tool; aliases are a powerful tool for making your system easier to use.

Labels

A *label* is a category to which you assign a file or folder. If the monitor on which your menu bar appears is a color monitor, each category name is also associated with a color. Labeling files or folders is one way to group objects. Once labels have been applied, you can arrange list views of disk contents by label, making it easier to keep track of related files and folders.

System 7 provides seven labels. To apply one to a file or folder, select the object and then choose the label/color from the Finder's label menu (Figure 4.21).

FIGURE 4.21
The Finder's Label menu

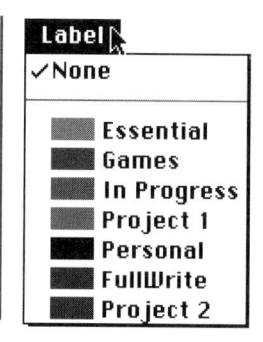

Label
✓None
▪ Essential
▪ Games
▪ In Progress
▪ Project 1
▪ Personal
▪ FullWrite
▪ Project 2

The label name and color that is associated with a given label is controlled by the Labels control panel (Figure 4.22). To change the color associated with a label:

1. Double-click on the color. A color wheel appears (see Figure 4.23).
2. Click the mouse pointer anywhere in the color wheel to select the desired color.
3. Press **Enter** or click **OK** to save your choice.

To change the text of a label, edit the existing text in the Labels control panel window.

FIGURE 4.22
The Labels control panel

Labels
▪ Essential
▪ Games
▪ In Progress
▪ Project 1
▪ Personal
▪ FullWrite
▪ Project 2

Aliases

As you read earlier, an alias is a pointer to the actual location of a file or folder. An alias has the same icon as the file or folder from which it was created; however, its name appears in italics rather than plain text. You work with an alias just as you would the original; any actions you take with the alias affect the original. For example, double-clicking on the alias of an application program launches the program; double-clicking on the alias of a folder opens the folder.

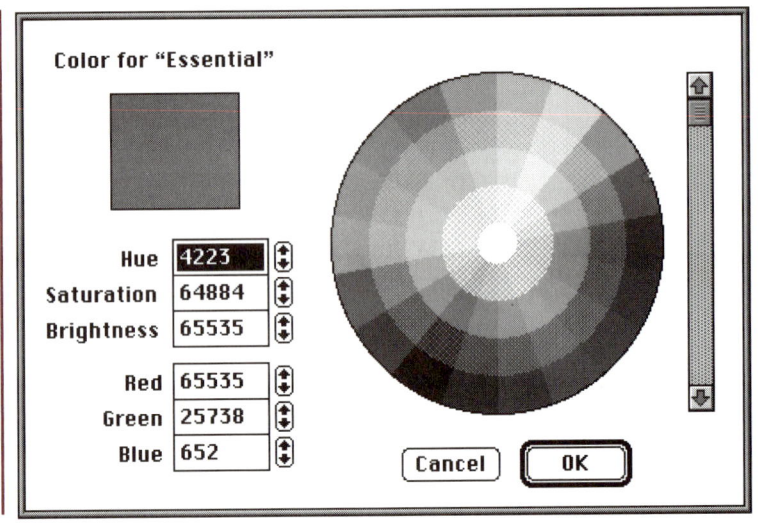

FIGURE 4.23
A color wheel for choosing a label's color

Because its contents include little more than the pathname of the file or folder it represents, an alias takes up very little space (between 1K and 4K). You can therefore feel free to scatter aliases wherever it is handy to have access to a file while storing the files wherever you have space. Some typical ways in which you can use aliases to make file access easier include:

- Place aliases for commonly used programs on the Desktop so they're always visible.

- Place aliases for commonly used programs on a disk whose window is always open. (This is the arrangement in Figure 4.1, where the startup disk contains little else besides the System folder, some essential utilities, and aliases.)

- Place aliases for commonly used programs in the Apple Menu Items folder so they will appear as part of the menu.

- Place trash can aliases at strategic locations on your Desktop. This is particularly useful if you have a large monitor or more than one monitor. Keep in mind, however, that only the original trash can gets "fat" when you put something in it; the aliases stay "thin."

If you need to get to the file or folder on which an alias is based, you needn't thread your way through the disk hierarchy. Instead, select the alias and press ⌘-I to open its Get Info window (Figure 4.24). Then, click the **Find Original** button.

The Macintosh operating system opens the window in which the original resides and selects it.

FIGURE 4.24
The Get Info window for an alias

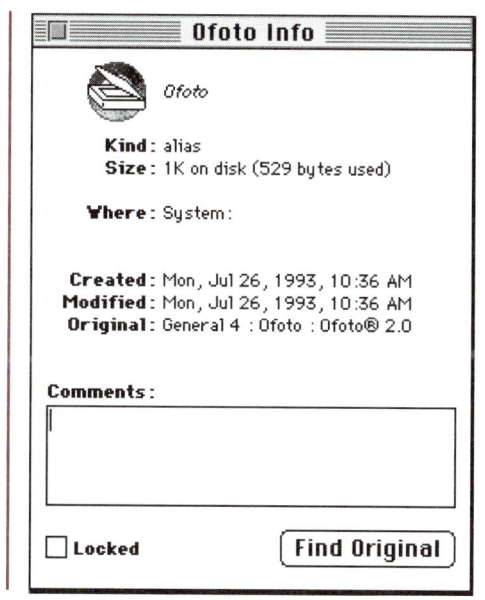

```
┌─────────────── Ofoto Info ───────────────┐
│                                          │
│    📄  Ofoto                             │
│                                          │
│    Kind: alias                           │
│    Size: 1K on disk (529 bytes used)     │
│                                          │
│   Where: System:                         │
│                                          │
│                                          │
│  Created: Mon, Jul 26, 1993, 10:36 AM    │
│ Modified: Mon, Jul 26, 1993, 10:36 AM    │
│ Original: General 4 : Ofoto : Ofoto® 2.0 │
│                                          │
│                                          │
│ Comments:                                │
│  ┌────────────────────────────────────┐  │
│  │                                    │  │
│  │                                    │  │
│  └────────────────────────────────────┘  │
│                                          │
│  ☐ Locked            ( Find Original )   │
└──────────────────────────────────────────┘
```

An alias represents a "hard" link to a file. In other words, the alias's pointer to the original consists of the pathname of the original. The benefit of this type of link is that aliases aren't restricted to the same file system, or volume, as the original. In fact, you can create an alias for a file or folder on removable media. The alias can exist even if the volume on which the original is stored isn't mounted; the Macintosh operating system will ask you to insert the correct volume when you access the alias.

There is, however, one major drawback to hard links: If you move the original or rename any object in its pathname, the alias can't find it. Therefore, if you change the name of any volume, folder, or file involved in creating the pathname for an alias, you must delete the alias and create a new one.

USEFUL ADD-ON

SpeedyFinder 7 (shareware by Victor Tan) adds some command key equivalents to the Finder's menus that make working with aliases and the trash can a bit easier. As you can see in Figure 4.25, Make Alias becomes ⌘-M and Empty Trash becomes ⌘-T. You can also use QuicKeys to create additional command key equivalents for Finder menu options.

FIGURE 4.25
SpeedyFinder 7's menu options

LOCATING FILES AND FOLDERS

The more files you have, the harder it becomes to keep track of where they are. The Macintosh operating system provides two ways to locate an object. Which you use depends on how much you already know about the file or folder's location.

Searching a Window

If you know the folder in which a file or folder is located, there are some keyboard shortcuts you can use to select the one you want:

- Type the first letter of the icon's name. The Macintosh operating system selects the first file that starts with the letter.
- Press **Tab** to move to the alphabetically next file.
- Press **Shift-Tab** to move to the alphabetically previous file.

Searching All Disks

Knowing the folder in which an object is located is far less common than having absolutely no idea where a file or folder might be lurking. The Finder's Find command can help by searching one or all mounted volumes. To find a file:

1. Choose **Find** from the Finder's File menu or press ⌘-**F**. The default window (Figure 4.26) appears.

FIGURE 4.26
Searching all volumes to find a file or folder

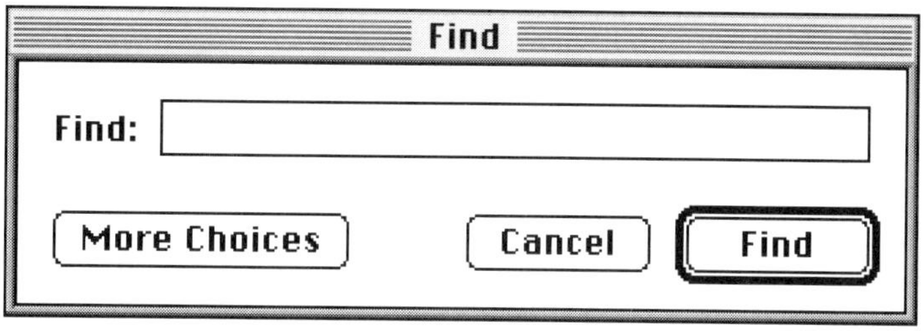

2. Type the name of the file or folder you want to find.

3. Press **Enter** or click the **Find** button. The Macintosh operating system searches all mounted volumes, stopping at the first file or folder whose name contains the characters you have entered into the dialog box.

4. To see the next match, choose **Find Again** from the Finder's File menu or press ⌘-**G**.

To gain more control over the way in which the file search is processed, click the **More Choices** button in the Find dialog box. The dialog box expands (see Figure 4.27). The leftmost pop-up menu lets you choose to search by name, size, type, date of creation, date of modification, label, comments, and whether the file is locked. The middle pop-up chooses how the search will match the characters typed at the right: contains (search text appears anywhere), starts with (search text appears at the left), ends with (search text appears at the left), is (search text is an exact match), is not (search text is anything except an exact match), and doesn't contain (search text doesn't appear anywhere).

FIGURE 4.27
Controlling the search for a file or folder

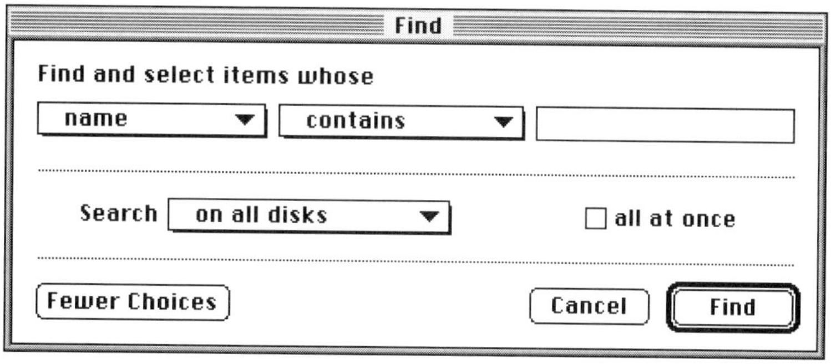

Using Find to Print Disk Directories

You can combine the Find command with the outline view of disk contents to print a directory of all files and folders on a disk volume. The procedure is as follows:

1. Press ⌘-F to open the Find dialog box. Click the **More Choices** button so that the dialog box appears as in Figure 4.27.

2. Configure the dialog box so that it looks like Figure 4.28 ("kind contains folder"). Check the "all at once" box.

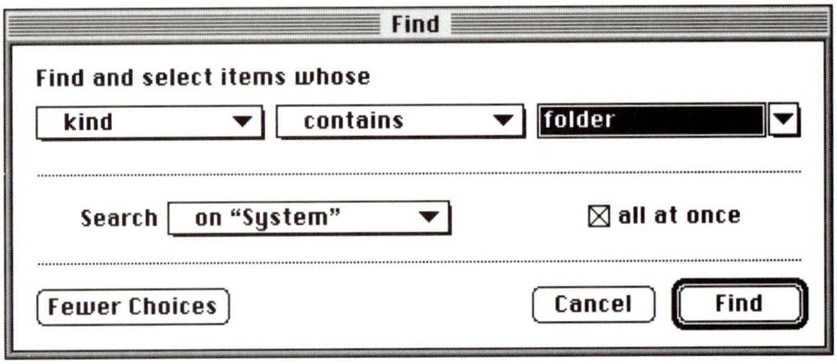

FIGURE 4.28
Finding files to get a directory of all files on a disk volume

3. Choose the disk volume to search.

4. Click the **Find** button or press **Enter**. Sit back and wait while the Macintosh operating system assembles the disk window in a list view.

5. When the disk window appears, press ⌘-← to expand every folder.

6. Turn on your printer.

7. Choose **Print Window** from the File menu.

To collapse the folder when printing is finished, press ⌘-→.

CHANGING ICONS

If you aren't satisfied with the icons for your files and folders, there is an easy way to change them:

- Copy the new icon onto the Clipboard. (There are many sources for custom icons. Perhaps the best is user groups and on-line services, which have icons in their public domain software collections.)

- Open the Get Info window for the file or folder whose icon you want to change.

- Click on the icon at the top left of the window to select it, as in Figure 4.29.

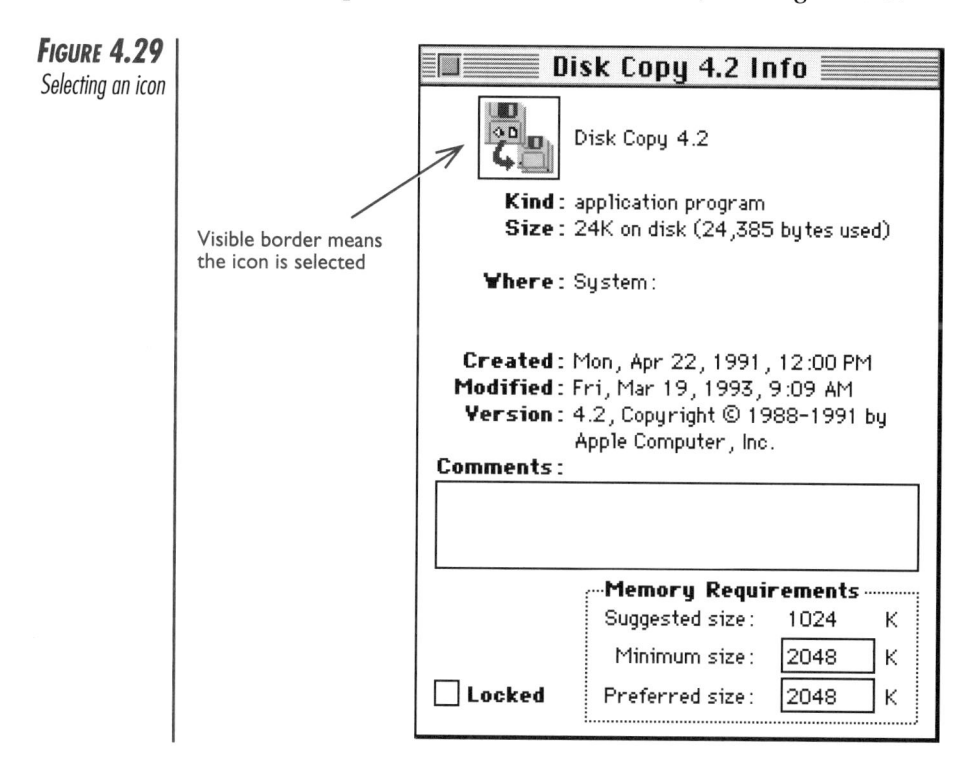

FIGURE 4.29
Selecting an icon

Visible border means the icon is selected

Disk Copy 4.2 Info

Disk Copy 4.2

Kind: application program
Size: 24K on disk (24,385 bytes used)

Where: System:

Created: Mon, Apr 22, 1991, 12:00 PM
Modified: Fri, Mar 19, 1993, 9:09 AM
Version: 4.2, Copyright © 1988-1991 by Apple Computer, Inc.
Comments:

Memory Requirements
Suggested size: 1024 K
Minimum size: 2048 K
☐ **Locked**   Preferred size: 2048 K

- Paste the new icon from the Clipboard.

Pasting a custom icon into the Get Info window doesn't really replace the original icon. The custom icon is stored separately and used instead of the original icon. If you cut the custom icon from the Get Info dialog box, the original icon reappears.

When you replace a volume icon with a custom icon, the custom icon is maintained in an invisible file called Icon, which is stored at the top level of the volume's hierarchy. The Finder sets a flag so it knows to use an icon in the file. If the Icon file is inadvertently deleted, the volume will mount with a generic document icon. However, when you try to paste in another custom icon, the Finder says, "The command cannot be completed because it cannot be found." This message occurs because the flag is set indicating that an Icon file exists but the Finder can't find it. The solution is to use a utility such as ResEdit to make the Icon file visible

104 NAVIGATING SYSTEM 7: Understanding The Macintosh Operating System

on another volume and then copy it to the problem volume. (Making invisible files visible is discussed at the very end of this chapter.) You will then be able to paste in the icon you want.

> **USEFUL ADD-ON**
> If you would like to design your own icons, consider using Icon 7, a system extension from Inline Design. Once Icon 7 is installed in the Extensions folder within the System folder, double-clicking on an icon in the Get Info dialog box launches the icon editor (for example, Figure 4.30). The drawing tools at the left of the dialog box can be used to modify the icon in any way you choose. You can also select an icon from one of Icon 7's icon libraries.

FIGURE 4.30
Editing an icon with Icon 7

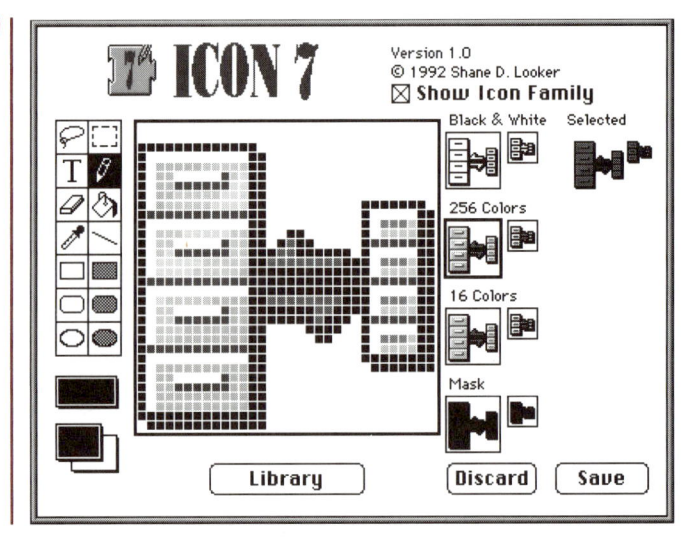

> **USEFUL ADD-ON**
> Many custom icons are available in the software libraries of on-line services such as America Online and CompuServe. There are, for example, more than 500 folder icons in the 3D Folders collection, created by many different people. 3D Folders, as shown below, are installed by pasting them into a folder's Get Info window as described in this chapter.

THE OPERATING SYSTEM'S VIEW

An operating system must have some way of physically storing and keeping track of files on a disk. As you will see, the way in which the Macintosh operating system views disk storage is considerably different from the way in which a disk is actually laid out. This portion of the chapter therefore begins by looking at how disks are laid out and then at the data structures used by the Macintosh operating system to keep track of disk usage and contents.

DISK FORMATTING

When you purchase an unformatted disk, it is truly a blank surface. Most disk media are sold in this way because they can then be formatted to the specifications of the drive in which they will be used. *Formatting* a disk does the following:

- Lays down the pattern of *tracks* and *sectors*. Each surface on which data are stored is divided into concentric circles called tracks (see Figure 4.31). The tracks are numbered beginning with 0, starting from the outside edge of the disk. At the same time, each surface is divided into pie-shaped sections known as sectors. As you can see in Figure 4.31, a single sector is therefore a portion of a single track. On Macintosh disks, each sector is 512 bytes in size. The more tracks on a disk (the more densely the tracks are packed), the more data can be stored on the disk. For example, 1.4Mb disks have more tracks than 800K disks, even though both use the same 3.5-inch media.

FIGURE 4.31
The physical layout of disk media

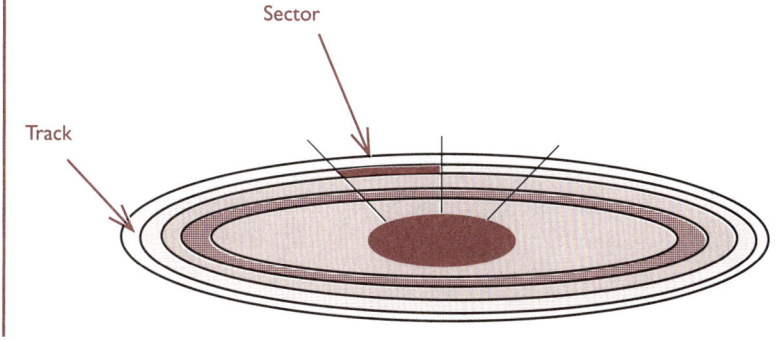

BY THE WAY! Because the tracks are packed so tightly on a 1.4Mb disk, the media must be of higher quality than 800K media. (Manufacturing standards are more exacting for 1.4Mb media.) Although it is possible to drill a second hole in an 800K disk and reformat it to hold 1.4Mb, you shouldn't do so. You run the risk of media failure and the loss of all the data on the disk.

- Initializes track 0 (the outermost track) to hold data structures that describe the contents of the disk. Because formatting creates a new set of these data structures, reformatting a disk makes any existing files on the disk inaccessible. It does not, however, actually erase those files.

- Checks for and marks bad sectors. Sectors that are damaged are flagged so they won't be used.

BY THE WAY! By the way: If you accidentally reformat a disk, don't panic—and don't make any changes to the disk. As long as you don't write to a reformatted disk, your chances of recovering its contents are good. To effect the recovery, you'll need a disk utility such as Norton Utilities that can examine the disk and reconstruct the original data structures that describe the disk's contents.

- Sets the *disk interleave*. The interleave determines whether data in a given track are written to adjacent sectors, every other sector, or every third sector. Early, relatively slow Macintoshes such as the Plus and SE work well with a 1:3 interleave (data written every third sector); other Macintoshes need a 1:1 interleave for best performance (data written to adjacent tracks).

Formatting a disk is not the same as "erasing" a disk. When you choose **Erase Disk** from the Finder's special menu, the Macintosh operating system doesn't reformat the disk; it initializes the volume by recreating the data structures that describe the contents of the disk, effectively making the files on the disk inaccessible. Unlike formatting, it doesn't check for bad blocks, lay down tracks and sectors, or set the interleave.

BY THE WAY! The Macintosh operating system uses the word *initialize* as a synonym for format. However, most third-party disk management utilities use the term "format."

Logical Disk Organization

Each hard disk is divided in *logical blocks* of 512 bytes. To make it easier to work with disk space, logical blocks are grouped together into *allocation blocks*. An allocation block is some multiple of the logical block size. For example, an allocation block might be 1,024 bytes. The size of an allocation block is set when a disk is formatted; it cannot be changed without reformatting. It is the smallest amount of space that can be added to a file at one time by any program. As you will see later in this chapter, the size of the allocation block is related to the size of drive.

To make it easier to allocate contiguous space on a disk, allocation blocks are grouped together into larger units called *clumps*. A clump is the smallest amount of space added to a file whenever a program needs more space than what is currently available. The clump size can be set by an application program, which means that different programs can allocate space in different sized chunks (although never less than an allocation block).

Disk Partitioning

Once a hard disk is formatted, it can be partitioned. (Floppy disks cannot be partitioned.) As you know, a partition is a section of a hard disk that appears on the Macintosh desktop as a separate volume. In most cases, you can speed up disk operations by partitioning a large hard disk (generally, one greater than 200Mb). Each partition has its own Desktop file. Because the Desktop file is smaller, locating and copying files is faster. In addition, partitions can make it easier to organize and back up files, especially if the sizes of the partitions are multiples of the size of your backup media.

Partitions on the same hard disk can be formatted for use by different operating systems. For example, one hard disk can be used for both Macintosh operating system and A/UX volumes. The structure of A/UX hard disk volumes is different from that of Macintosh operating system volumes and can't be mounted by the Macintosh operating system. However, A/UX can mount both its own partitions (there are several types) and Macintosh operating system partitions.

Disk Volume Organization

Each volume has an organization similar to that in Figure 4.32. (Don't forget that a volume can be an entire disk or a disk partition.) Notice that the logical blocks are numbered beginning with the first physical blocks on the volume. However, allocation blocks actually begin their numbering with the fourth physical block. The contents of each area on a volume are described in the following sections.

FIGURE 4.32
The organization of a Macintosh disk volume

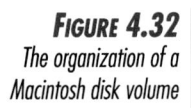

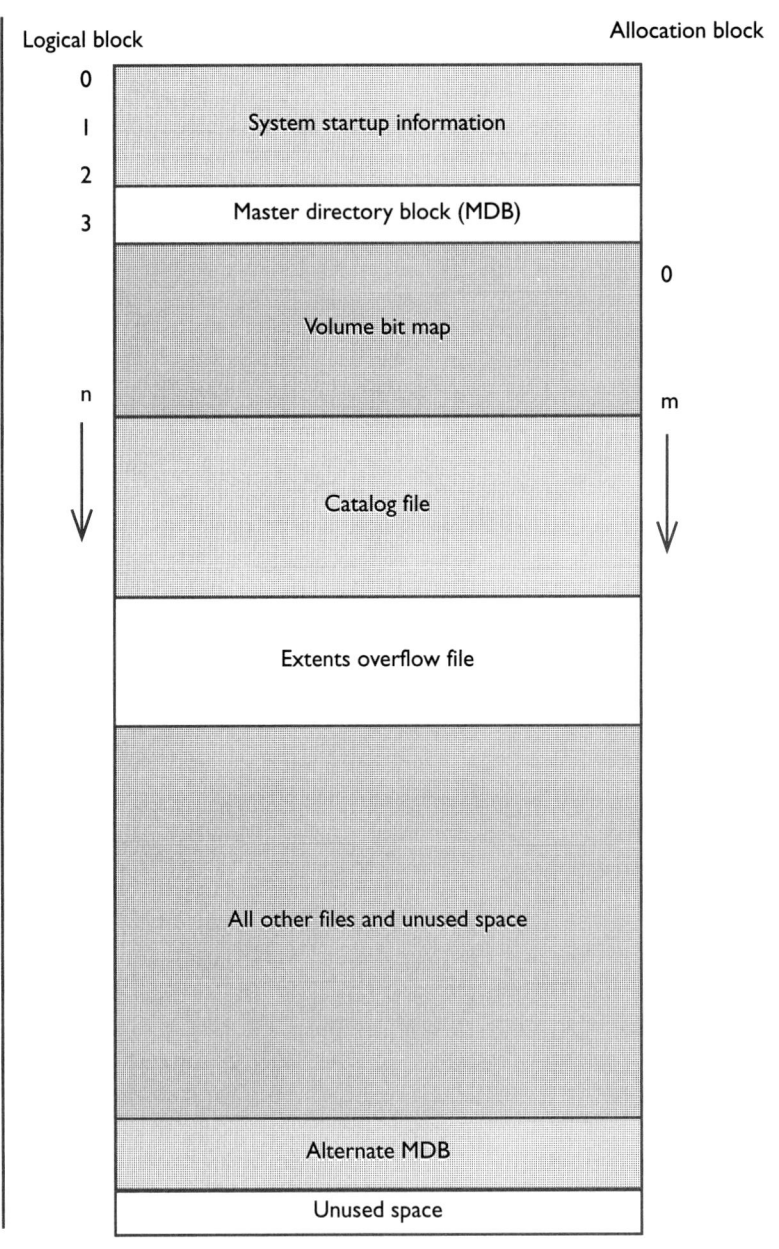

Logical block		Allocation block
0		
1	System startup information	
2		
3	Master directory block (MDB)	
	Volume bit map	0
n ↓		m ↓
	Catalog file	
	Extents overflow file	
	All other files and unused space	
	Alternate MDB	
	Unused space	

> **BY THE WAY!** The Desktop file, which keeps track of things like file/folder icons and the comments entered in a file/folder's Get Info box, isn't a part of the disk organization. Instead, it's a file used and maintained by the Finder.

Boot Blocks

The first two logical block of each disk volume are filled with system startup information. These *boot blocks* may contain information needed to boot the computer from the disk. If the volume isn't a startup volume (in other words, it contains no System folder), then the boot blocks are filled with zeros.

The boot blocks contain information such as:

- Name of the System file,
- Name of the Finder file,
- Name of the file containing the startup screen,
- Name of the startup program, the program to be run when the computer is booted (usually the Finder),
- Name of the system scrap file (usually the Clipboard), and
- Memory configuration parameters.

The boot blocks actually also include program code that can be used to execute the System file and start up the computer. However, in most cases the computer boots from program code that is part of the System file.

Master Directory Blocks

A *master directory block* (MDB), or *volume information block* (VIB), contains a wide range of information about what is stored on the volume. Its contents include:

- Date and time when the volume was created,
- Date and time when the volume was last modified,
- Attributes that indicate whether the volume is locked by hardware or software and whether it was mounted successfully,

NAVIGATING SYSTEM 7: Understanding The Macintosh Operating System

- Number of files and directories in the top level directory,

---

BY THE WAY! Don't forget that as far as the user is concerned, a disk directory is a folder.

- Number of directories and files on the volume,
- Location of the first block in the volume bitmap (discussed shortly),
- Location of the first block in the catalog file (discussed shortly),
- Size of allocation blocks,
- Number of allocation blocks in the volume,
- Clump size to use unless a program instructs otherwise,
- Size of catalog and extents overflow files (discussed shortly), and
- Volume name.

Each Macintosh volume maintains a copy of the MDB in the next-to-the-last block on the volume. This copy is for use by disk utility programs (especially those that are designed to recover accidentally deleted files or reformatted disks).

To keep the MDB clean and accurate, always use the Finder's **Shutdown** command before turning off your Macintosh. In the most benign circumstances, a dirty shutdown (one without executing the **Shutdown** command) makes the boot process take longer the next time you start up your computer. However, in some circumstances, it may trip a rather nasty bug in the Macintosh operating system that can prevent your Macintosh from booting.

On startup, the operating system writes a "dirty" flag to volume information block. When you use the **Shutdown** command, that flag is cleared. If the flag wasn't cleared, on next boot the operating system knows that the shutdown wasn't complete and therefore performs operations to clean up the volume's file system. This bug in the operating system can be tripped when booting a dirty volume: The operating system examines the extents file (discussed later in this chapter) and, even if the extents file is OK, reports a problem and refuses to boot the drive.

Before you panic the next time you experience an unexpected power outage, keep in mind that this problem only surfaces under very specific circumstances related to extents files greater than 786,432 bytes, large volume sizes, lots of fragmented files on disk, and dirty shutdown. If this should occur on your system, run a utility like Norton Utilities on the affected disk; Norton Utilities doesn't report the problem but fixes it anyway. Better yet, always shut down properly. For more specifics on circumstances when this bug occurs, see Ric Ford's column "Knowing bug's tricks helps keep it in check," *MacWEEK*, 3-1-93.

Volume Bitmap

The *volume bitmap* keeps track of which allocation blocks are in use and which are available. It contains one bit for every allocation block on the volume. If an allocation block is in use, its bit in the volume bitmap is 1; if an allocation block is available, its bit in the volume bitmap is 0. Note that this says nothing about which files are occupying the allocation blocks.

The size of the volume bitmap depends on the size of the disk and the size of the disk's allocation blocks. However, it has a maximum size of 65,535 bits. That means that there can't be more than 65,535 allocation blocks on a disk volume. If the allocation block size is equal to the logical block size (512 bytes), then a volume can be no larger than 32Mb. Larger disk volumes (up to a maximum of 2Gb) are supported by increasing the size of the allocation block. For example, if the allocation block is four logical blocks (2,048 bytes), then the maximum volume size is 128Mb.

There is one drawback to larger allocation blocks. Even if a program needs to store only one byte beyond the current end of its current file, it must expand the file by an entire allocation block. The result can be wasted space. You can keep the allocation block size relatively small by partitioning a large hard disk.This can help avoid the wasted space of large allocation block sizes as well as speed up disk access.

Catalog File and Extents Overflow File

The actual structure of the files and directories on a disk are maintained in the *catalog file*. In addition to storing the relationships between files and directories, the catalog file stores the following information about each file and directory:

- Type of catalog entry (for example, file or directory),
- Date and time file or directory was created,
- Date and time file or directory was last modified,

- First allocation block in a file,
- Location of the end of the file,
- Name of the file or directory,
- Identification of the directory containing the file or directory (its "parent" directory), and
- The first three *extents* allocated to the file (extent is another word for a group of allocation blocks used by a file).

If the list of blocks used by a file becomes too long to fit into the catalog file, it can overflow into the *extents overflow file*.

> **USEFUL ADD-ON** If you want to get a bit more information out of your floppy disk icons, try SpeedyFinder 7's "cool options" (Figure 4.33). Notice that the color disk icons show the capacity of the disk (SS, DD, or HD) as well as whether a disk is locked or damaged.

FIGURE 4.33
SpeedyFinder 7's "cool options"

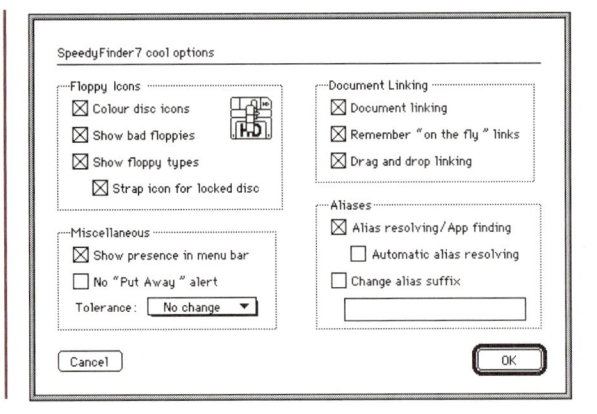

THE DESKTOP FILE

Under System 7, the Desktop file is actually a pair of invisible files—Desktop DB and Desktop DF—that the operating system uses to store file/folder icons and comments on each volume. The Desktop file therefore doesn't play a role in actually organizing the disk but is instead used to hold data for the Finder's use.

The Desktop file is modified each time a file or folder is created or deleted. As files and folders are added to the volume, the Desktop file grows in size to accommodate them; it doesn't necessarily shrink when a file or folder is deleted. Over time, the Desktop file not only consumes more space than necessary, but it can become corrupted. The usual evidence that you've got a problem is that custom icons disappear; application icons are replaced by the generic diamond and document icons are replaced by the page with a dog-eared corner. Another sign that there's a Desktop problem is double-clicking on a document file to open it and getting a message from the Finder that the application that created the file can't be found, even though the application is actually present on the computer.

The solution is to rebuild the Desktop, something that should be done on a regular basis anyway. To rebuild it on hard disk volumes, hold down the ⌘ and **Option** keys while the Macintosh is booting. You will be asked whether you want to rebuild the Desktop on each mountable hard disk volume. To rebuild the Desktop on a floppy, hold down the ⌘ and **Option** keys and insert the disk. When the operating system asks you if you want to rebuild the Desktop, choose the **OK** button.

> **BY THE WAY!**
> You won't be able to rebuild the Desktop on a floppy using the ⌘-Option method unless there is at least one file on the disk. To take care of a disk without files, use the Finder's **Erase Disk** command, which rebuilds all the disk's data structures.

Unfortunately, rebuilding Desktop by holding down ⌘ and **Option** keys during booting doesn't always recover missing icons. You may need to delete the Desktop DB and Desktop DF files. (Making invisible files visible is discussed later in this chapter.) Then, reboot with the ⌘ and **Option** keys held down.

> **USEFUL ADD-ON**
> A freeware application from MicroMat, TechTool (Figure 4.34), can make it easier to rebuild the Desktop. TechTool first deletes the invisible Desktop DB and Desktop DF files. It then reboots the Macintosh, forcing the operating system to recreate the Desktop files from scratch.

FIGURE 4.34
Using TechTool to rebuild the Desktop

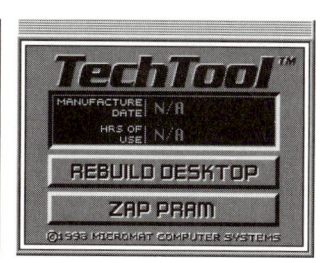

114 NAVIGATING SYSTEM 7: Understanding The Macintosh Operating System

Disk Fragmentation

When you begin to store files on a newly formatted disk, the Macintosh operating system places files in contiguous sectors (in other words, sectors that are right next to each other). However, as the disk fills up, there may not be enough contiguous space to store entire files. In that case, the operating system uses whatever space it can find, including space vacated by deleted files. Some files may be spread over sectors that are widely separated. When this occurs, a disk is said to be *fragmented*. The more fragmented a disk becomes, the slower the access to files on the disk.

To defragment a disk, placing all files in contiguous sectors, you'll need a disk utility such as Speed Disk (part of the Norton Utilities package). Speed Disk (Figure 4.35) checks a disk for fragmentation and then gives an indication of the degree of fragmentation. Defragmentation coalesces the empty space into larger blocks and writes fragmented files to contiguous sectors.

Figure 4.35
Using Norton Utilities's Speed Disk to defragment a disk

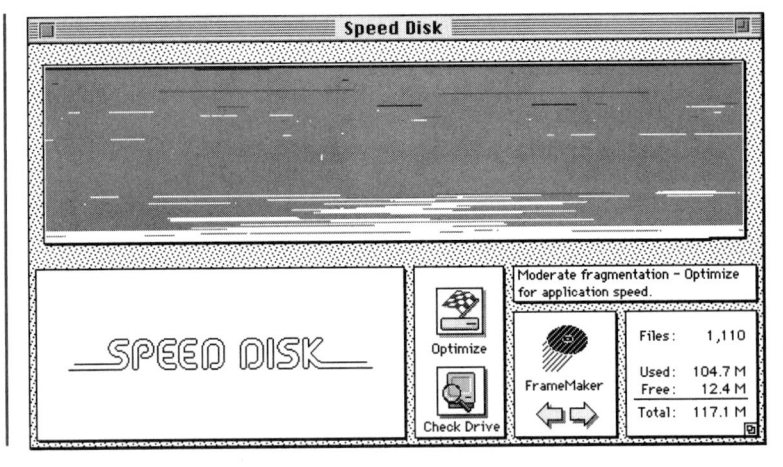

BY THE WAY!

Defragmenting a disk is not the same as optimizing a disk. Disk optimization organizes files to minimize access time. Applications and system files, which are rarely modified, are placed together at the beginning of the disk. Document files, which tend to be modified frequently, are placed at the end of the disk. Because optimization requires rewriting large portions of a disk, it is time consuming and cannot be performed on a disk with open files; defragmentation is relatively fast and can be done on a disk with open files. Like other disk utility programs, Speed Disk can optimize disks as well as defragment them.

MAKING INVISIBLE FILES VISIBLE

Some of the techniques you've read about in this chapter require working with invisible operating system files. Of course, to handle those files in any way you need to make them visible. There are many utility programs that do that for you. The instructions that follow are for ResEdit, a powerful, useful utility program that can be used to customize the Macintosh in a variety of ways.

To use ResEdit to make an invisible file visible:

1. Launch ResEdit.

2. Click the mouse button anywhere in the startup picture to make it disappear. An Open File dialog box appears.

3. Choose the file you want to make visible.

4. In some cases, ResEdit warns you that the file has no resource fork and that opening it will create one (see Figure 4.36). (The resource fork is the part of a file that is used to contain resources rather than data.) Respond **OK**.

FIGURE 4.36
Using ResEdit to open a file without a resource fork

> The file 'Desktop DB' has no resource fork. Opening it will add one. Do you wish to open it?
>
> [Cancel]   [OK]

5. Choose Get Info from ResEdit's File menu. The Info dialog box appears (see Figure 4.37). Notice that the Invisible box is checked. Click on that box to remove the check mark and close the dialog box.

FIGURE 4.37
The ResEdit Get Info dialog box

```
╔═══════════════ Info for Desktop DB ═══════════════╗
│ File  [Desktop DB                              ]  │
│ Type  [BTFL]              Creator [DMGR]          │
│  ☐ System      ☒ Invisible    Color: [Color 8 ▼]  │
│  ☐ On Desk     ☐ Inited       ☐ Bundle   ☐ Letter │
│  ☐ Shared      ☐ No Inits     ☐ Alias    ☐ Stationery │
│  ☐ Always switch launch       ☐ Use custom icon   │
│ ─────────────────────────────────────────────────  │
│  ☐ Resource map is read only            ☐ File Protect │
│  ☐ Printer driver is MultiFinder compatible  ☒ File Busy │
│                                         ☐ File Locked │
│  Created  [5/30/93  2:18:06 PM]                   │
│  Modified [7/27/93 10:55:54 AM]                   │
│      Size  286 bytes in resource fork             │
│            32768 bytes in data fork               │
╚═══════════════════════════════════════════════════╝
```

6. ResEdit asks if you want to save your changes. Respond Yes.

7. Quit ResEdit.

When you return to the Finder, you'll discover that you can now see the invisible file.

USEFUL ADD-ON

If, like many people, you find using ResEdit a bit daunting, consider using the shareware program Attributes instead. Attributes, which is included on the disk that comes with this book, lets you modify the characteristics of one or more files at the same time. As you can see in Figure 4.38, you can change a file's type and creator as well as the creation and modification date and time. You can also make a file invisible, lock it so it can't be deleted or moved, or turn it into a stationery pad. Applications can be turned into aliases.

One small word of caution is necessary with regard to invisible files. Because Attributes works by dragging file and/or folder icons onto the Attributes program icon, you won't be able to work with an invisible file. (You won't be able to see its icon!) Therefore, once you've used Attributes to make a file invisible, you'll need something like ResEdit to make it visible again.

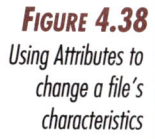

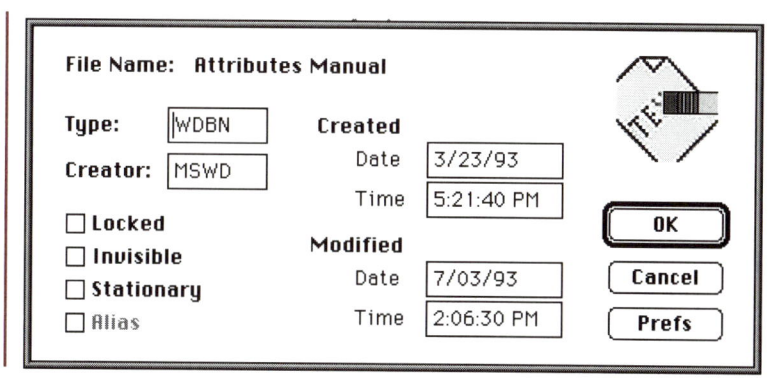

FIGURE 4.38
Using Attributes to change a file's characteristics

DISK AND FILE COMPRESSION

Sooner or later, every Mac user runs into a space problem. You may run short of hard disk space; you might need to use a floppy disk to transfer a file that's larger than the disk's capacity. Both of these problems can be handled by compressing files, although the way in which the compression is managed depends on our goal.

If you want to compress files simply to make them fit in a smaller space, use a file compression utility such as StuffIt or Compact Pro. However, if you want to automatically compress and decompress files as you work to expand what you can store on your hard disk, use a disk compression utility such as AutoDoubler.

There is one important thing to consider before embarking on disk or file compression: You can't use a file when it has been compressed. To access a compressed file, you must first decompress it. That means you must have enough storage space to hold the decompressed file. You must also wait for the decompression to occur.

BY THE WAY! Some operating systems (for example, MS DOS 6.0) include disk compression. However, disk compression has never been a part of the Macintosh operating system.

FILE COMPRESSION

File compression removes unused space from within a file or group of files, often squeezing files to half their original size. File compression and decompression

118 NAVIGATING SYSTEM 7: Understanding The Macintosh Operating System

isn't automatic; you must explicitly add files to or extract files from an archive. File compression therefore isn't a good solution to everyday disk space problems. On the other hand, it is excellent for archival storage (storage of files that you don't need to keep on your hard disk but don't want to discard entirely) and for transferring files over telecommunications lines.

Although there are many file compression programs, two are generally accepted as standards for data communications use: StuffIt, whose archives are identified by a ".sit" extension, and Compact Pro, whose archives are identified by a ".cpt" extension.

StuffIt (Figure 4.39) is a commercial program. As you add files to an archive, StuffIt automatically compresses them. StuffIt provides several types of compression. The amount of compression varies depending on the type of file being compressed and the type of compression used. You may therefore want to try each type of compression to see which squeezes files the most.

Figure 4.39
Creating a StuffIt archive

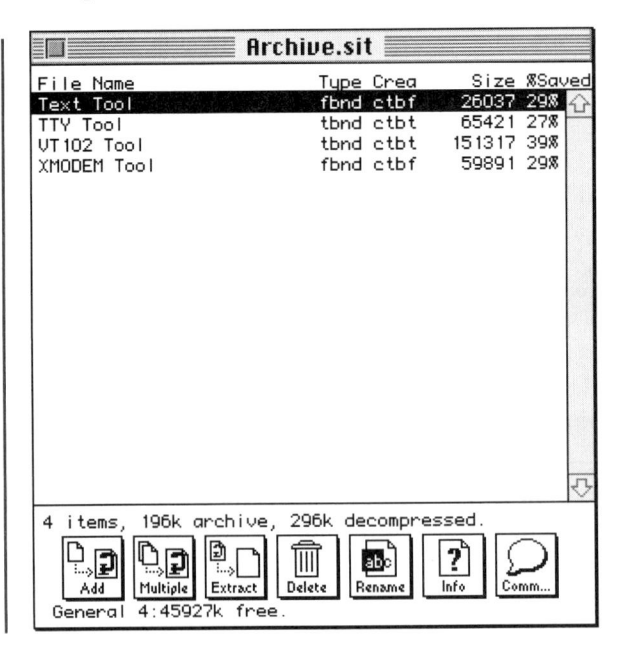

```
┌─────────────── Archive.sit ───────────────┐
│ File Name            Type Crea   Size %Saved │
│ Text Tool            fbnd ctbf  26037  29%   │
│ TTY Tool             tbnd ctbt  65421  27%   │
│ VT102 Tool           tbnd ctbt 151317  39%   │
│ XMODEM Tool          fbnd ctbf  59891  29%   │
│                                              │
│ 4 items, 196k archive, 296k decompressed.    │
│  [Add] [Multiple] [Extract] [Delete] [Rename] [Info] [Comm...] │
│ General 4: 45927k free.                      │
└──────────────────────────────────────────────┘
```

Although StuffIt is a commercial program, a subset of StuffIt's capabilities is available as freeware. The freeware application (StuffIt Expander) lets users extract files from a StuffIt archive. However, it cannot be used to build new archives. StuffIt archives can also be created to be self-extracting; that means that the unstuffing code is built into the archive. A user double-clicks on the archive icon and all files are extracted. A self-extracting archive is larger than one without the extraction code but means that the archive's recipient needs no other software to gain access to the files.

Compact Pro (Figure 4.40) is shareware. Although not as widely used by online services as StuffIt, Compact Pro does achieve high degrees of compression and is therefore often a good choice for permanent archiving or squeezing files for transmission to individuals. Unlike StuffIt, Compact Pro does not compress files as you add them to the archive, but instead waits until you issue a Save command. Compact Pro does not have a separate decompression program. However, Compact Pro archives can be made self-extracting.

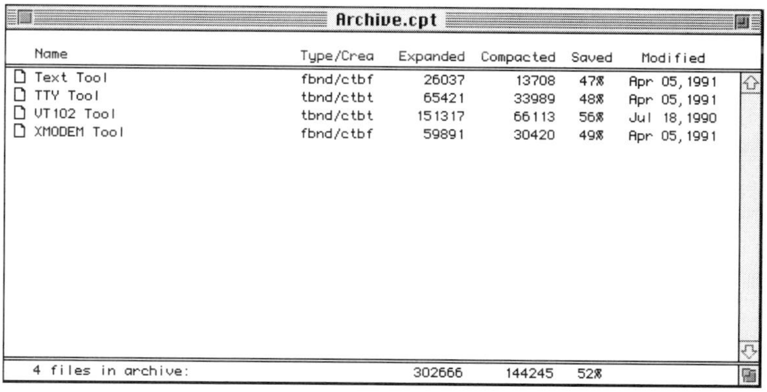

FIGURE 4.40

Creating a Compact Pro archive

Name	Type/Crea	Expanded	Compacted	Saved	Modified
Text Tool	fbnd/ctbf	26037	13708	47%	Apr 05, 1991
TTY Tool	tbnd/ctbt	65421	33989	48%	Apr 05, 1991
VT102 Tool	tbnd/ctbt	151317	66113	56%	Jul 18, 1990
XMODEM Tool	fbnd/ctbf	59891	30420	49%	Apr 05, 1991
4 files in archive:		302666	144245	52%	

DISK COMPRESSION

Disk compression is somewhat different from file compression. The purpose of disk compression is to transparently compress and decompress the files on a disk to increase what can be stored on a disk while you are working. The Macintosh operating system does not provide disk compression capabilities; they must therefore be added with third-party utilities such as AutoDoubler. Although disk compression does somewhat slow down opening and saving files, it can provide a cost effective way to increase your storage space.

AutoDoubler (Figure 4.41) installs at system startup and then transparently and automatically compresses and decompresses files. If you access a compressed file, AutoDoubler automatically decompresses it; compression occurs during idle times (not in the background). By default, AutoDoubler compresses files on a volume. However, you can exclude files from compression by name, size, or label.

FIGURE 4.41
The AutoDoubler control panel

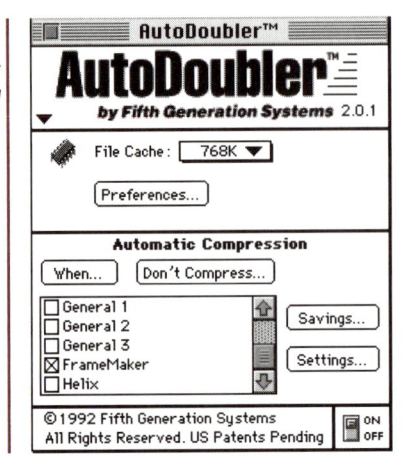

AutoDoubler can be configured to achieve a variety of compression goals (see Figure 4.42). In most cases, you will want to maintain as much free space as possible. However, you can also set a target for the amount of free disk space.

FIGURE 4.42
AutoDoubler compression settings

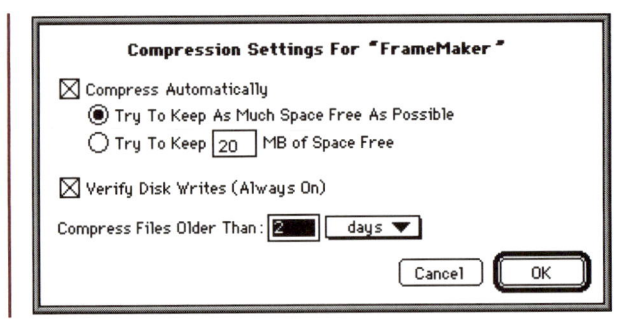

Be somewhat careful when you embark on a disk compression project. Some applications won't work properly if their support files are compressed. You may therefore want to leave application programs uncompressed and compress only your document files.

DISK BACKUP

There's no better way to protect the data you have stored on a disk than to make backup copies. Disks do fail, simply from excessive use; in the long run, there's nothing you can do to prevent it. However, as long as you have recent backups, you won't lose any valuable data.

> **BY THE WAY!** Some operating systems (for example, UNIX) include file archiving utilities. However, disk backup has never been a part of the Macintosh operating system.

How often should you back up your disks? How many backup copies should you keep? There is no definitive answer. General wisdom says that you should keep three backup copies of everything. When you want to make a new backup, you reuse the oldest of the three backups. In some cases, however, three backup copies probably aren't necessary. Consider the following backup guidelines:

- Make one backup copy of each disk that is shipped with commercial software. Lock the originals and put them away. Use the copies to install your software. Because you have the locked originals, you probably don't need more than one working copy.

> **BY THE WAY!** In the early days of the Macintosh, most commercial software was copy protected, making it impossible to make floppy disk copies. Business users, however, insisted on their right to make backup copies of their legally purchased software. As a result, only a few games retain copy protection. You will be able to make backup copies of nearly all productivity application software.

- Keep three copies of important files that change often. However, don't simply back up an entire disk volume every time a few files on that volume are modified. Over time, hard disk sectors can become damaged and unreadable. The typical way of detecting this damage is attempting to read a file and discovering that it's inaccessible. If you have regularly been backing up the entire disk volume, you may inadvertently destroy your last readable copy of an old file. Once you have three copies of a file, don't make another backup of it until the file is modified in some way.

The most straightforward way to make backup copies is to use the Finder to place copies of your files on some type of removable media such as a floppy disk, optical disk, or SyQuest cartridge. There are several problems with this strategy. First, you must drag each file from its original location to the backup media. Second, you must pay attention to how much space you have on the backup media. When you fill a backup disk, you must make another backup disk available, formatting it if necessary. Third, there is no way to split very large files between smaller disks. Finally, you need to keep track of when you made backups and what files were backed up.

Backup software can make it easier to manage the process. Retrospect, for example, can transfer files to tape or other removable disk media such as floppy disk, optical disk, or SyQuest cartridge. Retrospect keeps track of the files stored in a backup copy (an "archive") in a disk file known as a "catalog." Each catalog file contains data about which files were backed up when. (Should the disk on which a catalog file is stored become damaged, the catalog can be reconstructed from the archive itself.)

Retrospect takes over the file copying process. For example, the disk volume backed up in Figure 4.43 contains 139.5Mb of files. However, the tapes used to hold the archive store only 60Mb. Retrospect therefore takes care of splitting large files between tapes and, when necessary, formats tapes in the middle of the backup process. All the user needs to do is have enough media available.

FIGURE 4.43
Backing up a hard disk volume with Retrospect

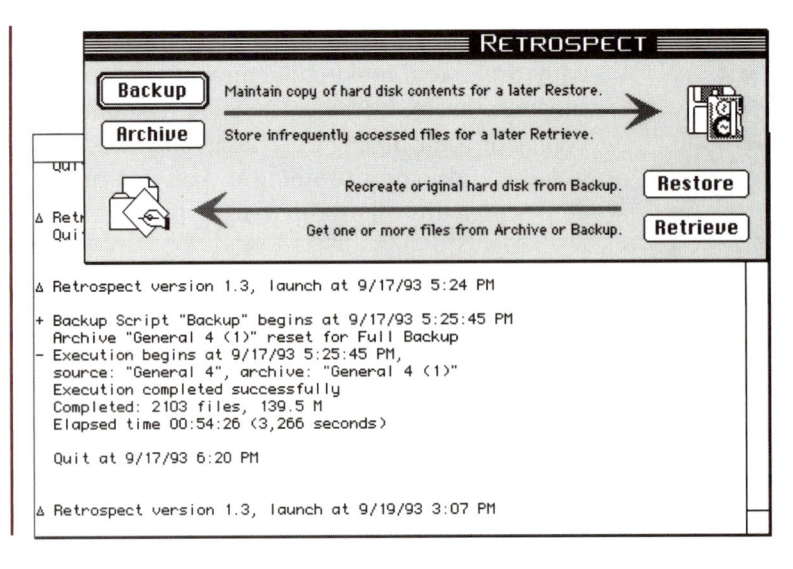

```
══════════════════════ RETROSPECT ══════════════════════

[ Backup  ]   Maintain copy of hard disk contents for a later Restore.
[ Archive ]   Store infrequently accessed files for a later Retrieve.

              Recreate original hard disk from Backup.    [ Restore  ]
              Get one or more files from Archive or Backup. [ Retrieve ]

△ Retrospect version 1.3, launch at 9/17/93 5:24 PM
+ Backup Script "Backup" begins at 9/17/93 5:25:45 PM
  Archive "General 4 (1)" reset for Full Backup
- Execution begins at 9/17/93 5:25:45 PM,
    source: "General 4", archive: "General 4 (1)"
  Execution completed successfully
  Completed: 2103 files, 139.5 M
  Elapsed time 00:54:26 (3,266 seconds)

  Quit at 9/17/93 6:20 PM

△ Retrospect version 1.3, launch at 9/19/93 3:07 PM
```

CHAPTER 5
Applications and Process Management

This chapter looks at how the Macintosh operating system executes and manages application programs, focusing on what happens when you run more than one application at a time. You'll also read about background operations and discover what you can do when your Macintosh crashes or hangs.

UNDERSTANDING MULTITASKING

An operating system that is capable of multitasking can have more than one program executing at the same time. To effect multitasking, an operating system must:

- Allocate RAM to each process as it is launched.
- Protect the RAM occupied by each process from all other processes running at the same time.
- Have some mechanism for determining which process gains control of the CPU and how long a process retains control.
- Be able to freeze a process that is giving up control of the CPU so that execution can begin exactly where it left off the next time the process has access to the CPU.

Processes can run in the *foreground* or *background*. At any given time, there is one foreground process, the process with which the user is currently interacting. There may also be any number of background processes that are executing without user intervention. If a background process needs user input, it must be brought to the foreground, sending the current foreground process to the background.

There are many types of programs that it makes sense to run in the background. As far as the Macintosh is concerned, probably the most common is printing. PrintMonitor, the application that manages background printing to laser printers, works like other background processes in that it gets control of the CPU whenever the foreground application isn't using it. In addition to printing, applications can perform activities such as recalculating values on a spreadsheet or retrieving data from a database in the background.

> **BY THE WAY!** Nonmultitasking operating systems such as MS DOS can also do background printing using a technique known as *cycle stealing*. This same technique was used by some third-party Macintosh applications to implement background printing before the introduction of MultiFinder.

Removing one process from the CPU and bringing another process into the CPU is known as a *context switch*. The Macintosh recognizes two types. A *major switch* occurs when a background process is given control of the CPU and brought to the foreground; a *minor switch* occurs when a background process is given control of the CPU without being brought to the foreground.

As you read in Chapter 1, there are two types of multitasking: preemptive and cooperative. The difference between them has to do with deciding which process has control of the CPU at any given time. Understanding this difference is important to understanding the strengths and limitations of the Macintosh operating system.

Preemptive Multitasking

Preemptive multitasking is used in multi-platform operating systems such as UNIX (including Apple's A/UX) and most minicomputer and mainframe operating systems. A preemptive operating system takes complete control of process management. It has some scheme for deciding which process gets to use the CPU at any given time.

The length of time that a process can run before it must vacate the CPU is known as a *quantum*. The operating system maintains a clock (the *interval timer*) that indicates when a quantum has expired, forcing a context switch.

> **BY THE WAY!** With a preemptive operating system, a process may be forced to give up control of the CPU before its quantum expires if an interrupt occurs. An *interrupt* is an event, such as the completion of an I/O operation, that requires the computer's immediate attention.

The order in which processes are given control of the CPU varies from one preemptive operating system to another. A typical scheme, known as *round robin scheduling*, maintains a list of processes that are ready to run (in other words, should the CPU become available, they would be able to execute without waiting for I/O). When the CPU becomes available, the process at the head of the list is given control. When the operating system requires that process to give up the CPU, the "next" process in the list is switched into the CPU and the process switched out of the CPU is placed back at the end of the list.

Regardless of the scheme a preemptive operating system uses to decide which process gets control of the CPU, it is always the operating system that decides. The operating system also determines when a process must give up control of the CPU. Programs are written as if they were to run as the only program executing; all multitasking is managed by the operating system.

Under a preemptive operating system, any program can run in the background. When a user launches a program, he or she can indicate that the program should be placed in the background, freeing the user to work with another application in the foreground. The important thing to recognize here is that programs don't need to be written specifically for background operations.

> **BY THE WAY!** Preemptive multitasking is essential for a *multi-user* operating system (an operating system that supports more than one person working with the computer at one time). Preemption means that each user can have a foreground application running at his or her workstation, along with any number of background processes. Each of these processes gets a turn at the CPU, using a process scheduling scheme such as the round robin scheduling discussed earlier so that all processes are treated relatively fairly. Because CPUs operate at such high speeds, most of the time it appears to

each user that he or she is using the computer alone. (When there are many processes running and a multi-user system becomes loaded, a user may well notice a slowdown.)

Cooperative Multitasking

Cooperative multitasking requires cooperation between the operating system and application programs to manage multitasking. The foreground application—the program whose windows are active and with which you are currently working—has highest priority with the CPU. The operating system gives background processes, such as printing, CPU time whenever the foreground process is idle.

To get the Macintosh operating system to perform a major switch, you either click on a background process's window or choose its name from the Application menu (the menu at the far right of the menu bar whose name is the icon of the current foreground process). The operating system does not have an interval timer to force a context switch when a quantum has expired.

When the foreground process is idle (not using the CPU), the Macintosh operating system performs a minor switch and gives a background process (if any are in memory) a chance to execute. However, because there is no interval timer, it is up to the application program to voluntarily give up the CPU so that the foreground process or another background process can run. In other words, the scheduling of processes into and out of the CPU is based on cooperation between the operating system and application programs.

BY THE WAY! It is certainly possible for a software developer to write a program that hogs the CPU when the program is running in the background. However, most software developers realize that users wouldn't be very tolerant of such badly behaved programs and therefore wouldn't be likely to purchase them.

Not every Macintosh program can run in the background; it must be written specifically to do so. A foreground-only application looks for events in the event queue using a program found in the Macintosh ROM called GetNextEvent, which functions only when the program is in the foreground. On the other hand, programs written for background operations use WaitNextEvent, which lets them check the event queue for events directed at them when the program is in the background. A program that can run in the background must also include its own timer to tell it when to relinquish the CPU.

Because cooperative multitasking places some of the burden for process management on application programs, some people believe that cooperative multitasking isn't true multitasking and that the only real form of multitasking is preemptive multitasking. There isn't any definitive answer to this controversy. However, keep in mind that under the Macintosh operating system, whether an application program can execute in the background and how it behaves in the background depends on the way the application program has been written, not on the operating system.

LAUNCHING APPLICATIONS

The traditional way to launch a Macintosh application is to double-click on the application's icon. (You can also launch an application by selecting an icon and then choosing **Open** from the File menu. However, most people get beyond that point very quickly.) If an application is written according to Apple's guidelines, it will either open an untitled document or give you the choice of opening an existing document or creating a new one.

One of the most innovative features of the first Macintosh operating system was its ability to link documents to the applications that created them. That means you can double-click on a document to open it. If the application that created the document isn't running, the operating system launches the application; otherwise, it simply opens the document. The secret behind this capability is two four-character strings attached to every Macintosh file: the file's *type* and *creator*.

A file type indicates the type of file. For example, APPL indicates an application that can be launched. The documents created by an application have a creator string that identifies the application. For example, Microsoft Word documents have a creator string of MSWD; Aldus Freehand documents have a creator string of FHA3. When you double-click on a document, the Macintosh operating system looks for the application associated with a document's creator string.

An application also stamps a document file with a type string. Documents formatted for use by a specific application have types unique to the application. For example, Microsoft Word documents have a type of WDBN; Aldus Freehand documents have a type of FHD3. To help avoid duplication, software developers must register their type and creator strings with Apple.

In addition to the application-specific type strings, there are some generic document types that can be opened by more than one application. These include TEXT (files containing only ASCII character codes and no formatting commands), PICT (graphics files that use QuickDraw commands to describe an image), TIFF (bitmapped graphics files in tag image file format), PTNG (bitmapped paint files), and ESPF (encapsulated PostScript graphics files that use PostScript commands to describe an image).

By default, the Macintosh operating system maps TEXT and PICT files to TeachText, a text editor that ships with the operating system and many application programs. If you double-click on a document file for which the operating system can't find a creator, you are given a chance to choose an application with which to open the document (see Figure 5.1).

FIGURE 5.1
Choosing an application to open an document

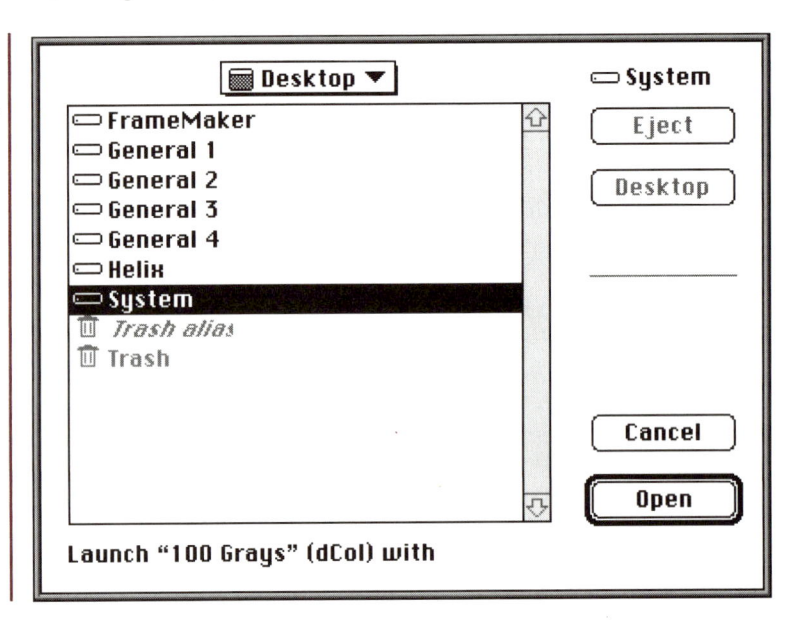

FLASH BACK — Prior to System 7, if you double-clicked on a document for which the Macintosh operating system couldn't find an application, the operating system displayed an alert saying that it couldn't find a program to open the document. Your only alternative was to launch the application with which you wanted to open the document and then use the application's Open command to open the document.

System 7 provides an alternative to the dialog box in Figure 5.1 for choosing the application with which you want to open a document: *drag and drop*. To use drag and

CHAPTER 5: Applications and Process Management

drop, drag a document icon onto the icon of the application with which you want to open it. Drag and drop works between volumes as long as you are dragging onto an application icon. However, if you are working with the alias of an application, drag and drop only works when the document and application alias are on the same volume; it will not work if the application alias is a different volume from the document.

USEFUL ADD-ON
SpeedyFinder 7 (shareware by Victor Tan) provides additional flexibility in linking file types to application types. As you can see in Figure 5.2, file types are matched to applications actually present on the system. For example, if TeachText isn't present, TEXT files are opened by Microsoft Word. By the same token, TIFF files are opened by BrushStrokes. This makes it much easier to work with generic file types such as TEXT, TIFF, PICT, PNTG, and EPSF.

FIGURE 5.2
Using SpeedyFinder 7 to link document types to applications

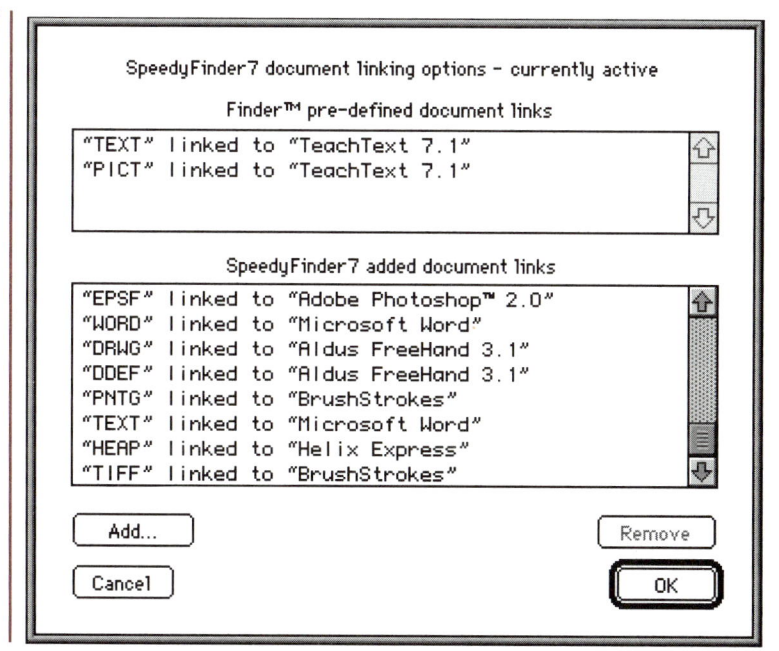

```
SpeedyFinder7 document linking options - currently active

        Finder™ pre-defined document links
    ┌─────────────────────────────────────────┐
    │ "TEXT" linked to "TeachText 7.1"        │
    │ "PICT" linked to "TeachText 7.1"        │
    │                                         │
    └─────────────────────────────────────────┘

        SpeedyFinder7 added document links
    ┌─────────────────────────────────────────┐
    │ "EPSF" linked to "Adobe Photoshop™ 2.0" │
    │ "WORD" linked to "Microsoft Word"       │
    │ "DRWG" linked to "Aldus FreeHand 3.1"   │
    │ "DDEF" linked to "Aldus FreeHand 3.1"   │
    │ "PNTG" linked to "BrushStrokes"         │
    │ "TEXT" linked to "Microsoft Word"       │
    │ "HEAP" linked to "Helix Express"        │
    │ "TIFF" linked to "BrushStrokes"         │
    └─────────────────────────────────────────┘

    [ Add... ]                    [ Remove ]
    [ Cancel ]                    [   OK   ]
```

USEFUL ADD-ON
One way to simplify launching applications and/or opening documents is to use OneClick, a shareware application by Rick Christianson that creates floating palettes of application and document icons (for example, see Figure 5.3). Once an application or

document has been linked to a tile on a palette, you can launch the application or open the document by clicking on the tile containing the appropriate icon. Palettes can be sized to show between three and 12 tiles; you can have multiple palettes open at the same time.

FIGURE 5.3
A OneClick palette

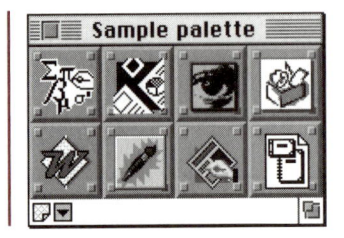

OPENING AND SAVING DOCUMENTS

The Open File and Save File dialog boxes have been a part of the Macintosh operating system since 1984, although they have been changed somewhat to make them easier to use. System 7 introduces several new features.

As you can see in Figure 5.4, the name of the current folder that appears above the scrolling file and folder list is actually a menu containing the path of the current folder. Choosing a folder name from this menu makes the chosen folder the current folder. The top level in the path is always Desktop. Choosing **Desktop** from the menu, or clicking the **Desktop** button, displays the names of all mounted disk volumes.

FIGURE 5.4
The Open File dialog box

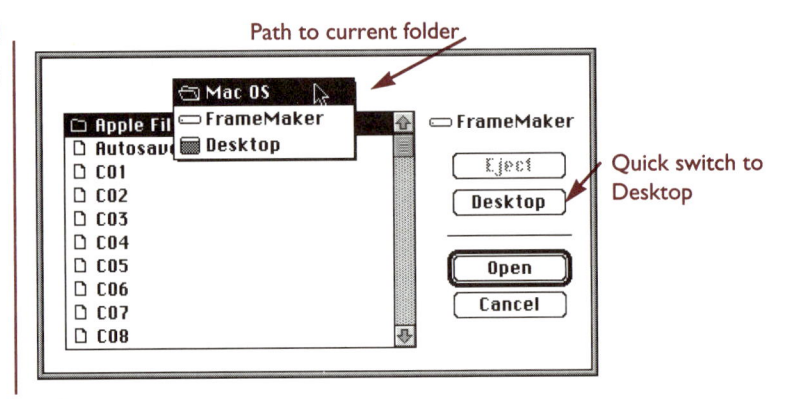

CHAPTER 5: Applications and Process Management   **131**

> **FLASHBACK**
>
> Prior to System 7, the **Desktop** button read Drive. Its function was to cycle through mounted volumes one at a time, making each one the current volume in turn.

Once the contents of the folder you want are displayed in the scrolling list, you can use the mouse to scroll to and select the file or folder you want to open. You can speed up the process a bit by typing the first letter of the file or folder. The Macintosh operating system highlights the first item in the list that begins with the letter typed. If no item in the list begins with the letter typed, the operating system highlights the item whose first letter is closest to the letter typed.

The Save File dialog box (Figure 5.5) provides the same menu at the top of the scrolling list of files and folders and the **Desktop** button. You can also scroll quickly to a folder in the scrolling list by typing its first letter. However, because the Save File dialog box also has a box for entering the name of a file, typing the first letter to locate a folder only works when the scrolling list is surrounded by a heavy border (as it is in Figure 5.5). To switch between the scrolling list and the box for entering the file name, press **Tab**.

FIGURE 5.5
A Save File dialog box

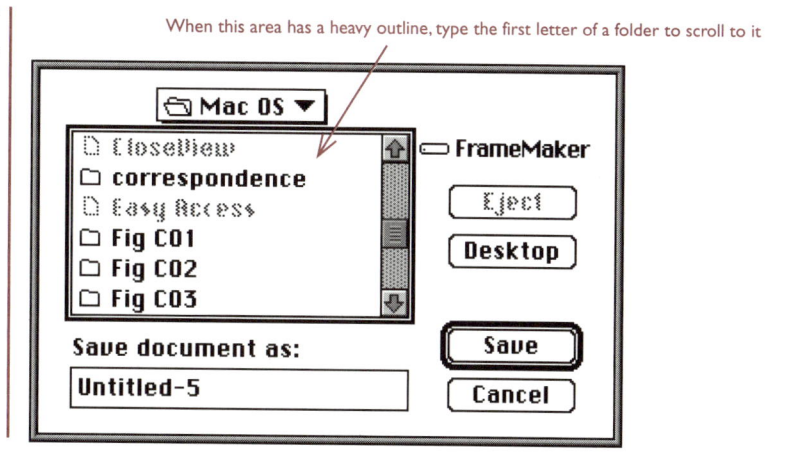

When this area has a heavy outline, type the first letter of a folder to scroll to it

FLASH BACK: Like the System 6 Open File dialog box, the System 6 Save File dialog box has a **Drive** rather than a **Desktop** button. The System 6 Save File dialog box also doesn't support scrolling to a folder by typing its first letter.

USEFUL ADD-ON: One of functions of SuperBoomerang, part of the Now Utilities suite, is to add versatility to the Open File and Save File dialog boxes. As you can see in Figure 5.6, an Open File or Save File dialog box gets a menu bar of its own. The Folder menu contains a list of the most recent folders you've accessed; the file menu contains a list of the most recent files you've accessed. This can make your life much easier if, for example, you need to switch repeatedly between two or more folders.

FIGURE 5.6
An Open File dialog box as modified by SuperBoomerang

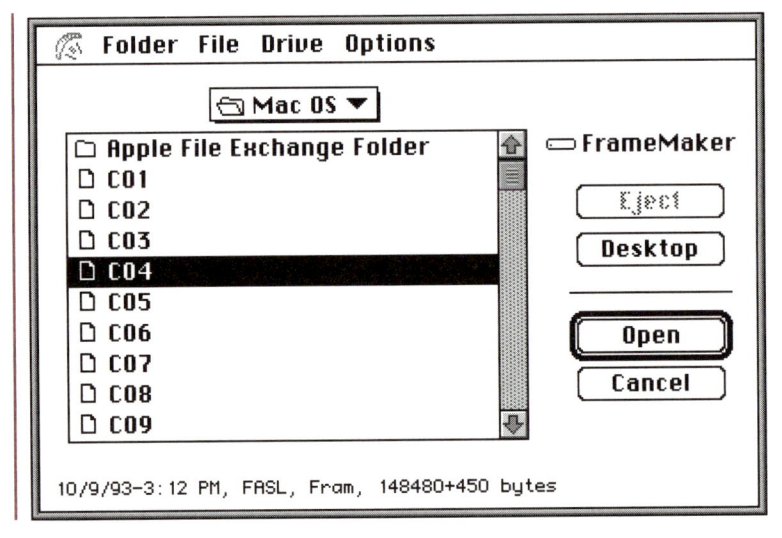

SuperBoomerang also remembers the last file you accessed. That means that when you display an Open File or Save File dialog box, the most recent file you accessed is highlighted. If at first the usefulness of this doesn't seem obvious, consider what the Macintosh operating system does: It always highlights the *first* item in the scrolling list of files and folders. If you happen to be processing all the items in a folder, in order, then scrolling to the next item each time you want to open a file or folder can be very tedious.

SWITCHING APPLICATIONS

As you have read, the Macintosh operating system performs a major switch whenever you indicate that you want to change the foreground application. Assuming the application that is to be the new foreground application is already running, there are several ways to do so:

- Choose the application's name from the Applications menu (the menu at the far left of the menu bar whose name is the icon of the current foreground application).
- Click on any open window of the application.
- Double-click on the application's icon.

> **FLASHBACK:** Prior to System 7, double-clicking on the icon of a running application produced an error. Under System 7, it simply does a context switch.

One common problem with running multiple applications is that windows tend to overlap and hide one another on your monitor. Windows can end up hiding floppy disk icons and even the trash can. The Macintosh operating system therefore lets you temporarily hide windows of running applications. To do so, go to the Applications menu, from which you can hide either the windows of the current foreground application or all other applications (see Figure 5.7).

To make windows visible again, you can choose **Show All** from the Applications menu, which restores all hidden windows. Alternatively, choose the name of a hidden application from the Applications menu. This not only shows the hidden windows but makes the window the foreground application.

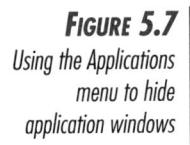

FIGURE 5.7
Using the Applications menu to hide application windows

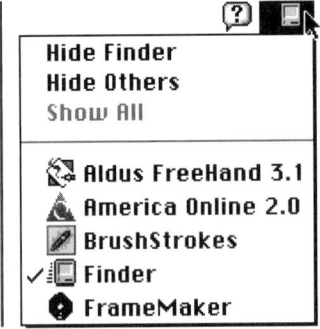

```
Hide Finder
Hide Others
Show All

  Aldus FreeHand 3.1
  America Online 2.0
  BrushStrokes
✓ Finder
  FrameMaker
```

There are a couple of shortcuts that can make switching and hiding windows a bit easier:

- To hide the current application, Option-click in any other application's window. The application whose window you clicked in becomes the foreground application.

- To hide the current application and show one that's hidden, hold down the **Option** key and choose the hidden application from the Applications menu. The application whose name you choose becomes the foreground application.

BACKGROUND PRINTING

Many Macintosh applications have been written to perform at least some of their functions in the background. The most common background application, however, is probably PrintMonitor, the operating system program that manages background printing to laser printers.

HOW BACKGROUND PRINTING WORKS

Background printing uses a technique known as *spooling*. In its broadest sense, spooling means using some sort of external storage (most commonly a disk drive) as a temporary holding area for input and/or output operations. For example, some mainframe operating systems use spooling to hold programs that are waiting to be loaded into main memory for execution. More typically, however, spooling is used for printed output.

Printers operate much more slowly than computers. This means that once a user issues a command to print a file, the user must waste considerable time waiting while the file is printed before proceeding with other work. The problem becomes particularly acute with a multi-user operating system or on a network, where more than one user is competing for access to the same printer.

The solution is to temporarily store the print job somewhere so that the user can continue to work without having to wait for the printer to become available. Therefore, when the user requests printing, the file to be printed isn't sent directly to the printer. Instead, it is written to a special area on disk (the *print queue* or *spool queue*). Once the file has been transferred to the print queue, the user regains control of his or her computer and can continue with other work.

Background printing software keeps track of items in the print queue and sends them to the printer as the printer becomes available. After a file is printed, it is deleted from the queue.

The Macintosh operating system stores *spool files* (files waiting to be printed) in a folder named PrintMonitor Documents in the System folder. The number of files that can be in the spool queue at any given time is limited only by available disk space. You should therefore be sure to leave space on your startup volume for spooling. Most moderate-sized files take less than 1Mb of spool space; small files take only a few kilobytes. However, if you work with files that contain a lot of color or grayscale graphics (for example, scanned photographs) and/or downloadable fonts, you may need as much as 10Mb of space for spooling some files.

TURNING ON BACKGROUND PRINTING

By default, the Macintosh does not print in the background; you must explicitly turn on background printing. To do so:

1. Select **Chooser** from the menu. The Chooser dialog box opens (Figure 5.8).
2. Click on any laser printer icon.
3. Click the **Background Printing On** radio button.
4. Close the dialog box.

FIGURE 5.8
Turning on background printing

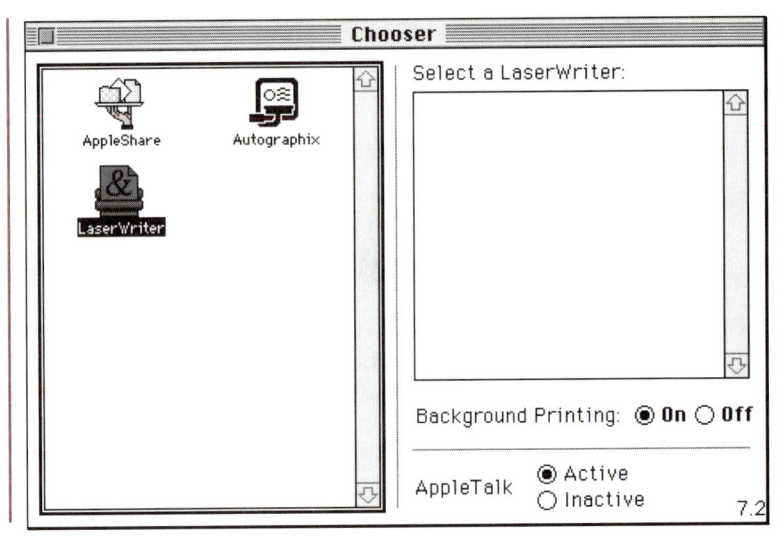

USEFUL ADD-ON: If you want background printing for a printer other than a laser printer, consider purchasing a commercial print spooling utility such as SuperLaserSpool. SuperLaserSpool implements background printing with ImageWriters, LaserWriters, Hewlett-Packard DeskWriters, and PostScript printers that use Apple printer drivers. Printers can be connected through an AppleTalk network or through one of the Macintosh's serial ports. It functions very much like the Macintosh operating system's PrintMonitor.

Managing the Print Queue

Assuming that background printing has been turned on, printing a document spools the file and returns control of the Macintosh to you so that you can continue working. If there are no other documents waiting to be printed, the Macintosh operating system launches PrintMonitor in the background.

Once PrintMonitor is running, you can bring it to the foreground just like any other application so that you can manage the files in the print queue. As you can see in Figure 5.9, the PrintMonitor dialog box displays the document that is currently printing at the top. All other files in the print queue appear in the scrolling list in the middle. The bottom of the dialog box is used for printer status messages. Use this dialog box to cancel the currently printing file, remove other files from the print queue, and delay and reschedule printing.

FIGURE 5.9
Working with the currently printing document

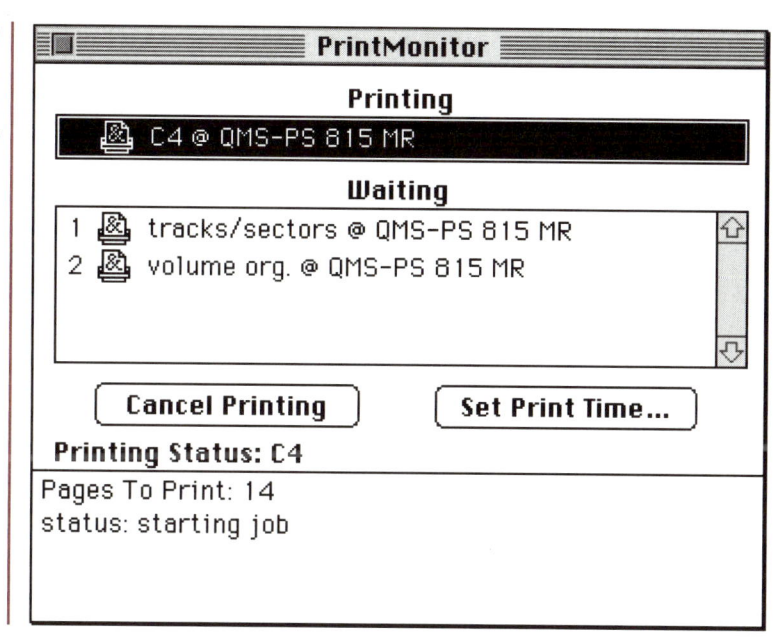

> **By the Way!** Don't leave the PrintMonitor dialog box open unless you are actually working with it. Leaving it open slows down overall system performance because the Macintosh operating system is continually checking the PrintMonitor Documents folder to see if there are any more spool files that it should add to the list in the middle of the dialog box.

Canceling the Currently Printing File

To cancel the file that is currently printing, do the following:

1. If the currently printing file isn't highlighted, click on its name at the top of the PrintMonitor dialog box.
2. Click the **Cancel Printing** button.

Removing Other Files From the Print Queue

To remove any other file from the print queue, do the following:

1. Click on the name of the file to highlight it. The **Cancel Printing** button changes to Remove From List (see Figure 5.10).

2. Click the **Remove From List** button.

FIGURE 5.10
Removing a spool file from the print queue

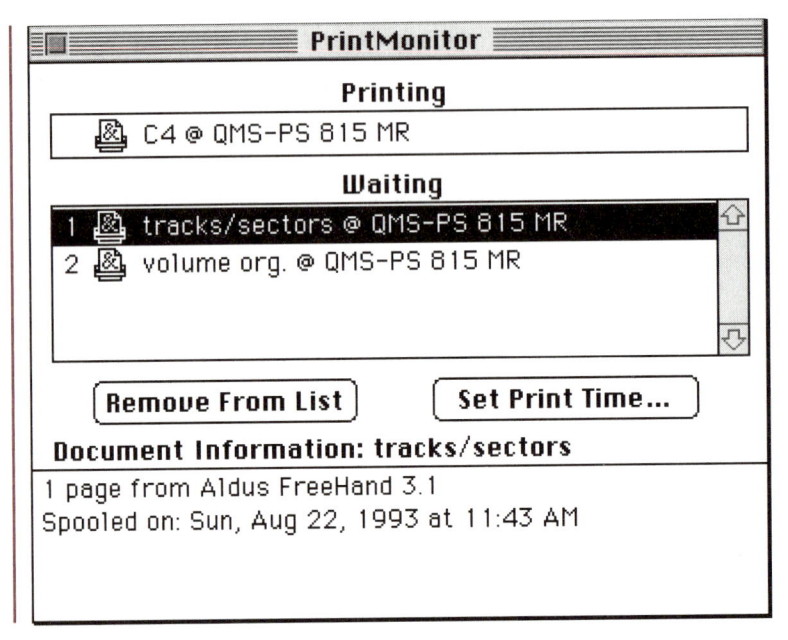

Delaying and Rescheduling Printing

The **Set Print Time** button lets you delay and reschedule printing. To delay printing until a later time:

1. Click on the file to be displayed to highlight its name.

2. Click the **Set Print Time** button. The dialog box in Figure 5.11 appears. The Macintosh operating system fills in the current date and time as the print time.

FIGURE 5.11
Setting the time at which a file should be printed

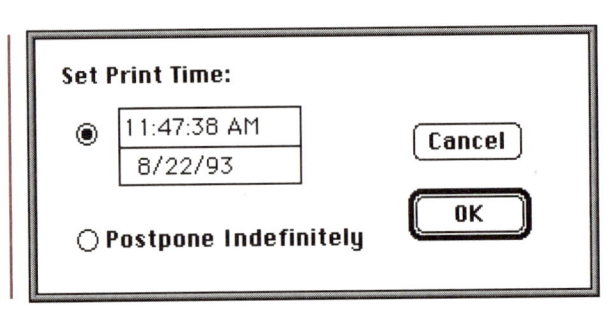

3. Change the print time and date as desired or click the **Postpone Indefinitely** radio button.

4. Click the **OK** button or press **Enter** to close the dialog box.

Postponing printing indefinitely leaves a file in the print queue; the Macintosh operating system makes no attempt to print it. Unfortunately, this can present a bit of a problem. PrintMonitor can't be launched like other applications (for example, by double-clicking on its icon). That means that if you don't have any current files in the print queue, there is no way to get to print files that have been delayed indefinitely. The solution is to print a document so that the Macintosh operating system launches PrintMonitor. Then you can make PrintMonitor the foreground application and set the print time for the delayed files.

To reschedule a postponed print job:

1. Make PrintMonitor the foreground application.
2. Click on the name of the file to highlight it.
3. Click on the **Set Print Time** button.
4. Click the **Set Print Time** radio button.
5. If you don't want to print the file immediately, replace the default date and time with the date and time you want the file printed.
6. Click **OK** to close the dialog box.

PRINTMONITOR MEMORY PROBLEMS

PrintMonitor can be a timesaver. However, it has some annoying shortcomings, one of which is its use of memory. Regardless of how you configure PrintMonitor, it always starts up in 80K of RAM. That simply isn't enough space to print some large files. When PrintMonitor runs out of space, it notifies you that it has a problem and gives you the option of restarting in a larger memory partition (see Figure 5.12).

This is all well and good, but restarting with more memory isn't as satisfactory a solution as it might sound. First, the new memory partition will only be 10K bigger than the previous one. If the new partition isn't big enough, PrintMonitor will need to restart again, increasing its space by another 10K. This continues until there's enough memory to print your file. To make matters worse, PrintMonitor can't pick up where it left off; it has to start over. In other words, if PrintMonitor runs out of memory on page 19 of a 20-page document, restarting PrintMonitor also restarts printing from page 1.

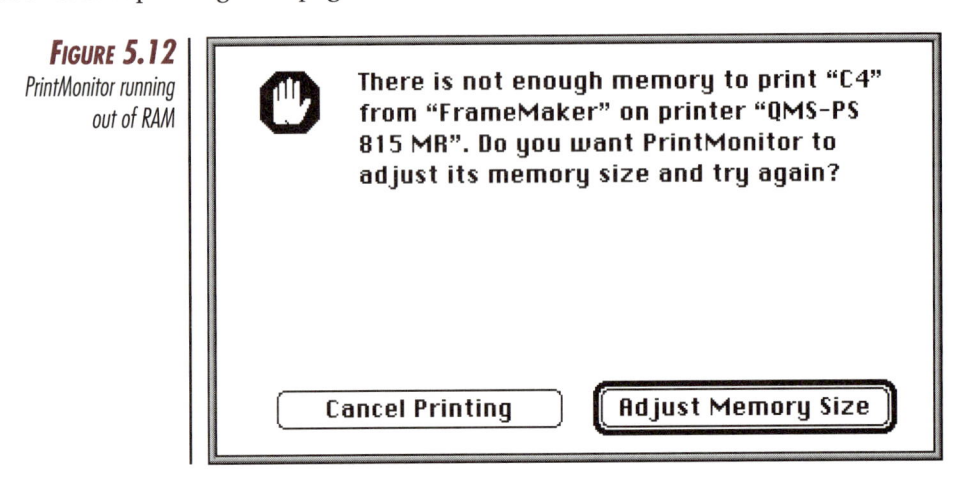

FIGURE 5.12
PrintMonitor running out of RAM

> There is not enough memory to print "C4" from "FrameMaker" on printer "QMS-PS 815 MR". Do you want PrintMonitor to adjust its memory size and try again?
>
> [Cancel Printing] [**Adjust Memory Size**]

PROCESS PROBLEMS: CRASHES AND HANGS

No program is perfect. Regardless of how carefully it was tested, there is always some combination of actions that will cause it to fail. A *crash* occurs when the Macintosh encounters an error from which it cannot recover. There are many causes, including INIT conflicts (discussed in Chapter 8), bugs in an application program, and problems with reading or writing to a disk.

The Macintosh's typical response to a crash is to display a "bomb" box (that dreaded alert with the little bomb in the upper left corner and a cryptic message about some sort of system error, as in Figure 5.13). When this occurs, the most obvious recourse is to click the **Restart** button to reboot the Macintosh. Unfortunately, if you do that, you lose all work in progress. There are, however, some alternatives, which you will see shortly.

A program can *hang* as well as crash. A hang usually occurs because a program becomes stuck repeating the same action and has no way to stop the repetition. (Programmers will recognize this as an infinite loop.) A hung program is as serious as a crashed program. You can't switch to the Finder or any other program; the mouse pointer may also be frozen. Fortunately, all isn't lost.

CHAPTER 5: Applications and Process Management **141**

FIGURE 5.13
The dreaded bomb box

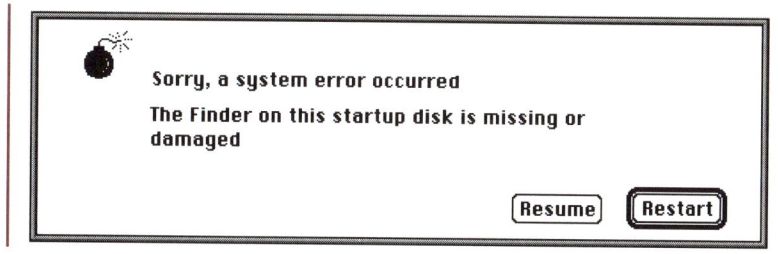

> Sorry, a system error occurred
> The Finder on this startup disk is missing or damaged
>
> [Resume] [Restart]

The Macintosh operating system provides two ways out of a crash or a hang. The first is a *forced quit*. If a program crashes or hangs, press ⌘-**Option**-**Esc**. This attempt to quit the problem program takes you back to the Finder. If you are successful, you will be able to reach any other programs you may have running at the time and save work in progress. (You won't be able to do anything with the problem program). Then restart the computer.

Some crashes and hangs don't display the bomb box, but throw you into the operating system's debugger. If you see a box like that in Figure 5.14, you may be able to reach the Finder and recover work in progress before restarting. To do so:

1. Type **SM 0 A9F4** (note: zero (0), not O).
2. Press **ENTER**.
3. Type **G 0** (note: zero (0), not O).
4. Press **ENTER**. At this point the debugger box should disappear and you should be back at the Finder.

FIGURE 5.14
The debugger dialog box

> \>

BY THE WAY!

You can also reach the debugger box by pressing the interrupt button on the programmer's switch. This is handy when forced quit doesn't work.

USEFUL ADD-ON

The system extension Crash Barrier from Cassidy & Greene provides a friendly way to deal with system crashes and hangs. Whenever a system error occurs, Crash Barrier intercepts the bomb box and displays its own dialog box instead. In "beginner mode" (Figure 5.15) you can ask Crash Barrier to attempt to repair the problem, quit to the Finder, or restart the computer. If the Fix option succeeds, you will be able to save what you were doing with the crashed application. If Crash Barrier can't get the crashed program going again, you can at least reach the Finder and save other work before restarting.

FIGURE 5.15
Crash Barrier beginner mode options

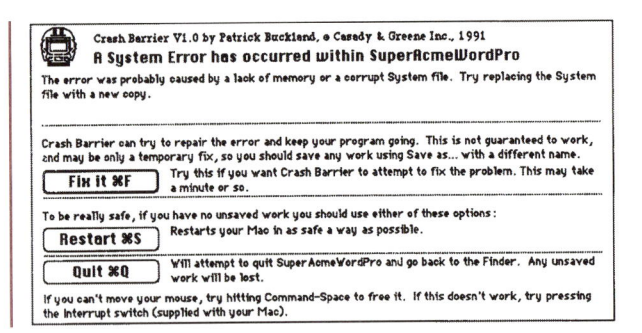

Crash Barrier's "expert mode" (Figure 5.16) provides extra flexibility. For example, if the crashed program has been written so that it can resume after a system error, Crash Barrier will trigger the program code that resumes execution.

FIGURE 5.16
Crash Barrier expert mode options

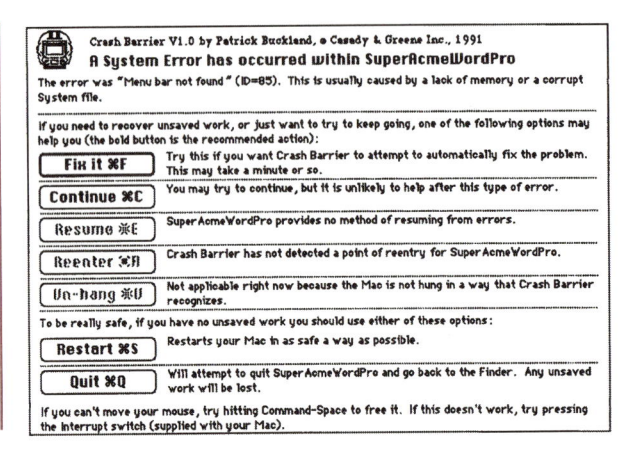

Crash Barrier is particularly useful when a program hangs. Either dialog box can be invoked with a sequence of keystrokes, so that even if the mouse pointer is frozen, you can access the extension's capabilities.

CRASHES AND THE 68040 CACHES

One source of software crashes is an incompatibility between the data caches in the Motorola 68040 microprocessor and some application programs. To understand this problem and how you might solve it, you first need to know something about CPU caches and how the 68040 is different from the 68030.

> **BY THE WAY!** The 68020 has an instruction cache, but no data cache. The 68000 has no caches at all.

A *CPU cache* is a type of high-speed RAM. Reading something from or writing something to cache memory is much faster than accessing the type of RAM used as main memory. A CPU therefore attempts to keep data and program instructions that it is likely to use next in cache memory to help speed up program execution.

There are two ways to handle changes to the data in a *data cache* (a cache that holds data on which a program is operating). A CPU can write the changed data to the cache and also immediately write the change to main memory. This is known as a *write-through cache* and is found in the 68030.

The problem with a write-through cache is that the CPU wastes time writing to main memory. The 68040 therefore gains additional processing speed by using a *copy-back*, or *write-back*, cache. Instead of writing changes immediately to main memory, the 68040 writes data changes only to the data cache. It writes the changes to main memory during idle periods or when the program quits.

Some application software is incompatible with the copy-back caching scheme. Although most applications have been updated to work properly with the 68040, you may run across some older programs that are still incompatible. You can either stop using the incompatible program or you can turn off the 68040 copy-back caching.

The Macintosh operating system provides a control panel (Cache Switch in Figure 5.17) that disables the 68040 caches. This is a rather brute force solution because it affects everything you do, not just a single application. It also defeats the purpose of having the faster 68040 CPU, since you will experience a performance slowdown with the caches disabled. Nonetheless, it will let you use older software with your 68040 Macintosh.

FIGURE 5.17
The Cache Switch control panel

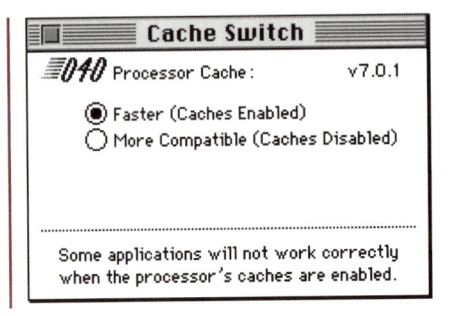

```
┌─────────────── Cache Switch ───────────────┐
│  040  Processor Cache:          v7.0.1     │
│                                            │
│     ● Faster (Caches Enabled)              │
│     ○ More Compatible (Caches Disabled)    │
│                                            │
│   ........................................ │
│   Some applications will not work correctly│
│   when the processor's caches are enabled. │
└────────────────────────────────────────────┘
```

CHAPTER 6
Memory

As you have read, one of the major tasks of an operating system is memory management. In a multitasking operating system like the Macintosh operating system, memory management tasks include:

- Allocating memory for each application as it is launched.
- Protecting the memory used by each application from the actions of all other applications.

This chapter looks at how the Macintosh operating system deals with memory within its cooperative multitasking environment. In particular, it looks at the concepts behind 24- and 32-bit addressing.

INTRODUCING MACINTOSH MEMORY

To understand some of the issues surrounding Macintosh memory management, you need to have some background in memory concepts. This includes things like how memory is measured and the hardware and software features that limit the amount of memory your Macintosh can access.

MEASURING MEMORY

To measure main memory (and to store numbers and characters), a computer uses the *binary* numbering system. Binary, or base 2, uses only the digits 0 and 1. Because the circuits in today's computers carry either a high voltage or a low voltage, the voltage of a circuit is a convenient way to represent a binary digit (a *bit*).

Counting in binary is similar to counting in base 10, the decimal system we use every day. However, while in base 10 each place in a number represents a power of 10, in binary each place represents a power of 2. As an example, look at the binary number in Figure 6.1. This number is an *integer*, a whole number with no fractional portion to the right of the *binary point* (the binary equivalent of the decimal point.) Notice that the rightmost digit represents 2^0, or 1. (Any number raised to the 0 power is the number itself.) Each digit to the left represents 2 raised to the next highest power. Because bits are always numbered beginning with 0, the leftmost bit will always have the place value 2^{n-1}, where *n* is the number of bits in the number.

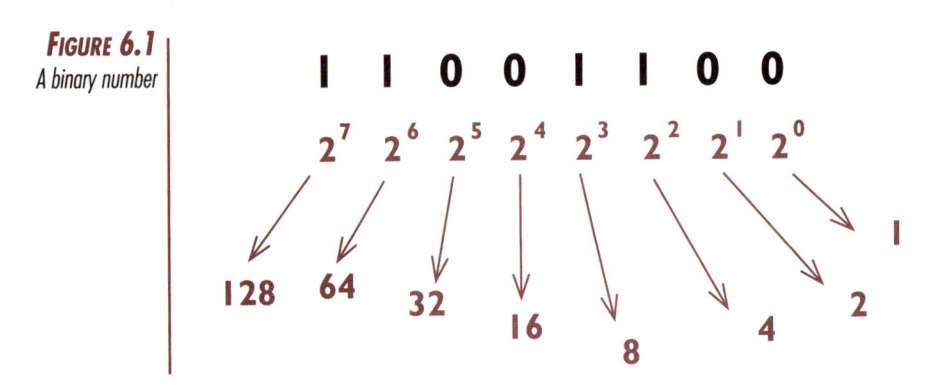

FIGURE 6.1
A binary number

1 1 0 0 1 1 0 0

2^7 2^6 2^5 2^4 2^3 2^2 2^1 2^0

128 64 32 16 8 4 2 1

To convert a binary number to its value in base 10, add the base 10 place values for each binary place that has a 1 in it. In Figure 6.1, the conversion becomes:

4 + 8 + 64 + 128 = 204

Some powers of 2 useful to Macintosh users can be found in Table 6.1.

Like most computers, the Macintosh doesn't access each bit individually, but instead works with groups of bits. The smallest grouping is a *byte* (eight bits). A byte, which can store values in the range 0 through 255, is used to measure main memory.

TABLE 6.1
Powers of 2

n	2^n
0	1
1	2
2	4
3	8
4	16
5	32
6	64
7	128
8	256
9	512
10	1,024
11	2,048
12	4,096
13	8,192
14	16,384
15	32,768
16	65,536
20	1,048,576
30	1,073,741,824
31	2,147,483,648
32	4,294,967,296

BY THE WAY! There is an easy way to figure out the decimal equivalent of the maximum number that can be stored in any number of bits: Take the place value of the next highest power of 2 and subtract 1. For example, keeping in mind that the least significant bit is always 2^0, the leftmost bit in a byte has the place value 2^7. Therefore, the maximum value that can be stored in a byte is $2^8 - 1$, or 256 - 1 (255).

Because computer storage is typically measured in thousands, million, and trillions of bytes, computer people use term *kilobyte* (abbreviated *K*) to mean roughly 1,000 bytes, *megabyte* (abbreviated *M*, *Mb*, *meg*, or *Mbyte*) to mean roughly 1,000,000 bytes, and *gigabyte* (abbreviated *Gb* or *G*) to mean roughly a trillion bytes. Today's

Macintoshes have at least 4Mb of RAM. 4Mb is really the minimum for useful work under System 7, but more RAM is certainly better.

> **BY THE WAY!** Technically, a kilobyte is 2^{10}, or 1024, bytes. A megabyte is 2^{20}, or 1,048,576, bytes and a gigabyte is 2^{30}, or 1,073,741,824, bytes.

The bytes of storage in main memory are numbered, beginning with zero. This gives each byte a unique *address*. Computer programs can then access main memory by specifying the address from which they want to read something or the address at which they wish to write something. The total range of addresses that a computer can access is known as its *address space*.

> **BY THE WAY!** If you can program in a high-level language like BASIC, Pascal, or C, then you might be interested to know that a program variable is nothing more than a label on a storage location in main memory. Variables mean that the programmer doesn't have to be concerned with actual addresses; the compiler or interpreter that translates the program to machine language takes care of assigning a unique main memory address to each variable.

In addition to a byte, a computer works with a grouping of bits known as a *word*. A word is the number of bits that the computer typically handles as a unit. Although the size of a byte doesn't vary from one type of computer to another, the size of a word does. The Macintosh has a 32-bit word. As you will see shortly, although all Macintoshes can operate on 32-bit quantities within their CPUs, not all of them can transfer a word at a time between the computer's components.

The Relationship between Memory and the System Bus

The major components of a computer—the CPU, main memory, ROM, and so on—are connected by an electronic pathway known as the *system bus*, which carries signals from one component to another. The size of the system bus has a direct relationship to the amount of memory a Macintosh can access and has a major impact on the interaction of the operating system and application programs.

A bus is actually a collection of electronic circuits, called *lines*, running in parallel. Each line in the bus is assigned a special purpose. Some lines carry addresses, in which case they are part of the *address bus*. Lines that carry data are part of the *data bus*. The remaining lines carry control signals, such as timing pulses from the CPU's internal clock and instructions to the computer's components (for example, "read" or "write").

Each line in the address and data buses represents one bit. A Macintosh address bus has either 24 or 32 lines. When the lines are viewed together as the bits of a binary number, a 32-bit address bus can carry values from 0 through 2^{32-1} (4,294,967,296 or 4Gb), each of which corresponds to a numbered byte. The maximum amount of memory that any Macintosh can address is therefore 4Gb.

However, Macintoshes with a 68000 microprocessor have only a 24-bit address bus, even though the CPU operates internally on 32-bit quantities. A 24-bit address bus can access 2^{24-1} bytes (16,777,215 or 16Mb). In the early days of the Macintosh, no one imagined that the Macintosh operating environment would need anywhere near a 16Mb address space; people thought that there was plenty of excess capacity.

Because they thought the missing eight upper bits of the address bus would never be used, many programmers used those extra eight bits for purposes other than addressing main memory. Programs that do this will bomb when used in an environment that expects 32-bit rather than 24-bit addresses and are often called *32-bit dirty*. Programs that don't play tricks with the upper eight bits and run without a problem in a 32-bit environment are known as *32-bit clean*.

Whether your Macintosh can use 32-bit addresses depends on several things. First, it must have at least a 68020 microprocessor, which ensures that it has a 32-bit address bus. Second, it must have 32-bit clean ROMs or software that compensates for the presence of 32-bit dirty ROMs. Macintoshes from the LC onward have 32-bit clean ROMs. Other 68020 or 68030 Macintoshes need to install Mode32, an INIT developed by Connectix Corp.

BY THE WAY! Apple has licensed Mode32 for free distribution to owners of 68020 or 68030 Macs with dirty ROMs. To obtain a copy, call the Apple Customer Assistance Center at 1-800-SOS-APPL.

> **BY THE WAY!**
> System 7.1 comes with a system extension that theoretically replaces Mode32. However, some users report problems with the system extension. Mode32 works beautifully. Therefore, you may want to stick with it at least until the bugs have been worked out of the Apple-written extension.

Assuming that your Macintosh has a 32-bit address bus, the Macintosh operating system can operate in either 24- or 32-bit mode. When running in 24-bit mode, you will be able to use programs that are 32-bit dirty but, as you will see in the next section, you will be limited in the amount of RAM you can access.

Memory Allocation

Regardless of whether your Macintosh can use 24- or 32-bit addressing, not all of its address space can be allocated to RAM. ROM must have its own unique set of addresses. In addition, the Macintosh uses *memory-mapped I/O*. When a program wants to perform some input or output, it reads from or writes to a main memory address, rather than to a specific I/O device. These addresses don't physically correspond to RAM or ROM, but instead provide a mechanism for *device-independent I/O*. A program simply reads from or writes to the main memory addresses set aside for the device, using the same input and output commands regardless of the type of device. The actual input and output is handled by a device driver, which as you know is software written specifically for each I/O device that handles the physical transfer of data. The beauty of this arrangement is that a Macintosh needs only one device driver for each I/O device, whether supplied as a part of the Macintosh operating system (for example, the LaserWriter driver) or by the manufacturer of the I/O device.

> **BY THE WAY!**
> If you've ever installed software on an MS DOS computer, you'll remember that each piece of MS DOS software supplies its own set of device drivers.

By the same token, a programmer doesn't need to write a device driver or, in many cases, even be concerned with the specific I/O device which the program will ultimately use. For example, most Macintosh software will run on any size monitor with any number of colors, without having to install a device driver for the specific monitor attached to the computer. (The major exception to this statement are some games and high-end graphics software that require a monitor that can display a specific number of colors or shades of gray.)

The Macintoshes that have a 68000 CPU—for example, the Plus, SE, and Classic—have a 24-bit address bus and generally allocate RAM as in Figure 6.2. Note that the addresses that appear at the right of the figure are expressed in hexadecimal (indicated by the dollar sign preceding the number). *Hexadecimal,* or base 16, is used primarily as a shorthand for binary. Each hexadecimal digit represents a power of 16; each hexadecimal place must therefore represent the values 0 through 15. Because we don't have single digits for 10, 11, 12, 13, 14, and 15, hexadecimal uses letters (A = 10, B = 11, C = 12, D = 13, E = 14, and F = 15).

Each hexadecimal place represents four binary places. (This works because 2^4 = 16.) A hexadecimal number is therefore one-quarter the length of a binary number, making a very convenient shorthand for working with large binary numbers.

The maximum address that can be handled by a 24-bit address bus—$0100 0000—is equal to 16Mb. RAM is allocated to the address range $0000 0000 through $0040 0000, a total of 4Mb. That is why the maximum RAM that a compact Macintosh such as the Plus, Classic, or SE can use is 4Mb; the rest of the address space is allocated to ROM, I/O devices, and expansion slots.

The Macintosh II line, LC III, and 68040 Macintoshes use a general RAM allocation like that in Figure 6.3. RAM is given the first 1Gb of space, even though the maximum RAM that any current Macintosh can use is 256Mb. (This limit is imposed by the maximum size of RAM chips, not by the Macintosh operating system.) Just as with the 68000 Macs, the remaining address space is used by ROM, expansion slots, and I/O devices.

When a 32-bit Macintosh is used in 24-bit mode, the operating system translates 24-bit addresses into 32-bit addresses, using an allocation like that in Figure 6.4. Notice that 8Mb are allocated to RAM, producing the 8Mb RAM limit for Macintoshes with a 32-bit address bus that are operating in 24-bit mode. The 6Mb expansion slot space was originally designed for the Mac II, providing 1Mb of RAM for each NuBus slot.

FIGURE 6.2
Memory map for 68000 Macintoshes

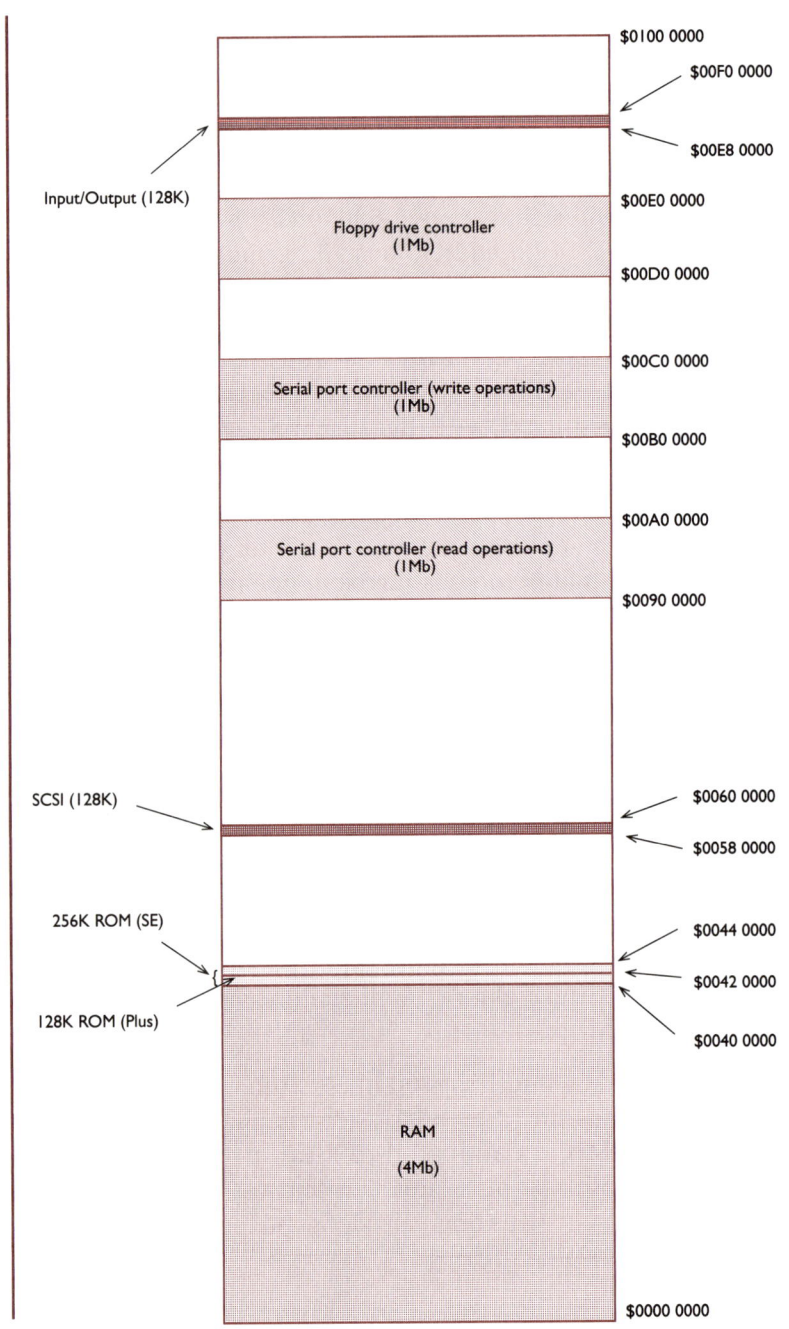

$0100 0000	
$00F0 0000	
$00E8 0000	Input/Output (128K)
$00E0 0000	Floppy drive controller (1Mb)
$00D0 0000	
$00C0 0000	Serial port controller (write operations) (1Mb)
$00B0 0000	
$00A0 0000	Serial port controller (read operations) (1Mb)
$0090 0000	
$0060 0000	
$0058 0000	SCSI (128K)
$0044 0000	256K ROM (SE)
$0042 0000	128K ROM (Plus)
$0040 0000	
$0000 0000	RAM (4Mb)

FIGURE 6.3
32-bit RAM allocation

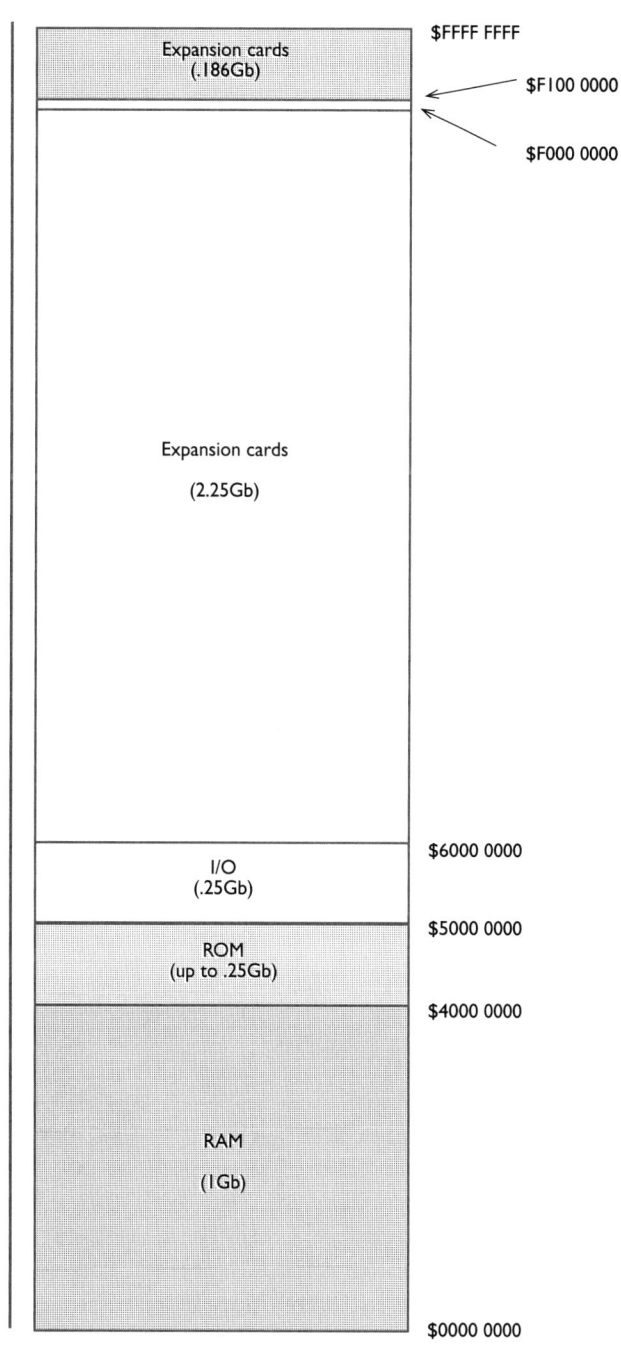

Address	Region
$FFFF FFFF	Expansion cards (.186Gb)
$F100 0000	
$F000 0000	Expansion cards (2.25Gb)
$6000 0000	I/O (.25Gb)
$5000 0000	ROM (up to .25Gb)
$4000 0000	RAM (1Gb)
$0000 0000	

FIGURE 6.4
Translating 24-bit to 32-bit addresses

32-Bit Address Space

Expansion cards (1.86Gb) — $FFFF FFFF
$F100 0000
$F000 0000

Expansion cards (2.25Gb)

24-Bit Addresses

$00FF FFFF
$00F0 0000
I/O (1Mb)

Expansion cards (6Mb)

$0090 0000
$0000 0000
ROM (1Mb)

I/O (.25Gb) — $6000 0000
$5000 0000
ROM (up to .25Gb)
$4000 0000

RAM (8Mb)

$0080 0000

RAM (1Gb)

$0000 0000

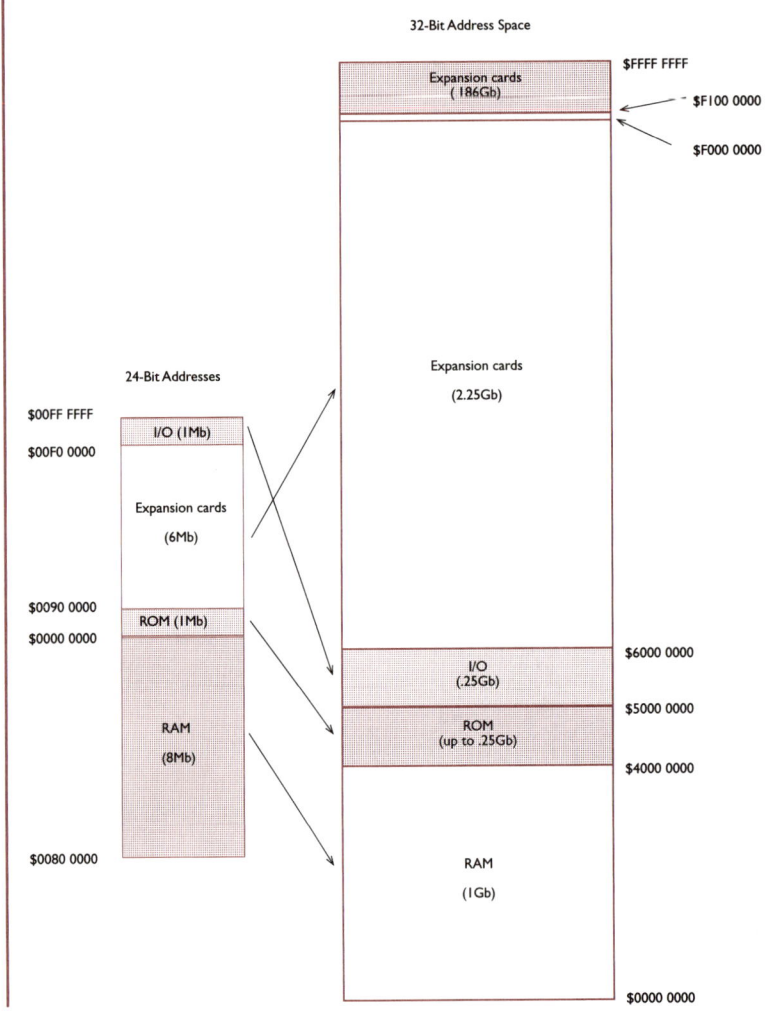

BY THE WAY!

Some software, such as Virtual from Connectix, can take the address space allocated to unused expansion slots and use it for virtual memory addresses. With Virtual, a 68020 Macintosh (equipped with a paged memory management unit, or PMMU), 68030 Macintosh, or 68040 Macintosh can address up to 15Mb RAM when using virtual memory in 24-bit mode. The limit of 8Mb of physical RAM is still present.

Although the remaining Macintoshes (LC, LC II, Classic II, Performa 200, Color Classic) have 32-bit address buses, they allocate their RAM differently from the rest of the 32-bit Macintoshes. As you can see in Figure 6.5, this memory mapping provides only 10Mb for RAM. Even though it may be possible to install more than 10Mb of physical RAM in one of these machines, the computer will only access 10Mb.

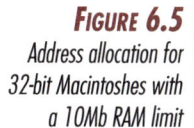

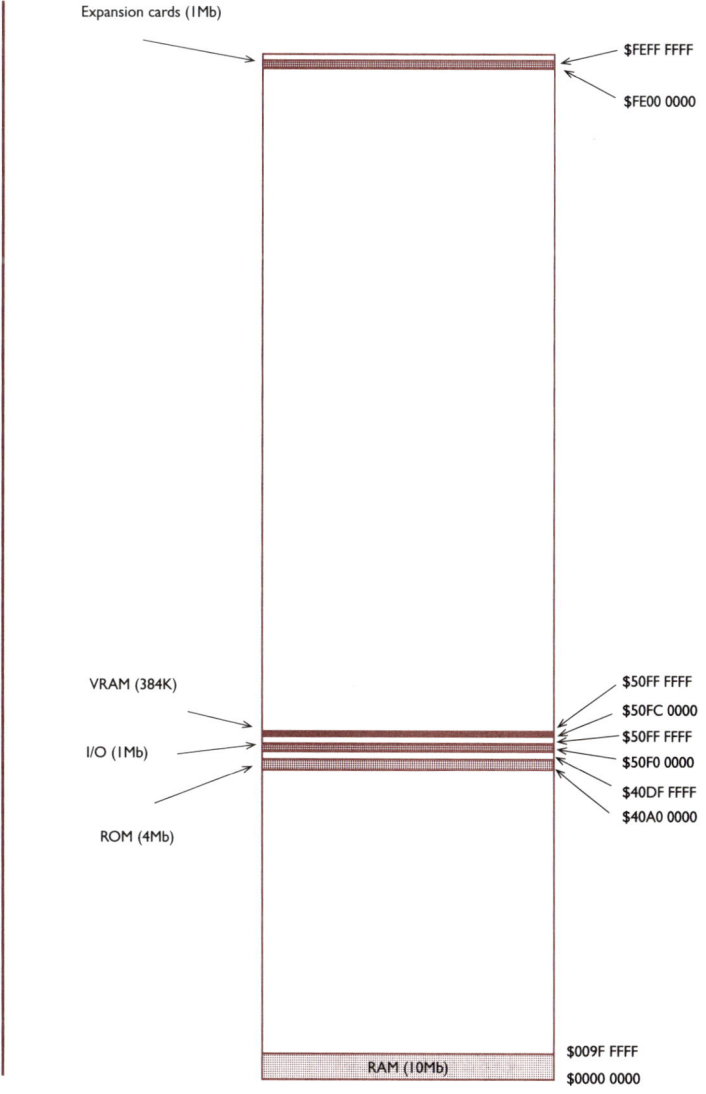

FIGURE 6.5
Address allocation for 32-bit Macintoshes with a 10Mb RAM limit

Expansion cards (1Mb) — $FEFF FFFF / $FE00 0000
VRAM (384K) — $50FF FFFF / $50FC 0000
I/O (1Mb) — $50FF FFFF / $50F0 0000
ROM (4Mb) — $40DF FFFF / $40A0 0000
RAM (10Mb) — $009F FFFF / $0000 0000

Notice in Figure 6.5 that 384K of RAM has been set aside as *video RAM* (VRAM). If no VRAM is installed in the computer's VRAM slot, the Macintosh can use this space for storing the memory map of the display screen. However, using regular RAM instead of VRAM limits you to a 13-inch monochrome monitor.

OPERATING SYSTEM MEMORY MANAGEMENT SCHEMES

To execute, a program must be in RAM. Therefore, the first step in running a program is to allocate a block of RAM (a *partition*) to the program, something which isn't as simple as it may seem. When a team of programmers writes an operating system, they must decide on a memory management scheme. The questions that must be answered include:

- Should all RAM partitions be the same size or should they vary in size?
- Should the partitions be permanent or created as they are needed?
- Should programs run in specific partitions or can they run in any partition in which they will fit?
- If a program is too big to fit into any single partition, can it be split between multiple partitions? If a program can be split, must the multiple partitions be contiguous (right next to one another)?

Early multitasking operating systems required programs to run in the same fixed-size partitions in which they were compiled. Today's operating systems, however, support variable size partitions; programs can run in any available. In most cases, programs can occupy multiple, non-contiguous partitions. (This is essential for virtual memory, which is discussed later in this chapter.)

The Macintosh operating system uses variable-sized memory partitions that are created dynamically as programs are launched. For a program to execute, there must be a contiguous block of memory available that is large enough to hold the entire program. If enough space isn't present, the Macintosh operating system asks you if you want to attempt to launch the program in available memory. Attempting to run an application in less memory than recommended by the software developer may or may not work, depending on the program.

> **BY THE WAY!** As you will see later in this chapter, when virtual memory is in use, the block of memory in which a program is launched must consist of *logically* contiguous RAM but not necessarily physically contiguous.

Memory Fragmentation

One of the problems with variable-partition memory allocation is that memory tends to become fragmented. To see how this occurs, consider what happens when you first load programs into the Macintosh RAM (see Figure 6.6). The operating system loads programs one after the other, filling up memory. All the unused space is clustered together in one contiguous block.

Figure 6.6 Loading programs into RAM

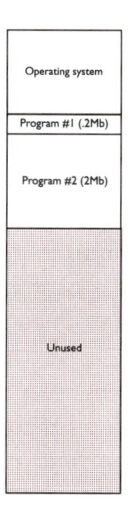

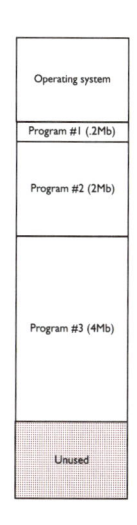

However, once you begin quitting programs, holes begin to appear in RAM. In operating system terms, a "hole" is nothing more than a block of space left unused when a program is no longer using that space. Figure 6.7 represents a session at the Macintosh in which a user launches and quits applications. Notice that when the user quits Program #1, a small hole (200K) is left at the top of memory. Quitting Program #3 leaves a rather large hole (4Mb) that can be used by three smaller programs. However, when the user quits Program #5 and Program #7, memory has several small holes instead of one small hole and one large hole. At this point, the user wants to run a program that requires 3Mb of RAM. Although there is a bit more than 3Mb of free memory, it is scattered in three holes, rather than in a single block. This fragmentation means that the Macintosh can't launch the program; it must have a contiguous block on memory into which a program will fit.

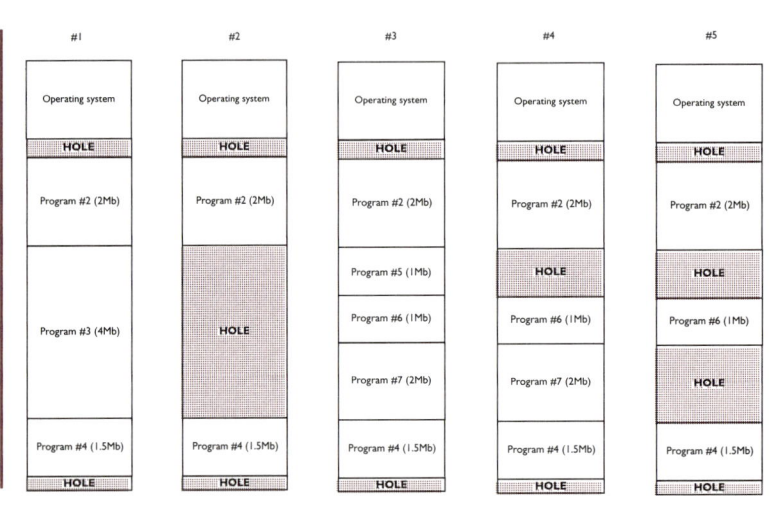

FIGURE 6.7
Memory fragmentation

#1	#2	#3	#4	#5
Operating system	Operating system	Operating system	Operating system	Operating system
HOLE	HOLE	HOLE	HOLE	HOLE
Program #2 (2Mb)	Program #2 (2Mb)	Program #2 (2Mb)	Program #2 (2Mb)	Program #2 (2Mb)
Program #3 (4Mb)	HOLE	Program #5 (1Mb)	HOLE	HOLE
		Program #6 (1Mb)	Program #6 (1Mb)	Program #6 (1Mb)
		Program #7 (2Mb)	Program #7 (2Mb)	HOLE
Program #4 (1.5Mb)	Program #4 (1.5Mb)	Program #4 (1.5Mb)	Program #4 (1.5Mb)	Program #4 (1.5Mb)
HOLE	HOLE	HOLE	HOLE	HOLE

What can you do when memory becomes fragmented? First, try quitting every running program so that only the Finder is running. Then relaunch your applications. If that doesn't solve the problem, you will need to restart the Macintosh.

BY THE WAY! Some operating systems can take care of memory fragmentation without requiring the user to quit and relaunch programs. This process, known as *garbage collection*, involves moving all programs in memory so that they occupy a contiguous block of RAM and coalescing all holes into one large contiguous hole. Unfortunately, the Macintosh operating system currently can't perform garbage collection.

MANAGING MEMORY USE

Although the Macintosh operating system takes care of most memory management, the user still has a role to play. You can view memory allocation, set the size of an application's memory partition, and turn 32-bit addressing on and off.

VIEWING MEMORY USE

You can see how the Macintosh has allocated memory to running applications at any time by returning to the Finder. Choose **About This Macintosh** from the menu. A dialog box similar to that in Figure 6.8 appears. Notice that it shows the amount of RAM used by each running program, the total available RAM as well as the size of the largest contiguous unused block of RAM. Because a program must be launched into a contiguous block, this measurement lets you know how much space is left for additional programs.

FIGURE 6.8
Viewing memory allocation

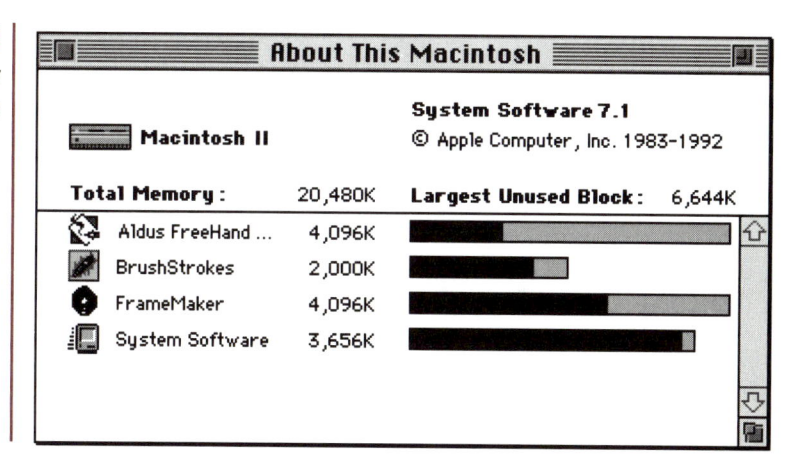

About This Macintosh	
Macintosh II	System Software 7.1 © Apple Computer, Inc. 1983-1992
Total Memory: 20,480K	Largest Unused Block: 6,644K
Aldus FreeHand …	4,096K
BrushStrokes	2,000K
FrameMaker	4,096K
System Software	3,656K

The amount of RAM used by System Software is a bit misleading. It doesn't show just the size of the System file, but all memory not available to applications. This includes the System file, the disk cache, any RAM disk, and system extensions. If more than 8Mb RAM are installed but 32-bit addressing isn't on, the remainder of RAM shows up here too. The problem, of course, is that you can't tell how system memory is allocated.

SETTING APPLICATION MEMORY SIZE

The size of an application's RAM partition is set in the program's Get Info box. As you can see in Figure 6.9, the software developer sets a suggested memory partition size; this value can't be changed. When you first install an application, the minimum size and preferred size will usually be equal to the suggested size. However, in many cases you will want to increased the preferred size (the amount of RAM the application will use if enough RAM is available).

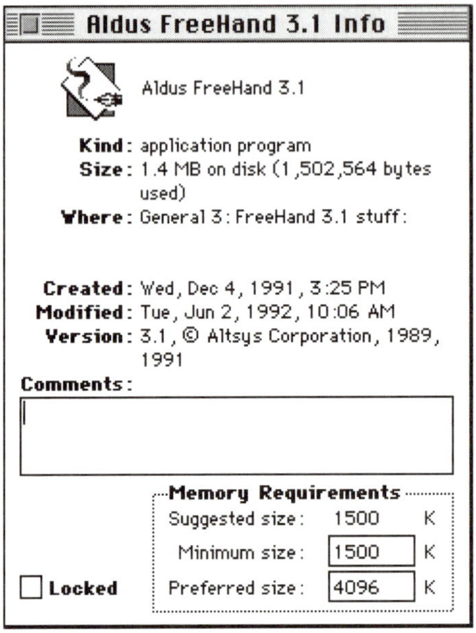

FIGURE 6.9
Setting application memory partition size

```
┌──────────────────────────────────────────────┐
│ ▤▤    Aldus FreeHand 3.1 Info                │
├──────────────────────────────────────────────┤
│   📄    Aldus FreeHand 3.1                   │
│                                              │
│      Kind: application program               │
│      Size: 1.4 MB on disk (1,502,564 bytes   │
│            used)                             │
│     Where: General 3: FreeHand 3.1 stuff:    │
│                                              │
│   Created: Wed, Dec 4, 1991, 3:25 PM         │
│  Modified: Tue, Jun 2, 1992, 10:06 AM        │
│   Version: 3.1, © Altsys Corporation, 1989,  │
│            1991                              │
│  Comments:                                   │
│  ┌────────────────────────────────────────┐  │
│  │                                        │  │
│  └────────────────────────────────────────┘  │
│          ┌─Memory Requirements─────────┐     │
│          │ Suggested size:  1500   K   │     │
│          │   Minimum size: │1500│  K   │     │
│  ☐ Locked│ Preferred size: │4096│  K   │     │
│          └─────────────────────────────┘     │
└──────────────────────────────────────────────┘
```

A larger RAM partition often means you can work with larger documents, particularly for applications that keep an entire document in RAM. Notice in Figure 6.9, for example, that Aldus FreeHand, a PostScript graphics program, is to be launched into a 4Mb partition (4096K). This lets the user work with more objects and more colors than would be possible if less memory were available.

Some application programs—especially word processors—keep as much of a document in RAM as will fit in the current memory partition. The rest of the document is placed temporarily in a disk file. The application shuffles portions of the document between RAM and disk as needed. This I/O activity slows down performance. Therefore, if you can allocate enough RAM to the program to keep an entire document in RAM, you will get better overall performance.

Under System 7.1, if there is no contiguous block of memory large enough for an application's preferred memory size, but there is a block of at least the minimum memory size, the Macintosh operating system launches the application in the minimum size partition. However, if there is no contiguous block as large as an application's minimum memory size, the operating system can't launch the application. You will see an alert telling you that there is a problem, although the exact text depends on the state of other running applications. For example, the alert in Figure 6.10 gives the user the option of automatically quitting all running applications that have no open windows to make enough room to launch the new application. If there aren't any applications with no open windows, the operating system suggests quitting one or more specific running applications (usually the applications that were last used).

FIGURE 6.10
An alert indicating that there isn't enough memory to launch an application

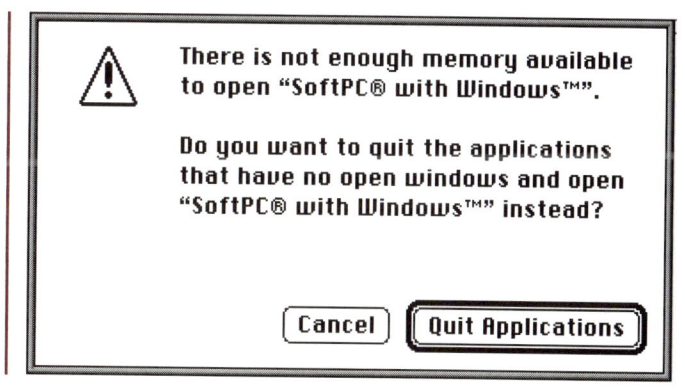

> There is not enough memory available to open "SoftPC® with Windows™".
>
> Do you want to quit the applications that have no open windows and open "SoftPC® with Windows™" instead?
>
> [Cancel] [[Quit Applications]]

BY THE WAY!

Running out of memory works a bit differently under System 7.0. If there is less than the minimum amount of memory, you will simply see an alert telling you that the application can't be launched. If there is more than the minimum amount but less than the preferred amount, you will be asked if you want to launch the application in available memory.

Running applications are not the only thing that can affect whether there is enough free RAM to launch an application. Each application's clipboard is stored in RAM in the application's memory partition. Only the most recent cut or copy ends up in the Clipboard file on disk (the System Clipboard). When you launch a new application, its clipboard is loaded with the contents of the System Clipboard. If that happens to be very large, you might get a message saying there isn't enough memory to launch the application, even though you've got plenty of contiguous memory according to the Finder. To fix the problem, do a copy of a single character (for example, from the Note Pad) so that the System Clipboard becomes very small.

The Memory Control Panel

Most of the remaining memory management functions are handled by the Memory control panel. There are actually four versions; which one you see depends on which Macintosh you have. The complete control panel can be found in Figure 6.11. The top section—disk cache—is available with every Macintosh. The second section—virtual memory—appears only with those Macintoshes that are capable of virtual memory (virtual memory is discussed later in this chapter). The 32-bit addressing section appears only for those Macintoshes that can handle 32-bit addresses; you will learn more about working with 32-bit addresses shortly. The RAM disk at the bottom of the control panel is available only with PowerBooks; RAM disks are discussed later in this chapter.

FIGURE 6.11
The complete Memory control panel

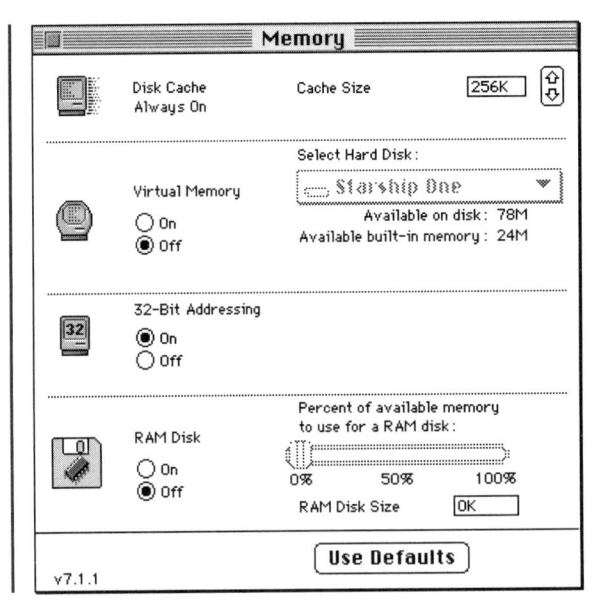

Working with 32-Bit Addressing

As you read earlier, any Macintosh with a 32-bit address bus can use 32-bit addressing. However, you must also have 32-bit clean ROMs. If you don't, you need to either add Mode32 or the System 7 extension that compensates for the 32-bit dirty ROMs. The status of the ROMs in Macintosh that can access more than 8Mb RAM can be found in Table 6.2. (Other Macs do have 32-bit clean ROMs, but because they can't access more than 8Mb RAM, the issue is moot.)

Table 6.2
ROM status of Macintoshes that can access more than 8Mb RAM

Model	Type of ROM
II, IIx, IIfx, IIcx, IIci	dirty
SE/30	dirty
Classic II/Performa 200	clean
Color Classic	clean
LC	clean
LC II, Performa 400, 405, and 430	clean
LC III, Performa 450	clean
IIsi	clean
IIvi, IIvx, Performa 600	clean
Centris 610, 650, and 660av	clean
Quadra 700, 800, 840av, 900, 950	clean
PowerBook 160	clean
PowerBook 180	clean
PowerBook 165c, 180c	clean
PowerBook Duo 210, 230	clean

Just having 32-bit clean ROMs or an extension that compensates for 32-bit dirty ROMs isn't quite enough to work in 32-bit mode. You must first turn it on. To do so, open the Memory control panel and click the 32-bit addressing "on" button. If you are using Mode32, you must also turn Mode32 on. To do so, open the Mode32 control panel and click the **Enabled** button (see Figure 6.12).

Figure 6.12 The Mode32 control panel

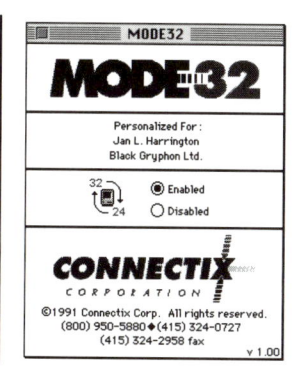

Virtual Memory

In the computer world, virtual means "simulated." *Virtual memory* is therefore a technique for simulating more RAM than is physically installed in your computer. In this section you will find out how virtual memory works, whether it is available on your Macintosh, and some of the pros and cons of using it.

How Virtual Memory Works

When working in a virtual memory system, the computer has two address spaces. The *real address space* represents memory that is physically present in the computer. The *virtual address space* represents the memory being simulated; it is represented by a file on a hard disk. Hardware known as a *paged memory management unit* (PMMU) takes care of translating virtual address to real addresses.

In a virtual memory scheme, real memory (physically installed RAM) is divided into fixed size blocks known as *page frames*. The disk file that simulates the virtual memory address space is also divided up into blocks of the same size (*pages*). With System 7, pages and page frames are 4K in size. The operating system swaps pages from real memory page frames to disk and back again, as pages are needed in real memory for program execution. The PMMU takes care of locating pages both in real memory and in the virtual memory disk file.

> **BY THE WAY!** To be completely accurate, a virtual memory scheme doesn't have to allocate memory in fixed size blocks. When the blocks vary in size, they are known as *segments*. Segmented virtual memory is more difficult to manage than paged virtual memory and isn't used widely on microcomputers.

In the sample in Figure 6.13, real memory has four page frames. However, the virtual address space has room for 16 pages. Therefore, only four pages can be in main memory at one time. Of course, the actual number of page frames in any given Macintosh depends on the amount of physical RAM installed.

Notice that a virtual page can be loaded into any available page frame. That means that the parts of a program might be scattered all over main memory. The operating system, working with the PMMU, however, handles the program as if it were in one contiguous block of memory. This is what is mean when we say that when virtual memory is active, an application can be launched into any "logically contiguous" block of memory that is large enough to hold it. As far as virtual RAM is concerned, the program is in a single block of memory. However, the page frames containing that block of RAM when the program is in real storage may not be contiguous; the operating system nonetheless acts as if the program were in physically contiguous memory.

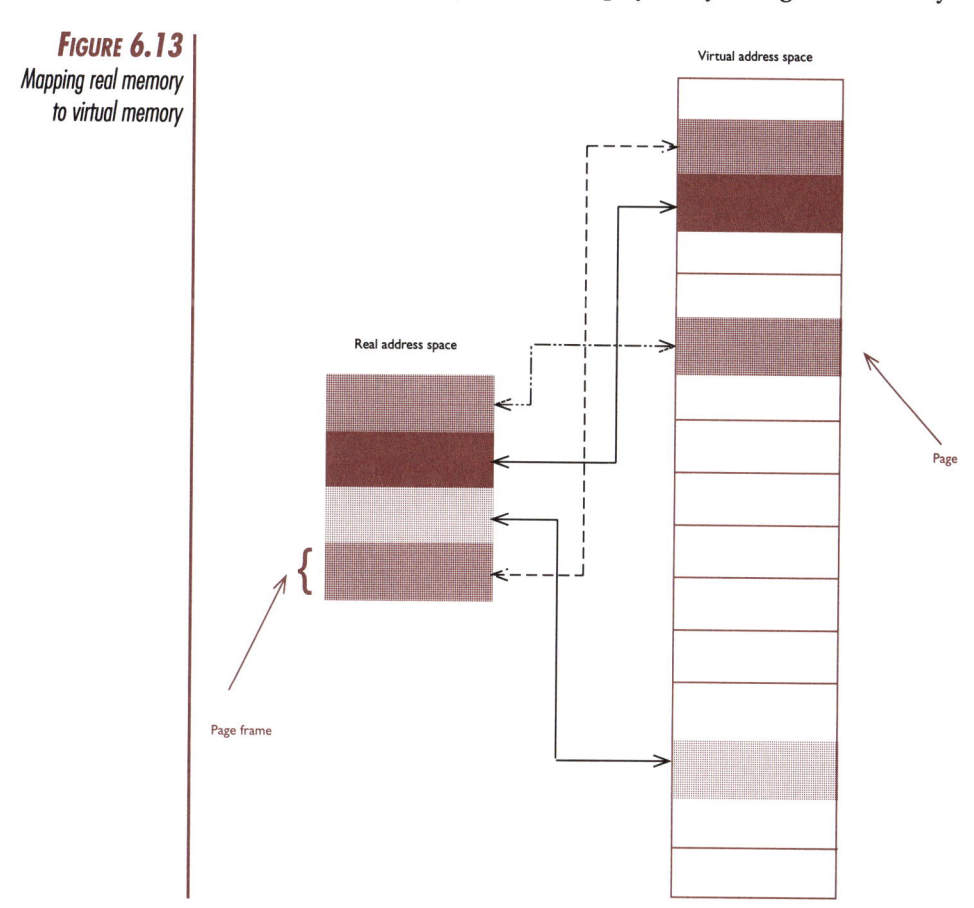

FIGURE 6.13
Mapping real memory to virtual memory

The amount of RAM you can simulate with virtual memory is limited by the maximum amount of RAM your Mac can access and how much free disk space you have. To implement virtual memory, the Macintosh needs a file as big as the entire virtual address space. When a page is swapped from real memory to disk, it is written to the virtual memory file in the location that corresponds to the page's virtual address. In essence, the virtual memory file is a picture of the contents of the entire virtual address space.

> **BY THE WAY!** Virtual memory adds considerable complexity to an operating system, especially one that supports multitasking (more than one program in the execution phase at a time). The operating system must not only keep track of what is in which page frame and work with the hardware to perform address translation, but must also know the program to which each page frame belongs. In addition, it must protect real memory used by one program from real memory being used by another.

The Pros and Cons of Virtual Memory

Virtual memory has one big benefit and a couple of drawbacks. Its big benefit is that it lets you extend your RAM for very little cost. If you happen to have lots of available hard disk space, then running virtual memory can let you run more applications at the same time or work with larger documents.

The major drawback, however, is that because virtual memory requires disk access, it slows down the operation of your Macintosh. To make the best use of virtual memory, you should have enough physical RAM to hold the largest application you use in addition to space for system software. For example, if your system software typically uses between 3 and 4Mb of RAM and your largest application runs in a 4Mb partition, you should have at least 8Mb of physical RAM installed. This means that swaps between disk and main memory will occur only when you switch applications, not while you are working with a single application.

Virtual memory can also present a security problem. The file used to hold the image of the virtual address space is just a text file; you can read it with any text editor or word processor. If you happen to be working with sensitive data, then leaving the virtual memory file on disk makes whatever data was last in a given page frame available. This includes encrypted data on which you might have been working in decrypted form.

Virtual Memory and Specific Macintosh Models

To support virtual memory, a Macintosh must have a PMMU. The Motorola 68000 microprocessor that is found in Macintoshes such as the Plus, SE, Classic, and PowerBook 100, however, cannot accept one. Any 68000 Macintosh is therefore unable to use virtual memory.

A PMMU is built into the 68030 and 68040 microprocessors. If you have a machine with either of those CPUs, then you will be able to use virtual memory. The original Mac II and LC, however, have a 68020 CPU. The 68020 can accept a PMMU as an add-on chip. Therefore, if you are planning to use virtual memory with either of these computers, you must upgrade your machine with the PMMU. PMMUs are readily available for the Mac II, but not for the LC.

> **BY THE WAY!** Apple is no longer selling a PMMU for the Mac II. However, many vendors that sell RAM for Macintoshes have PMMUs available.

USING VIRTUAL MEMORY

Virtual memory is controlled by the Memory control panel. To start virtual memory:

1. Open the Memory control panel. If your computer supports virtual memory, the control panel's window will include the virtual memory section.

2. Click the **Virtual Memory "on"** button.

3. Use the pop-up menu to choose a hard disk volume that has more space available than you have physical RAM installed (see Figure 6.14). The control panel displays a default size for the virtual memory address space.

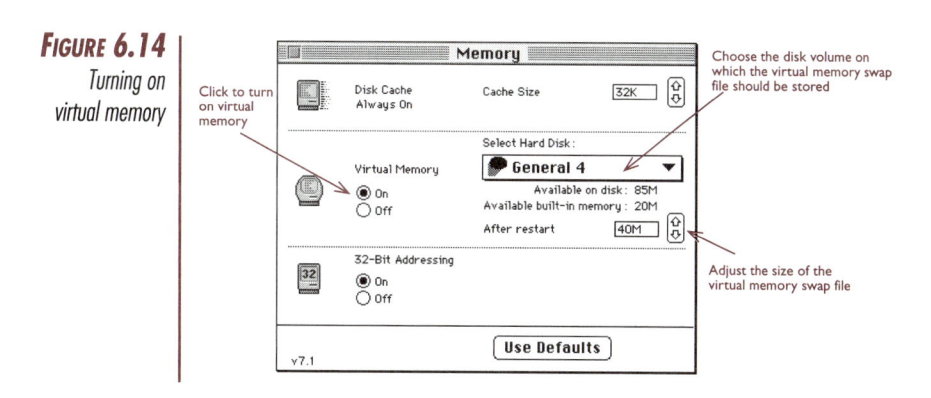

FIGURE 6.14
Turning on virtual memory

4. Enter the size of the virtual memory address space or use the up and down arrows to change the default.

5. Close the Memory control panel and restart your Macintosh.

The amount of virtual memory you can use depends on two things: the amount of free disk space and the maximum amount of memory your Macintosh can access. The Macintosh in Figure 6.14, for example, can access 128Mb of RAM, but because there are only 85Mb free on the hard disk volume, the virtual memory address space is limited to 85Mb.

USEFUL ADD-ON Before System 7, System 6 users obtained virtual memory capabilities with a system extension called Virtual. Although System 7 does provide virtual memory, there are still some circumstances under which Virtual is useful. In particular, Virtual can give Macintoshes with limited address spaces access to more virtual memory (usually 14 or 15Mb). This is particularly useful for machines such as the Classic II, which have limited RAM capacities even though they have 32-bit address buses.

The Disk Cache

A *cache* is a temporary holding area for data or the instructions that make up a computer program. The 68020, 68030, and 68040 microprocessors have special cache memory that speeds up program execution. In addition, System 7 provides a software-based disk cache that can speed up disk access.

How a Disk Cache Works

A *disk cache* is a portion of RAM set aside to hold the "next" data a program will need from disk. Because access to RAM is faster than access to disk, a program will execute faster whenever it can take data from RAM rather than having to read it from disk.

How does the operating system decide what the "next" data needed will be? The theory is that the most recently used data will be the data most likely to be used again in the near future. (There is a great deal of research that indicates that this is a very good scheme for predicting the "next" data.) In practical terms, this means that the disk cache usually holds the mostly recently used data. When a program needs data, it looks first in the disk cache. If the data aren't there, then it reads them from disk.

A disk cache can indeed speed up program execution. However, keep in mind that the disk cache uses up part of your RAM. If you are working with a Macintosh that has limited RAM, then a large disk cache may have impact on the number of programs you can have running at the same time.

DISK CACHE SIZE

By default, System 7 sets the disk cache to 32K. You can increase it in 32K increments. However, there is no definitive answer as to how big the disk cache should be. Some Macintosh experts recommend setting aside 32K for every 1Mb of RAM. That means, for example, that a 10Mb Macintosh should use a 320K disk cache and a 128K Macintosh should use a 4096K (4Mb) disk cache.

Unfortunately, you can't simply follow that rule. There is a point of diminishing returns after which additional disk cache space brings little or no performance benefits; this point is usually application-dependent. In addition, some application programs don't benefit from disk caching at all. The first place to look for advice is in the documentation that comes with your application programs; many will indicated suggested disk cache sizes for best performance. Without any such guidance, you will generally do well to leave the disk cache relatively small (500K or less).

USING THE SYSTEM 7 DISK CACHE

To set the size of the disk cache, open the Memory control panel. Use the up and down arrows at the right of the disk cache section of the window to increase or decrease the cache size (see Figure 6.15). As mentioned earlier, the cache size changes in 32K increments.

> In System 6, use of the disk cache was optional. Under System 7, it is always on.

FIGURE 6.15
Changing the size of the disk cache

[Memory control panel showing: Disk Cache Always On, Cache Size 256K; Virtual Memory Off, Select Hard Disk: Starship One, Available on disk: 78M, Available built-in memory: 24M; 32-Bit Addressing On; RAM Disk Off, Percent of available memory to use for a RAM disk: 0%, RAM Disk Size 0K; Use Defaults button; v7.1.1]

Click here to change the size of the disk cache

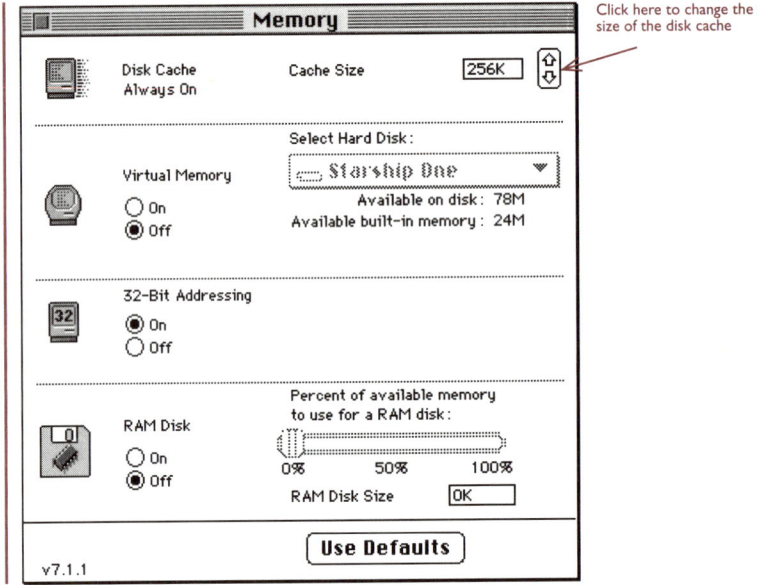

RAM Disks

A *RAM disk* is a portion of RAM set aside to act as a high-speed disk drive. Because access to RAM is significantly faster than access to a hard disk, I/O operations involving a RAM disk can speed up overall system performance. RAM disks are created and maintained by software. Once created, a RAM disk appears on the Desktop like any other disk volume; it is also used just like any other disk volume.

In most cases, you gain the most benefit from a RAM disk by placing a system folder and applications that periodically load portions from disk onto the RAM disk. However, it often doesn't pay to place a document on a RAM disk. Many documents are loaded from disk into memory when opened; they remain in main memory until you issue a **Save** command. Therefore, placing such documents on a RAM disk doesn't contribute much to increasing system speed.

There are, however, some drawbacks to using a RAM disk. First, a RAM disk uses part of your installed RAM. That means that whatever RAM you allocate to the RAM disk is no longer available for the operating system or applications. Even a minimal System 7 System folder occupies more than 2Mb; an average System folder, which includes a variety of control panels and system extensions, is closer to 10Mb. If you have less than 20Mb RAM, a useful RAM disk may require so much RAM that you don't have enough space for the applications you need to run.

> **BY THE WAY!** Even if you are using virtual memory, a RAM disk must occupy physical RAM; placing it in the virtual memory address space where it would be shuffled between disk and physical RAM would negate the value of having a RAM disk.

Second, the contents of a RAM disk are volatile. When power is removed from the RAM occupied by the RAM disk, its contents are lost. If you are using a PowerBook, you are far less vulnerable to power loss; putting the PowerBook to sleep (as opposed to shutting it down) preserves the contents of RAM. However, Macintoshes that get their power directly from an electrical outlet will lose RAM disk contents as the result of a power failure. That means that you must make provisions for periodic backup of your RAM disk to more permanent storage. The more often you copy from the RAM disk to a hard disk, the safer you'll be. However, each copy to the hard disk slows down system operations.

Using the System 7 RAM Disk

If you are using a PowerBook, the Memory control panel contains a bottom section that provides for a RAM disk. (The System 7 RAM disk isn't supported on other Macintosh models.) As you can see in Figure 6.16, there are a pair of radio buttons used to turn the RAM disk on and off as well as a slider to set the RAM disk's size (see Figure 6.16). As you allocate a percentage of available RAM to the RAM disk, the Memory control panel shows the actual number of kilobytes in the RAM disk.

The System 7 RAM disk can survive a restart, but not a crash or power failure. It also has no provisions for automatically copying files from the RAM disk to a hard disk; you must do that yourself before shutting down the computer. (Keep in mind, however, that if you put a PowerBook to sleep, the RAM disk is preserved; the sleep state continues to send a minimal amount of power to RAM.)

Files are copied to and deleted from a System 7 RAM disk just as with any other disk volume. However, if you want to delete the RAM disk, you must first delete all files from it. Then you can either drag the RAM disk's Desktop icon to the trash or use the Memory control panel to turn it off.

To change the RAM disk's size, first delete all files from it. Then open the Memory control panel and use the slider to adjust the size.

FIGURE 6.16
Configuring the System 7 RAM disk

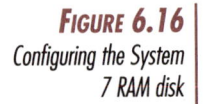

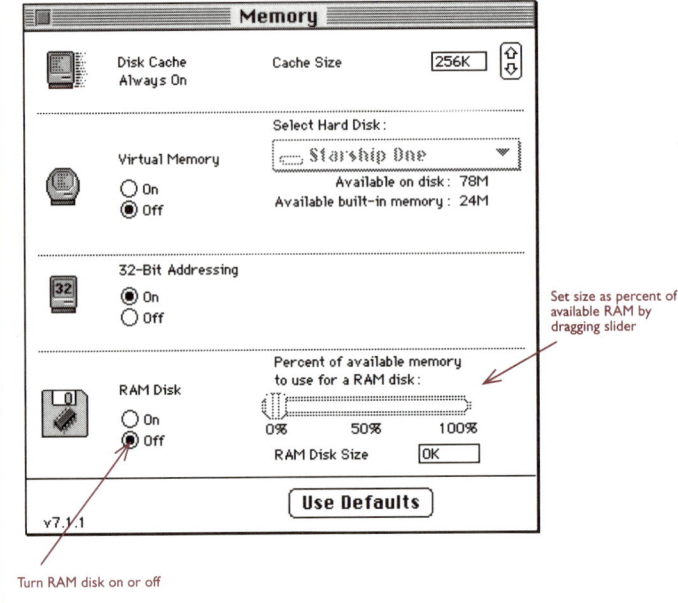

[Memory control panel screenshot showing: Disk Cache Always On with Cache Size 256K; Virtual Memory with Select Hard Disk: Starship One, Available on disk: 78M, Available built-in memory: 24M, On/Off radio buttons (Off selected); 32-Bit Addressing On/Off (On selected); RAM Disk On/Off (Off selected) with Percent of available memory to use for a RAM disk slider 0%–50%–100%, RAM Disk Size, OK button; Use Defaults button; v7.1.1. Annotations: "Set size as percent of available RAM by dragging slider" and "Turn RAM disk on or off"]

RAM Disks for Macintoshes that Don't Support the System 7 RAM Disk

If you don't have a PowerBook, you can't use the System 7 RAM disk. However, you aren't out of luck; there are shareware and commercial applications that provide RAM disk capabilities. One of the commercial products is Maxima, developed by Connectix (the same company that created Mode32).

Maxima's RAM disk, although vulnerable to a complete power failure, can survive a system crash and reset. As long as there is power to the Macintosh, it will retain its contents. Like other RAM disks, Maxima places an icon for a disk on the desktop (see Figure 6.17).

Maxima installs first during system startup. Its RAM disk can therefore be used to start up the computer. In other words, the first thing that happens during the startup process is that the System folder is copied into RAM. Because the rest of the startup operations happen from RAM rather than from disk, startup is faster than it would be otherwise.

Maxima can be configured to automatically save the RAM disk's contents at system Shutdown (see Figure 6.18). It also maintains separate configurations for 24- and 32-bit addressing. Under 24-bit addressing, Maxima can take memory not used by expansion cards as additional RAM ("Extended RAM"). This lets a Macintosh use up to 15Mb of RAM when working in 24-bit mode. (The maximum amount of memory is 15Mb minus 1Mb for each expansion board installed in a slot.)

FIGURE 6.17
The Maxima RAM disk on the Desktop

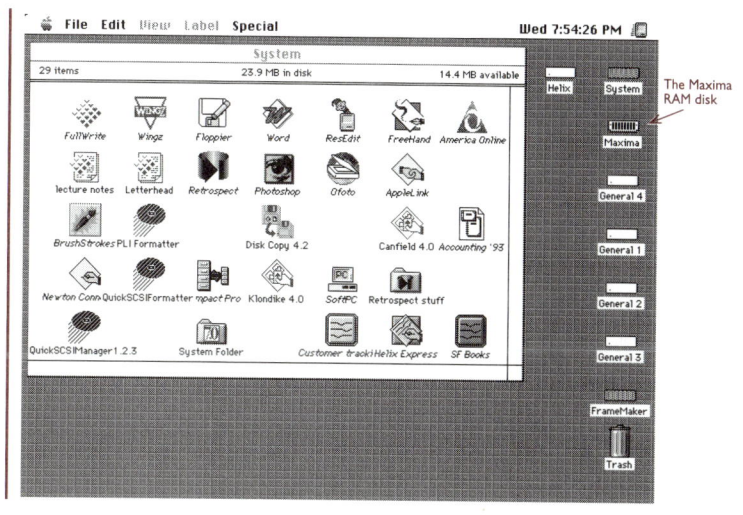

FIGURE 6.18
The Maxima control panel

There is also shareware RAM disk software. AppDisk, for example, works with any Macintosh. AppDisk is different from Maxima in that it runs as an application. That means that you can reclaim the RAM used by AppDisk at any time by simply quitting the program, which runs in the background as long as you have a RAM disk open. However, AppDisk cannot survive crashes or resets nor can it be used to start up the system.

CHAPTER 7
Fonts

In the beginning, there were bitmapped fonts, and they were good. Then Adobe begat PostScript and PostScript fonts, and they were good. Finally, Apple begat TrueType fonts, and they weren't bad either. All kidding aside, there *are* three types of fonts used on the Macintosh. Although font support is provided by the operating system, which type of font you use at any given time depends on the type of printer you are using as well as the application software you're using.

One of the things that made the Macintosh stand out from other computers back in 1984 was its ability to work with different fonts. (One of the first things most early purchasers did was to create documents with as many fonts as they could; most people have learned better.) Fonts have matured considerably since then, but the way in which fonts are represented on the screen hasn't changed much. This chapter therefore looks at Macintosh fonts, including the way in which fonts are described and measured, the types of fonts, and how you can organize a large collection of fonts and still not lose your mind. You'll also read about a way to use software that requires a PostScript printer with printers that don't support PostScript.

TYPOGRAPHIC TERMINOLOGY

To a typographer, a *font* is a single typeface in a single size. The *typeface* refers to the style of type, such as Times or Courier or Garamond. A typeface may be plain type, like the body text of this book, or it may be **boldface**, *italic*, or ***bolditalic***.

The size of a font refers to the space from the lowest *descender* (a character such as "y" or "g" that drops below the line) to the highest *ascender* (a character such as "h" or "k"), measured in *points* (1/72-inch). When considering fonts, keep in mind that a font size says nothing about the width of the font or about how high characters such as "o" or "c" rise. Because these characteristics can vary widely, two fonts of the same size may take up very different amounts of space. For example, compare 12-point Benguiat, with 12-point Garamond, a font typically used for the body of documents:

This is 12- point Benguiat

This is 12-point Garamond

Notice that although both fonts are the same height, Benguiat is much wider. Characters such as "c" and "o" are also higher, making Benguiat look larger. The height of such characters is known as the *x-height* because it is determined by the height of the letter "x."

Fonts of the same typeface are grouped into font families. For example, all sizes and styles of Times are considered a font family. Many Macintosh users refer to a font family with the term "font." Although technically incorrect, this use of the word generally doesn't cause problems unless you happen to be purchasing fonts to add to your Macintosh and discover that though you thought you were buying an entire font family, you only purchased a portion of it.

TYPES OF MACINTOSH FONTS

Until the introduction of the LaserWriter in 1986, there was only one type of Macintosh font—bitmapped. Since then, font technology has improved with the introduction of outline fonts—PostScript and TrueType. Nonetheless, bitmapped fonts have a continuing, important role for the Macintosh.

BITMAPPED FONTS

A bitmapped font is a font in which the character is created as a pattern of dots. All Macintosh printers, which physically form their images with patterns of dots (even ink-jet and laser printers), can print bitmapped fonts. When printed, bitmapped fonts tend to have jagged edges, especially when scaled to large sizes. Bitmapped fonts therefore provide the poorest-quality printed output from a Macintosh.

> **BY THE WAY!** The term "poorest" in the preceding paragraph is rather relative. Even the Apple ImageWriter, a dot-matrix printer, can produce quite acceptable hard copy in its "best" mode from a bitmapped font. The output just isn't as good, for example, as that produced by TrueType fonts on the same printer.

Bitmapped fonts are also used to create images on the Macintosh screen for both bitmapped and PostScript fonts. Changing the size of a screen bitmap produces a poor display. You get the best results by installing a bitmapped screen font for each size you want to use. Consider, for example, Figure 7.1, in which you can see two examples of the Bookman font. Bitmaps are installed for 10-, 12-, 14-, 18-, and 24-point. The 14-point sample therefore appears quite readable and looks very similar to what will appear on paper. However, if the bitmapped is sized to 16-point, for which no bitmap is available, the characters are out of proportion and do not resemble what will be printed.

FIGURE 7.1
The effect of scaling a bitmapped font

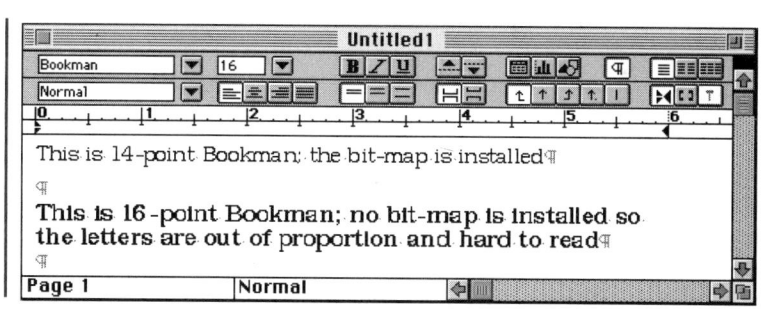

Bitmapped fonts can be installed as individual font files (one typeface in one size) or collected together into *suitcases*. In most cases, suitcases (named for the shape of their icon) contain all or part of one font family. For example, in Figure 7.2 the suitcase BI Times BoldItalic contains five bitmaps for Times bold italic in five sizes.

A suitcase works much like any other folder. To add a font file, drag it to the suitcase icon. To remove a font file from a suitcase, open the suitcase's window and drag the font out.

FIGURE 7.2
The contents of a font suitcase

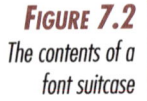

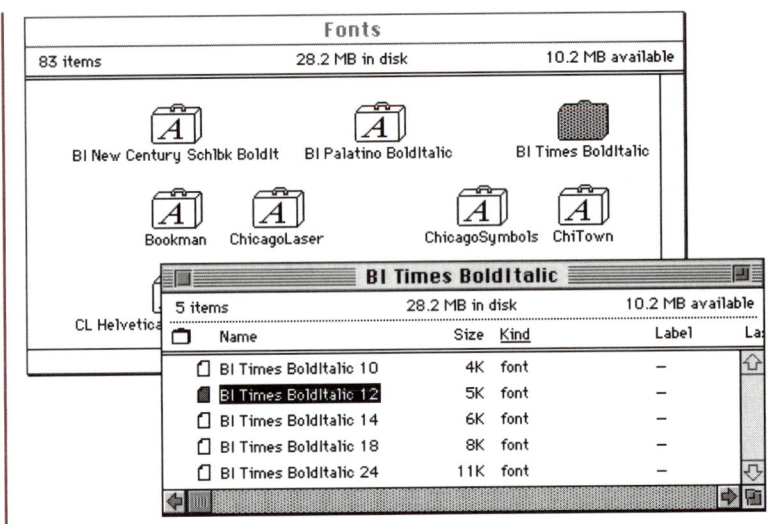

Although fonts don't need to be grouped into suitcases, keeping them grouped makes it easier to work with large collections of fonts. In addition, the Macintosh operating system has a limit of 128 open font files. "Font files" means either font suitcases or font files not stored in suitcases. Therefore, if you have a very large collection of fonts, you can have more fonts available at any one time if you group them into suitcases. As long as you don't have any individual font files lying about, you can 128 font suitcases open.

PostScript Fonts

The arrival of the LaserWriter in 1986 included an exciting new type of font—the PostScript font. *PostScript* is a *page-description language*, a special programming language used to describe a page to a printer. Rather than describing an image as a pattern of dots, PostScript describes the outline of shapes that make up the image. PostScript fonts, which are a type of *outline font*, include definitions for drawing the outside edges of each character; the outlines are then filled in by the printer. The beauty of this is that a character can be drawn in any size and still appear with smooth edges.

There are two types of PostScript fonts: Type 1 and Type 3. Type 1 fonts, the most common, include all fonts produced by Adobe and most of the fonts from Linotype, Agfa-Compugraphic, Varityper, Monotype, and Autologic. Type 3 fonts are generally older fonts created before Adobe made the Type 1 font specifications public. When you have a choice, purchase Type 1 fonts; they usually produce better looking output than Type 3 fonts.

The drawback to PostScript fonts is that you must have a printer that can handle PostScript. Printers such as the ImageWriter and the StyleWriter cannot; some of the personal Apple LaserWriters also don't have PostScript. Because PostScript is the property of Adobe Systems, the manufacturer of printers that use PostScript must pay a licensing fee for the language; PostScript printers therefore cost more than non-PostScript printers.

> **BY THE WAY!** Printer prices have dropped so dramatically that you can purchase a PostScript laser printer for less than $1,000 with more capabilities than the original LaserWriter, which sold for $5,000.

Without the help of an add-on program, PostScript fonts can't be used to create screen images; they are for output only. A PostScript font therefore consists of two files: the bitmapped screen font and the PostScript printer font. The printer font may be in ROM in the printer, on a hard disk attached to a printer, or stored on a Macintosh's hard disk. PostScript printer fonts stored on the Macintosh's hard disk are *downloaded* to the printer as needed and stored in the printer's RAM. Such *downloadable fonts* are erased from the printer's memory when the printer is turned off.

Most application programs automatically download PostScript fonts as needed. However, if you encounter a program that doesn't download the fonts, you can send them to the printer with the LaserWriter Font Utility, a program that is shipped with System 7. LaserWriter Font Utility lets you select a group of fonts for downloading at one time (see Figure 7.3). In addition, it can display or print the fonts in a printer's ROM or on a printer's hard drive as well as send a PostScript file to a printer.

Figure 7.3
Selecting a group of fonts for downloading at one time

BY THE WAY!

A PostScript file is a text file that contains commands in the PostScript language. To generate one, change the destination in the Print dialog box from Printer to PostScript file (see Figure 7.4).

FIGURE 7.4
Using the Print dialog box to create a PostScript file

```
LaserWriter  "QMS-PS 815 MR"                         7.1.2    [ Save ]
Copies: 1           Pages: ● All  ○ From:     To:            [Cancel]
Cover Page:   ● No ○ First Page ○ Last Page
Paper Source: ● Paper Cassette  ○ Manual Feed
Print:          ○ Black & White     ● Color/Grayscale
Destination:   ○ Printer            ● PostScript® File
```

In most cases, PostScript files are created for printing on 1200- or 2400-dots-per-inch imagesetters. It much less usual to receive a PostScript file for printing on a 300- or 600-dots-per-inch laser printer.

USEFUL ADD-ON

If you want to get rid of the jagged bitmaps for PostScript Type 1 fonts, consider using Adobe Type Manager (ATM). As well as improving screen display, ATM also makes it possible to print Type 1 PostScript fonts on non-PostScript printers. (If you want to print anything other than a Type 1 PostScript font to a non-PostScript printer, see the discussion of Freedom of Press, which follows shortly.)

ATM's effect is most noticeable when using odd font sizes for which bitmaps aren't available. For example, in Figure 7.5 you can see 42-point GillSans (the typeface used to add annotations to many of the illustrations in this book). There is no 42-point bitmap. Therefore, the upper sample, which was generated without the benefit of ATM, contains jagged, hard-to-read characters. The bottom sample, however, was generated with ATM turned on. It provides smooth, readable characters even in an unusual size.

FIGURE 7.5
The effect of Adobe Type Manager on screen display of Type 1 PostScript fonts

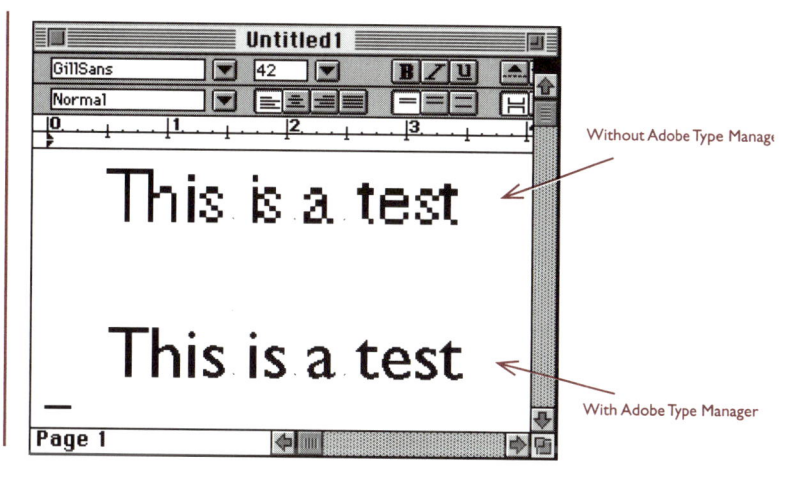

ATM installs as a control panel (Figure 7.6). Once installed in memory, it can be turned on and off from the control panel as needed. Changes take effect immediately; there is no need to reboot the Macintosh.

FIGURE 7.6
The Adobe Type Manager control panel

PostScript and Application Programs

Most Macintosh applications support printing to any printer for which you have a printer driver. However, there are some that require a PostScript output device (either a laser printer or an imagesetter). These programs include high-end graphics software such as Adobe Illustrator and Aldus Freehand as well as some document processing software such as Interleaf Publisher.

The Macintosh operating system has no provisions to translate the output of PostScript-based software into a form that non-PostScript printers can accept. You will therefore be unable to print from such programs on your non-PostScript printer unless you invest in an add-on program. (See the following "Useful add-on" for details.)

USEFUL ADD-ON

If you want to print from an application that requires a PostScript output device on a non-PostScript printer, you can do it with Freedom of Press. Freedom of Press intercepts the PostScript printer descriptions and translates them into QuickDraw commands, which every Macintosh printer can understand.

Freedom of Press supports a large selection of Apple, Hewlett Packard, Canon, and PCL printers. Once a printer has been selected (as in Figure 7.7), Freedom of Press handles printing whenever you issue a print command from within an application. You can also print PostScript files directly from the Freedom of Press program.

Figure 7.7
Choosing a non-PostScript printer using Freedom of Press

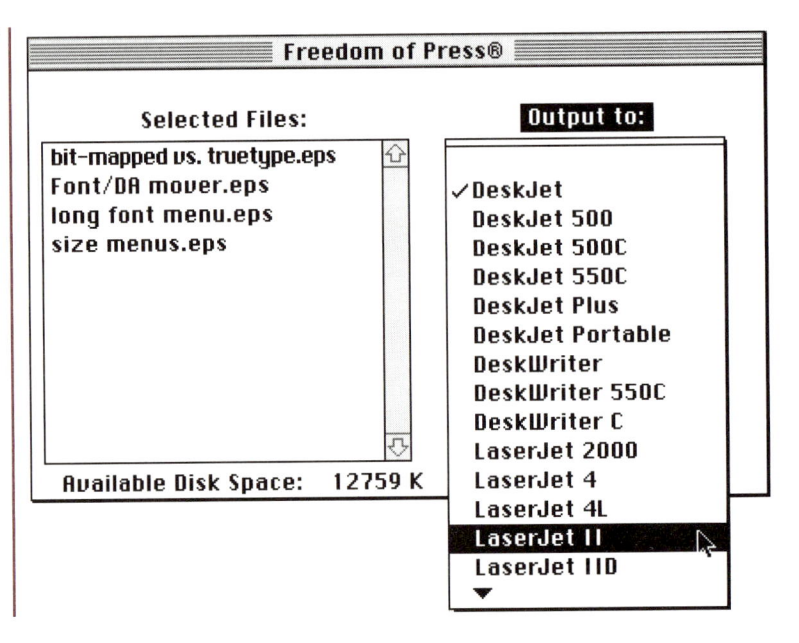

TrueType Fonts

TrueType is an outline font technology that made its official debut with System 7. Like PostScript, TrueType fonts are scalable; they can be used in any size needed and still produce smooth characters. However, TrueType fonts don't need separate screen and printer files. TrueType fonts also provide smooth output on non-PostScript printers such as the Apple ImageWriter and most ink-jet printers (for example, the Apple StyleWriter and the HP DeskJet).

> **BY THE WAY!** Although TrueType was developed by Apple, it has been licensed by other computer manufacturers. For example, Microsoft Windows supports TrueType fonts.

How can you tell a TrueType font from a bitmapped font? There are several ways. As you can see in Figure 7.8, there are two differences in their files. First, a TrueType font file name is just the name of the font; a bitmapped font file name is followed by the size of the bitmap. Second, when you open a TrueType font file, you will see samples in a variety of sizes; a bitmapped font file window shows a sample only in the size of the bitmap.

FIGURE 7.8 Distinguishing TrueType and bitmapped font files

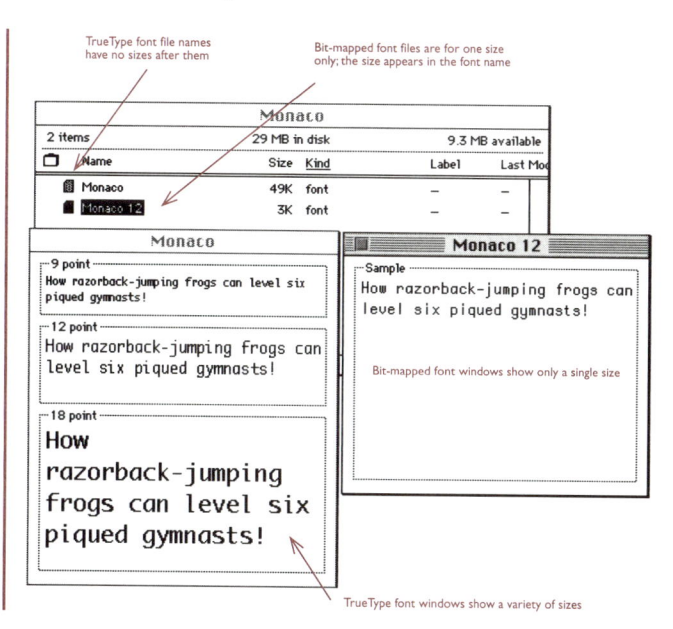

You can also tell whether you're working with a TrueType or a bitmapped font from the Size menu. When you are working with a bitmapped font, sizes are outlined only for those sizes for which bitmaps are present (see Figure 7.9). However, because TrueType fonts are scalable, all sizes are available; every size in the Size menu is therefore outlined.

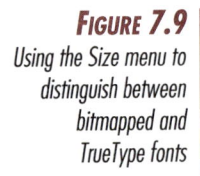

FIGURE 7.9
Using the Size menu to distinguish between bitmapped and TrueType fonts

Sizes are outlined only for those sizes for which bit-maps exist

All sizes are outlined because the TrueType font is scalable

Size menu for bit-mapped font

Size menu for TrueType font

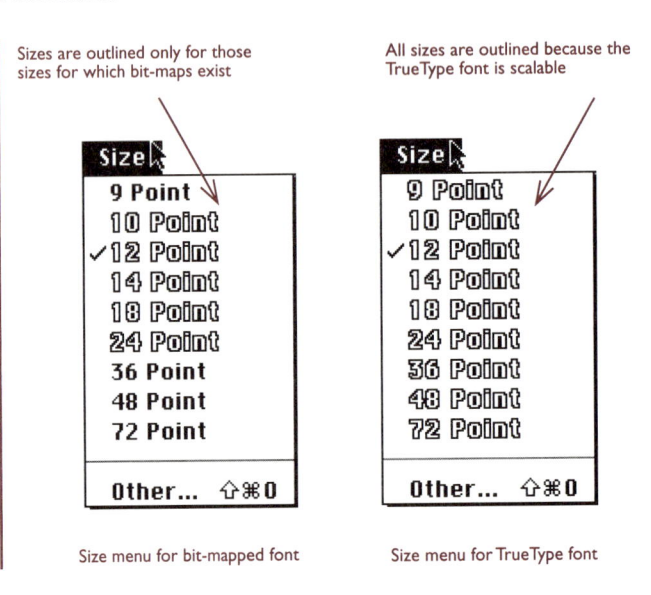

If you still aren't sure whether you're working with a bitmapped or TrueType font, try typing some text in a size that doesn't appear in the size menu. For example, in Figure 7.10 the 16-point Geneva looks smooth because it's a TrueType font. However, the 16-point TTY100 (a font used by a data communications program) doesn't look smooth at all; it's a bitmapped font for which no 16-point bitmap file exists.

FIGURE 7.10
Using an unusual font size to distinguish between bitmapped and True-type fonts

This is 16-point Geneva. It looks smooth because it's a TrueType font.

This is 16-point TTY100. It looks pretty awful because it's a bit-mapped font and no bit-map is available in this size.

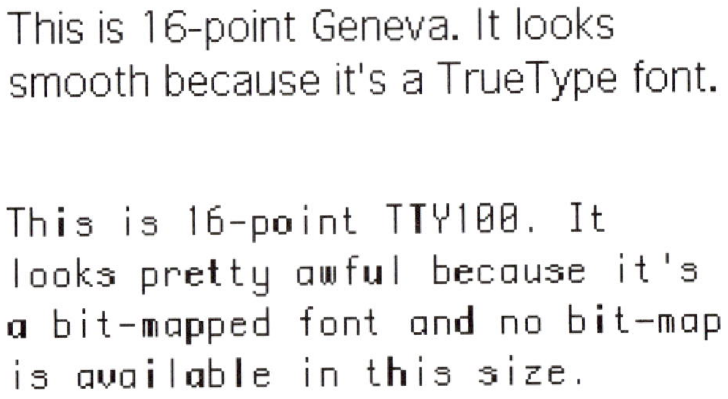

OBTAINING FONTS

There are literally thousands of bitmapped, PostScript, and TrueType fonts. Some bitmapped and TrueType fonts are shipped as part of the Macintosh operating system. (The Macintosh operating system font set can be found in Table 7.1.) Several of the TrueType fonts—Courier, Helvetica, New York, Palatino, Symbol, Times—are usually built into PostScript-compatible printers. The TrueType fonts therefore can double as screen fonts for some PostScript printer fonts.

> Many of the fonts in Table 7.1—Athens, Cairo, Chicago, Geneva, London, Los Angeles, Monaco, New York, San Francisco, and Venice—began life as bitmapped fonts in 1984. Those that haven't been rendered as TrueType fonts are called "classic" Macintosh fonts.

TABLE 7.1
The Macintosh operating system default font set

Font Name	Type
Athens	Bitmapped
Cairo	Bitmapped
Chicago	TrueType
Courier	TrueType
Geneva	TrueType
Helvetica	TrueType
London	Bitmapped
Los Angeles	Bitmapped
Mobile	Bitmapped
Monaco	TrueType
New York	TrueType
Palatino	TrueType
San Francisco	Bitmapped
Symbol	TrueType
Times	TrueType
Venice	Bitmapped

PostScript printers have a collection of PostScript font outlines in ROM. The bitmaps for those fonts are usually provided on floppy disk by the printer manufacturer.

Additional fonts are available as freeware or shareware from on-line services or user groups. Most, however, are commercial products. If you are looking for an inexpensive, wide-ranging collection of moderate-quality fonts, consider purchasing KeyFonts. KeyFonts, available either on floppy disk or CD-ROM, includes more than 100 TrueType and PostScript fonts. Typesetting-quality fonts can be purchased from software vendors or from the type manufacturer. Monotype, for example, distributes a CD-ROM containing PostScript fonts from several manufacturers. The fonts are "locked." Once you pay for a font, you receive a password that unlocks the font so you can install both the bitmaps and the PostScript outline on your own disk.

INSTALLING AND REMOVING FONTS

The procedures for installing and removing fonts differs a bit between System 7.0 and 7.1. (Keep in mind that under 7.0, fonts are stored as resources in the System file; under 7.1 they can reside in a separate Fonts folder.) The process also depends on whether you are installing bitmapped, TrueType, or PostScript fonts.

> Prior to System 7, the only way to get fonts into the System file (where they were stored along with sounds and desk accessories) was to use the Font/DA mover. As you will see, this program has only limited use under System 7.

INSTALLING BITMAPPED AND TRUETYPE FONTS

To install bitmapped and TrueType fonts under either 7.0 or 7.1, drag them to the System folder. The Macintosh operating system recognizes the files as font files and asks you if they should be placed in the Fonts folder. If you respond **OK**, they will be placed in the System 7.1 Fonts folder. (Under 7.0, they'll end up in the System file.)

INSTALLING POSTSCRIPT PRINTER FONTS

If you drag PostScript font outlines to the System folder, they will also end up in the System 7.1 Fonts folder. (Under system 7.0, they'll be placed in the System file but not within any other folder.) However, this is the wrong location for them; if you leave PostScript fonts in the Fonts folder, the operating system won't be able to find them when you print. PostScript font files containing outlines that will be downloaded to a PostScript printer during printing should go in the Extensions folder. That means that to properly install a PostScript font outline, you should open the System folder and explicitly drag the PostScript font file to the Extensions folder.

Removing Fonts Under System 7.0

There are two ways to remove fonts under System 7.0. Which you use depends on whether the System file containing the fonts is the current System file. (In other words, is it the System file that was used to boot the computer?) If the System file containing the fonts *is* the current System file, then you must use the Font/DA Mover to remove fonts:

1. Open the Font/DA Mover. (Be sure to use version 4.1 or later; earlier versions aren't compatible with System 7.) The fonts currently installed in the System file appear at the left of the program's window (see Figure 7.11).

Figure 7.11
The Font/DA Mover

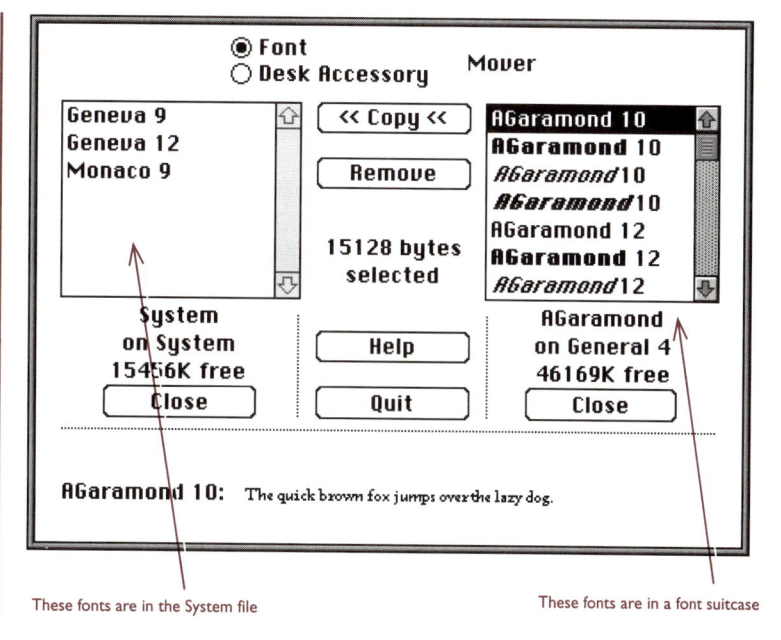

These fonts are in the System file

These fonts are in a font suitcase

2. Highlight the fonts or fonts you want to delete.

3. Click the **Remove** button.

If the System file in which the fonts are stored isn't the current System file, then you can remove fonts by dragging them out of the System file. To do so:

1. Double-click on the System file's icon to open its window.

2. Drag the font file or files you want to delete to the trash.

3. Empty the trash.

> **BY THE WAY!** Don't try to use the Font/DA Mover to remove Geneva 9, Geneva 12, or Monaco 9 from the System file. (These fonts won't appear when you open the System file's window.) The Macintosh operating system uses these fonts for Finder displays.

Removing Fonts Under System 7.1

To remove fonts under System 7.1, drag the font files from the Fonts folder to the trash. Fonts can only be removed from the Fonts folder in the current System folder if no applications are running.

Creating Font Suitcases

As you have read, fonts that belong to the same family are often gathered into suitcases. This can not only help organize a large font collection but make more fonts available at any one time. Getting a font file into an existing suitcase is easy: Just drag the file to the suitcase. However, if you want to create a new suitcase, you'll need to use the Font/DA Mover.

To create a new font suitcase:

1. Launch the Font/DA Mover.

2. Click the **Open** button at the right of the program window. A Save File dialog box appears.

3. Use the Save File dialog box to select a disk location for the new suitcase. Click the **Open** button to close the Save File dialog box. The New Font File dialog box appears.

4. Enter a name for the new suitcase (see Figure 7.12) and click the **Create** button.

FIGURE 7.12
Creating a new font suitcase

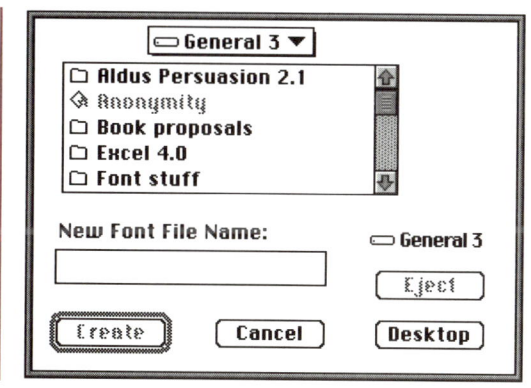

5. Quit the Font/DA Mover.
6. Drag font files into the new suitcase.

ORGANIZING FONTS WITH SUITCASE

Macintosh users who do a lot of word processing or desktop publishing tend to accumulate large collections of fonts. When those fonts are installed in the System folder, they are loaded into RAM at system startup, consuming RAM even if they aren't used. In addition, bitmaps and outlines take up space on a startup volume, space that might otherwise be saved for spooling print files. A large font collection also creates a long Font menu that can be inconvenient to use. For example, the font menu in Figure 7.13 fills a 13-inch monitor but only has room to display fonts beginning with the letters "A" and "B." (Keep in mind that bitmaps are displayed in alphabetical order.)

For all of these reasons, many Macintosh users have looked for an alternative way to manage fonts. The most widely used font-management program is Suitcase, which also can be used to organize and manage resources such as fonts and sounds. Suitcase not only lets you create sets of fonts for use with specific applications, but gets bitmaps and outlines out of the System folder and only opens fonts when you ask for them, freeing up RAM for other uses.

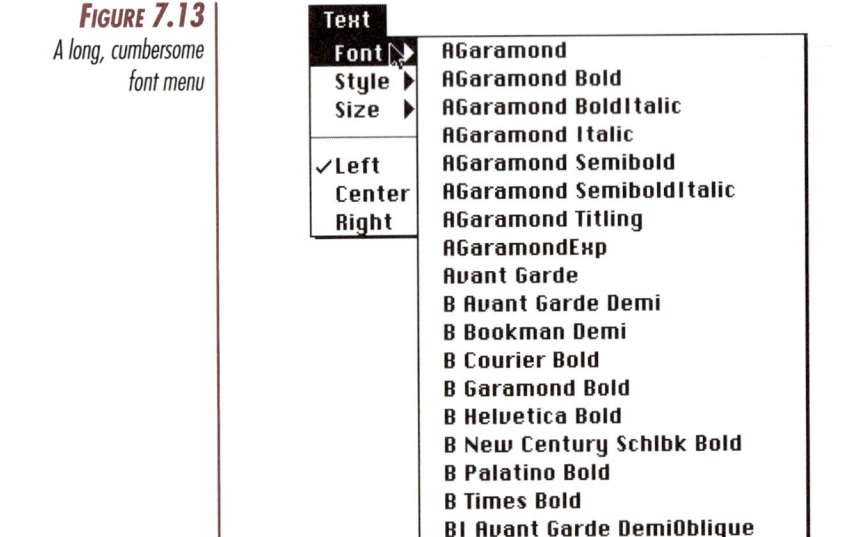

FIGURE 7.13
A long, cumbersome font menu

| Text |
| Font ▸ |
| Style ▸ |
| Size ▸ |
| ✓ Left |
| Center |
| Right |

AGaramond
AGaramond Bold
AGaramond BoldItalic
AGaramond Italic
AGaramond Semibold
AGaramond SemiboldItalic
AGaramond Titling
AGaramondExp
Avant Garde
B Avant Garde Demi
B Bookman Demi
B Courier Bold
B Garamond Bold
B Helvetica Bold
B New Century Schlbk Bold
B Palatino Bold
B Times Bold
BI Avant Garde DemiOblique
BI Bookman DemiItalic
BI Courier BoldOblique
BI Garamond BoldItalic
BI Helvetica BoldOblique
BI New Century Schlbk BoldIt
BI Palatino BoldItalic
BI Times BoldItalic
Bookman
▼

Down arrow means there are more fonts

Suitcase groups resources into units called "sets" that are accessible from the Suitcase control panel (see Figure 7.14). The Permanent Set contains resources that are opened at system startup. The resources in this set are therefore available to all applications at all times. If you don't want to further customize your font setup, you can nonetheless cut down on RAM use and move fonts out of the System folder by simply installing all fonts in the Permanent Set. Suitcase also lets you place bitmaps and outlines in the same folder.

If you want to create special groups of fonts for use with specific groups of applications, use Suitcase to create your own sets. Add to a given set only those fonts you want to appear in the font menu. (Fonts can belong to multiple sets). Then use the Suitcase control panel to open the set when you need its fonts. In addition to the Permanent Set, which is always open, you can open as many custom sets as you need.

FIGURE 7.14
The Suitcase control panel

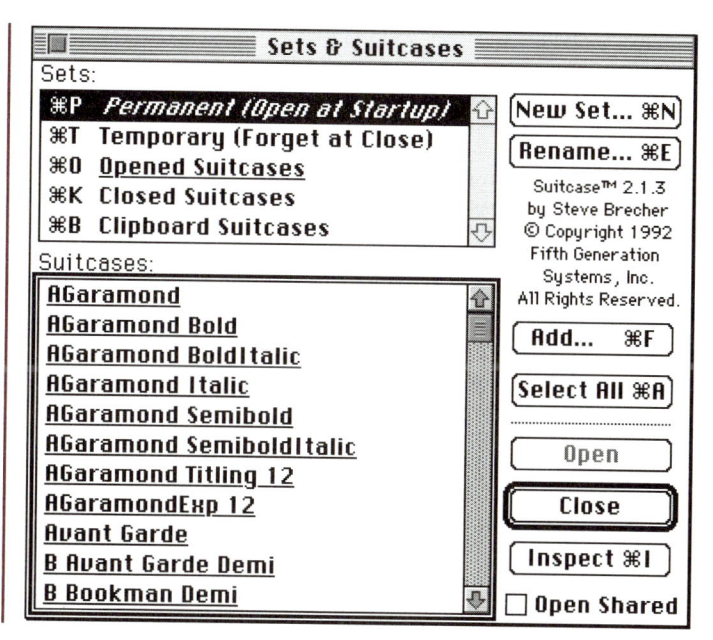

> **BY THE WAY!** If you have a large collection of sounds, you can use Suitcase to organize and open them just as you would fonts. There are two advantages to doing so. The sounds can be removed from the System file and placed anywhere you like, and the sounds aren't loaded into RAM at system startup, saving memory.

Cleaning up the Font Menu

Do your Font menus look like Figure 7.15? In other words, do your Font menus list the name of every bitmap you have installed in your Fonts folder? Figure 7.15, for example, shows six bitmaps for the Adobe Garamond font family, one for each style. (AGaramond Titling and AGaramondExp are part of related, but distinct, font families.) If you have more than a few fonts, your Font menu becomes very long and very hard to use. What most people would prefer is to see one entry for each font family, as in Figure 7.16. Then you could use the Style menu to choose the variation of the font.

FIGURE 7.15
A Font menu showing every installed bitmap

```
Font
AGaramond
AGaramond Bold
AGaramond BoldItalic
AGaramond Italic
AGaramond Semibold
AGaramond SemiboldItalic
AGaramond Titling
AGaramondExp
Avant Garde
B Avant Garde Demi
B Bookman Demi
B Courier Bold
B Garamond Bold
B Helvetica Bold
▼
```

FIGURE 7.16
A Font menu showing only font family names

```
Font
Adobe Garamond
Adobe Garamond Expert
Avant Garde
Bookman
Bordeaux
Boston
Chicago
Chicago Laser
Chicago Symbols
Courier
Garamond
Geneva
Gilde
Gill Sans
▼
```

The Macintosh operating system does not group font bitmaps by family, although some high-end word processing and desktop publishing programs have been written to do so. Therefore, if you want your fonts grouped by family in all applications, you will need an add-on program. Two alternatives are Font Harmony, which comes with Suitcase, and Adobe Type Reunion.

Both programs ask the user to choose a font suitcase whose bitmaps should be "harmonized." The problem with this is that if you happen to organize your bitmaps differently from someone with whom you are sharing files, the fonts that you used to create your documents may not be the fonts that appear when the documents are opened on another Macintosh. This can wreck havoc when you are taking documents to a service bureau to be printed. (To get around this problem, service bureaus often ask you to bring all your fonts with you or to provide PostScript files instead of original documents.)

BY THE WAY! System 7.1 frequently can't open harmonized font suitcases. You should therefore proceed with caution when deciding whether to use a font harmonizing utility under 7.1.

CHAPTER 8
INIT Management

Throughout this book you've read about a lot of programs that add functionality to the Macintosh operating system. Some, such as system enablers, may be absolutely required before your system will run. Others, such as Mode32, can add significant capabilities to your system. There is also a third group that, while not necessary, makes working with your Macintosh easier and/or more fun. The wide variety of add-on programs available today can make it hard to decide which you should install. You may also find that add-ons conflict with one another, either preventing your Macintosh from starting up or causing your system to crash.

This chapter looks at the whole issue of managing such add-on software. It looks at the types of add-ons you might encounter, whether you should use them, and handling conflicts between them. The chapter ends with two lists of suggested add-ons (a minimal set and an expanded set).

TYPES OF ADD-ON PROGRAMS

There are three types of programs that can be added to a Macintosh. Two of these—system extensions and control panels—are loaded into RAM at system startup and are therefore commonly known as *INITs*. The third type—desk accessories—has lost its place as a special type of program under System 7.

System Extensions

True system extensions extend the operating system by adding functions to it. You can't run a system extension by double-clicking on its icon (see the warning in Figure 8.1). Once loaded at system startup, you generally don't have access to them. Stored within the Extensions folder, most system extensions have an icon that looks like a jigsaw puzzle piece (see Figure 8.2).

FIGURE 8.1
The result of double-clicking on a system extension icon

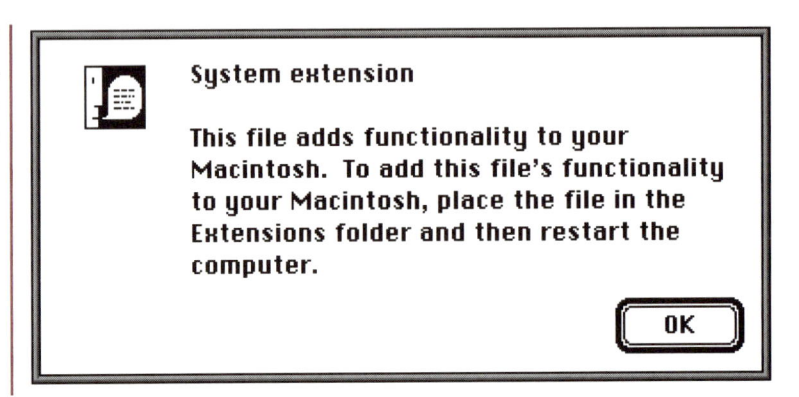

> **System extension**
>
> This file adds functionality to your Macintosh. To add this file's functionality to your Macintosh, place the file in the Extensions folder and then restart the computer.
>
> [OK]

FIGURE 8.2
Control panel and system extension icons

After Dark, QuicKeys™, Labels, Map, Sharing Setup, Sound

CEToolbox, Control Panel Handler, File Sharing Extension, Network Extension

Control panel icons are usually rectangular with sliders at the side

Extension icons usually look like jigsaw puzzle pieces

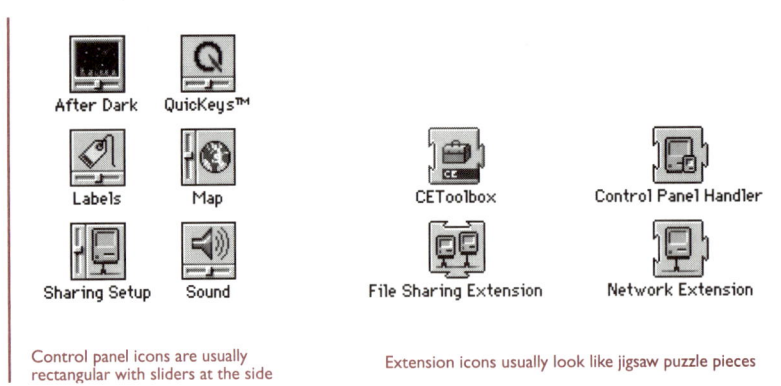

Control Panels

Control panels are designed to let you configure your working environment. Changes made through control panels may take effect immediately (for example, changes made through the General Control panel) or may require restarting the system before taking effect (for example, using the Monitors control panel to change the startup monitor). Although loaded at system startup, a control panel can be accessed while the Macintosh is running by double-clicking on its icon.

An alias for the Control Panels folder is placed inside the Apple Menu Items folder. When you choose Control Panels from the menu, the Control Panels folder opens. (Control panels icons typically are rectangular with sliders on the side and/or bottom, as in Figure 8.2.) You must then double-click on the icon of the control panel you want to use. As you read earlier in this book, a system add-on that creates hierarchical menus out of folder contents (for example, HAM or NowMenus) can give you access to individual control panels directly from the menu.

Desk Accessories

The third type of add-on is a desk accessory. As you read earlier, System 7 more or less eliminates desk accessories as a special category of program. No longer installed in the System file, desk accessories behave like small application programs. You can double-click on a desk accessory's icon to run it or, if it has been placed in the Apple Menu Items folder, run it by choosing its name from the menu. Desk accessories don't load into RAM at system startup; they are loaded into RAM when launched, just like any other application program. That means that they don't contribute to startup problems and therefore have far less impact on system stability than system extensions or control panels. Desk accessories take up space on a disk but otherwise have no special overall effect on your system; treat them like application programs.

Converting Older Desk Accessories for System 7 Use

If you are upgrading to System 7 from any version of System 6, then your desk accessories appear in suitcase files, just like families of fonts. Because System 7 handles desk accessories like other applications, you need to remove them from their suitcases. To prepare your older desk accessories for System 7 use:

1. Double-click on the suitcase to open its window.

2. Drag the contents of the suitcase outside the suitcase window.

3. Discard the empty suitcase window.

4. If you want the desk accessory to appear in the menu, drag the desk accessory or an alias for the desk accessory to the Apple Menu Items folder inside the System folder.

> **BY THE WAY!** Many desk accessories were written to run under earlier versions of the Macintosh operating system and may not be compatible with System 7. Feel free to try any desk accessories you want, but be aware that older ones may crash or hang your system.

FKEYs

An *FKEY* (pronounced "ef-key") is a small add-on program that is activated by a single keystroke combination such as ⌘-**Shift-3**. (As you know, that key combination takes a screen shot). Unlike other programs, FKEYs don't stay running after being launched. They perform the action they are programmed to perform and then quit.

FKEYs have been around since the early days of the Macintosh, when no Macintosh keyboard had function keys and before the availability of keyboard macro programs like QuicKeys and scripting languages like AppleScript. Because the Macintosh environment has matured significantly, FKEYs aren't used frequently today. However, you can use them if you so choose and find they are compatible with System 7.

FKEYs are resources that must be installed in the System file. When they were more common, there were utility programs that moved them. However, those utilities are no longer compatible with the Macintosh operating system. That means that if you want to install an FKEY, you will have to do so with ResEdit. Alternatively, you can maintain your FKEYs outside the System file using Suitcase.

INITs: To Use or Not To Use?

There are at least two schools of thought about using INITs. The "minimalist" approach suggests that you should use only those INITs that are absolutely necessary to make your system function. There are two advantages to this point of view. First, you avoid most INIT conflicts. Second, you don't use up megabytes of precious RAM loading INITs that are infrequently used. The drawback to this is that you aren't taking advantage of the added capabilities that INITs can bring to your computing environment.

The opposite of the minimalist approach is to use as many INITs as you want and can manage to load without running into conflicts. This gives you the most flexibility in configuring your system and can make working with your Macintosh easier and more fun. However, the more INITs you use, the more RAM that is consumed by system software. Every INIT you add also increases the possibility of an INIT conflict.

Regardless of which approach you take to choosing INITs, there are some that you *must* have. These include:

- The system enabler without which your system cannot function. As you will remember from Chapter 2, not all Macintoshes require system enablers; use only the enabler designed specifically for your Macintosh model.

- Device drivers for hardware such as scanners, CD-ROM players, tape drives, SyQuest drives, printers, and so on. Without these drivers, your Macintosh won't be able to interact with your hardware device.

- System extensions such as QuickTime that are required by application software. Without the system extensions, the application software that relies on them won't be able to run. Such extensions are usually included with the application programs that require them.

- System extensions that are required by the operating system. For example, many of the functions of System 7 Pro are provided as system extensions. Without them, you won't have access to System 7 Pro's capabilities.

- Other extensions that provide hardware support, such as Mode32, which enables 32-bit addressing for Macintoshes with 32-bit dirty ROMs.

LOADING INITS

By definition, an INIT loads during the system startup process. Most Macintosh users have multiple INITs, which load in a predetermined order. The default loading order is governed by the following rules:

- System enablers always load first.
- INITs load alphabetically within a folder.

- INITs in the Extensions folder load first, followed by Control Panels, and finally any INITs not nested within any folder in the System folder.

Why should you care about INIT loading order? As you will read shortly, some INITs can't coexist in RAM at the same time. Your system may crash or hang during startup. On some occasions, you can get around such conflicts by changing the order in which INITs load. In particular, place a character like a period or ~ in front of an INIT file name to make it fall last in the alphabetical sequence so that it will load last within its folder group. For example, Adobe Type Manager contains a ~ in front of its same so that it will always load last.

INIT Conflicts

As you have just read, not all INITs can coexist peacefully in RAM. An *INIT conflict* can manifest itself during startup as a crash or hang. It can also appear as a crash or hang when you attempt to access a control panel. In some cases, INIT conflicts can be responsible for random system problems. Adding to the problem is that there is no way to get information about where INITs are loaded in main memory. INIT conflicts therefore are often hard to diagnose.

USEFUL ADD-ON

Although you can't get a memory map of where your INITs have loaded, you can get a good handle on how much memory they are using with the shareware program Symbionts. Symbionts, which is included on the disk that comes with this book, installs in two parts, a control panel and a system extension. The file name of the system extension begins with the character ! so that it loads as early as possible.

As INITs are loaded, Symbionts displays the number of bytes used by each file. Once the startup process is finished, you can view a summary of what happened from the Symbionts control panel. Notice in Figure 8.3 that the Symbionts preferences screen indicates the total number of INITs loaded and the total amount of memory used.

Symbionts also keeps track of how much memory is occupied by each individual INIT. Figure 8.4, for example, shows system extensions in the order in which they were loaded. Notice that the sizes of Crash Barrier and Now ToolBox are unknown. This is because those two INITs load *before* Symbionts.

FIGURE 8.3
Viewing a summary of installed INITs

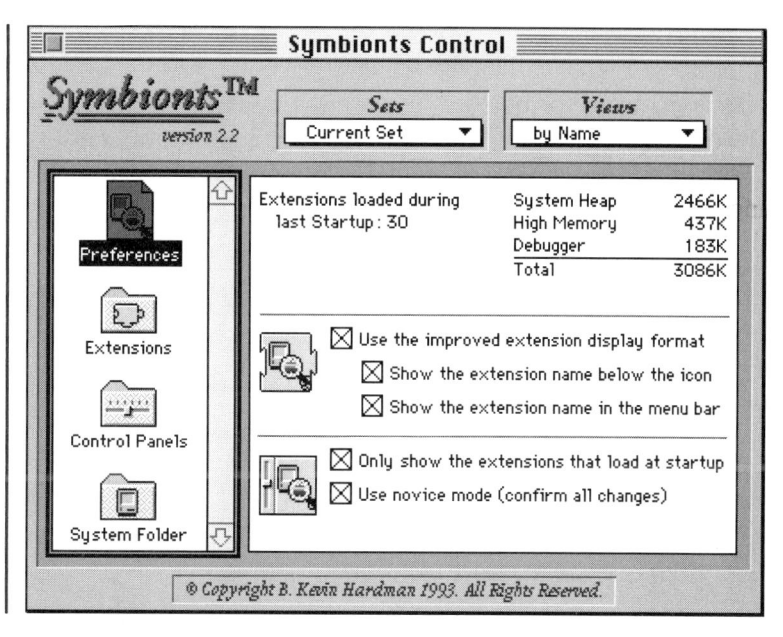

FIGURE 8.4
Looking at the memory occupied by specific INITs

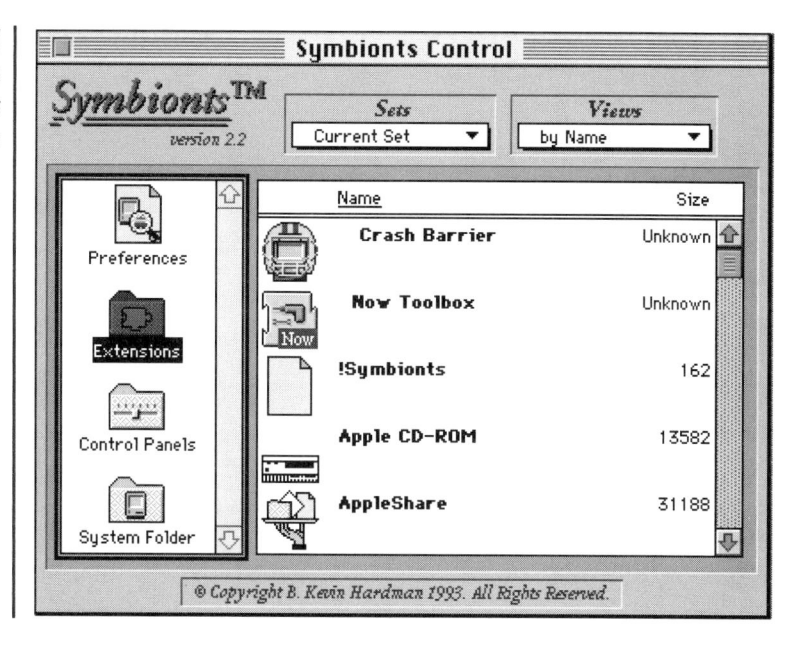

There are several ways to diagnose an INIT conflict and figure out which INIT is responsible for the problem. To be certain that you do have an INIT conflict, you can restart your computer with all INITs disabled. Hold down the **Shift** key when booting. (Enablers aren't affected because a Macintosh requiring an enabler won't boot without it.) Then repeat whatever actions resulted in a problem. If the problem doesn't recur, then you are almost certainly dealing with an INIT conflict. However, if the trouble happens again, then you should look for problems such as a corrupted System file, a damaged disk, or application program conflicts.

Once you are certain you are dealing with an INIT conflict, you need to figure out exactly which INIT is at fault. It can be done without utility programs with the following process:

1. Boot the Macintosh from a floppy disk. (Use a System 6 system disk, if you like; it will work for these purposes.)
2. Remove all INITs but one from the System folder on your hard disk. The removed INITs don't need to be deleted from the startup disk, but simply removed from the System folder.
3. Restart the Macintosh.
4. If no problem occurs, replace one more INIT into the System folder.
5. Repeat steps 2 and 3 until the problem recurs. The last INIT placed in the System folder is the culprit.

Once you've identified the problem INIT, you have several choices. The easiest is to simply stop using the culprit. If you must have the INIT, you can try changing the order in which it loads. Sometimes having it load last will solve the problem. If you must have the INIT and changing the load order doesn't work, call the manufacturer of the INIT to see if an upgrade is available.

The biggest problem with the preceding procedure for identifying a problem INIT is that it's time consuming and a royal pain. If you happen to have a lot of INITs, it can take a long time to replace them one by one, rebooting each time. To make matters worse, if you used a System 6 floppy to boot the machine at any point, returning to System 7 means that the Macintosh will rebuild the Desktop of any volumes modified under System 6. The solution is to use software that helps you manage your INITs. The rest of this section looks at several programs that do just that.

USING EXTENSIONS MANAGER

The disk that accompanies this book contains a copy of Extensions Manager, a freeware utility distributed by Apple. Extensions Manager can help you determine which INIT is responsible for an INIT conflict. It also lets you group INITs into "sets" and determine which sets will be loaded at system startup.

Extensions Manager groups INITs into two categories: enabled and disabled. Disabled INITs are placed in a folder named Disabled Extensions within the System folder. Anything inside the Disabled Extensions folder isn't loaded at system startup.

Installing Extensions Manager

To install Extensions Manager, drag its control panel and system extension to the System folder. Then restart your Macintosh. Once loaded, the Extensions Manager control panel (Figure 8.5) lists all INITs, grouped by type. Extensions appear first, followed by control panels, and finally the System folder.

FIGURE 8.5
The Extensions Manager control panel

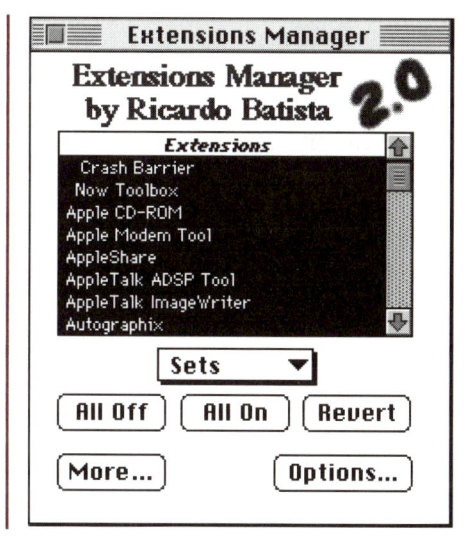

Disabling INITs

Extensions Manager helps you identify INIT conflicts by making it easier to enable and disable extensions. You can use Extensions Manager rather than dragging INITs into and out of the System folder.

To disable an INIT:

1. Open the Extensions Manager control panel.
2. Click on the name of the INIT you want to disable. When the name is unhighlighted, it is disabled.

Enabling INITs

To enable a previously disabled INIT:

1. Open the Extensions Manager control panel.

2. Click on the name of the INIT you want to enable. When the name is highlighted, it is enabled.

Using the Extensions Manager at System Startup

Extensions Manager can also solve the problem of a Macintosh that crashes during system startup because of an INIT conflict. The trick is therefore to have the Extensions Manager control panel available during system startup, before any INITs start to load. To gain access to the Extensions Manager control panel during startup, hold down the space bar as your Macintosh boots. After the control panel appears, enable or disable INITs as needed.

Extensions Manager Sets

A "set" is a collection of INITs that can be enabled or disabled as a whole. To create a set:

1. Open the Extensions Manager control panel.

2. Enable those INITs that you want in the set. Disable those INITs that you don't want in the set.

3. Choose **Save Set** from the Sets menu (Figure 8.6).

FIGURE 8.6
The Extensions Manager Sets menu

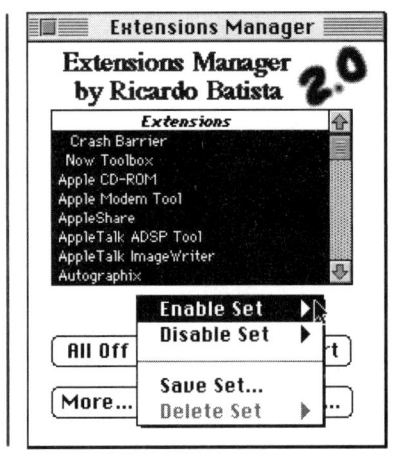

4. Enter a name for the set (Figure 8.7). Once the set has been named, its name appears in the Sets menu's Enable Set and Disable Set submenus.

FIGURE 8.7
Naming an Extensions Manager set

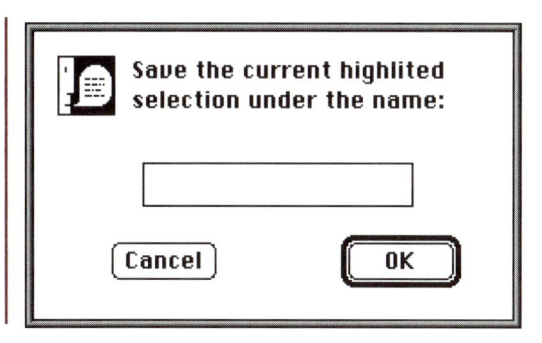

> Save the current highlited selection under the name:
>
> [Cancel]   [OK]

To enable a set, choose its name from the Enable Set submenu. To disable a set, choose its name from the Disable Set submenu. To delete a set, choose the set's name from the Delete Set. Note that deleting a set only removes the name given to a group of INITs along with the names of the INITs in the group; it doesn't affect the INIT files.

COMMERCIAL INIT MANAGERS

Commercial INIT managers provide a variety of features that can make it easier to identify INIT conflicts and handle the problem. Three of those are Startup Manager, Conflict Catcher, and INITPicker 3.

Startup Manager

The Startup Manager (Figure 8.8) is part of the Now Utilities package. INITs are enabled and disabled by clicking on their names in the Startup Manager control panel; disabled INITs are left in their original location. (There is no equivalent of the Extensions Managers Disabled Extensions folder). Startup Manager also supports sets of INITs that can be enabled or disabled as a whole.

If your Macintosh crashes or hangs during the startup process, Startup Manager disables the INIT that was loading when the crash or hang occurred. Reboot the computer by pressing the reset switch. When the boot process reaches the disabled INIT, the Startup Manager control panel appears, telling you what happened. At that point you can either re-enable the disabled INIT or continue starting up without it.

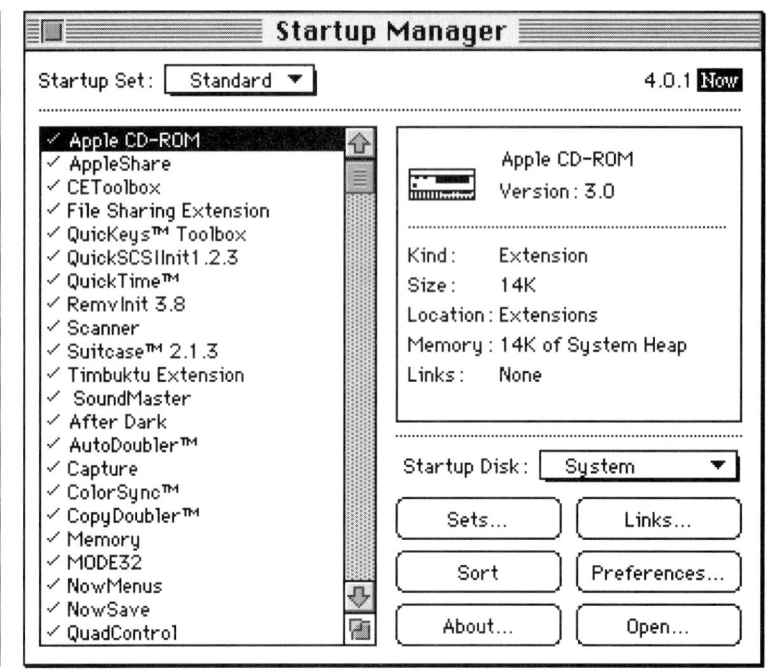

Figure 8.8
The Startup Manager control panel

Conflict Catcher

Conflict Catcher (Figure 8.9) is particularly handy for identifying the INITs responsible for INIT conflicts. When a crash or hang occurs during system startup, Conflict Catcher disables half your INITs. If a reboot doesn't present a problem, then the problem INIT is in the disabled INITs. Conflict Catcher disables all enabled INITs and enables half the disabled INITs. The process is repeated, always enabling half of the group of INITs that contain an INIT causing a problem, continuing until the single INIT responsible is isolated.

INITPicker 3

The technique of placing special characters in front of an INIT file's name works only within the INIT's folder. INITPicker 3 (Figure 8.10), however, gives you complete control over INIT loading order. To change the order, you simply drag the name of INIT to the position in the list where you want it to load. INITPicker 3 also provides disabling and enabling of INITs and grouping of INITs into sets.

CHAPTER 8: INIT Management

FIGURE 8.9
The Conflict Catcher control panel

FIGURE 8.10
The INITPicker 3 control panel

Choosing INITs

There are literally hundreds of INITs available. Which ones should you install? There is no one right answer. As you read earlier, you can adhere to the minimalist school of thought and only use those INITs that are absolutely necessary. Alternatively, you can be more adventurous and load your system with INITs.

To help get you started with choosing INITs, consider the lists that follow. These lists were assembled from an informal (and decidedly unscientific) poll of people who frequent the Macintosh Utilities forum on America Online. Each participant was asked for two lists, one of the INITs that he or she couldn't live without and others that were "nice but not essential." The recommendations printed here are therefore a compilation of what the America Online users suggested.

Keep in mind that there are some INITs about which you don't really have a choice whether to use. These include any system enablers your Macintosh might require, system extensions that are a part of the Macintosh operating system (for example, those used by System 7 Pro), Mode32 or the System 7 extension that enables 32-bit addressing on Macintoshes with 32-bit dirty ROMs, and any device drivers you need to access hardware. Beyond these, however, it's all up to you.

The following INITs (or categories of INITs) appeared on most people's "must have" lists:

- An INIT manager (for example, Extensions Manager)
- A virus checker
- A menu bar clock (for example, Reminder)
- QuicKeys
- SuperBoomerang
- Suitcase
- A utility to provide hierarchical menus

The following "nice to have" INITs appeared on most people's lists:

- A RAM disk
- A screen saver

- A utility for installing Desktop patterns
- A file and/or disk compression utility
- Adobe Type Manager

Considering all the INITs available, it's interesting that both these lists are relatively short. Choose and test your INITs carefully; don't be afraid to try an INIT for a while and later discard it if it conflicts with other software or if you find you aren't using it.

CHAPTER 9
Publish and Subscribe

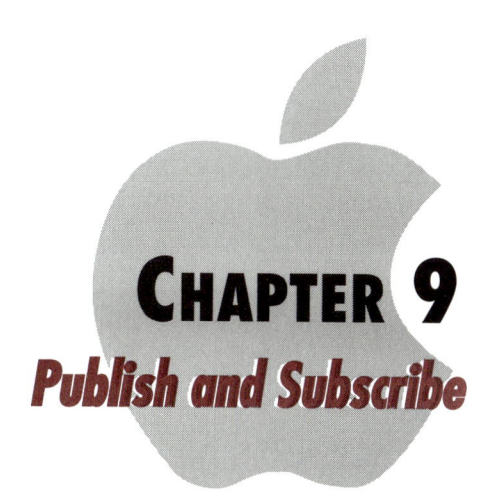

"Publish and subscribe" is a phrase used to describe a type of interapplication communication provided by the Macintosh operating system. Its purpose is to let you embed part of one document within another so that when the embedded section is updated in its original file, it is updated in the document in which it is embedded as well. This chapter looks at working with publish and subscribe to create "hot links" between your documents.

How Publish and Subscribe Works

The part of a document that you want to share with other documents is called an *edition*. It is written to disk in a file known as an *edition container*; each edition you create, even if you create multiple editions from the same document, resides in its own edition container (a separate file). Edition containers have icons like that in Figure 9.1.

FIGURE 9.1
An edition container icon

An edition is created by *publishing* it; when you use a published edition in another document, you *subscribe* to that edition. Not every Macintosh program can publish and/or subscribe to editions; the application must be written specifically to do so. However, as application programs are updated, more and more are capable of supporting this unique feature of System 7.

> **BY THE WAY!** Publish and subscribe is provided by a special part of the Macintosh operating system known as the Edition Manager. Because the Edition Manager must open and close documents, it must be able to recognize and respond to Apple Events. You will find more about Apple Events in Chapter 11.

Publishing Parts of a Document

To publish all or part of a document for embedding in another document, do the following:

1. Make sure that the application programs you are planning to use support publish and subscribe. (You can tell by looking in the Edit menu for the options **Create Publisher**, **Publisher Options**, and **Subscribe To**.)
2. Select the portion of the document you want to publish.
3. Choose **Create Publisher** from the Edit menu. The Create Publisher dialog box appears (Figure 9.2). Notice that it has a thumbnail preview of the edition at its left but otherwise looks much like a Save File dialog box.
4. Choose the location in which the edition container should be stored.
5. Enter a name for the edition container. (Use any name you want, but like file names, edition names that give clues to their contents and purpose are extremely useful.)
6. Click the **Publish** button or press **Enter**.

At this point, the edition is surrounded by a gray border in its document (see Figure 9.3). However, the edition container hasn't been saved. In most cases, edition files are updated when you save the document containing the edition. If you don't save the document, the edition isn't saved either.

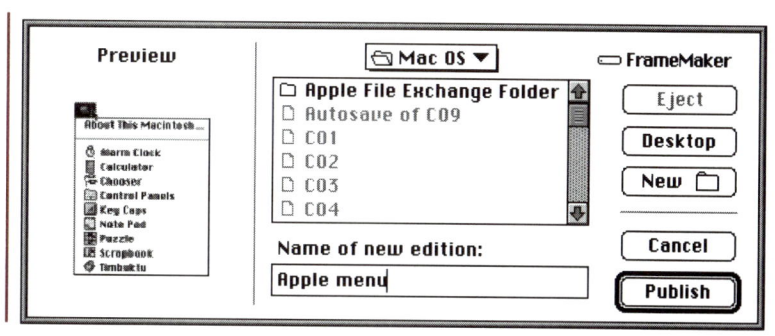

CHAPTER 9: Publish and Subscribe   **213**

FIGURE 9.2
Publishing a portion of a document

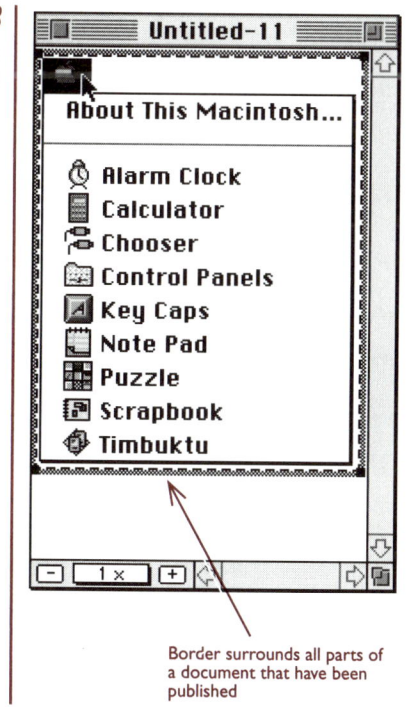

FIGURE 9.3
A published edition in its original document

Border surrounds all parts of a document that have been published

Most programs give you choices about when editions are updated. To gain access to those options, choose **Publisher Options** from the Edit menu. As you can see in Figure 9.4, you can either save editions automatically when the source document is saved or save them manually. If you choose to save an edition manually, you can use the **Send Edition Now** button to write the edition to disk. Notice that you can also use the Publisher Options dialog box to cancel an edition.

FIGURE 9.4
Publisher options

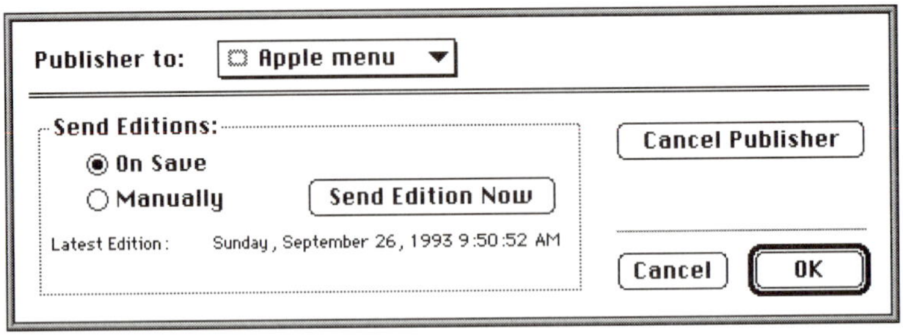

SUBSCRIBING TO PUBLISHED EDITIONS

Subscribing to an edition means that you are creating a link between the edition stored on disk and the document that subscribes to it. The edition is copied into the subscribing document. However, whenever the Macintosh operating system detects that the edition contained has been modified, any documents subscribing to that edition will be updated to reflect the changes as well.

To subscribe to an edition:

1. Make certain that the application you are using supports publish and subscribe.
2. Open the document that will be subscribing to the edition.
3. Move the insertion point to the location in the document where the edition should appear.
4. Choose **Subscribe To** from the Edit menu. The Subscribe To dialog box appears (Figure 9.5).

FIGURE 9.5
Subscribing to a published edition

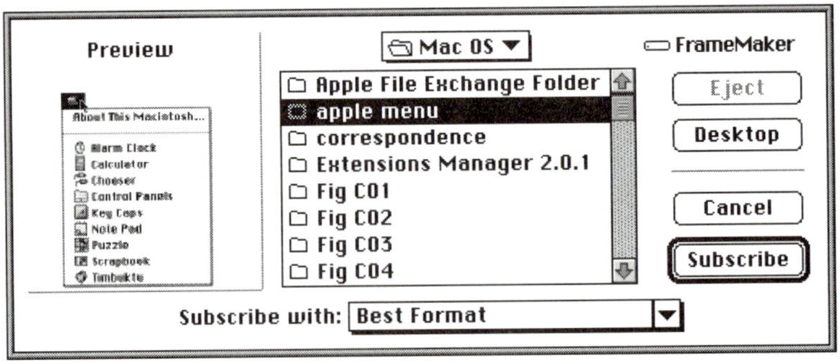

5. Highlight the name of an edition container. A preview of that edition appears at the left of the dialog box. Notice that other than the preview, the Subscribe To dialog box is very much like an Open File dialog box.

6. Click the **Subscribe** button or press **Enter**. The edition appears in the document at the current insertion point.

Like editions in their source documents, editions to which you subscribe are surrounded by a gray border (see Figure 9.6). The link to the edition is saved when you save the subscribing document.

FIGURE 9.6
A document with an edition to which it has subscribed

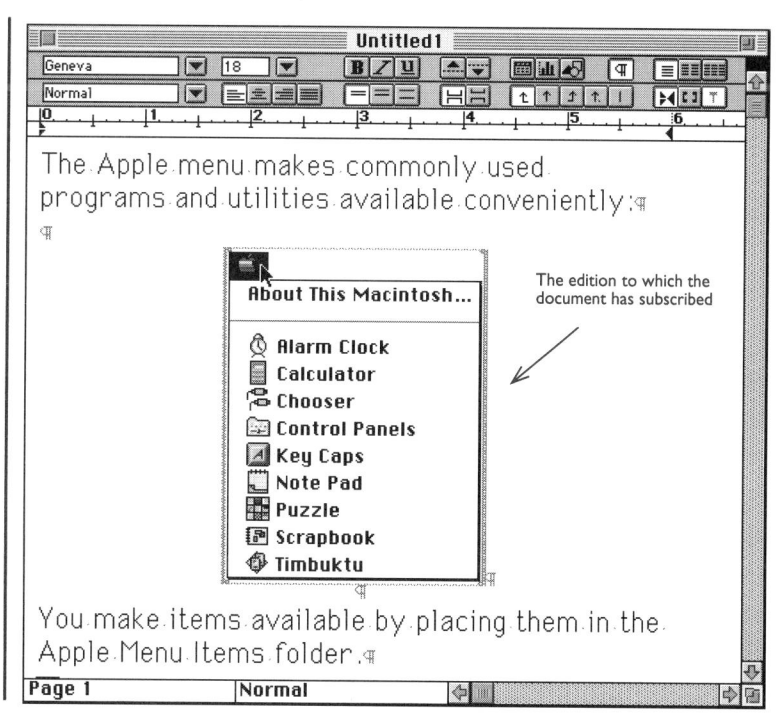

By default, editions are updated when you open a document. The Macintosh operating system looks for those edition containers that have been modified since you last worked with the subscribing document and replaces the previously saved version of the edition with the more recent version. You can gain additional control over the edition updating process through the Subscriber Options dialog box (Figure 9.7).

FIGURE 9.7
The Subscriber Options dialog box

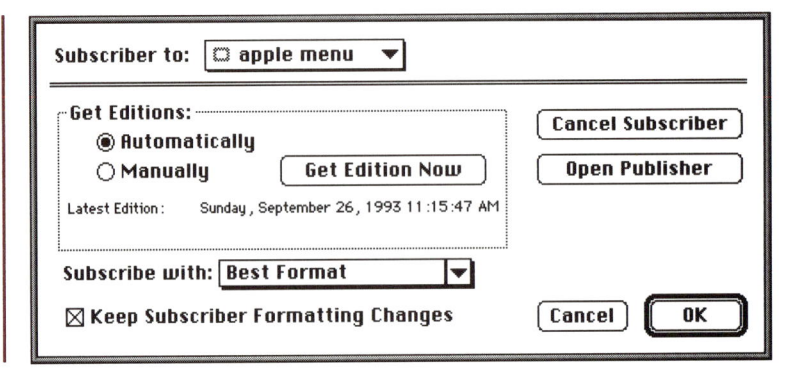

Selecting the **Manually** button in the Get Editions box means that automatic updating won't occur. Instead, use the **Get Edition Now** button to force the Macintosh operating system to read the contents of an edition container. Notice also that the Subscriber Options dialog box contains an **Open Publisher** button. This button opens the source document for an edition so that you can work on it.

Handling Subscriber/Edition Links

The links between a subscriber and editions are hard links based on the edition container's path name, just like the links between aliases and their original files. If you move or rename an edition container, any documents that subscribe to it won't be able to find the file.

Because editions are actually copied into subscribing documents, a missing edition file won't cause you to lose the edition entirely. However, it will no longer be updated. How can you tell if an edition is missing? Look in the Subscriber Options dialog box. As you can see in Figure 9.8, the name of the edition is grayed out in the Subscriber To menu. The Get Editions box also indicates that the edition file can't be found.

FIGURE 9.8
The Subscriber Options dialog box for a missing edition

CHAPTER 9: Publish and Subscribe   **217**

HANDLING EDITION CONTAINERS

An edition container is a bit different from other files on disk. If you double-click on its icon, you will see a preview of the contents of the edition (see Figure 9.9). Click on the **Open Publisher** button to work with the edition's source document. If the application that created the source document is already running, the Macintosh operating system simply opens the source document. Otherwise, it launches the application and opens the source document.

FIGURE 9.9
Working with an edition container

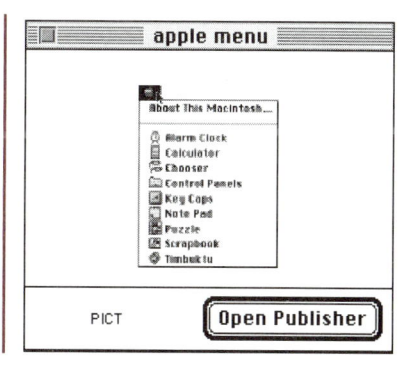

CHAPTER 10
Networks and File Sharing

The Macintosh's networking capabilities made their debut with the Macintosh Plus, the first Macintosh model to provide *AppleTalk*. As network use has grown, the Macintosh has expanded to not only support a variety of network media, but to provide additional networking capabilities through its operating system. This chapter begins by looking at the types of networks supported by the Macintosh and then at the networking features provided by System 7. It concludes by discussing several techniques for sharing files with MS DOS computers.

> **BY THE WAY!** Many of the concepts presented in this chapter are fundamental to working with PowerTalk, the electronic document transfer capabilities added to the Macintosh operating system by System 7 Pro.

MACINTOSH-FRIENDLY NETWORKS

Although the Macintosh can be used on many types of local area network media, using it with either *LocalTalk* or *Ethernet* is the easiest because the Macintosh hardware and software provides significant support for both platforms. To give you a foundation for System 7's networking features, this section covers some Macintosh network basics.

> **BY THE WAY!** The Macintosh operating system does provide extensions for *Token Ring* networks, the network used by many MS DOS computers. However, at this time less than 5% of Macintoshes are connected to Token Ring networks.

Hardware versus Software

Any type of computer network requires the cooperation of hardware and software. Network hardware must do the following:

- Provide a connection between the Macintosh and the network.
- Provide a medium over which data can travel between the devices on the network. (Keep in mind that a computer network includes devices such as printers and modems as well as computers.)

The software must run on top of whatever hardware is available. Its tasks include:

- Accepting data from the computer and transforming it into a form that can travel on the network.
- Managing access to the network media.
- Accepting data sent to the computer from another device on the network and translating it into a form the computer can understand.

Network software accomplishes its tasks by following a series of *protocols*. A network protocol is a set of rules that governs procedures for access to and data transfer over a network. Once a protocol has been made public and accepted as a standard for a given type of network, any software that adheres to that protocol will be compatible with other hardware and software that uses the same protocol.

AppleTalk is a set of software protocols. The networking features of System 7 are based on them. However, the AppleTalk protocols can run over several types of hardware, including LocalTalk, PhoneNet, and Ethernet.

AppleTalk Network Configuration

Macintosh networking is based on a *bus* configuration. As you can see in Figure 10.1, the bus itself is a straight line, open at either end, to which all devices are connected. Each device is connected to the bus through an interface box. The easiest (and cheapest) way to set up an AppleTalk network is to use either a *LocalTalk* connector or a *PhoneNet* connector (see Figure 10.2). The difference between the two lies in the type of cable they use.

FIGURE 10.1
An AppleTalk bus network

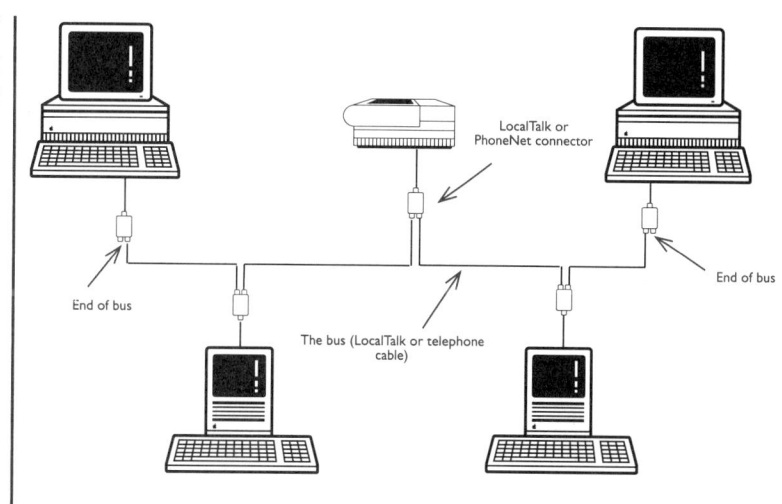

FIGURE 10.2
A PhoneNet connector (Photo courtesy Farallon Corp; Scott Peterson, photographer)

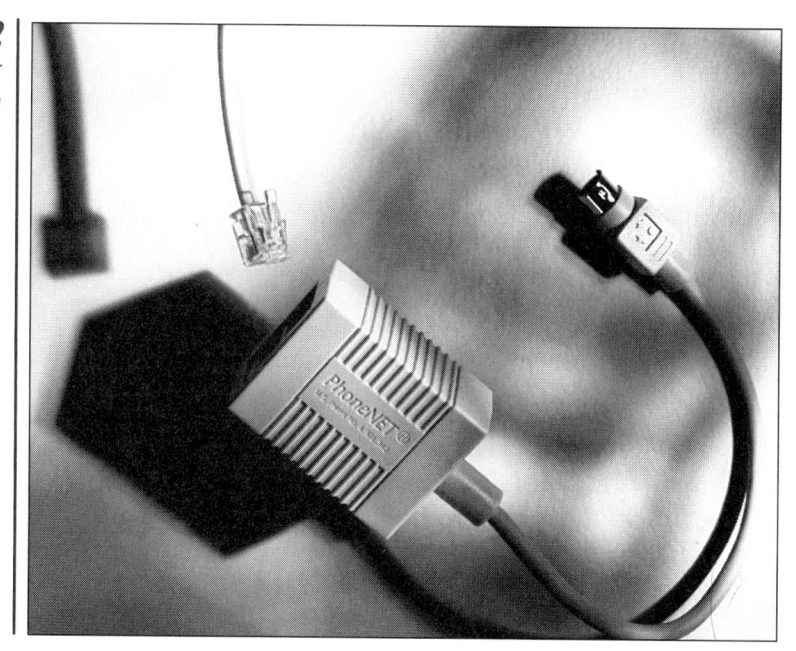

LocalTalk uses proprietary cabling. PhoneNet, on the other hand, uses standard telephone wire. Notice in Figure 10.2, for example, that the telephone cable has the typical RJ 11 jack used to connect telephones, modems, and fax machines to the telephone system. Although PhoneNet can't *share* wiring with a telephone, a network based on PhoneNet cabling can take advantage of *unused* telephone wiring already in a building. It is also possible to mix PhoneNet and LocalTalk connectors in the same network by using a cable that has an RJ 11 jack on one end and a LocalTalk jack on the other.

> **BY THE WAY!** The PhoneNet alternative to LocalTalk was developed by Farallon Corp. However, today other manufacturers also produce connectors that are compatible with the PhoneNet standard.

The software to transfer data from a Macintosh to an AppleTalk network and to receive data from the network is built into the Macintosh ROM. The LocalTalk or PhoneNet connector takes care of making sure the network is available and transferring data over the network.

ETHERNET NETWORK CONFIGURATIONS

Running over LocalTalk or PhoneNet cabling, AppleTalk is relatively slow. Its maximum speed is around 256,000 bits per second (256Kbps). For a network of more than a few devices, that is just too slow. Larger networks are therefore commonly based on Ethernet., which provides speed of up to 10 million bits per second (10Mbps). In most cases, the AppleTalk protocols run over Ethernet hardware and cabling, using system software extensions known as EtherTalk.

Ethernet hardware is built into some Centris and Quadra Macintoshes. It can be added to other Macintoshes either through an expansion board (for example, Figure 10.3) or through an external SCSI device.

Ethernet uses one of three types of cabling. *Thin* Ethernet uses the type of coaxial cable used with cable television; it connects to the computer with the same F-connector. *Thick* Ethernet uses a heavier coaxial cable with a nine-pin connector. For example, the top connector in Figure 10.3 is for thick Ethernet cabling.

FIGURE 10.3
An Ethernet expansion board (Photo courtesy of Farallon Corp.; Kim Harrington, photographer)

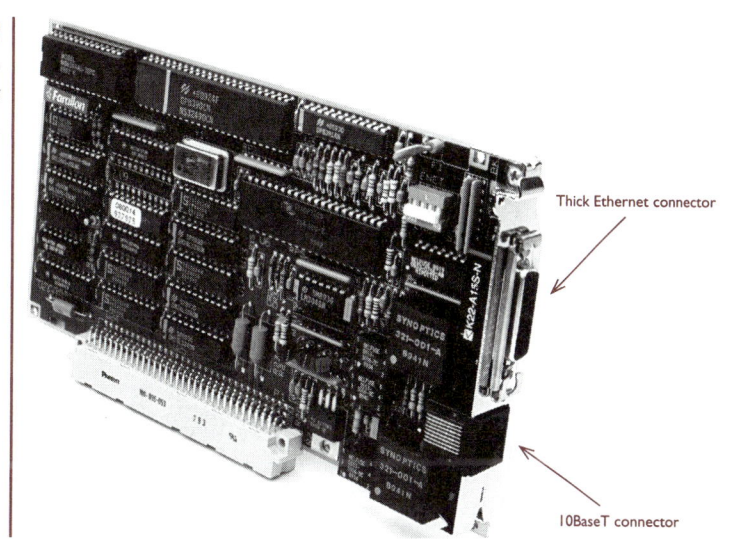

Thick Ethernet connector

10BaseT connector

The third type of cabling, *10 BaseT*, uses what appears to be a telephone jack (the bottom connector in Figure 10.3). However, it is larger than a standard RJ 11 jack and uses heavier wire than standard telephone wire. A 10 BaseT network also requires a different type of network architecture—a *star*. As you can see in Figure 10.4, the center of the star is a *hub* or *star controller*. Rather than traveling along a bus, messages are passed to the hub and from there transmitted to the receiver.

FIGURE 10.4
A star configuration for a 10 BaseT Ethernet network

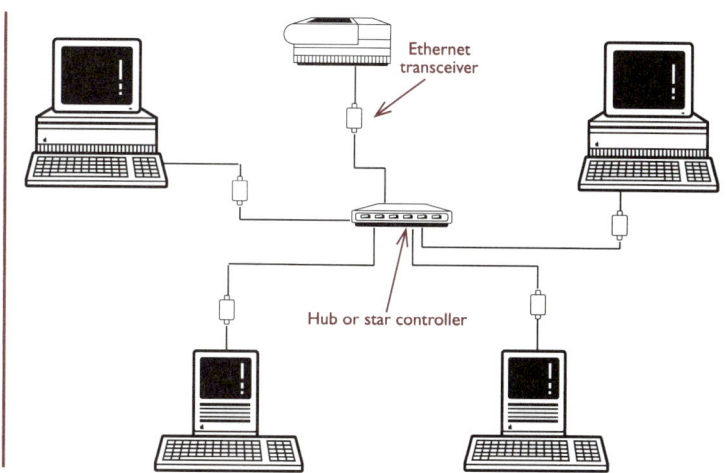

Ethernet transceiver

Hub or star controller

Regardless of the type of cabling you use for an Ethernet network, the computer is connected to the network with a *transceiver* (Figure 10.5). The transceiver manages access to the network, passing messages between the network and the Ethernet hardware in the computer. You can think of a transceiver as performing functions similar to those of a LocalTalk or PhoneNet connector.

FIGURE 10.5
An Ethernet transceiver (Photo courtesy of Farallon Corp.; Scott Peterson, photographer)

BY THE WAY! Networking is one of the fastest changing areas within computing; there is an exception to every rule. For example, Farallon has just announced hardware (EtherWave) that connects 10BaseT Ethernet in a bus rather than a star.

CONNECTING NETWORKS: ZONES

An AppleTalk network is limited to 32 devices. As you might guess, performance degrades to unacceptable levels long before you have that many pieces of hardware connected. The solution to the problem is to break the network into *zones* with fewer devices. The zones can be connected together through either a *bridge* or a *router*. Bridges and routers can also be used to connect LocalTalk zones to Ethernet zones, creating mixed networks. As you will see later in this chapter, the Macintosh operating system makes it easy to access data stored in any zone on your network.

> **BY THE WAY!** At one time there was a distinct difference between a bridge and a router. However, many of today's bridges have capabilities formerly only found in routers, making it increasingly hard to distinguish between them.

The zones in an AppleTalk network have names. Assuming that you are sitting at your Macintosh, you can refer to the zone to which your Macintosh is connected (your "local" zone) with an asterisk (*). If your network has only one zone (in other words, all hardware is connected to the same network without the intervention of a bridge or a router), then its name is always *. However, if your Macintosh is part of a network with more than one zone, then your local zone has a name by which it is known to users whose Macintoshes are connected to other zones.

As an example, consider the network in Figure 10.6. This network has three zones connected by a single router. The router accepts a message addressed to a server, Macintosh, or printer in a zone other than the zone in which the message originated. The router then checks the address of the message and then sends it on to the zone where the recipient is located.

FIGURE 10.6
An AppleTalk network with three zones

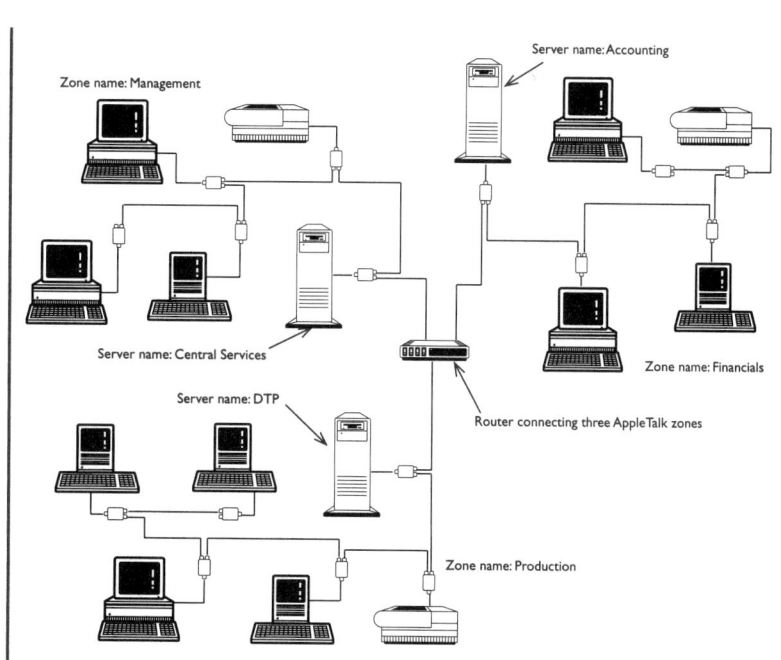

Assume that your Macintosh in located in the zone named Production and that you have given your computer the network name ExpertDTP. A user in one of the other zones can send your Macintosh a message or share files on your Macintosh by first selecting the zone in which your computer is located and then selecting your computer by name. In most cases, this is done through the Chooser. You may also use special electronic mail software (for example, PowerTalk, System 7 Pro's electronic document transfer facility) that lets you indicate the zone in which the recipient of a message is located.

Notice in Figure 10.6 that the server in each zone has a name. This becomes important when you want to access data stored on an AppleShare server or use a PowerShare to send electronic mail and documents. Mounting volumes from an AppleShare server is discussed later in this chapter; PowerShare is discussed in Chapter 11.

SYSTEM 7 NETWORKING CAPABILITIES

There are two types of networking that you are likely to run into when using a Macintosh: *client/server* and *peer-to-peer*. Client/server networking means that one or more computers (most commonly, but not necessarily, Macintoshes) have been designated as repositories for programs and files that are available for sharing over the network. Network users (*clients*) log onto a *server* to use the programs and files to which they have been given access rights. The software that provides client/server networking is called *AppleShare*. The client portion of AppleShare is part of the Macintosh operating system. However, the part that maintains the server is not; it must be purchased separately.

Peer-to-peer networking views all Macintoshes on a network as equals; there are no permanent servers and no permanent clients. Instead, a Macintosh can function as a client by mounting a disk volume belonging to another Macintosh on the network. The mounted volume, which appears on the Desktop as in Figure 10.7, can then be used just like any other mounted volume. The same Macintosh can function as a server by letting another Macintosh mount one of its volumes. In fact, a single Macintosh can act as a client and a server at the same time.

Client/server networking using an AppleShare server is set up by a network administrator. The administrator will give you a user name and password for logging on to each server to which you have access. You will see how to log on later in this chapter.

FIGURE 10.7
A remote volume mounted on a Desktop using peer-to-peer neworking

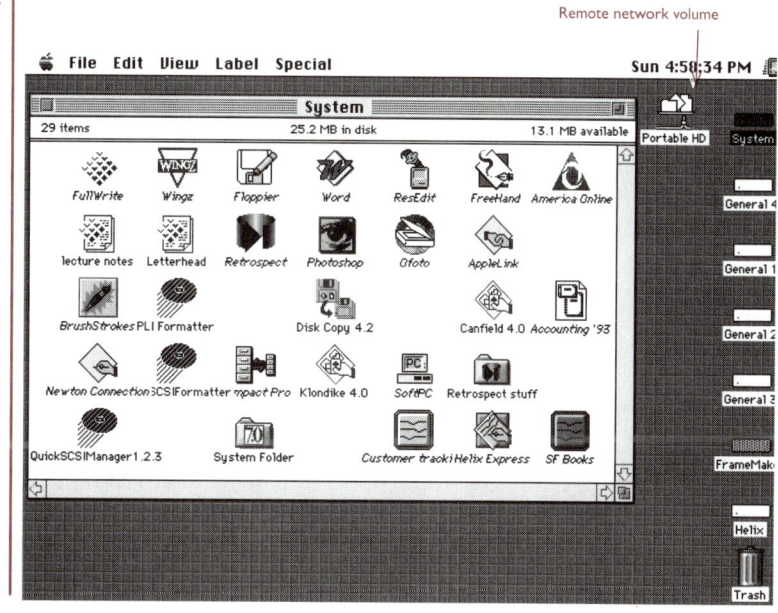

Peer-to-peer network capabilities are built into the Macintosh operating system via AppleShare. As you will see in the next section of this chapter, you can control who has access to your Macintosh and which volumes, or parts of volumes, can be shared over the network. Because System 7 networking essentially involves sharing files, it is often simply called "file sharing."

PREPARING A MACINTOSH FOR FILE SHARING

As the "owner" of your computer, you have control over who has access to which files on your disk volumes. You also have control over what others can do with those files. Gaining that control means that you must do some preparation before your disks can be shared.

NAMING THE MACINTOSH

The first step in preparing your Macintosh for file sharing is to give it a "network identity." To do this:

1. Open the Sharing Setup control panel (Figure 10.8).

FIGURE 10.8
The Sharing Setup control panel

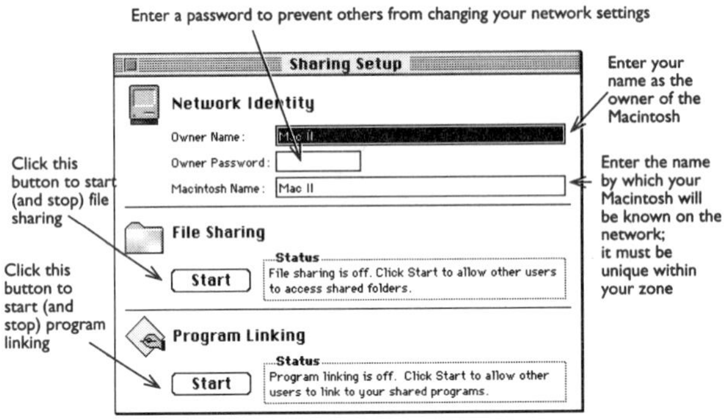

2. Enter your name, or the name by which you as person want to be known on the network, in the "Owner Name" box.

3. Enter a password in the "Owner Password" box. This password will let you access your Macintosh from a remote location and give you all access rights associated with being the owner.

4. Enter the name by which your Macintosh will be known on the network in the "Macintosh Name" box.

TURNING ON FILE SHARING

The second step is to enable file sharing on your Macintosh. This makes your Macintosh eligible for file sharing, but it does not give anyone access to your disk volumes; you must do that separately.

To turn on file sharing:

1. Open the Sharing Setup control panel.

2. Click the **Start** button in the center section of the control panel (see Figure 10.8). The **Start** button turns into a **Cancel** button. Use this button to abort sharing startup.

File sharing starts up as soon as you click the **Start** button. However, the more disk volumes that have been made sharable, the longer it will take. You can tell that the sharing startup process has finished when the **Cancel** button changes to **Stop**. Nonetheless, you don't need to leave the Sharing Setup control panel open until that point. File sharing startup will continue in the background even if the control panel is closed.

> **BY THE WAY!**
>
> There's technically no reason that you can't turn on file sharing and leave it turned on. However, if you leave it on, file sharing starts up each time you boot your Macintosh, which can significantly lengthen the startup process. If you aren't going to be sharing files every time you use your Mac, consider turning off file sharing before you shut down and turning it on only when you know you are going to need it.

CREATING USERS AND USER GROUPS

The access that you allow to your Macintosh's disk volumes can be tailored to specific users and groups of users. To set up users, do the following:

1. Open the Users & Groups control panel. Notice that instead of the usual control panel window, you see a folder window (Figure 10.9). By default, there are two icons in the window. The icon with the dark border (Mac II in Figure 10.9) represents the owner of the Macintosh; its name is taken from whatever was entered as the owner in the Sharing Setup control panel. The second icon is named <Guest>, representing all users who haven't been specifically allowed to sign on the computer.

FIGURE 10.9
The Users & Groups control panel window

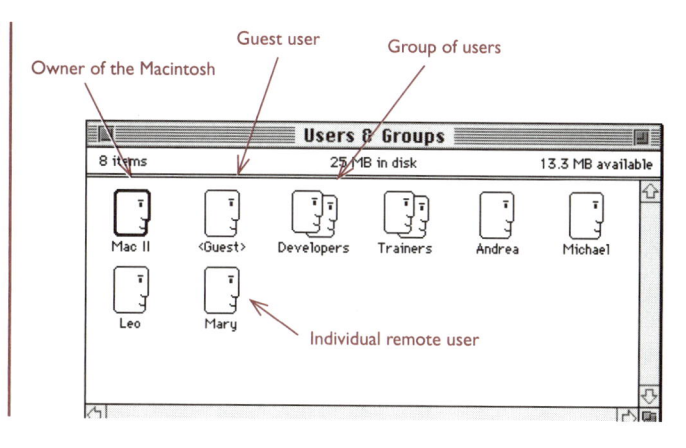

2. Create a user icon for each user who will be allowed to share files on your Macintosh. To do so:

   a. Press ⌘-N or choose **New User** from the File menu (see Figure 10.10). (The **New User** and **New Group** options are available only when the Users & Groups control panel is open and its window is the current window.)

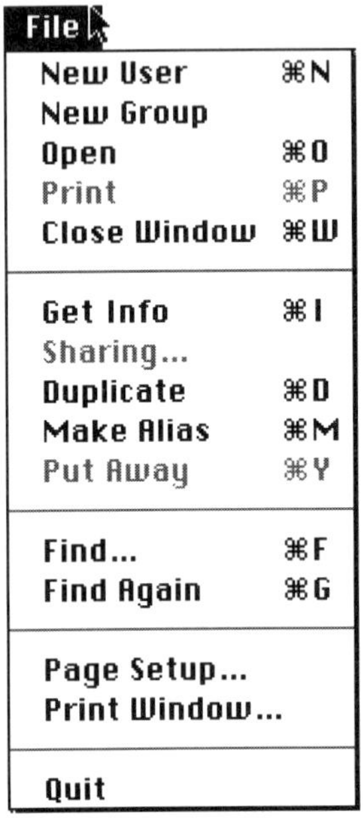

FIGURE 10.10
The Finder's File menu when the Users & Groups control panel window is open

```
File
New User       ⌘N
New Group
Open           ⌘O
Print          ⌘P
Close Window   ⌘W

Get Info       ⌘I
Sharing…
Duplicate      ⌘D
Make Alias     ⌘M
Put Away       ⌘Y

Find…          ⌘F
Find Again     ⌘G

Page Setup…
Print Window…

Quit
```

   b. Give the user icon a name. Make sure that the person who will be using this user name also knows the user icon's name.

   c. Double-click on the user icon to open its window (Figure 10.11). Enter a password for the user. Click the **"Allow user to connect"** check box to allow the user to sign on to your Macintosh. Click the **"Allow user to change password"** icon to allow the user to change his or her own password. If this box is not checked, the only way to change the password is for the owner of the Macintosh to return to the user icon window.

3. Create group icons for groups of users that will have the same access rights. (This can make it simpler to assign access rights to many people.) To create a new group and assign users to it:

FIGURE 10.11
Configuring access for a remote user

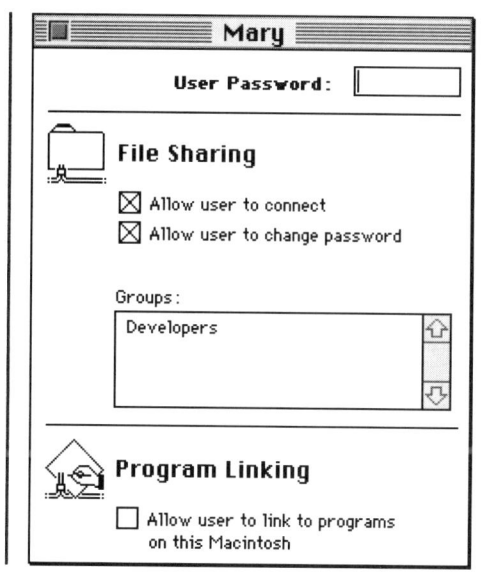

a. With the Users & Groups control panel open and active, choose **New Group** from the File menu. A group icon appears.

b. Give the icon a name.

c. To add a user to a group, drag the user icon to the group icon. Notice that the user icon doesn't disappear into the group icon as it would if you were transferring a file or folder into a folder. Instead, you a message saying "Transferring user UserName into group GroupName." Nonetheless, if you double-click on the group icon window, you will see that each user icon now exists within the group (for example, see Figure 10.12).

FIGURE 10.12
A group window

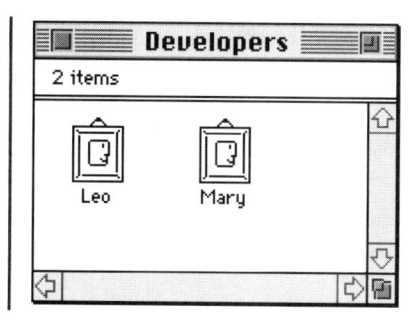

User and group icons are different from most other icons. User icons can only be dragged to group icons and to the trash to delete them. Deleting a user also deletes it from any groups to which it belonged. Group icons can only be dragged to the trash to delete them.

> **BY THE WAY!** If you remove a user icon from the trash and return it to the Users & Groups window, it will also be returned to any groups to which it belonged.

Setting Volume Permissions

As you read earlier, turning on file sharing doesn't provide access to specific disk volumes; you must grant such access specifically, volume by volume, to users and groups. There are three levels of access you can give a user and/or a group. You can allow a remote user to see the folders on a volume, to see the files on a volume, or to make changes to the contents of a volume.

Although at first it might not seem logical, it is possible to give a user the right to make changes to a volume without giving the user the right to see the files or folders on that volume. When you do that, you create the equivalent of a drop box, a place to which someone can copy or save files but not find out what other files or folders are on the volume.

To grant access rights:

1. Select the disk volume for which you want to enable file sharing.
2. Choose **Sharing** from the Finder's File menu. A Sharing window for the selected volume appears (for example, Figure 10.13).
3. Click the **"Share this item and its contents"** box to share the volume.
4. Use the Owner pop-up menu to choose the user icon that should be considered the owner of this volume. By default, the owner of the volume is the owner of the Macintosh that appears in the Sharing Setup control panel. Click the check boxes that correspond to the rights the owner should have.

Figure 10.13
Configuring remote access for a disk volume

5. Choose a user or group name from the User/Group pop-up menu. Click the check boxes that correspond to the rights the user or group should have.

6. Repeat step 5 for each user or group that should have rights to access this volume.

7. Click the check boxes in the "Everyone" row to indicate the rights that everyone else, including the <Guest> user, should have. (In most cases, the <Guest> user will have very limited rights.)

8. Close the Sharing window. The Macintosh asks if you want to save the changes. Click the **Save** button or press **Enter** to do so.

> **BY THE WAY!** You *can* share read-only volumes such as CD-ROMs. Set their access rights just as you would any other disk.

ACCESSING REMOTE VOLUMES

Accessing a remote volume is a somewhat involved process (lots of steps). Before beginning, be sure you know your user name and password for the remote Macintosh whose disk volume you are going to mount.

234 NAVIGATING SYSTEM 7: Understanding The Macintosh Operating System

MOUNTING REMOTE VOLUMES

To mount a remote volume on your Desktop, do the following:

1. Select **Chooser** from the menu to display the Chooser window.
2. Click on the AppleShare icon. A list of Macintoshes in the current zone for which file sharing has been turned on appears at the right of the window (see Figure 10.14). If your Macintosh has multiple zones and the Macintosh whose disk you want to mount is not in the same zone as your Macintosh, select the zone from the list of zones at the lower left of the Chooser window (see Figure 10.15).

FIGURE 10.14
Using the Chooser to begin mounting a remote volume on a network with one AppleTalk zone

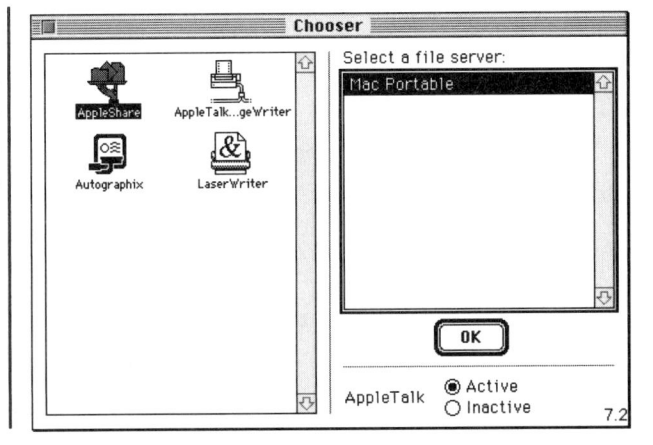

FIGURE 10.15
Using the Chooser to begin mounting a remote volume on a network with multiple AppleTalk zones (Courtesy Apple Computer, Inc.; copyright Apple Computer, Inc., 1993)

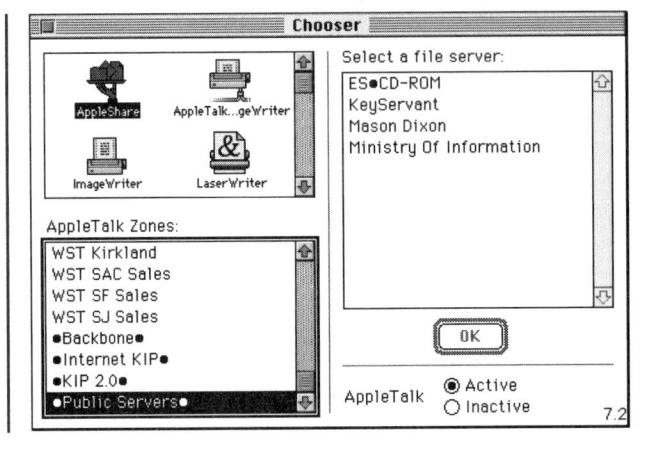

CHAPTER 10: Networks and File Sharing   **235**

> **BY THE WAY!** The Chooser lists all servers it can find on your network. The list in Figure 10.15, for example, contains the names of AppleShare servers as well as Macintoshes that are available for peer-to-peer file sharing.

3. Double-click on the name of the Macintosh whose volume you want to mount. A log-on dialog box appears (Figure 10.16).

FIGURE 10.16
Logging onto a remote Macintosh

4. If you have the right to change your password and you wish to do so, click the **Set Password** button. In the password dialog box (Figure 10.17), enter both your existing password and a new password. Click the **OK** button or press **Enter**.

FIGURE 10.17
Changing the password for user icon on a remote Macintosh

5. Click the **Guest** radio button if you are logging on as a guest. Otherwise, type your user name in the Name box; enter your password in the Password box.

236 NAVIGATING SYSTEM 7: Understanding The Macintosh Operating System

6. Click the **OK** button or press **Enter**. If your user name and password aren't recognized, you'll see the warning in Figure 10.18. If your user name and password are recognized, a dialog box listing volumes to which you have access on the remote Macintosh appears (Figure 10.19).

FIGURE 10.18
A failed remote log-on attempt

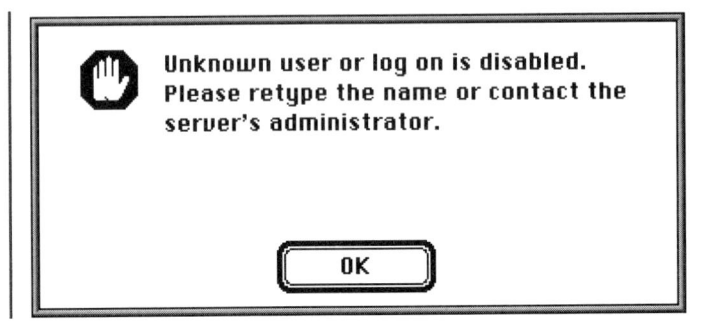

> Unknown user or log on is disabled. Please retype the name or contact the server's administrator.
>
> [OK]

FIGURE 10.19
Choosing a remote volume to mount

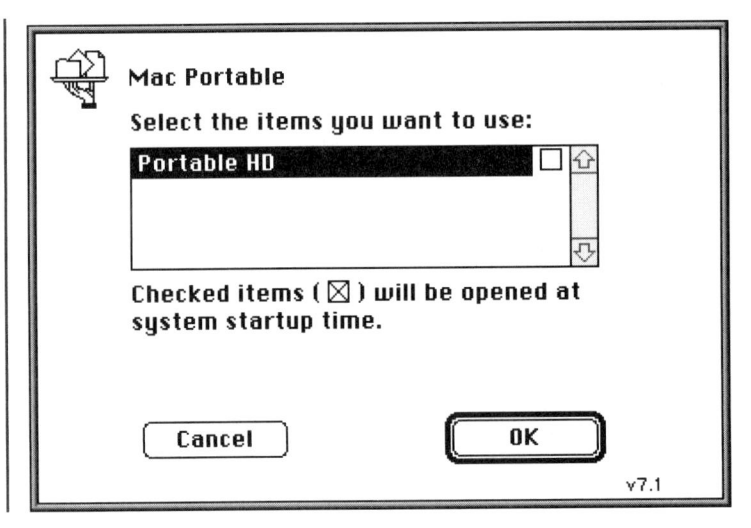

> Mac Portable
>
> Select the items you want to use:
>
> Portable HD
>
> Checked items (☒) will be opened at system startup time.
>
> [Cancel]   [OK]
>
> v7.1

BY THE WAY!

If you click the check box at the right of remote volume names, the Macintosh operating system will attempt to mount the checked volume(s) when you start up your system. Of course, this will fail if the remote volume isn't available when you boot your Mac.

---

7. Click on the name of the first volume you want to mount. Shift-click to select additional items.

8. Click **OK** or press **Enter**. The Macintosh operating system mounts the remote volume or volumes on your desktop, just as in Figure 10.7.

9. Return to the Chooser window. Click the icon for the printer you will be using. This will let you print while you are using remote volumes.

10. Close the Chooser window and begin using your remote volumes.

UNMOUNTING REMOTE VOLUMES

To unmount a remote volume, simply drag its icon to the trash. The unmount will fail, however, if the remote volume is the current volume for opening or saving files in any running application, even if you don't have any files on that volume open. This occurs when the last file or folder you saved or opened using any running application is on the remote volume. To get around this problem, you can:

- Quit the application that was using files stored on the remote volume.
- Choose **Save As** from the File menu and make a local volume (a volume on your Macintosh) the current volume.
- Choose **Open** from the File menu and make a local volume the current volume.

Depending on the application, you may need to actually save and/or open something to get the volume change to "stick."

> **BY THE WAY!** You can mount up to 10 remote volumes. Only 10 other users can mount any of your shared volumes.

PROGRAM LINKING

Program linking is a form of interapplication communication that is still not widely used. Programs that support Apple Events can be configured to allow other programs to link to them across a network to share data. Program linking is available only if *both* programs support Apple Events. To find out if a program can participate in linking, you must first enable program linking.

Turning on Program Linking

To allow others to link to your programs across a network, do the following:

1. Open the Sharing Setup control panel.

2. Click the **Start** button in the Program Linking section (see Figure 10.8). Linking starts up almost immediately. The **Start** button turns into a **Stop** button.

Like starting up file sharing, starting up program linking doesn't make linking available for any specific user, group, and/or file; it only provides the capability on your system. You must explicitly indicate which users, groups, and/or files can participate in linking.

Enabling Linking for an Application

Once you have turned on linking, you can identify which applications support linking and, if you want, allow linking to those applications. To find out whether a program can be linked and to enable linking:

1. Highlight the program's icon in a Finder window. (Don't use an alias—it won't work. You must use the original.)

2. Choose **Sharing** from the Finder's File menu. A Sharing dialog box appears. If linking is available, the box appears as in Figure 10.20. If linking is not available, the box appears as in Figure 10.21; notice that "Allow remote program linking" is dimmed.

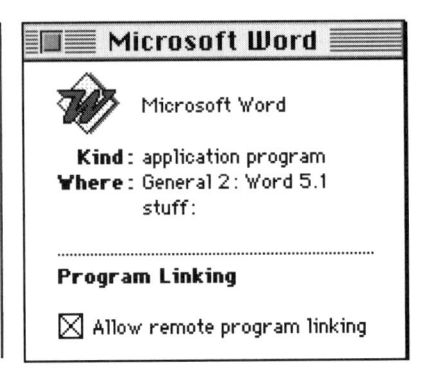

FIGURE 10.20
The Sharing dialog box for a program that supports linking

FIGURE 10.21
The Sharing dialog box for a program that doesn't support linking

3. To enable linking for an application that supports it, click the **"Allow remote program linking"** check box and close the Sharing dialog box.

ENABLING USERS TO LINK

The final step in permitting linking is to add linking permissions for users. To do so:

1. Open the user icon of a user who should be allowed to link to programs on your Macintosh.

2. Click the **"Allow user to link programs in the Macintosh"** check box at the bottom of the user window (look back at Figure 10.11).

3. Close the user window.

Keep in mind that this provides widespread linking access. A user who is allowed to link to programs on your Macintosh will be able to link to *any* application for which you have enabled linking. There is no way to restrict access for a single user to specific applications.

STOPPING FILE SHARING

To prevent users from sharing your files, do the following:

1. Open the Sharing Setup control panel.

240   NAVIGATING SYSTEM 7: Understanding The Macintosh Operating System

2. Click the **Stop** button in the middle section of the control panel to stop file sharing. The Macintosh operating system asks you how long you want to wait before turning off file sharing (see Figure 10.22).

FIGURE 10.22
Setting the delay until file sharing is stopped

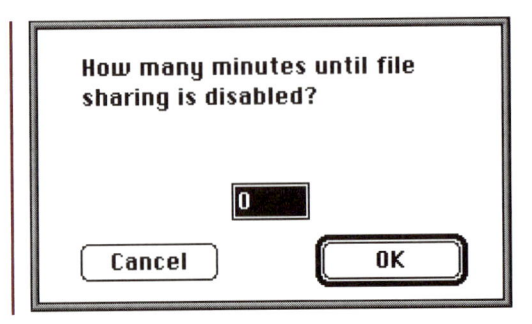

3. Enter the number of minutes before file sharing should be stopped. If you enter 0, file sharing is stopped immediately. Otherwise, the Sharing Setup control panel keeps track of how much time is remaining in the delay period, as in Figure 10.23. During the delay, you can click the **Cancel** button to abort disabling file sharing.

FIGURE 10.23
Timing the delay for the disabling of file sharing

Any users who are sharing your files will be warned that file sharing is shutting down (see Figure 10.24). If the users don't gracefully exit from whatever they are doing with shared files, their actions will be abruptly terminated when file sharing is turned off. The delay is therefore a courteous way to give remote users a change to save their work.

FIGURE 10.24
The warning received by a Macintosh sharing files on a Macintosh that is about to turn off file sharing

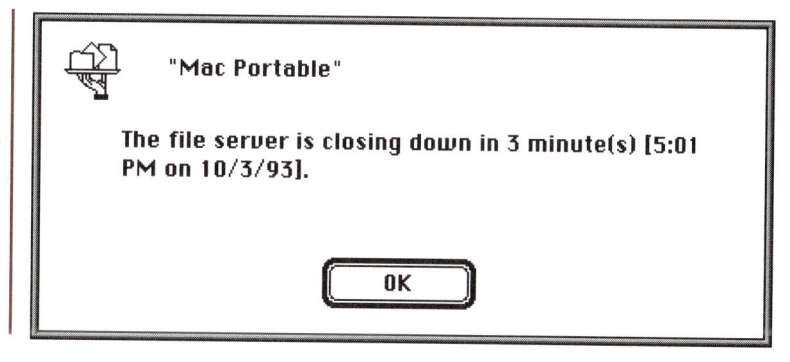

> "Mac Portable"
>
> The file server is closing down in 3 minute(s) [5:01 PM on 10/3/93].
>
> OK

STOPPING PROGRAM LINKING

Stopping program linking is much simpler (and less polite to remote users) than turning off file sharing. To stop program linking:

1. Open the Sharing Setup control panel.
2. Click the **Stop** button in the bottom section of the control panel.

Program linking is stopped immediately; remote users receive no delay or warning.

SEEING WHO'S CONNECTED

The Macintosh operating system provides a way to monitor who is connected to your Macintosh, sharing your files. To see file sharing activity, open the File Sharing Monitor control panel (Figure 10.25). Users connected to your Macintosh appear at the right of the dialog box; the thermometer at the bottom left of the window gives you a relative measure of how much file sharing is occurring.

If you want to disconnect a user, select the user's name in the Connected Users list. Then click the **Disconnect** button. You will be asked to specify a delay until the disconnect, just as you are asked for a delay in stopping file sharing.

FIGURE 10.25
Monitoring file sharing activity

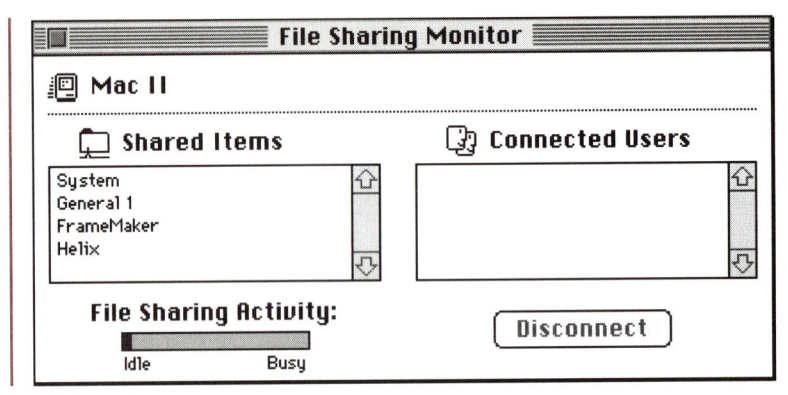

> **BY THE WAY!** The problem with the File Sharing Monitor control panel is that although it shows you what items are available for sharing and who is currently connected to your Macintosh, it doesn't tell you exactly who is doing what.

LOGGING ONTO AN APPLESHARE SERVER

If your Macintosh is part of a network that has one or more AppleShare servers, then you may be able to log on to those servers to use programs and documents stored there. As you read earlier in this chapter, you will need to obtain a user name and password from the network administrator for each server to which you have access.

Logging onto an AppleShare server is very similar to mounting a remote volume under peer-to-peer file sharing. To log on, do the following:

1. Open the Chooser.

2. Click on the AppleShare icon at the left of the dialog box. A list of all available file servers appears, as in Figure 10.26. Keep in mind that this list contains both Macintoshes that can be used for peer-to-peer networking (for example, Mac Portable in Figure 10.26) as well as AppleShare servers (for example, DTP and Central Services in Figure 10.26).

3. Double-click on the name of the server you want to use. A log-in window appears (Figure 10.27).

CHAPTER 10: Networks and File Sharing **243**

FIGURE 10.26
Selecting an AppleShare server

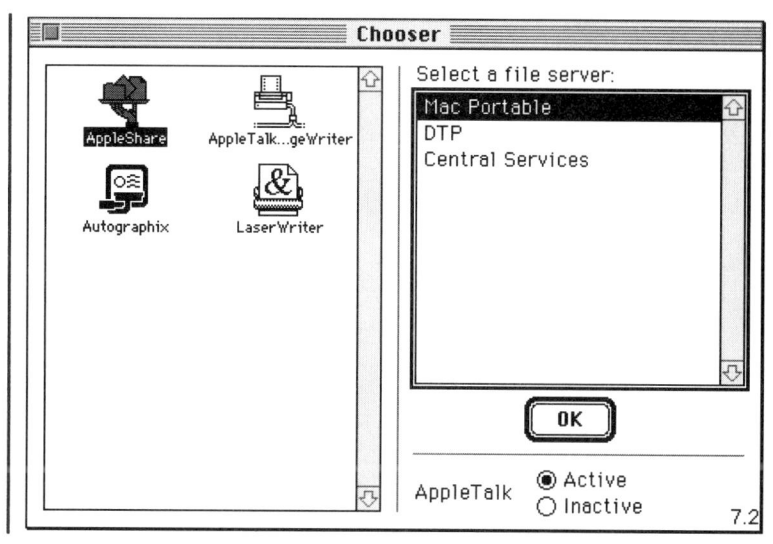

FIGURE 10.27
Logging onto an AppleShare server

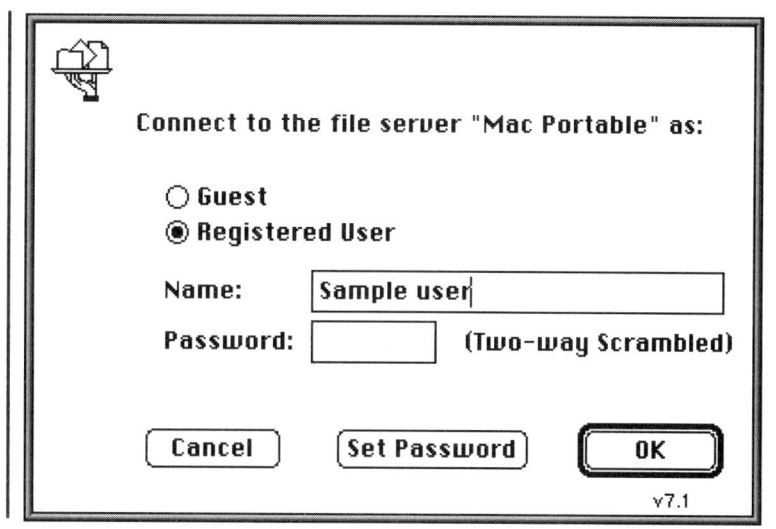

4. Enter your user name and password.

> **BY THE WAY!**
> You can use the **Set Password** button to change your password, just as you would if you were mounting a remote volume shared in a peer-to-peer manner.

5. Click the **OK** button or press **Enter**. The server information card appears, listing the disk volumes on the server (Figure 10.28).

FIGURE 10.28
An AppleShare server information card

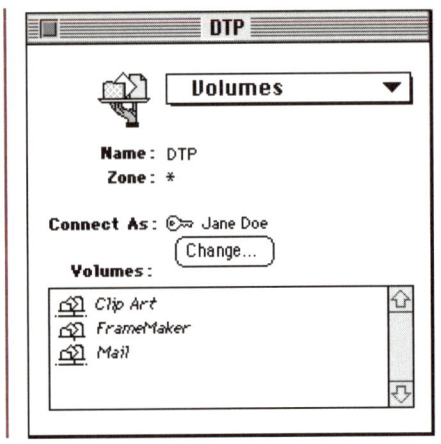

6. Double-click on the volume you want to use. The volume mounts on your Desktop, just like a volume mounted with peer-to-peer networking.

EXCHANGING AND SHARING FILES WITH MS DOS PCs

It's an unfortunate truth, but we don't live in a Macintosh-only world. You may very well need to exchange disks and files with someone who is working with a computer running the MS DOS operating system. The Macintosh operating system provides some facilities for working with MS DOS floppy disks and transferring files between Macintosh and MS DOS formats. The remainder of this chapter looks at those capabilities along with some add-ons that can smooth the process.

WHAT YOU CAN SHARE

Simply being able to read an MS DOS disk and gain access to the files on that disk doesn't mean that you can use those files. In particular, you won't be able to run programs meant for MS DOS computers. This is because MS DOS computers use microprocessors from a different manufacturer (Intel) than those used in the Macintosh (Motorola). The instructions that each manufacturer's microprocessors understand are different; their programs therefore can't be run on the other type of computer, even if the program file has been transferred. In addition, MS DOS programs make use of features of the operating system, just as Macintosh programs use programs from the Macintosh ToolBox. Unless the MS DOS system routines are available, a program written for the environment won't run.

> **BY THE WAY!** There are two ways to run MS DOS programs on your Macintosh. The software-only solution (SoftPC from Insignia Solutions) emulates an MS DOS computer. It is reasonably priced and compatible with most MS DOS software, but because it is an emulator, it runs relatively slowly. The hardware solution is a NuBus board from Orange MicroSystems (Mac386 or Mac486) that contains an Intel microprocessor, effectively placing a second computer inside your Macintosh. An Orange Micro Inc., board runs as fast as a stand-alone MS DOS computer; it also costs about the same.

What, then, can you share with an MS DOS computer? In most cases, you can share document files. Text files (those that contain only character codes, without any special formatting codes) can usually be transferred with few problems. Some graphic file formats (for example, TIFF and EPS) are also usually easy to transfer. In addition, you may find that some programs such as word processors that exist on both MS DOS and the Macintosh have compatible file formats. For example, the word processor WordPerfect uses the same file format on all types of computers. The same is true of many spreadsheets as well.

In many cases, MS DOS file formats that aren't the same as Macintosh file formats can be translated to similar Macintosh file formats. You will read more about file translation throughout the rest of this chapter.

Working with MS DOS Floppy disks

Without help, the Macintosh can't read floppy disks formatted by MS DOS computers. This is because the physical layout and encoding of the data are different from that used by the Macintosh. If you insert an MS DOS disk into a Macintosh disk drive, you'll see an alert telling you that the disk is unreadable and asking you if you want to initialize the disk. There are, however, several ways to get a Macintosh to recognize and read an MS DOS disk.

To handle MS DOS disks, you must have a SuperDrive (the high-density drive that can format disks to hold 1.4Mb). In addition, you will need software that can direct the SuperDrive to read the foreign disk formatting.

> **BY THE WAY!** Regardless of how you choose to read MS DOS disks, the Macintosh will view an MS DOS directory as a folder. You can therefore navigate through an MS DOS file system in the same way you navigate through the Macintosh file system.

If you are going to transfer a file from a Macintosh disk to an MS DOS disk, you must pay some attention to file names. Although the Macintosh isn't particularly choosey about how you name your files (the only character you can't use is a colon), MS DOS has some very strict file-naming rules to which you must adhere if you want the files to be recognized when the disk is used in an MS DOS computer. File names are limited to eight characters (uppercase letters, numbers, and the underscore) plus a three-character extension. The extension is separated from the file name by a period. In some cases, the extension indicates the type of file. For example, EXE and COM files are executable binary files. TXT represents a text file. A few MS DOS applications also use extensions to identify the documents they create.

Apple File Exchange

The oldest (and clumsiest) way to deal with MS DOS disks is to use Apple File Exchange. Apple File Exchange is an application that comes with the Macintosh operating system. It can read a variety of disk formats, including MS DOS and PRO-DOS (disks formatted by an Apple II operating system).

Apple File Exchange doesn't mount disks on the Macintosh Desktop. Instead, you must launch the application and then insert the disk you want to read. The application (Figure 10.29) lists the files and folders on both the source and destination disk. To transfer a file, you select its name in the scrolling at the right of the Apple File Exchange window and make the destination folder the current folder in the scrolling list at the left. Then, you click the **Translate** button.

It's no accident that the button that moves files from a foreign format disk to a Macintosh disk is named "Translate." Apple File Exchange was originally designed to provide file translation capabilities. Apple provided one or two sample translators and expected third-party developers to produce others. However, because Apple File Exchange doesn't work in a Macintosh-like manner—it doesn't mount foreign disks on the Desktop nor can it format MS DOS disks—it hasn't been a very popular program. Therefore, few translators have appeared. Instead, software developers have produced other file translation solutions, one of which is discussed shortly.

FIGURE 10.29
Using Apple File Exchange

```
╔══════════════ Apple File Exchange ══════════════╗
│  ╔═ FrameMaker ═╗                  ╔═ DOS Disk ═╗│
│  │ 📁 A/UX      ↑│                  │📁 GRAPHICS ↑││
│  │ 📁 Clip Art   │   ┌─────────┐    │📁 SS_DBASE  ││
│  │ 📁 Desktop Folder│ │Translate│    │📁 WORDPROC  ││
│  │ 📁 Dictionaries │ └─────────┘    │             ││
│  │ 📁 Filters    │   ┌─────────┐    │             ││
│  │ 📁 FrameMaker │   │ Remove  │    │             ││
│  │ 📁 Gryphon    │   └─────────┘    │             ││
│  │ 📁 gryphon.TIFF│                 │             ││
│  │ 📁 Help       │                  │             ││
│  │ 📁 Mac OS    ↓│                  │            ↓││
│       FrameMaker                       DOS Disk   │
│     49294K bytes available         194K bytes available│
│    ┌────┐ ┌─────┐                 ┌────┐ ┌─────┐  │
│    │Open│ │Drive│                 │Open│ │Drive│  │
│    └────┘ └─────┘                 └────┘ └─────┘  │
│    ┌──────────┐ ┌─────┐           ┌──────────┐ ┌─────┐│
│    │New Folder│ │Eject│           │New Folder│ │Eject││
│    └──────────┘ └─────┘           └──────────┘ └─────┘│
╚═════════════════════════════════════════════════╝
```

Macintosh PC Exchange

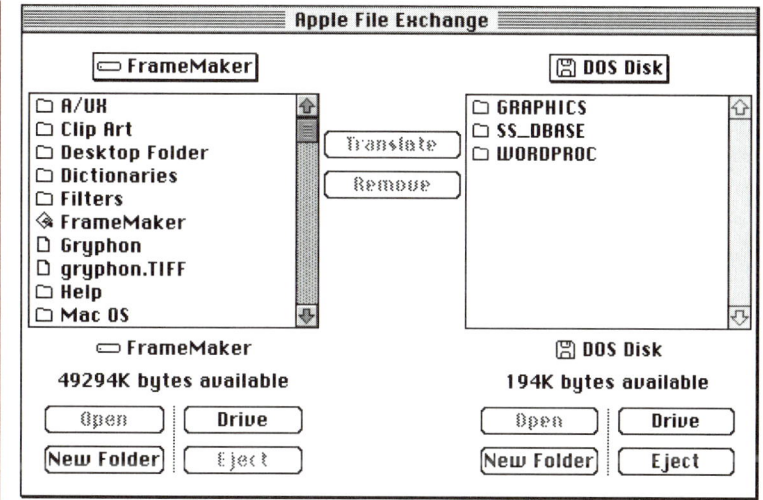

Macintosh PC Exchange is an Apple product that mounts MS DOS disks on the Macintosh Desktop. It also can format MS DOS disks and let you link MS DOS file extensions to Macintosh applications to make it easier to open MS DOS documents with Macintosh programs.

Macintosh PC Exchange installs as a control panel. Once it is loaded into main memory, you can simply insert an MS DOS disk into a SuperDrive. The disk appears on the Desktop with a special icon:

To view the disk's contents, you click on its icon, just as you would a Macintosh disk. To copy a file from an MS DOS disk to a Macintosh disk or from a Macintosh disk to an MS DOS disk, you drag the file's icon. You can also delete a file from an MS DOS disk by dragging its icon to the trash.

When Macintosh PC Exchange is loaded, the Erase disk command produces a dialog box that lets you choose the format for the disk (Figure 10.30). A double-sided disk (one with a single hole for write-protecting the disk) can be formatted as either an 800K Macintosh disk or a 720K MS DOS disk. (The Macintosh 400K format isn't available, although you will be able to read the older single-sided disks.) A high-density disk (one with a write-protect hole, a second hole on the opposite edge of the disk, and the letters "HD" on the disk) can be formatted as either a 1.4Mb disk or a 1.4Mb MS DOS disk.

FIGURE 10.30
Formatting a disk with Macintosh PC Exchange installed

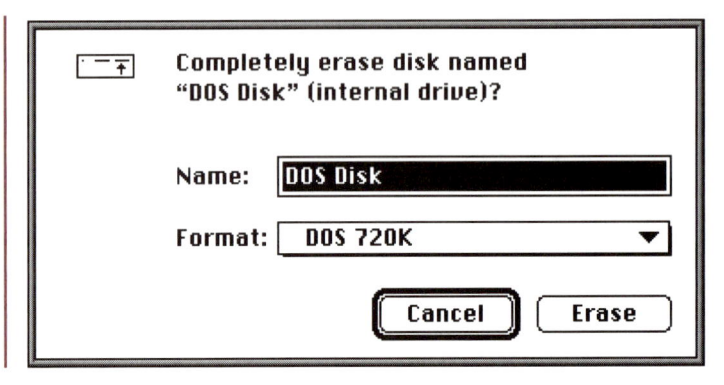

> Completely erase disk named "DOS Disk" (internal drive)?
>
> Name: DOS Disk
>
> Format: DOS 720K
>
> [Cancel] [Erase]

BY THE WAY!

Unlike some MS DOS computers, the Macintosh's SuperDrive is sensitive to the hole at the top left of high-density disks. If you insert a double-sided disk, the Macintosh expects it to be either a 400K or 800K Macintosh disk or a 720K MS DOS disk. If you insert a high-density disk, the Macintosh expects it to be either a 1.4Mb Macintosh disk or a 1.4Mb MS DOS disk. There is therefore one situation in which you will be unable to read an MS DOS disk, regardless of what software you have installed: An double-sided disk that has been formatted to hold 1.4Mb. (Some IBM PCs, in particular the PS/2s, aren't fussy about what type of floppy disk you use; the default formatting is 1.4Mb.)

Macintosh PC Exchange has one other function: It can make it easier to open MS DOS documents with Macintosh applications. Unlike Macintosh files, MS DOS files don't have types and creators that link the documents with the applications that created them. Although some applications do use the file extension to identify their own documents, there is no operating system support for document and application linking.

Macintosh PC Exchange lets you map MS DOS file extensions to Macintosh file types. You can then double-click on an MS DOS file and have the file opened by a Macintosh application that can manipulate it. The mapping of extensions to

Macintosh file types is handled through the Macintosh PC Exchange control panel (Figure 10.31). The **Add** button displays a dialog box for entering the MS DOS extension and choosing the Macintosh application and file type to which it should be linked. In Figure 10.32, for example, MS DOS files with the extension WD5 are linked to Microsoft Word as documents with the file type WDBN.

FIGURE 10.31
The Macintosh PC Exchange control panel

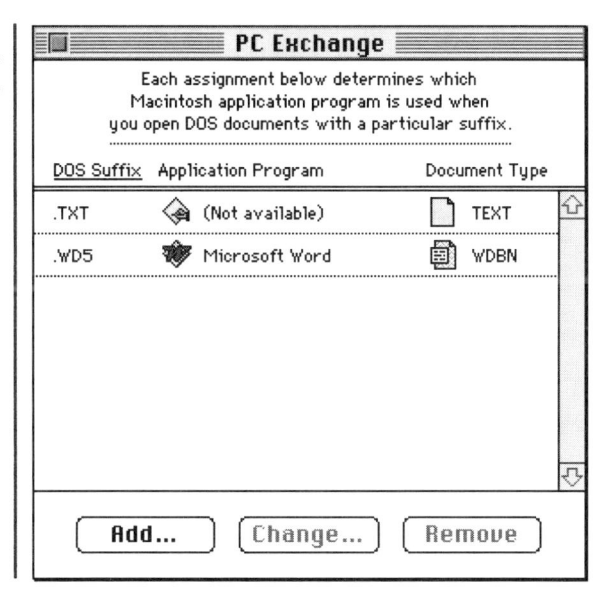

FIGURE 10.32
Linking an MS DOS file name extension to a Macintosh file type

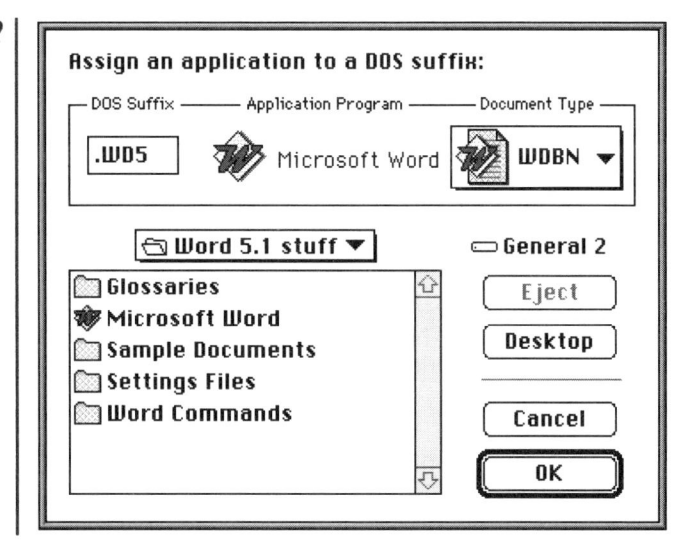

AccessPC

An alternative to Macintosh PC Exchange is AccessPC from Insignia Systems. AccessPC also installs as a control panel (Figure 10.33) and supports the linking of MS DOS file name extensions to Macintosh applications and file types. AccessPC also mounts MS DOS disks directly on the Desktop with the icon:

Figure 10.33: The AccessPC control panel

AccessPC has one advantage over Macintosh PC Exchange if you happen to be using SoftPC. SoftPC emulates up to two MS DOS disks by storing the contents of each disk in a single Macintosh file. AccessPC can mount such disks on the Macintosh Desktop, giving you access to the MS DOS files stored on it. Otherwise, the only way to get to those MS DOS files is through SoftPC.

> **BY THE WAY!** Both Macintosh PC Exchange and AccessPC work with all types of MS DOS removable media, including floppy disks, CD-ROMs, SyQuest cartridges, and Bernoulli cartridges.

File Opening with Easy Access

It isn't always feasible to map MS DOS file extensions to Macintosh applications and file types; a file may have no file extension or its extension may be arbitrary, with no relationship to the type of file. You may also be missing the application to which you have mapped a file extension. In either case, you have two alternatives: You can open the file from within a Macintosh application using the Open File dialog box or you can install Easy Access, an Apple product that simplifies identifying the application with which you want to open an MS DOS file.

Easy Access installs as a control panel. Once installed, its operation is transparent. When you double-click on the icon of an MS DOS file whose file name extension hasn't been mapped to a Macintosh application and file type, it displays the dialog box in Figure 10.34. The exact behavior of the dialog box depends on whether you have file translators installed. If you do, and the "Show only recommended choices" box is checked, you will see a list of available applications and translators. Otherwise, Easy Access lists all applications so that you can choose which should be used to open the document.

Figure 10.34
Choosing an application with which to open an MS DOS file using Easy Access

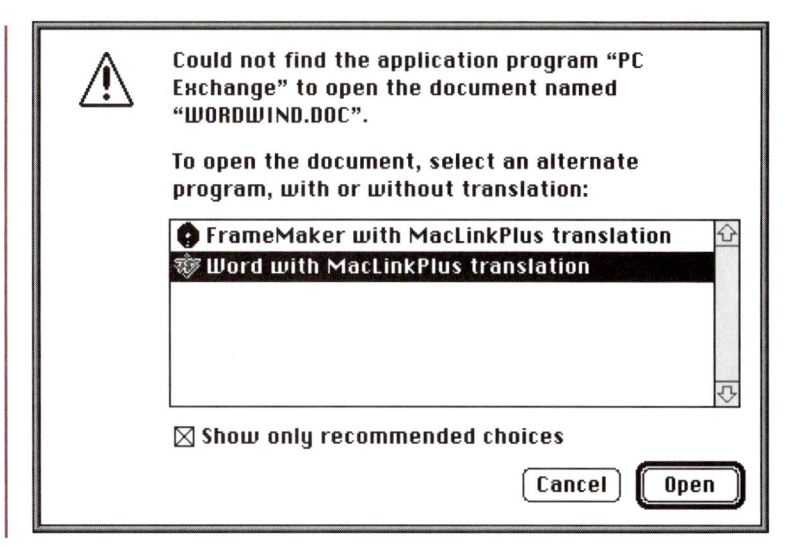

TRANSLATING MS DOS FILES

The final piece to the file-sharing puzzle is the translation of MS DOS file formats into Macintosh file formats. Although Apple File Exchange hasn't lived up to

Apple's original expectations for file translation software, other software developers have written collections of file translators. For example, MacLinkPlus/Translators provides more than 300 translators for word processing, spreadsheet, database, and graphics files.

The translators can be used in two ways. If Easy Access is installed, you can select a translator by double-clicking on the MS DOS file. Looking back at Figure 10.34, you can see that Easy Access displays the translators that are available for the selected file. In this particular example, a Microsoft Word for Windows document can be translated into either a Macintosh Microsoft Word document or a FrameMaker document. Once a translator has been chosen, Easy Access translates the file and opens it in the selected Macintosh application.

Alternatively, you can use the MacLinkPlus/Translators application to translate the file. Notice in Figure 10.35 that the file translation process actually makes a copy of the file (the **Transfer and Translate** option). Although it is theoretically possible to replace an MS DOS file with the Macintosh translated file, it would be unwise to do so. If something were to go wrong during the translation process, you would lose your original file. It therefore is much safer to store the translated document in a new file.

Figure 10.35
Using MacLinkPlus/Translators to translate an MS DOS file

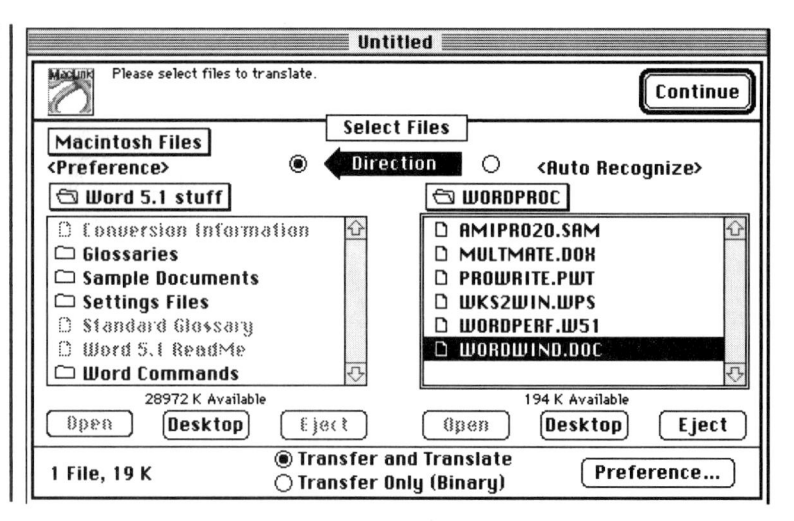

Chapter 11
System 7 Pro: Installation, QuickTime, and AppleScript

As you know, System 7 Pro is an upgrade to System 7.0 and 7.1 that includes three significant features: QuickTime, AppleScript, and PowerTalk. System 7 Pro is sold as a separate product. Therefore, the first question you probably want to ask yourself is: "Do I need it?" The answer is a qualified "it depends."

QuickTime, a system extension that supports movies, has been in use prior to its inclusion in System 7 Pro. Software that requires QuickTime usually includes the extension. Therefore, if all you want to do is play QuickTime movies, you probably don't need System 7 Pro.

AppleScript lets you customize your Macintosh environment by running programs written in the AppleScript language. You can write your own scripts or use those prepared by others. Even if you only want to run scripts written by someone else, you will need System 7 Pro to do so.

> **BY THE WAY!** There are some early versions of AppleScript scripts that will run without AppleScript installed. (They require the installation of a special library of support programs.) However, now that System 7 Pro has been released, those scripts are being rewritten to require that AppleScript be present. Therefore, you can't count on being able to run any scripts without AppleScript.

PowerTalk, which is discussed in depth in Chapters 12 and 13, brings electronic mail to the Macintosh Desktop. If you never use your Macintosh to communicate over a network, then PowerTalk won't be of much use to you. However, if you have access to any type of network to which other System 7 Pro users are connected, then all of you can reap significant benefits by using PowerTalk to communicate.

This chapter looks at installing System 7 Pro. It also introduces you to QuickTime and AppleScript, the two components of System 7 Pro you are likely to use even if your Macintosh isn't connected to a network.

System 7 Pro Installation

System 7 Pro uses the same Installer program as other versions of the Macintosh operating system. Theoretically, it should place the new operating system files in your existing System folder, replacing whatever version of the Macintosh operating system you are currently using. However, although the installation will usually be successful, you may find that you can't boot from System 7 Pro; the Finder will crash. If that occurs, you will need to do an ultra clean install, as described in Chapter 2.

Before beginning to install System 7 Pro, place any device drivers you need to access external disk drives (hard disks or removable media such as SyQuest or optical drives) in the System folder on the Disk Tools disk. If your initial installation fails, you will be prepared to reboot from the Disk Tools disk and do the clean install.

System 7 Pro includes a number of new operating system programs and files, including:

- Finder version 7.1.3: This new Finder recognizes Apple Events.
- System 7.1.1
- System Enablers 001, 003, 040, 088, 131, 201, 401, and 403
- QuickTime: This system extension adds QuickTime capabilities to the operating system.
- A collection of support files for AppleScript (discussed later in this chapter)
- A collection of support files for PowerTalk (discussed in Chapters 12 and 13)

QUICKTIME

The QuickTime system extension is used by application programs to play movies (video and sound). As a user, you don't interact with it directly. Instead, you place it in the System folder so that it is loaded into main memory at system startup. It is then accessible to any program that needs it.

Exactly what you see when a program includes a QuickTime movie varies from one application to another. However, in most cases the movie appears in its own window with a set of controls at the bottom. In Figure 11.1, for example, there are controls for the sound level, to pause the movie, to fast forward, and to rewind. (This demonstration movie is stopped by closing its window by clicking in the close box.) The slider in the middle lets you select the portion of the movie you want to view.

FIGURE 11.1
A QuickTime movie

APPLESCRIPT

AppleScript provides a powerful new way to customize your Macintosh. Scripts—programs written in the AppleScript programming language—can automate a wide variety of actions. For example, the *Move to Apple* script included on the disk that comes with this book makes it easy to place an application or an alias of an application in the Apple Menu Items folder. All you have to do is drag the files that should be moved to the Apple Menu Items folder onto the script's icon. You will then be asked whether you want to move the original file or an alias; the script does the rest of the work.

What Gets Installed

When you include AppleScript in your System 7 Pro installation, the Installer copies the following files to your startup disk:

- AppleScript™: a system extension that supports running scripts.
- Apple® Event Manager: a system extension that adds support for Apple Events to the operating system. (Apple Events are discussed shortly.)
- Record Button: a system extension used by Script Editor.
- AppleScript™ Utilities: a folder containing the following programs:
    — Script Editor: an application for writing and running scripts.
    — Scriptable Text Editor: a text editor that supports Apple Events that can be used to demonstrate and learn about scripting.

Apple Events

At the heart of AppleScript are Apple Events. As you will remember, the Macintosh operating system is event-driven. That means it responds to things that happen in its environment. Apple Events are a special category of event designed to make it possible for programs to exchange messages. In other words, they provide a mechanism for interapplication communication.

A program must be written explicitly to handle Apple Events. The Finder that is a part of System 7 Pro responds to Apple Events. Application programs are also beginning to be updated so that they, too, respond to Apple Events.

Programs that respond to Apple Events support groups of events known as *suites*. The Finder, for example, accepts any of the messages you can see in Figure 11.2. Notice that the Finder will respond to an AppleScript that asks it to open the about box, copy something, duplicate something, make an alias of something, move something, and so on. Each of the events in its suite corresponds to a command that a user can issue when working with the Finder.

Application programs must respond to a suite set of required events (open, print, run, quit) and a suite of core (or standard) events. The core events are events that can be used by most applications and therefore can form a platform on which interapplication communication can be built. In addition, an application may support other events that are specific to the application. Such events will only be useful in scripts that automate actions within the application that supports them. As an example, consider the events recognized by Microsoft Excel (Figure 11.3). Notice that it supports the require suite, a core suite, and three miscellaneous suites that are of use only within the application.

FIGURE 11.2
The Finder event suite

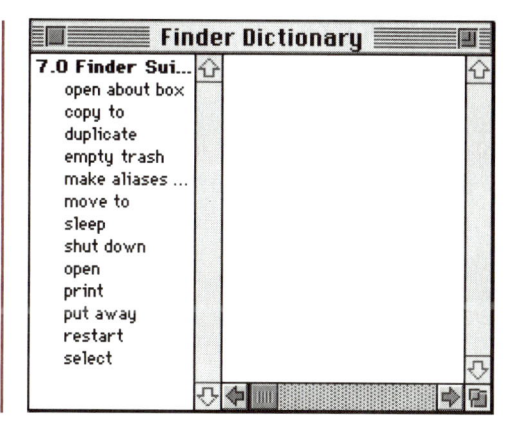

```
Finder Dictionary
7.0 Finder Sui...
   open about box
   copy to
   duplicate
   empty trash
   make aliases...
   move to
   sleep
   shut down
   open
   print
   put away
   restart
   select
```

FIGURE 11.3
Microsoft Excel's event suite

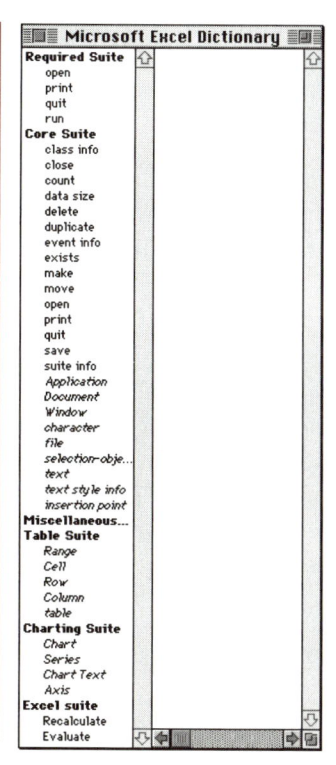

```
Microsoft Excel Dictionary
Required Suite
   open
   print
   quit
   run
Core Suite
   class info
   close
   count
   data size
   delete
   duplicate
   event info
   exists
   make
   move
   open
   print
   quit
   save
   suite info
   Application
   Document
   Window
   character
   file
   selection-obje...
   text
   text style info
   insertion point
Miscellaneous...
Table Suite
   Range
   Cell
   Row
   Column
   table
Charting Suite
   Chart
   Series
   Chart Text
   Axis
Excel suite
   Recalculate
   Evaluate
```

Determining Which Applications Support Apple Events

There's no magic formula for determining whether an application supports Apple Events (in other words, whether it is *scriptable*). In most cases, a software manufacturer wants to publicize Apple Event support as part of its software marketing effort. You are therefore likely to find reference to Apple Events in product literature, packaging, and documentation. If you still aren't sure, there is one fail-safe way to find out.

System 7 Pro provides an editor for creating AppleScripts. (You'll read more about using it shortly.) The Script Editor can also show you the events supported by a program (a program's *dictionary*). To open a dictionary:

1. Launch the Script Editor. (It can be found in the AppleScript Utilities folder.)
2. Choose **Open Dictionary** from the File menu. An Open File dialog box appears.
3. Make the folder containing the application whose dictionary you want to open the current folder. If the application has a dictionary (in other words, it supports Apple Events), its name will appear in the file list.
4. Double-click on the file name. The dictionary window opens.

If the application doesn't have a dictionary, then its name won't appear in the file list in the Open File dialog box. That is proof positive that the program can't handle Apple Events.

Recording Scripts

There are two ways to create AppleScript scripts. One involves programming. (See the section Writing Scripts for an overview.) The other lets you record your actions as a script. Recording can be used to create scripts involving any applications that are *recordable*. Unfortunately, not all scriptable applications are recordable. The only certain way to determine whether an application is recordable is to attempt to record a script involving a scriptable program. If you get a recording, then the program is recordable.

To create a recorded script, do the following:

1. Launch Script Editor. An untitled script window appears (Figure 11.4).

FIGURE 11.4
An empty script window

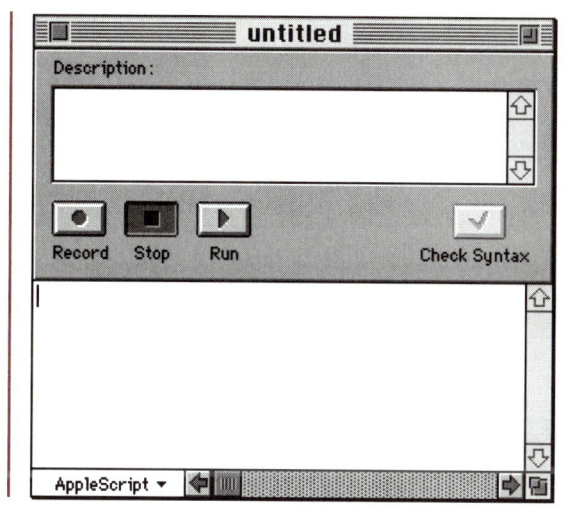

2. Click the **Record** button.
3. Perform whatever actions you want to record in the script.
4. When you are through recording actions, make Script Editor the current application.
5. Click the **Stop** button.

For practice, try the following with the Scriptable Text Editor that is stored in the AppleScript Utilities folder:

1. Open a new Script Editor document.
2. Type **"New document with styles"** in the Description box.
3. Turn on recording by clicking the **Record** button.
4. Make the Finder the current application.
5. Open the AppleScript Utilities folder.
6. Double-click on the Scriptable Text Editor icon to launch the program.
7. Choose "Times" from the Font menu.
8. Choose "12" from the Size menu.
9. Choose "Italic" from the Style menu.

10. Make Script Editor the current application.

11. Click the **Stop** button.

If everything has worked properly, your script should appear as in Figure 11.5. What you have created is a script that launches an application and sets the text styles. You could use such a script to set automatically the type characteristics you prefer each time you launch Scriptable Text Editor.

FIGURE 11.5
A recorded script

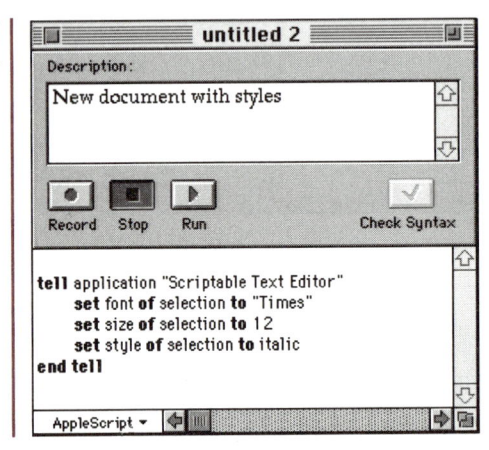

SAVING A SCRIPT

Script Editor is much like any other Macintosh text processing application: A new document is stored only in main memory until you save it for the first time. However, you have several choices to make when you save a script. First, you must choose whether to let the script be opened with Script Editor or to make it "Run-Only." A *run-only script* can be executed, like any other program, but no one can view the script itself. A run-only script can therefore be distributed to other users without fear that someone will copy or alter the code.

If you save a script so that it can be opened by Script Editor, there are three possible formats:

- Text: Saving a script as text creates a text file that can be opened by any program that reads files of type TEXT (for example, a word processor). A text script cannot be saved as run-only.

- Compiled: Saving a compiled script saves a bit of disk space over saving a script as text. A compiled script can be opened only by Script Editor. It can also be saved as run-only.

> **BY THE WAY!** A compiled run-only script isn't useful unless you are actually writing scripts in the AppleScript language. Such a script can't be opened by the Script Editor nor can it be run by double-clicking on its icon. However, it can be executed from *within* another script.

- Application: Saving a script as an application turns the script into a program that can be launched by double-clicking on its icon. A script saved as an application (sometimes also called an *applet*) can be opened only by Script Editor. It can also be saved as run-only.

Each type of script file format has its own icon. As you can see in Figure 11.6, an application uses the diamond icon typically associated with executable files as a background to a scroll. A compiled script has just the scroll as its icon. Scripts saved as text have a standard document icon with a scroll in the middle.

FIGURE 11.6
Script file icons

When you save a file as an application, you have two additional choices to make (see Figure 11.7). By default, an application script quits after it completes its work. However, if you want it to stay open so that it can accept a message from another script, click the **Stay Open** box. Click the **Never Show Startup Screen** if you want the script to run without the startup screen. (You'll see the startup screen shortly.)

RUNNING A SCRIPT

The way in which you run a script depends on how the script has been saved and/or what the current application happens to be:

FIGURE 11.7
Saving a script as an application

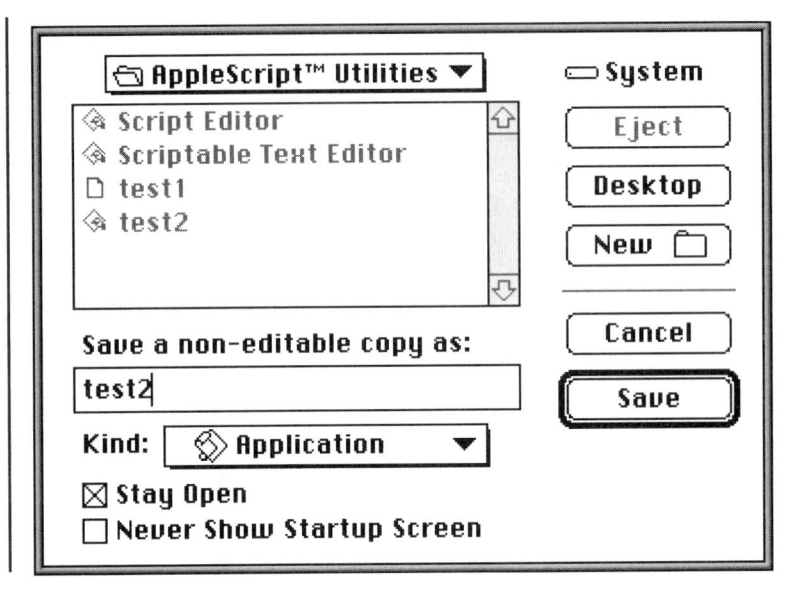

- If the script is open in Script Editor, click the **Run** button. The script runs and returns you to Script Editor.

- If the script has been saved as an application, return to the Finder and double-click on the script's icon. Unless "Never Show Startup Screen" was checked when the script was saved, the startup screen appears (see Figure 11.8). Click **Run** or press **Enter** to execute the script. Click **Quit** to return to the Finder.

There is one additional twist to running scripts that have been saved as applications. Some scripts, such as the *Move to Apple* script, have been written in a special way so that they function as drop boxes: You drag a file or folder icon on top of the script's icon and the script operates on those items. However, there is no way to tell from an applet's icon whether it is designed to function as a drop box. You must therefore check the documentation that comes with a script to find out if you should drop items on top of it or double-click on it to run it.

WRITING SCRIPTS

(This section is written for people who know how to program in a high-level programming language. If you don't program, you probably want to skip it.) A programmer can write scripts in the AppleScript language. In fact, writing scripts (as opposed to recording them) is the only way to take full advantage of AppleScript. Complete documentation for the language can be found in the *AppleScript Language Guide* (available from APDA; see the Product List at the end of this book for complete information).

FIGURE 11.8
An application script startup screen

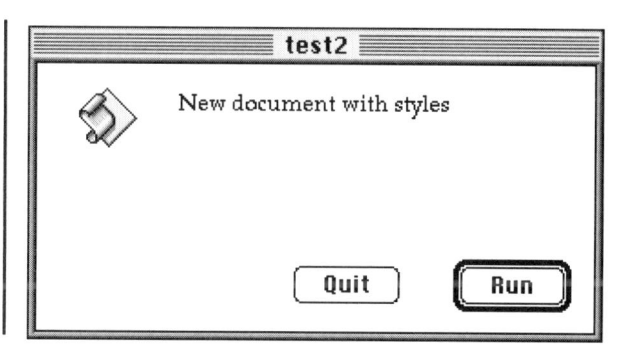

As an example, consider the code for the *Move to Apple* script, that appears in Listing 11.1. (If you have done any HyperScript programming, then you may notice similarities between HyperScript and AppleScript.) The basic unit of a script is a *handler,* a block of code that responds to and handles an Apple Event. The handler in Listing 11.1—delimited by the first line of the program and the statement "end open"—responds to dragging files onto the script's icon by opening the files and operating on them. (Scripts that begin with an "on open" handler are known as *droplets* because they are launched when you drop a file or folder on top of them.)

The remainder of the script contains programming language structures similar to those found in most structured languages, including looping ("repeat") and selection ("if/then/else"). The language also lets handlers call other handlers so that code can be organized with the equivalent of procedures or functions with parameter passing. In Listing 11.1, for example, the named handlers DragObjects and MakeAliasesForObjects are called by the handler that begins "on open names."

AppleScript variables are given values with the "set" command. Variables can contain a single value or a group of values. When a variable contains a group of values, AppleScript can be told which values separate (or "delimit") items within a string of text, making it possible to use a variable as if it were an array.

AppleScript scripts send messages to applications with the "tell" operator. For example, the DragObjects handler sends a "move" message to the Finder, telling it to move an object from one place to the other. The MakeAliasesForOjbects handler sends a "make aliases" message to the Finder, instructing the Finder to create aliases for the files and/or folders on which the script is operating.

AppleScript also provides support for elements of the Macintosh user interface. The "display dialog" statement in Listing 11.1, for example, creates a dialog box with a text string and three buttons. Notice that the "display dialog" statement also sets a default button.

LISTING 11.1
An AppleScript script to move an icon or its alias to the Apple Menu Items folder
(Move to Apple 2.0 courtesy of Greg Kearney)

```
on open names
    --ask if we want an alias or the real file
    set x to 1
    repeat (number of items in names) times
        activate
        display dialog "Do you wish to place the original or an alias of " & (item x of names) ¬
            & " into the apple Menu Items folder?" ¬
            buttons {"Cancel", "Original", "Alias"} ¬
            default button "Alias"
        get result
        if button returned of result is "Cancel" then
            exit repeat
        else
            if the button returned of result is "Original" then
                DragObjects((path to apple menu items), {item x of names})
            else
                if button returned of result is "Alias" then
                    set AppleScript's text item delimiters to {":"}
                    set origList to item x of names as string
                    set xx to number of text items of origList
                    set theList to (text items 1 through (xx - 1) of origList) as string
                    set theList to theList & ":"
                    set newItem to (item x of names) as string
                    set theAlias to newItem & " alias" as string
                    MakeAliasesForObjects((alias theList), {alias newItem})
                    DragObjects((path to apple menu items), {alias theAlias})
```

```
            end if
         end if
      end if
      set x to x + 1
   end repeat
end open


on DragObjects(dst, objs)
   tell application "Finder" to move to dst from objs
end DragObjects


on MakeAliasesForObjects(cont, objs)
   tell application "Finder" to make aliases for cont items objs
end MakeAliasesForObjects
```

Chapter 12
System 7 Pro: PowerTalk Setup and Configuration

PowerTalk is the first component of a group of software that will make up the *Apple Open Collaboration Environment* (AOCE). AOCE forms the framework for *collaboration services*, operations in which users share work and documents over a network. PowerTalk, the end-user portion of AOCE, provides electronic mail capabilities along with secure transfer of documents. Electronic mail can be sent via modem over telephone lines, transmitted over a peer-to-peer network, or implemented in a client/server network using PowerShare, the second component of AOCE. Apple envisions AOCE as maturing into a multiplatform environment, linking Macintoshes, MS DOS computers, DEC VAX computers, and UNIX computers.

The rest of this chapter looks at setting up PowerTalk from the end-user's point of view. It will show you how to configure PowerTalk and introduce you to some of PowerTalk's security features. Sending and receiving messages is discussed in Chapter 13, along with special provisions to ensure the security of the messages you send.

WHAT GETS INSTALLED

When you install PowerTalk as part of System 7 Pro, the following files are copied onto your startup disk:

- PowerTalk Folder: a folder placed on the top level of your startup drive that contains the following utility programs:

  —AppleMail: an application for sending, reading, and replying to electronic mail.

  —Untitled Info Card: a prototype card that you will duplicate to store data about the people with whom you share mail and documents.

  —DigiSign Utility: an application for requesting a private digital signature that can be used to authenticate messages, verifying that they came from you and that they haven't been modified since you sent them.

- Catalogs Manager, Mailbox Extension, PowerTalk Extensions, and PowerTalk Manager: System extensions that add support for PowerTalk to the operating system.

- PowerTalk Setup control panel: a control panel for configuring various aspects of the PowerTalk environment.

- Find in Catalog and Personal Catalog: two new items in the menu that provide access to PowerTalk catalogs.

- PowerTalk Data: a folder installed inside the System folder that holds resources used by PowerTalk.

Installing PowerTalk also places two new items on your Desktop. The first is an icon named Catalogs:

Catalogs

The Catalogs icon acts as a repository for data about users with whom you exchange electronic mail and other documents. You will learn how to create and use catalogs later in this chapter.

The second icon is initially named "Mailbox":

Mailbox

After you set up PowerTalk, the name of this icon will be changed to your name. The Mailbox has two parts, an in box for incoming mail and documents and an out box for outgoing mail and documents. You will see it in action in Chapter 13.

Although the Catalogs and Mailbox icons are Finder objects, they are different in some ways from volume icons and folder icons. For example, you can't change their names. Their Get Info dialog boxes are also somewhat different. The Catalogs icon's Get Info box (Figure 12.1) tells you only what kind of object it is and where it is located. The Mailbox icon's Get Info box (Figure 12.2) also tells you what kind of object it is and where it is located. In addition, it lets you set the maximum number of messages that can be stored in the mailbox at a time.

FIGURE 12.1
The Get Info dialog box for a Catalogs icon

FIGURE 12.2
The Get Info dialog box for a Mailbox icon

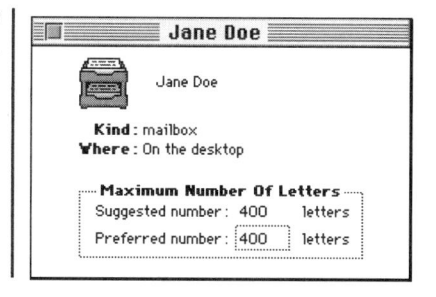

PowerTalk also adds two new options to the Special menu (see Figure 12.3). The **"I'm at ..."** option is used to choose a data communications configuration when you are using PowerTalk on the road. The **"Unlock Key Chain ..."** option is part of PowerTalk security.

SETTING UP POWERTALK

Before you can use PowerTalk, you must perform a sequence of setup operations that identify you as a PowerTalk user and provide some measure of security for the messages you will be sending and receiving.

FIGURE 12.3
The Special menu after PowerTalk has been installed

```
Special
Clean Up Window
Empty Trash

Eject Disk      ⌘E
Erase Disk...

I'm at...
Unlock Key Chain...

Restart
Shut Down
```

Before You Begin

Before you begin setting up PowerTalk, there are some system configuration activities you should perform. These activities include:

- Using the Date & Time control panel to set the current date, time, and time zone and to indicate whether your location uses Daylight Savings Time. This is vital for correct time-stamping of shared and mailed objects.
- Using the Chooser to turn on AppleTalk.
- Using the Sharing Setup control panel to give your Macintosh a network name.

Beginning PowerTalk Setup

Basic PowerTalk security is provided through a *Key Chain*. When a Key Chain is locked, PowerTalk services are unavailable from your Macintosh. When a Key Chain is unlocked, PowerTalk is available to anyone who has access to your Macintosh. To unlock a Key Chain, you supply the Key Chain's password. PowerTalk setup therefore includes defining a password for a Key Chain. To get started, do the following:

1. Make sure that all PowerTalk files have been installed on your startup hard disk.
2. Double-click on either the Catalogs or Mailbox icons. Alternatively, open the PowerTalk Setup control panel or choose **Unlock Key Chain** from the Finder's Special menu. Regardless of which you do, you will see the dialog box in Figure 12.4.

FIGURE 12.4
Beginning
PowerTalk setup

> **Welcome to PowerTalk™**
> the Apple Open Collaboration Environment
>
> The PowerTalk Key Chain lets you access multiple services using just one Access Code.
>
> [Cancel] [**Proceed**]
>
> Copyright 1989-1993, Apple Computer, Inc.

3. Click the **Proceed** button or press **Enter**. The dialog box in Figure 12.5 appears.

FIGURE 12.5
Indicating whether you have a PowerShare server account

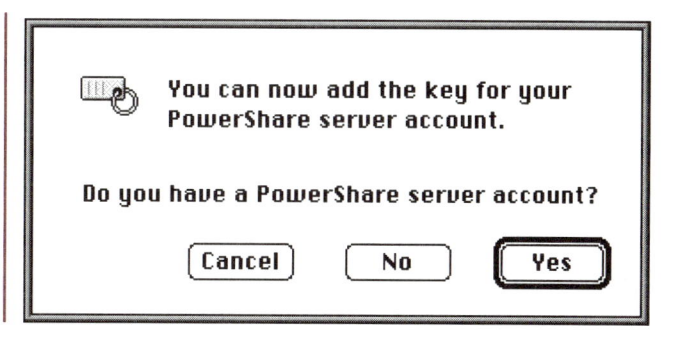

> You can now add the key for your PowerShare server account.
>
> Do you have a PowerShare server account?
>
> [Cancel] [No] [**Yes**]

4. If you will be using PowerTalk through a PowerShare server, click the **Yes** button or press **Enter**. If you will be using PowerTalk over a peer-to-peer network (no PowerShare server), click the **No** button.

The remaining steps in the setup process vary depending on whether you will be using a PowerShare server or working with PowerTalk in a peer-to-peer environment.

FINISHING SETUP FOR A POWERSHARE SERVER

Using a PowerShare server means that the mail and documents you share with other users are stored on a server. The items you send are placed on the server; the recipient retrieves them from the server. By the same token, items sent to you are placed on the server, from where you can retrieve them. This means that you must have two passwords, one to give you access to the server and one to give you access to PowerTalk services on your Macintosh. Access to a PowerTalk server requires an account name and a password; access to PowerTalk requires an Access Key.

When you indicate that you would be working a PowerShare server (as in step 4 above), PowerTalk checks the network to which your Macintosh is connected for all PowerShare servers. Then, it displays the dialog box in Figure 12.6, listing the servers it found.

FIGURE 12.6
A list of available PowerShare servers

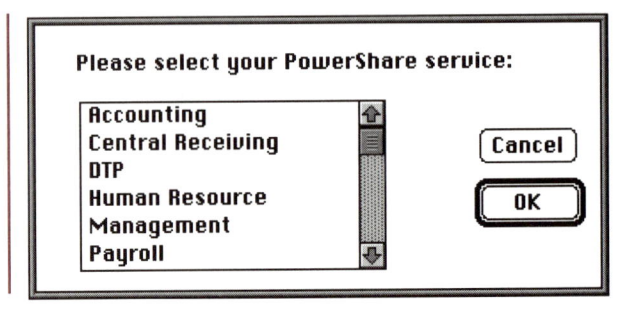

> Please select your PowerShare service:
>
> Accounting
> Central Receiving
> DTP
> Human Resource
> Management
> Payroll
>
> [Cancel] [OK]

To complete PowerTalk setup for use with a PowerShare server, do the following:

1. Get your PowerShare name and password from the person responsible for administering the PowerShare server you will be using.

2. Double-click on the name of the PowerShare server you will be using. The dialog box in Figure 12.7 appears.

FIGURE 12.7
Entering a PowerShare name and password

> To add your PowerShare key, please provide your account information.
>
> PowerShare service: DTP
> Name: Jane Doe
> Password: ••••••
>
> [Set Password] [Cancel] [OK]

3. Enter your PowerShare name and password.

CHAPTER 12: System 7 Pro: PowerTalk Setup and Configuration 273

4. Click the **OK** button or press **Enter**. PowerTalk sets your PowerShare name and password. It also initializes your PowerTalk Access Code to your PowerShare password.

> **BY THE WAY!** Beyond the setup phase, your PowerShare password and PowerTalk Access Code are independent. You can change one without affecting the other.

5. The dialog box in Figure 12.8 appears. Click the **OK** button or press **Enter**.

FIGURE 12.8
Finalizing setup for PowerTalk use with a PowerShare server

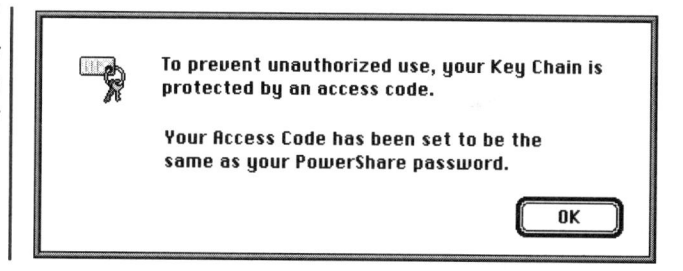

> To prevent unauthorized use, your Key Chain is protected by an access code.
>
> Your Access Code has been set to be the same as your PowerShare password.
>
> [OK]

At this point, PowerTalk is ready to use with a PowerShare server. You will notice that when you returned to the Desktop after dismissing the dialog box in Figure 12.8 that the name of the Mailbox icon has changed from "Mailbox" to the name you entered in the dialog box in Figure 12.7. You will also find a PowerTalk Key Chain icon on your Desktop:

PowerTalk Key Chain

> **BY THE WAY!** Like the Catalogs and Mailbox icons, you won't be able to change the name of the PowerTalk Key Chain icon.

Finishing Setup for a Peer-to-Peer Environment

If your network doesn't have a PowerShare server, you can still exchange electronic mail and documents with other users who have PowerTalk installed. Like System 7's peer-to-peer file sharing, using PowerTalk in a peer-to-peer environment means that messages pass directly between your Macintosh and the Macintosh with which you are exchanging information, without using a server as an intermediary.

> **BY THE WAY!**
>
> The biggest drawback to a peer-to-peer configuration is that the two Macintoshes exchanging messages must both be turned on during the message transfer. If a server is present on the network, only the server and either the sender or receiver need to be available.

When you click the **No** button in the dialog box in Figure 12.5, PowerTalk displays a second dialog box that collects information about your user name and Access Code. To use it to complete PowerTalk setup for use in a peer-to-peer environment, do the following:

1. Type your name and an Access Code (see Figure 12.9).

FIGURE 12.9
Entering a user name and Access Code for a PowerTalk Key Chain in a peer-to-peer environment

> To prevent unauthorized use, your Key Chain is protected by an Access Code.
>
> Please provide your name and Access Code:
>
> Name: Jane Doe
>
> Access Code: ••••••
>
> [Cancel] [OK]

2. Click the **OK** button or press **Enter**. A confirmation dialog box appears (Figure 12.10).

FIGURE 12.10
Confirming an Access Code

> Please reenter your new Access Code to make certain you typed it correctly the first
>
> Access Code: [••••••]
>
> [Cancel] [OK]

3. Enter the same Access Code once more.

4. Click the **OK** button or press **Enter**. The final dialog box appears (Figure 12.11).

FIGURE 12.11
Finalizing setup for PowerTalk in a peer-to-peer environment

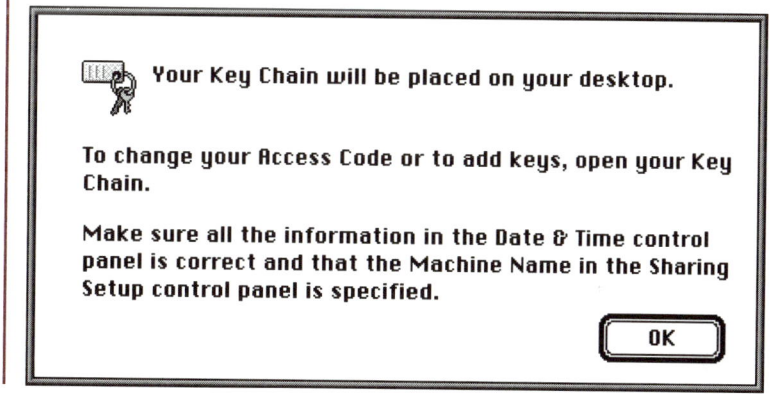

> Your Key Chain will be placed on your desktop.
>
> To change your Access Code or to add keys, open your Key Chain.
>
> Make sure all the information in the Date & Time control panel is correct and that the Machine Name in the Sharing Setup control panel is specified.
>
> [OK]

5. Click the **OK** button or press **Enter**. PowerTalk completes the setup by installing the PowerTalk Key Chain icon on the Desktop.

CONTROLLING POWERTALK ACCESS

Access to PowerTalk is controlled by the PowerTalk Setup control panel and your PowerTalk Key Chain. The control panel (Figure 12.12) provides a master control for PowerTalk. To make it completely inaccessible, click the **Off** radio button at the top of the dialog box.

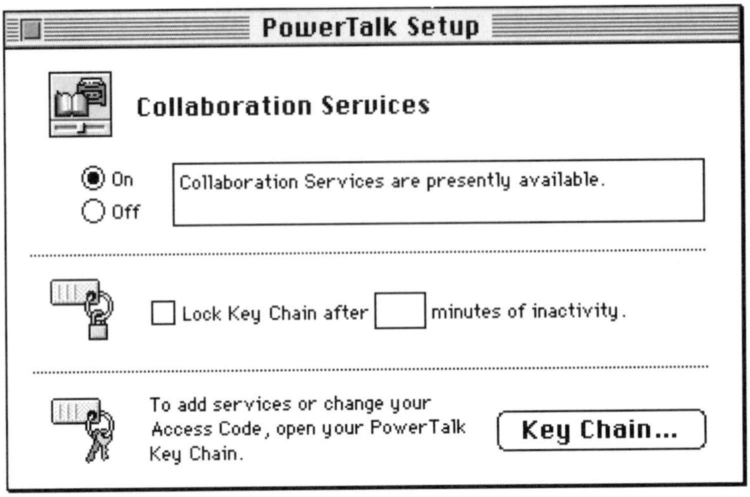

FIGURE 12.12
The PowerTalk Setup control panel

BY THE WAY! Although the PowerTalk Setup control panel can make PowerTalk inaccessible, anyone who has access to your Macintosh has access to the control panel to turn it back on.

BY THE WAY! Once PowerTalk is set up, your Macintosh will take longer to boot. The Catalogs and PowerTalk Key Chain icons appear on the Desktop right after icons for all mounted disk volumes. The Macintosh then pauses a minute or so to search for waiting mail. Open disk windows finally appear, followed by the Mailbox icon. If you find the delay annoying, keep PowerTalk turned off from the PowerTalk Setup control panel unless you are planning to use it.

The PowerTalk Key Chain provides password protection for all PowerTalk services. To gain access to PowerTalk, you unlock the Key Chain; to secure PowerTalk, you lock it again.

BY THE WAY! The Macintosh operating system automatically locks your Key Chain every time you shut down your computer. You will therefore need to unlock it each time you start up your computer.

UNLOCKING THE POWERTALK KEY CHAIN

To unlock the Key Chain and gain access to PowerTalk:

1. Choose **Unlock Key Chain** from the Finder's Special menu. The dialog box in Figure 12.13 appears.

FIGURE 12.13
Unlocking the PowerTalk Key Chain

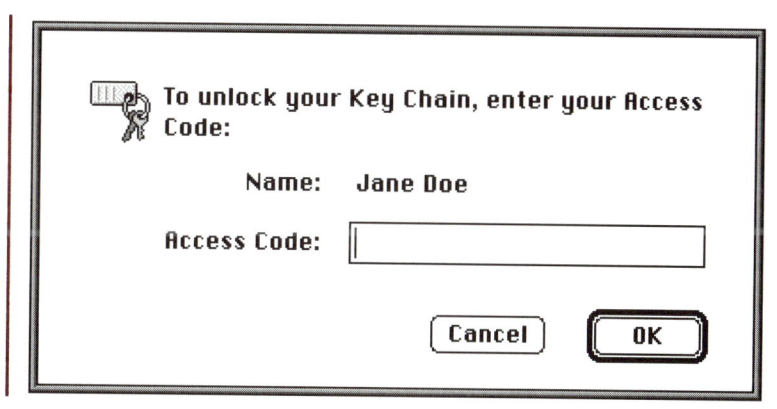

2. Enter your Access Code.
3. Click the **OK** button or press **Enter**. PowerTalk unlocks the Key Chain and changes the Special menu option to Lock Key Chain.

LOCKING THE POWERTALK KEY CHAIN

To lock the Key Chain so that PowerTalk is inaccessible, choose **Lock Key Chain** from the Finder's Special menu. No Access Code is required; the Key Chain is locked immediately.

If you think you might forget to lock the Key Chain when you walk away from your Macintosh (assuming the computer is left on, that is), you might want to configure PowerTalk to lock the Key Chain after a specified period of inactivity. To set a lock delay:

1. Open the PowerTalk Setup control panel.
2. Click the Lock Key Chain after check box.
3. Enter the number of minutes of inactivity that should elapse before PowerTalk is turned off.

Changing Your PowerTalk Access Code

To change your Access Code:

1. Open the PowerTalk Setup control panel (Figure 12.12).
2. Click the **Key Chain** button. The dialog box in Figure 12.14 appears.

FIGURE 12.14
Changing a PowerTalk Access Code

> Please type in your name, your old Access Code, and your new Access Code
>
> Name: Jane Doe
> Old Access Code:
> New Access Code:
>
> [Cancel] [OK]

3. Enter your current Access Code ("Old Access Code"). Press **Tab**.
4. Enter your new Access Code.
5. Click the **OK** button or press **Enter**.

> **BY THE WAY!** You can also gain access to the dialog box in Figure 12.14 from the PowerTalk Key Chain window. More about the contents of that window can be found later in the next section.

PowerTalk Services

There are three types of *PowerTalk services* you can use:

- Direct AppleTalk (peer-to-peer)
- PowerShare (client/server)

CHAPTER 12: System 7 Pro: PowerTalk Setup and Configuration   **279**

◆ **Direct Dialup Mail** (remote dialup over telephone lines)

At any given time, you can subscribe to many PowerShare services (one for each PowerShare server to which you have access). Each PowerShare service requires its own use name and password. When you add a new PowerShare service, a new key is added to your Key Chain. Regardless of the number of keys in your Key Chain, you will still have only one Access Code to unlock access to the entire Key Chain.

> **BY THE WAY!** Direct Dialup Mail is not a part of the System 7 Pro package. The Direct Dialup Mail Accessory Kit must be purchased separately.

The services you can use are specified in the PowerTalk Key Chain window. When you set up PowerTalk, your first service is entered for you. If you indicated that you will be using a PowerShare server, that server becomes your first service. If you indicated that you wouldn't be using a PowerShare server, then Direct AppleTalk becomes your first service.

To access the PowerTalk Key Chain window, double-click on the PowerTalk Key Chain icon. As you can see in Figure 12.15, the window displays each service you have installed. Double-click on the name of the service (for example, AppleTalk) to get information about the service (see Figure 12.16).

Figure 12.15
Using the PowerTalk Key Chain window to view available services

FIGURE 12.16
An information window about a PowerTalk service

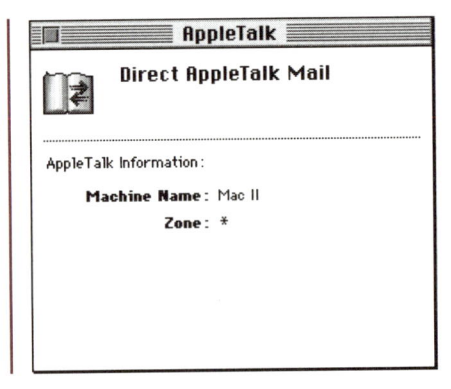

[AppleTalk window showing:
Direct AppleTalk Mail
AppleTalk Information:
Machine Name: Mac II
Zone: *]

> **BY THE WAY!** Clicking the **Change Code** button in the upper right of the PowerTalk Key Chain window displays the dialog box in Figure 12.14. Use it to change your PowerTalk Access Code.

ADDING OTHER SERVICES

As the network to which your Macintosh is connected changes, you may need to add PowerTalk services. To add a service:

1. Open the PowerTalk Key Chain window.
2. Click the **Add** button. A list of available service types appears (Figure 12.17).

FIGURE 12.17
Choosing a new PowerTalk service

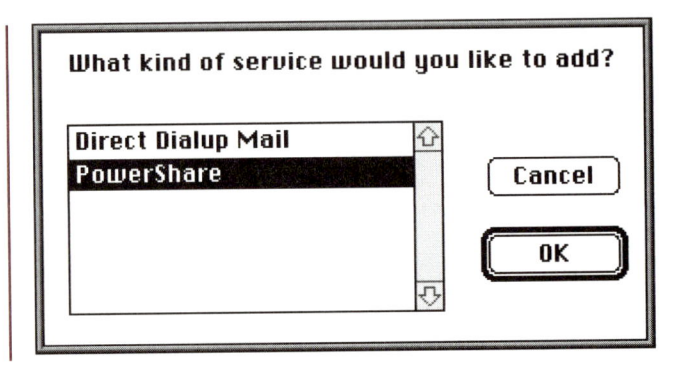

[Dialog: What kind of service would you like to add?
Direct Dialup Mail
PowerShare
Cancel / OK]

3. Double-click on the type of service you want to add.

4. If you have chosen a PowerShare service, PowerTalk checks the network for available PowerShare servers and displays a dialog box like that in Figure 12.6. Double-click on the name of the server you want to add. Enter your user name and password on the new server, just as you did when you were setting up PowerTalk.

The new service is added to the PowerTalk Key Chain window.

REMOVING SERVICES

If circumstances change and you want to remove a service, you can do so from the PowerTalk Key Chain window:

1. Open the PowerTalk Key Chain window.

2. Highlight the service you want to remove.

3. Click the **Remove** button. A confirmation dialog box appears (Figure 12.18).

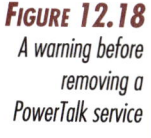

FIGURE 12.18
A warning before removing a PowerTalk service

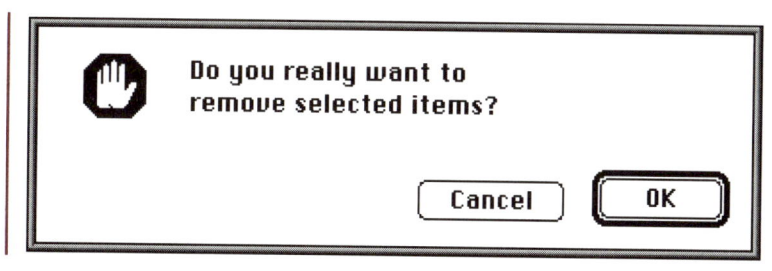

> Do you really want to remove selected items?
>
> [Cancel] [OK]

4. Click the **OK** button or press **Enter** to confirm the removal. Click the **Cancel** button to abort.

> **BY THE WAY!**
> You will be able to remove every service *except* the first one you installed.

Working with Information Cards and Catalogs

Information about the people and hardware with which you communicate are stored in *catalogs*. A catalog can contain data about users and groups of users, stored in *information cards*. Catalogs can also contain information about AppleShare servers, PowerShare servers, and other shared hardware such as printers.

There are three types of catalogs you may encounter:

- Personal: A personal catalog is a repository for information about other users. The contents of a personal catalog are under your direct control. When you install PowerTalk, the Installer places one personal catalog in the Apple Menu Items folder. You can open that catalog by choosing **Personal Catalog** from the menu. In addition, you can create other personal catalogs, which by default are placed on the Desktop.

- AppleTalk: AppleTalk catalogs are stored in the Catalogs icon on the Desktop. They store information about Direct AppleTalk Mail connections (peer-to-peer PowerTalk setups) and AppleShare servers. AppleTalk catalogs are shared by other Macintoshes on your network.

- PowerShare: PowerShare catalogs are stored in the Catalogs icon on the Desktop. They store information about the users who have accounts on the PowerShare servers to which you have access. PowerShare catalogs are shared by all those who have accounts on the same servers that you do.

AppleTalk and PowerShare catalogs are maintained by PowerTalk. They are created and deleted as you add and remove PowerTalk services. Most of the data in the information cards in AppleTalk and PowerShare catalogs aren't stored on your Macintosh, but on some other computer on your network. You therefore can use the contents of AppleTalk and PowerShare catalogs only when you are connected to a network. However, if you copy information cards or aliases of information cards from an AppleTalk or PowerShare catalog into a personal catalog, you will have access to those items even when you aren't connected to a network.

Catalogs and PowerTalk Addresses

The destination of any file or electronic mail message you send using PowerTalk is indicated by an electronic address. When PowerShare servers are involved, catalogs become an integral part of that addressing scheme.

If you are using PowerTalk in a peer-to-peer environment, without a PowerShare server, then an address has the format:

Macintosh network name@zone

In other words, you use the network name of the Macintosh to which you want to send a message, followed by the character @, followed by the AppleTalk zone in which the receiving Macintosh is located. If the recipient is in your local zone, then an address might appear as:

Jane Doe@*

However, if Jane Doe's Macintosh is in the Accounting zone, the address would appear as:

Jane Doe@Accounting

PowerShare addresses have a similar format, but the parts of the address have a different meaning. A generic PowerShare address therefore looks like the following:

User name@Catalog name

The first portion of the name corresponds to a user who is represented as an information card within a catalog. The name of the catalog follows the @ sign. If an information card for David Johnson is stored in the PowerShare catalog DTP, then David Johnson's PowerShare electronic address is:

David Johnson@DTP

Some PowerShare catalogs may be organized so that groups of users are placed in folders inside the catalog. Although you needn't specify the path through the folders where a given user can be found, you can speed up access if you do so. Folder names are separated from their catalog by colons. For example, if David Johnson's information card is stored in a folder named Imaging Specialists inside the DTP catalog, the electronic address would be:

David Johnson@DTP:Imaging Specialists

Given that there are two distinct forms of PowerTalk addresses, you will need to gather the following information if you are going to create information cards from scratch for the people with whom you will be exchanging messages:

- If you will be reaching someone via Direct AppleTalk, you will need the network name of his or her Macintosh.

284 NAVIGATING SYSTEM 7: Understanding The Macintosh Operating System

◆ If you will be reaching someone through a PowerShare server, you will need the name of the PowerShare catalog in which the person's information card is stored. You will also need the name of that information card. To get the best PowerTalk performance, you should also find out the names of any folders in which the user's information card is stored.

CREATING USER INFORMATION CARDS

Information cards are a special type of document that store a wealth of data about the users with whom you communicate. In addition, they play a part in sending files from one Macintosh to another. You may also wish to create group information cards to make it easier to send the same document to multiple users at the same time. (You'll see how to send files later in Chapter 13.)

> **BY THE WAY!** By the way: You won't necessarily have to create an information card for every user with whom you exchange messages. You will be able to copy some existing information cards from AppleTalk and PowerShare catalogs.

Information cards can be stored on the Desktop. More typically, however, they are stored in catalogs. To create a new information card, you must first open a catalog:

1. Choose **Personal Catalog** from the menu. The default personal catalog window opens (Figure 12.19). A new menu (the Catalogs menu in Figure 12.20) appears in the Finder's menu bar.

FIGURE 12.19
An empty personal catalog window

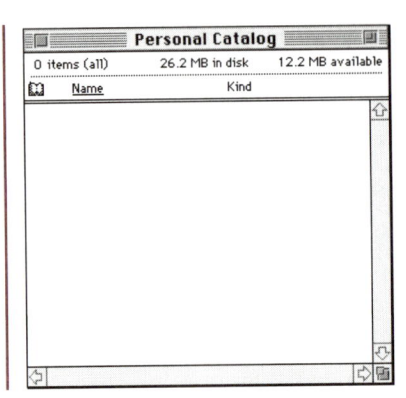

CHAPTER 12: System 7 Pro: PowerTalk Setup and Configuration **285**

FIGURE 12.20
The Catalogs menu

```
Catalogs
New Personal Catalog
Configure Catalogs

New Group
New User
```

2. Choose **New User** from the Catalogs menu. An untitled user information card icon appears in the catalog window (Figure 12.21).

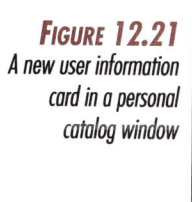

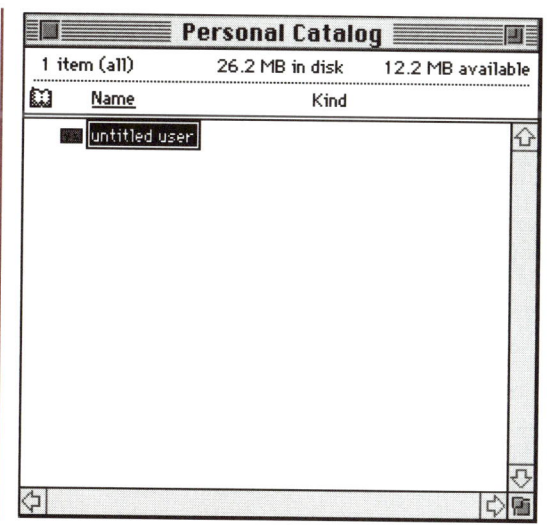

FIGURE 12.21
A new user information card in a personal catalog window

```
Personal Catalog
1 item (all)     26.2 MB in disk    12.2 MB available
   Name                   Kind
   untitled user
```

3. Type a name for the user information card. In most cases, this will be the name of the person whose data will be stored in the card.

4. Press **Enter** to store the information card's name.

Now that the information card has been created and named, you can open it and add data to it. An information card has four parts: Business Card, Personal Info, Phone Numbers, Electronic Addresses. To add data to the card:

1. Double-click on the information card icon. An empty information card window appears. As you can see in Figure 12.22, you are presented with a Business Card. Each word surrounded by < and > represents a field where you can enter data.

NAVIGATING SYSTEM 7: Understanding The Macintosh Operating System

FIGURE 12.22
An empty information card

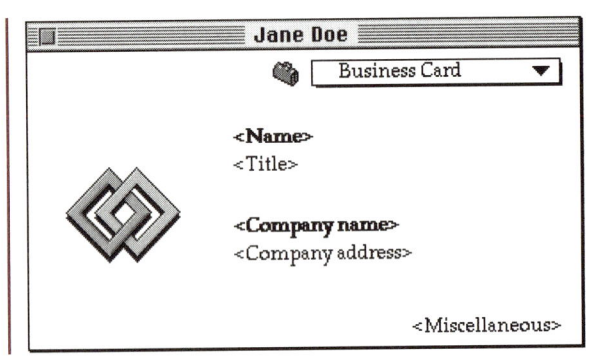

2. Click the mouse pointer in the <Name> field. Type the name of the person about whom the information card stores data.

3. Press **Tab** or click the mouse pointer in the <Title> field. Type the title of the person about whom the information card stores data. If you want to leave the field blank, press the space bar once. (If you don't enter at least a space in a field, a straight-line cursor remains in the field to mark its place.)

4. Press **Tab** or click the mouse pointer in the <Company name> field. Type the company with whom the person is associated or press the space bar to leave the field blank.

5. Press **Tab** or click the mouse pointer in the <Company address> field. Type the address of the company with whom the person is associated or press the space bar to leave the field blank.

6. Press **Tab** or click the mouse pointer in the <Miscellaneous> field. Type a short comment or press the space bar to leave the field blank. At this point, your information card might look something like Figure 12.23.

BY THE WAY!
By the way: If you press **Tab** once more, you will highlight the logo at the left of the Business Card. (A box appears around the logo.) To change the logo, copy a PICT or bitmapped graphic onto the Clipboard, highlight the logo on the Business Card, and paste.

The next step is to add any personal information you want to store about the person who is the subject of the information card:

FIGURE 12.23
A completed Business Card

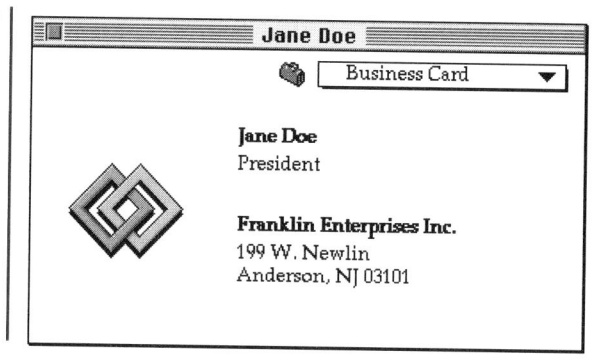

1. Choose **Personal Info** from the pop-up menu at the top right of the card. The information card now displays fields for entering personal information.

FIGURE 12.24
A Personal Info card

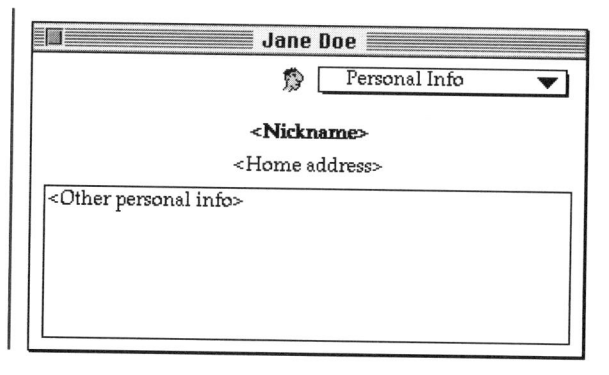

2. Enter a nickname, home address, and any other personal information you want to store about the person described by the information card.

The third part of an information card stores voice phone numbers that can be used to contact the person who is the subject of the information card:

1. Choose **Phone Numbers** from the pop-up menu. The information card now displays a screen for storing phone numbers (Figure 12.25). Notice that the format of this card is different from the Business or Personal Info card; there aren't any data fields.

2. To add a phone number, click the **Add** button. A list of phone number types appears (Figure 12.26).

FIGURE 12.25
An empty phone number card

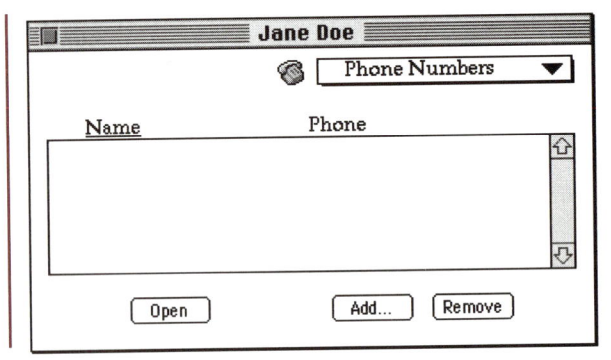

FIGURE 12.26
Choosing a phone number type

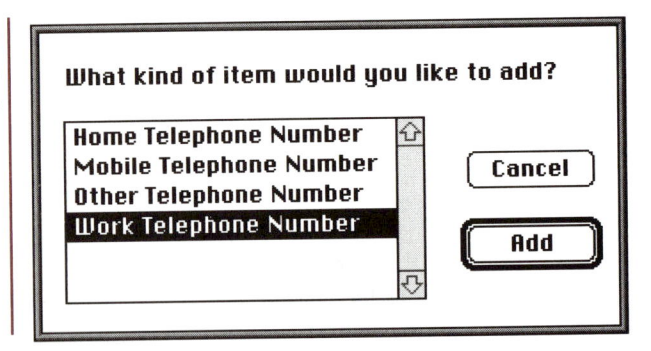

3. Double-click on the type of phone number you want to add. The dialog box in Figure 12.26 closes and fields for entering the phone number appear on the information card, as in Figure 12.27.

FIGURE 12.27
Fields for entering a new phone number

CHAPTER 12: System 7 Pro: PowerTalk Setup and Configuration **289**

4. If you want to change the value in the Name column, type a new value.

5. Click the mouse pointer in the <work number> field. (You can't tab into it.) Type the phone number.

6. Repeat steps 10 through 13 for any other phone numbers you want to add. A completed card might appear as in Figure 12.28.

FIGURE 12.28
A completed Phone Number card

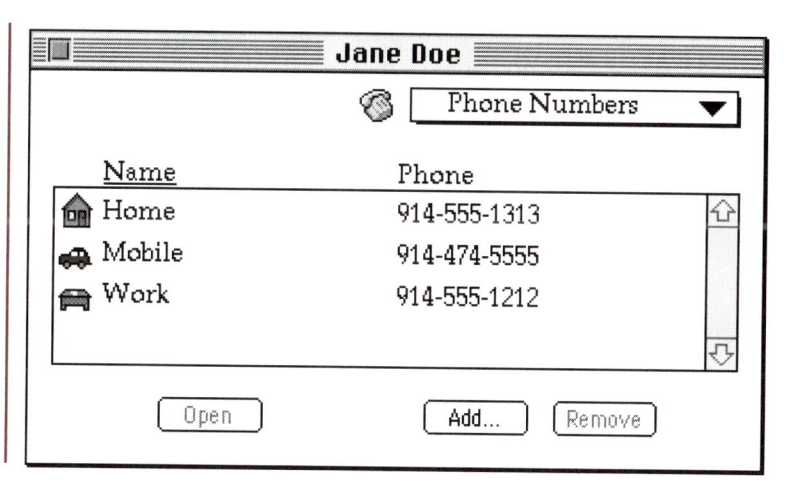

Name	Phone
Home	914-555-1313
Mobile	914-474-5555
Work	914-555-1212

The final part of an information card stores electronic addresses used to deliver electronic documents via PowerTalk:

1. Choose **Electronic Addresses** from the pop-up menu at the top right of the information card. A blank Electronic Addresses card appears (Figure 12.29).

FIGURE 12.29
An empty Electronic Addresses card

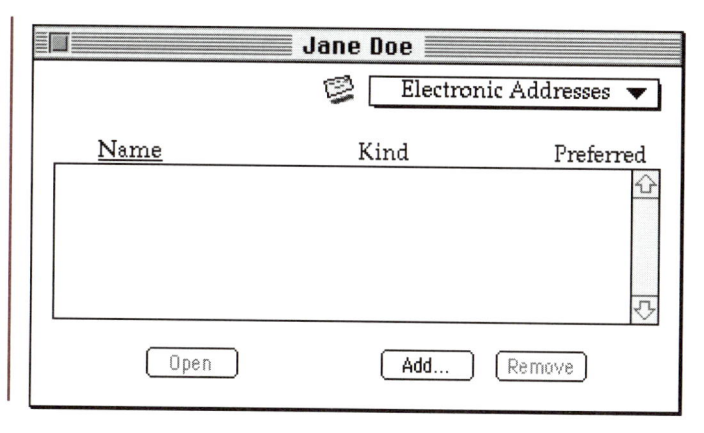

2. To add an electronic address, click the **Add** button. A dialog box listing the types of available PowerTalk services appears (Figure 12.30).

FIGURE 12.30
Choosing a type of electronic address to add to an information card

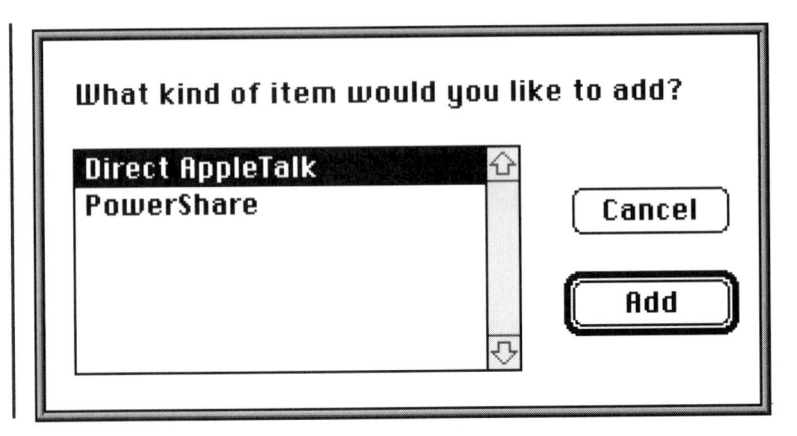

3. Double-click on the type of service for which you want to add an electronic address. The address is added to the card with a default name (see Figure 12.31). Replace the default name with something that clearly identifies the address to you. You might, for example, use the network name of a Macintosh for a Direct AppleTalk address and the name of a user and the catalog in which the user is stored for a PowerShare address.

FIGURE 12.31
A new electronic address

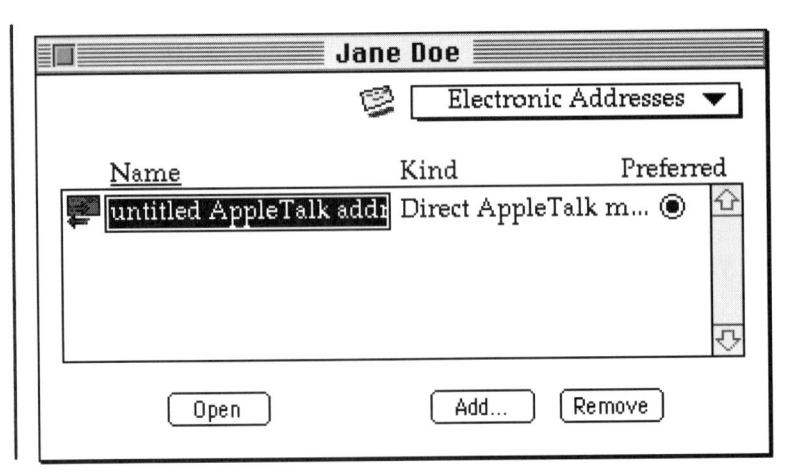

Notice in Figure 12.31 that the first electronic address added to an information card is designated as the "Preferred" electronic address. Unless you indicate otherwise, this is the address that will be used when you send mail or documents to the user this card describes. As you add other electronic addresses, each is given a radio button in the Preferred column (see Figure 12.32). You can change the preferred address at any time by clicking the radio button next to the address you want to make the preferred address.

FIGURE 12.32
A completed Electronic Addresses card

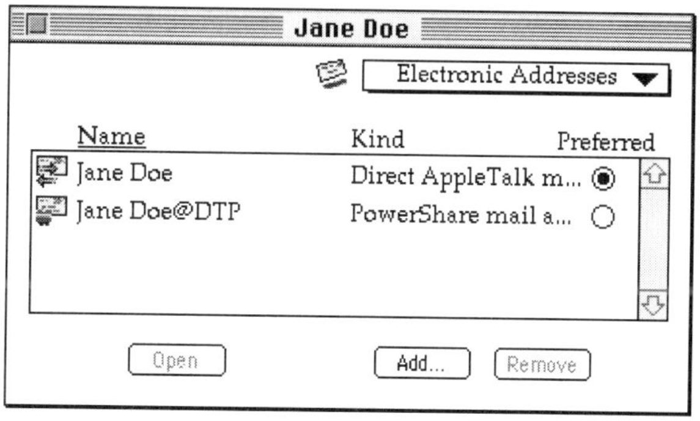

4. To store the complete electronic address associated with the entry on the Electronic Addresses card, double-click on the icon to the left of the Electronic address name. An electronic address info window opens, as in Figure 12.33.

FIGURE 12.33
An electronic address info window that shows the name of the Macintosh and its zone in separate fields

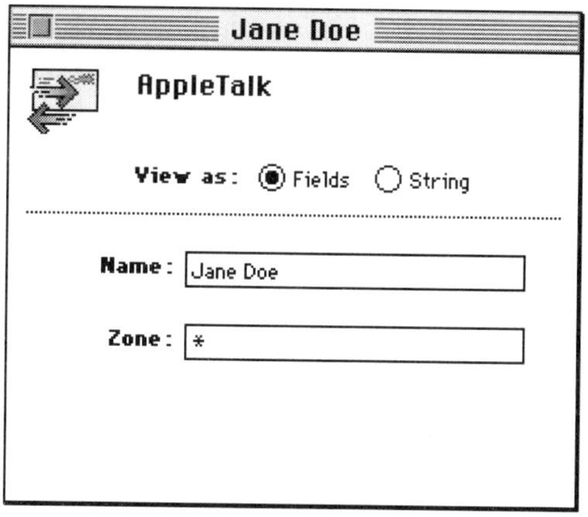

5. If this is a Direct AppleTalk address, enter the network name of the Macintosh to which this address applies. If this is a PowerShare address, enter the name of the user to whom this address applies.

6. If this is a Direct AppleTalk address, enter the zone in which the Macintosh is located. For your local zone, enter an asterisk (*). If this is a PowerShare address, enter the catalog (and optionally the folders) in which the user information card for this address is stored.

Note in Figure 12.33 that the Macintosh name and zone are viewed as fields. If you check the **String** radio button, the contents of the fields are assembled into a string that actually represents the electronic address (for example, see Figure 12.34).

FIGURE 12.34
An electronic address info window that shows the name of the Macintosh and its zone as an address string

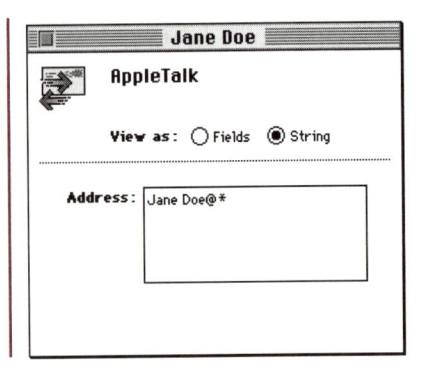

CREATING GROUP INFORMATION CARDS

A group information card is somewhat like a group network icon, in that it lets you work with multiple users at the same time. In this case, you will be able to send the same message to many users with one action, rather than having to send the messages individually.

To create a group information card:

1. Open a catalog window.
2. Choose **New Group** from the Catalogs menu. A group icon appears in the catalog window.
3. Type a name for the group icon.
4. To place a user in the group, drag the user's information card icon over the group icon. As with adding network users to a group, the user information card is copied, rather than moved, into the group. (To be completely accurate, the Macintosh operating system places an alias for the user information card in the group information card.)

To see the members of a PowerTalk group, double-click on the group information card icon. A group information card window opens, showing you the aliases for the user information cards that are part of the group (for example, see Figure 12.35).

FIGURE 12.35
A group information card window

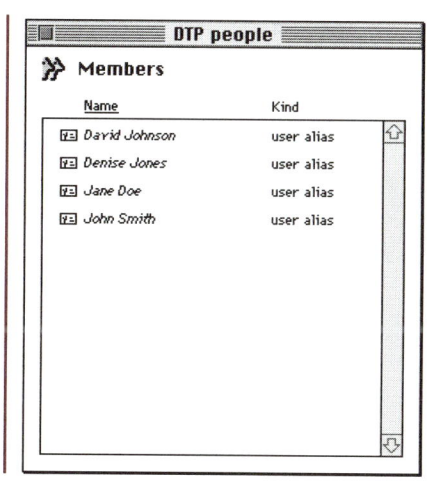

DTP people

Members

Name	Kind
David Johnson	user alias
Denise Jones	user alias
Jane Doe	user alias
John Smith	user alias

CREATING AND USING PERSONAL CATALOGS

Personal catalogs are the only type of catalog that you can create and delete at will. (AppleTalk and PowerShare catalogs are created and removed by PowerTalk as you add and remove PowerTalk services.) As you know, installing PowerTalk places a default personal catalog in the Apple Menu Items folder. However, you can create additional personal catalogs as needed, making it easy to organize the people with whom you communicate. Such catalogs are usually stored on the Desktop under a catalog icon with a stylized network "face" on the right page:

Friends

To create a new personal catalog, you must have access to the Catalog menu. That means that some catalog window (although it doesn't matter which) must be open:

1. Open any catalog window to display the Catalogs menu in the menu bar.

2. Choose **New Personal Catalog** from the Catalogs menu. PowerTalk creates the new personal catalog on the Desktop with the default name "untitled personal catalog."

3. Give the new personal catalog a name, just as you would any other icon.

> **BY THE WAY!** Although PowerTalk places a new personal catalog on the Desktop, you can move it from there to anywhere you want (for example, on a hard disk volume within a folder).

One of your personal catalogs is always designated as the "preferred" personal catalog. This is the catalog that application programs that support PowerTalk will use to find electronic addresses. The preferred catalog has a special icon (note the bookmark on the left page):

Personal Catalog

To make a catalog your preferred catalog:

1. Highlight the catalog icon.
2. Choose **Get Info** from the Finder's File menu or press ⌘-I. The catalog's Get Info window appears (see Figure 12.36).

FIGURE 12.36
A personal catalog Get Info box

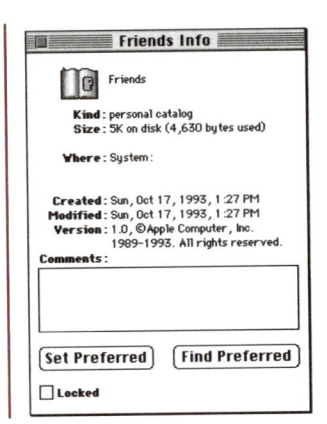

3. Click the **Set Preferred** button.

If you are unsure as to the location of the current preferred personal catalog, you can click the **Find Preferred** button.

There are several ways to add items to a personal catalog:

- Create new user and group information cards in the personal catalog.
- Open other personal catalog windows and drag items from those windows to the personal catalog.
- Create an alias for an item in an AppleTalk or PowerShare catalog and drag it to the personal catalog.
- Search for items using the **Find in Catalog** command (discussed shortly) and save the items found in a personal catalog.
- Save items in a personal catalog while working with the Mailer, an application that lets you create and send electronic mail. (The Mailer is discussed in Chapter 13.)

Once you have items stored in a personal catalog, you can delete them at any time by dragging them to the trash.

Using an AppleTalk Catalog

An AppleTalk catalog is created when you install Direct AppleTalk service. Stored inside the Catalogs icon on the Desktop, it contains information cards for the Macintoshes with which you can communicate peer-to-peer and lists the AppleShare servers on the network. In Figure 12.37, for example, there are three Direct AppleTalk users (Mac II, Jane Doe, and David Johnson) and two AppleShare file servers (DTP and Central Services).

Figure 12.37
An AppleTalk catalog window

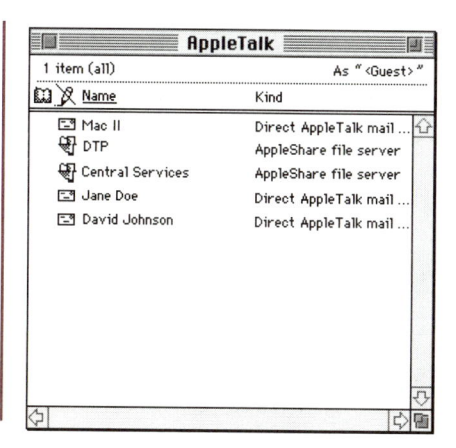

There are two major uses for the contents of an AppleTalk catalog, sending messages to other Macintoshes and logging on to AppleShare servers. To log on to an AppleShare server, double-click on the server's icon. The Macintosh operating system displays the Server Log-on dialog box in Figure 10.27. You can then complete the log-on in the normal manner.

> **BY THE WAY!** If your AppleTalk network has zones, each zone will appear in a folder in an AppleTalk catalog window. Double-click on the folder to see the contents of the zone.

PowerShare Catalog Notes

A PowerShare catalog, stored within the Catalogs icon on the Desktop, contains information cards for all users who have PowerShare accounts on that server. You will have one PowerShare catalog for each PowerShare server to which you have access. As you will see shortly, you will be able to use the information cards in PowerShare catalogs to send messages to other users.

Searching Catalogs

As the network to which your Macintosh is attached grows, so will the contents of your catalogs. To help you locate specific information cards that are in catalogs accessible to your system, PowerTalk provides a catalog search utility. To search your catalogs:

1. Choose **Find in Catalog** from the menu. The Find in Catalog window appears (Figure 12.38).

2. Pick the type of item for which you want to search from the leftmost pop-up menu. As you can see in Figure 12.38, you can search for all items or restrict the search to users, file servers, or miscellaneous types of items.

3. Pick where you want to search. As you can see in Figure 12.39, you can search "everywhere," in a specific catalog (in this case, AppleTalk or DTP), on all mounted disk volumes, or on a specific disk volume. (If you can narrow the search to a single catalog or disk volume, you can significantly speed up the search.)

FIGURE 12.38
The Find in Catalog window

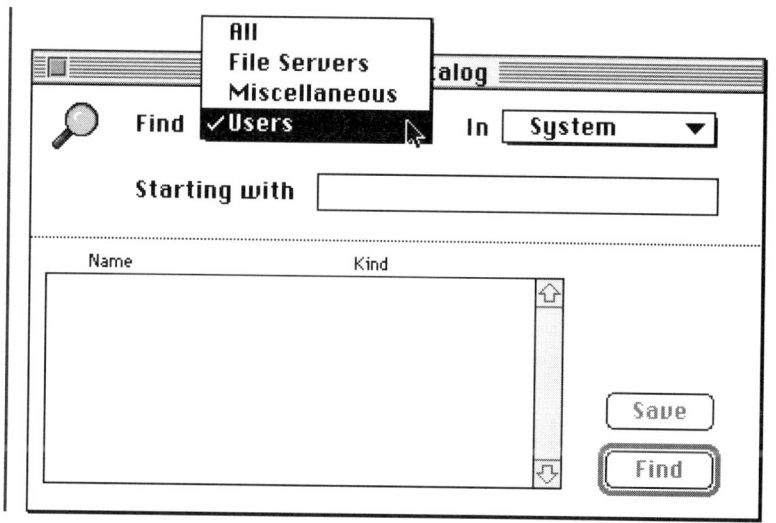

FIGURE 12.39
Choosing where to search

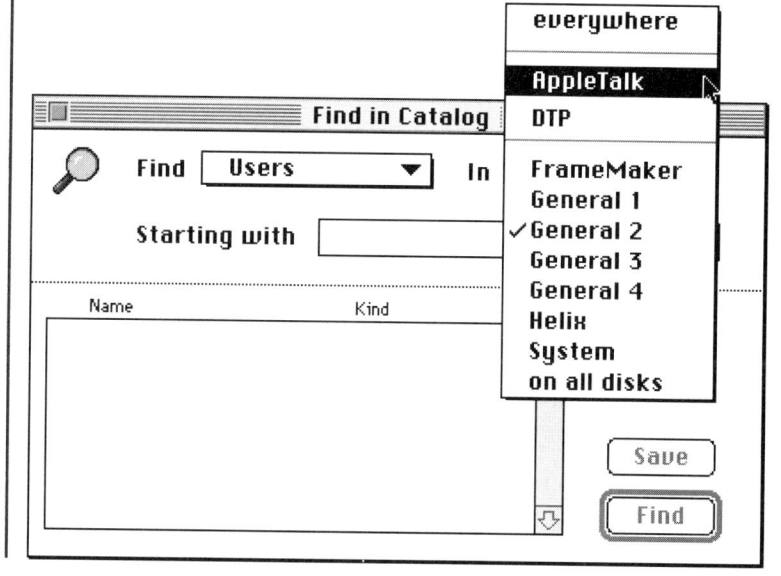

4. Type the first part of the name of the item you want to find. (The more characters you enter, the more accurate the search will be.)

5. Click the **Find** button or press **Enter**. PowerTalk searches for the type of item you've requested in the location(s) you've requested. The results of the

search appear in the scrolling list at the bottom left of the Find in Catalog dialog box, as in Figure 12.40.

FIGURE 12.40
An information card located by Find in Catalog

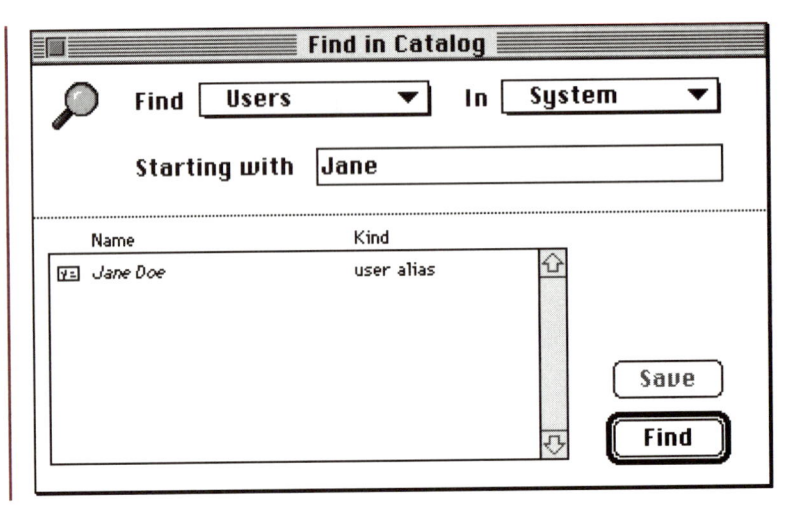

![Find in Catalog dialog showing Find: Users, In: System, Starting with: Jane, with result Jane Doe / user alias, and Save and Find buttons]

BY THE WAY! When PowerTalk is searching, the **Find** button turns into a **Stop** button. You can click it at any time to stop the search.

There are two things you can do with items that you've found:

- Highlight an item and drag it from the Find in Catalog window to wherever you want to store a copy of the item.

- Highlight an item and click the **Save** button. A copy of the item is placed in your preferred personal catalog.

CHAPTER 13
System 7 Pro: Sending and Receiving Messages with PowerTalk

PowerTalk's greatest strength is its ability to transmit virtually any Finder object (a file, a folder, or an information card) across an AppleTalk network. As you will see in this chapter, sending Finder objects is as easy as drag-and-drop.

PowerTalk also provides electronic mail capabilities. The Mailer, an application that was installed with PowerTalk, can be used directly from the Finder. In addition, many application programs have integrated the Mailer. You can then send formatted documents directly from that application as electronic mail. In this chapter you will learn how to use the Mailer and see how it can been integrated into an application program.

SENDING ITEMS: FINDER OBJECTS

You can send any Finder object to any user or group of users for which you have an information card directly from the Finder. To send a Finder object:

1. Open whatever objects and/or folders necessary so that you can see the information card for the recipient of the item you're going to send.

2. Open whatever disks and/or folders necessary so that you can see the item you're going to send.

3. Drag the item you're going to send to the information card of the recipient. PowerTalk asks you to confirm that you intend to send the item (Figure 13.1).

FIGURE 13.1
Confirming sending a Finder object with PowerTalk

> ⚠ Do you want to send "Letterhead" to the Direct AppleTalk mail address "Mac II"?
>
> [Cancel] [OK]

4. Click the **OK** button or press **Enter** to confirm the transmission. PowerTalk sends the item for you. If the recipient is a group information card, every user in that group receives a copy of the item transmitted.

BY THE WAY! The only transmission you can't make by dragging is sending an information card to a group information card recipient. PowerTalk thinks you're trying to add the information card to the group! The solution is to place any information cards you want to send via a group information card into a folder. Then you can drag the folder to the group information card without a problem.

SENDING ITEMS: LETTERS AND THE APPLE MAILER

Inside the PowerTalk folder on your startup hard disk is a program called AppleMail. As a stand-alone program, AppleMail lets you create, send, and receive electronic mail. Documents that are to be sent over a network using PowerTalk are known as *letters* and have their own Desktop icon:

C10 letter

A portion of AppleMail has also been integrated into a number of mainstream application programs, making it possible to send and receive electronic mail without leaving the program. (You will see an example of how later in this chapter.) The remainder of this section assumes that you are using AppleMail as a stand-alone application. However, the procedures for sending and receiving mail are the same regardless of the application with which you are working.

Introducing the Mailer

AppleMail has a two-part window (see Figure 13.2). The *mailer* is the top portion of the window, above the empty area where you enter the contents of the document to be mailed. (The mailer is the portion that is integrated into application programs.) By default, the name of the person who has unlocked the PowerTalk Key Chain appears in the mailer's From box. To send mail, you must select at least one recipient (there are four ways to do so) and enter a subject. You may also decide to attach one or more files to your message (*enclosures*).

Figure 13.2
The AppleMail window

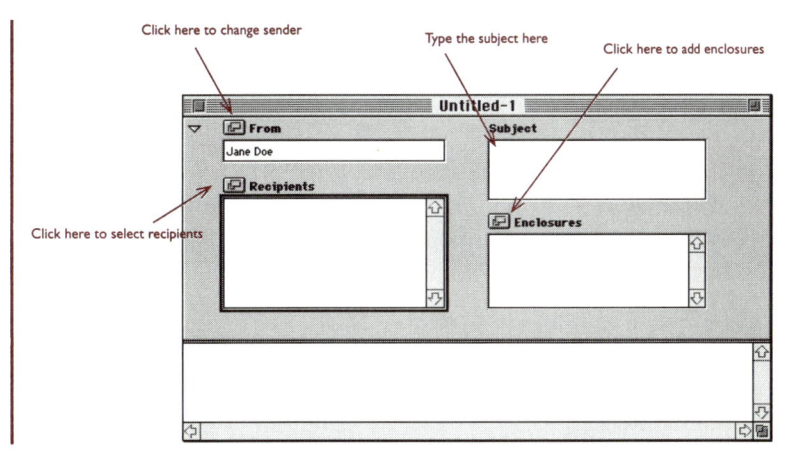

AppleMail's text editor is more capable than a basic text editor like TeachText, but has far fewer features than a word processor. You can choose the typeface, size, and style of text characters using the typical Font, Size, and Style menus, but you won't be able to control formatting such as the placement of margins, tab stops, or page breaks. However, you can paste any PICT or bitmapped graphic (black-and-white, grayscale, or color) into the mailer.

302 NAVIGATING SYSTEM 7: Understanding The Macintosh Operating System

AppleMail supports the typical File and Edit menu commands you expect to find in any Macintosh application (see Figure 13.3). In addition, you will find File commands related to using letterheads, which you will read about shortly.

FIGURE 13.3
AppleMail's File and Edit menus

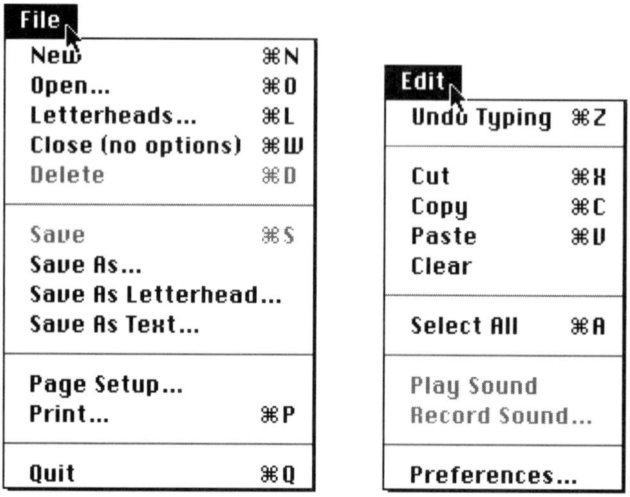

File	
New	⌘N
Open...	⌘O
Letterheads...	⌘L
Close (no options)	⌘W
Delete	⌘D
Save	⌘S
Save As...	
Save As Letterhead...	
Save As Text...	
Page Setup...	
Print...	⌘P
Quit	⌘Q

Edit	
Undo Typing	⌘Z
Cut	⌘X
Copy	⌘C
Paste	⌘V
Clear	
Select All	⌘A
Play Sound	
Record Sound...	
Preferences...	

CHANGING THE SENDER

The sender of a message must either be the person who controls the Key Chain on the Macintosh from which the message is being sent, someone with a valid PowerShare account, or the current guest user. A guest user is someone for whom you have set up a visitor's mailbox. (You will see how to do this later in this chapter.)

To change the sender:

1. Click the button at the top left of the mailer (see Figure 13.2). The dialog box in Figure 13.4 appears. Assuming you have already unlocked your Key Chain, PowerTalk fills in your name.

2. Click the **More Choices** button. The dialog box expands to show you the options in Figure 13.5.

3. Click the **Choose Catalog** button to select the PowerShare catalog in which the new sender is stored.

4. Enter the new sender's name and password.

5. Click the **OK** button or press **Enter**.

FIGURE 13.4
The default "Change sender" dialog box

> To change the sender of this letter, enter your PowerTalk Key Chain Access Code:
>
> Name: Jane Doe
>
> You have already entered your Access Code.
>
> [More Choices]   [Cancel]   [OK]

FIGURE 13.5
Changing the sender of a message

> To change the sender, please provide the appropriate PowerShare account information:
>
> ○ Guest
> ● PowerShare account
> ○ Key Chain Access Code
>
> PowerShare service: [Choose Catalog...]
> Name: [Jane Doe]
> Password: [   ]
>
> [Fewer Choices] [Set Password] [Cancel] [OK]

CHOOSING RECIPIENTS

There are four ways to choose recipients and attach their electronic addresses to the message you are sending: selecting from a personal catalog, selecting from a shared catalog, searching catalogs, and entering the address directly. To begin, click the button above the Recipients area in the mailer (look back at Figure 13.2). The dialog box in Figure 13.6 appears in the right half of the mailer. Notice that there are four buttons down the left side. Each provides access to one method of selecting a recipient.

304 NAVIGATING SYSTEM 7: Understanding The Macintosh Operating System

FIGURE 13.6
Choosing a recipient from a shared catalog

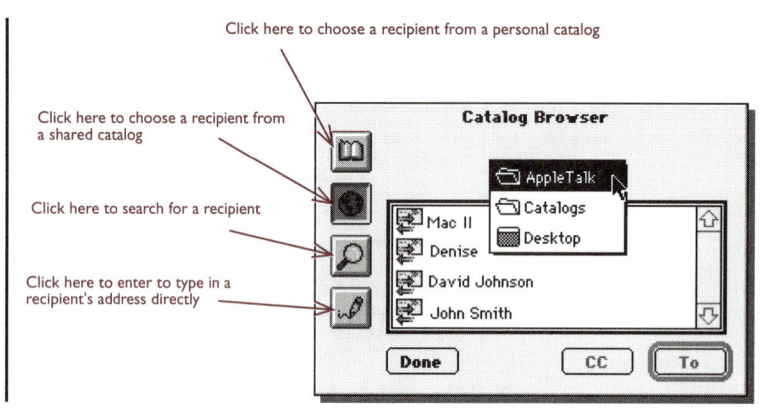

- Click here to choose a recipient from a personal catalog
- Click here to choose a recipient from a shared catalog
- Click here to search for a recipient
- Click here to enter to type in a recipient's address directly

Choosing Recipients from a PowerShare Catalog

By default, PowerTalk highlights the **Shared Catalogs** button (the second from the top). To select one or more recipients from a PowerShare or AppleTalk catalog:

1. Use the pull-down menu at the top center of the dialog box to choose the catalog from which you want to select recipients. The information cards in the catalog appear in the scrolling list.
2. Highlight a recipient.
3. Click the **To** button or press **Enter**.

> **BY THE WAY!**
> If you want someone to receive a "carbon copy" rather than to be a primary recipient of a messages, click the **CC** button instead of the **To** button.

4. Repeat steps 1 through 3 for each recipient of the message who will come from a shared catalog.
5. Click the **Done** button.

Choosing Recipients from a Personal Catalog

To choose recipients from a personal catalog:

CHAPTER 13: System 7 Pro: Sending and Receiving Messages with PowerTalk **305**

1. Click the top left button at the left side of the Recipients dialog box. The dialog box changes to list the information cards in your preferred personal catalog (Figure 13.7).

FIGURE 13.7
Choosing message recipients from your preferred personal catalog

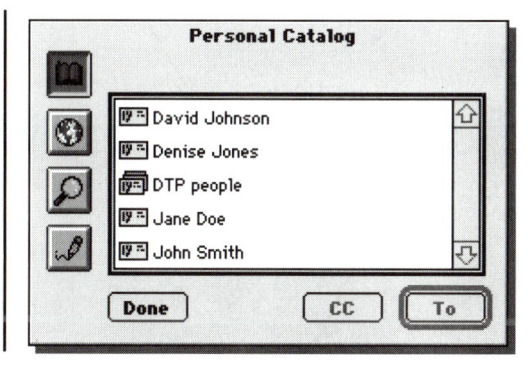

2. Click on an information card (either a user or group card).
3. Click the **To** or **CC** button.
4. Repeat steps 2 and 3 for each recipient in your preferred personal catalog.
5. Click the **Done** button.

Searching for Recipients

The mailer's search capabilities are very similar to the Find in Catalog application about which you read in Chapter 12. To use it from within the mailer:

1. Click the third button at the left side of the Recipients dialog box. The dialog box changes to let you enter search text and define where you want to search (Figure 13.8)
2. Type the text for which you want to search in the Find box.
3. Use the Search pop-up menu to select the disk or catalog in which you want to search.
4. Click the **Find** button. The information cards that PowerTalk locates appear in the scrolling list in the middle of the dialog box. The **Find** button also changes to a **To** button.
5. Highlight the name of a recipient.

FIGURE 13.8
Searching for a recipient

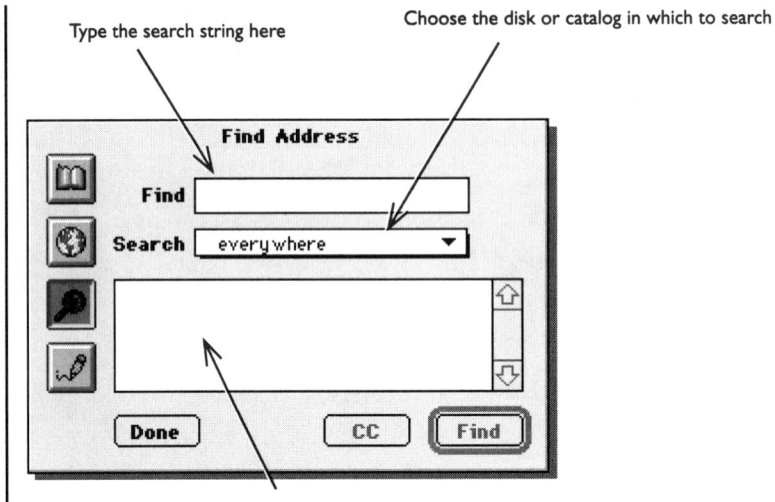

Type the search string here

Choose the disk or catalog in which to search

Information cards that match the search criteria appear here

6. Click the **To** or **CC** button.

7. Repeat steps 5 and 6 for all recipients you want to add.

8. Click the **Done** button.

Entering an Address Directly

If you know the electronic mail address of a recipient, you can enter the address directly into the Recipients dialog box. To do so:

1. Click the bottom button at the left side of the Recipients dialog box. The dialog box changes to let you enter the address (Figure 13.9).

FIGURE 13.9
Entering an electronic mail address directly

CHAPTER 13: System 7 Pro: Sending and Receiving Messages with PowerTalk   **307**

2. Use the Catalog pop-up menu to choose the type of service (PowerShare or AppleTalk) for which you will be entering an address.

3. Type the electronic mail address in the Address box.

4. Click the **To** or **CC** button.

5. Repeat steps 2 through 4 for each address you want to enter.

6. Click the **Done** button.

ENTERING A SUBJECT

Before the mailer will let you send a message, you must enter a subject. To so do, click and mouse pointer in the Subject box and type an appropriate phrase or sentence.

ADDING ENCLOSURES

Enclosures are any files you want to send along with your message. There are two ways to add enclosures. The first is to simply drag the icon of the file or folder you want to send into the Enclosures box. This inserts a copy of the enclosure into the AppleMail document; the original enclosure isn't moved or deleted.

Alternatively, you can identify an enclosure with an Open File dialog box:

1. Click the **Enclosures** button (see Figure 13.2). A slightly modified version of an Open File dialog box appears (Figure 13.10).

FIGURE 13.10
Choosing an enclosure to add to a message

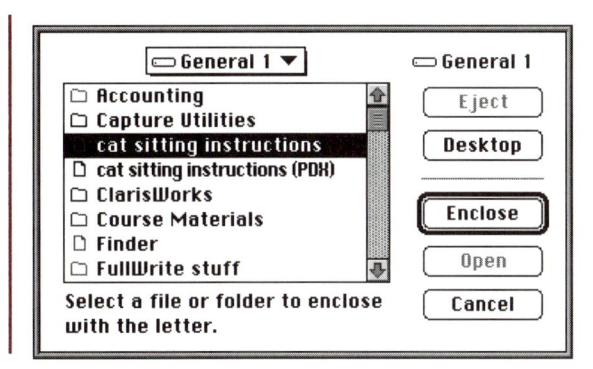

2. Locate the file or folder you want to enclose.

3. Click the **Enclose** button or press **Enter**.

4. Repeat steps 1 through 3 for each file or folder you want to enclose.

When an enclosure has been added to a message, a tiny paperclip appears at the top right of the mailer, as in Figure 13.11.

FIGURE 13.11
A complete letter with an enclosure

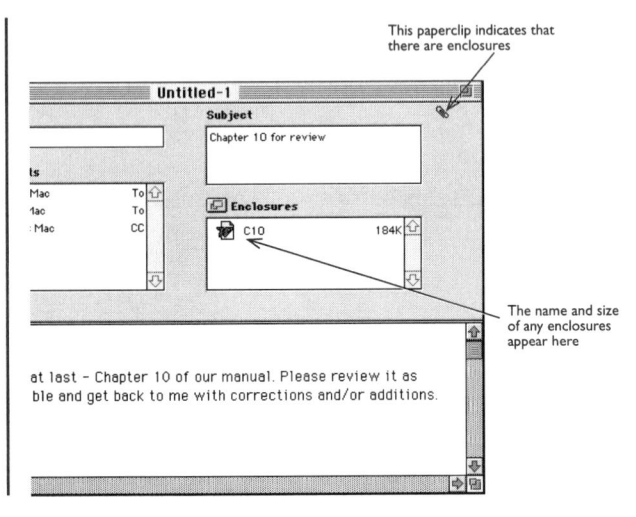

SENDING THE LETTER

Once you have chosen at least one recipient and entered a subject for your message, you can send the mail. To do so:

1. Choose **Send** from the Mail menu (Figure 13.12) or press ⌘-**M**. The Send dialog box appears (Figure 13.13).

FIGURE 13.12
The mailer's Mail menu

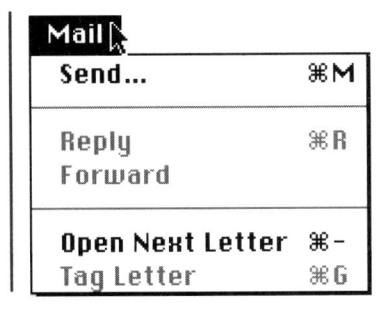

FIGURE 13.13
The Send dialog box

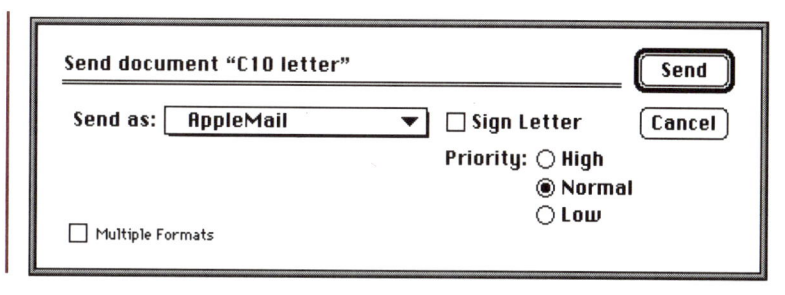

2. Choose the format for the message from the Send as pop-up menu. The available formats vary depending on the Application in which the mailer is embedded. When you are working with AppleMail, you can either send it as an editable message or as a *snapshot*. A snapshot is a bitmapped version of a letter than can be viewed and printed but not edited.

3. Choose the message's priority by clicking one of the **Priority** radio buttons.

4. Click the **Send** button or press **Enter**. PowerTalk tries to send the message immediately.

> **BY THE WAY!** The Sign Letter check box lets you add a digital signature to a message to verify that it has come from you and that it hasn't been altered during transmission. Digital signatures are discussed in depth at the end of this chapter.

> **BY THE WAY!** If PowerTalk can't send your message immediately (because either you or the message's recipient aren't connected to the network), the message is placed in your Out Tray. You will see how to work with it shortly.

SAVING AND USING LETTERHEADS

A *letterhead* is a template for an AppleMail message. AppleMail comes with a selection of letterheads, including the "blank" letterhead that appears in Figure 13.2. Other letterheads include graphics that make messages a bit more interesting. For example, you might use the "Daily News" letterhead in Figure 13.14 to create a newsletter that circulates to all PowerTalk users. The "Hot News" letterhead (Figure 13.15), complete with color chili peppers, might be used to grab a recipient's attention.

FIGURE 13.14
The "Daily News" letterhead

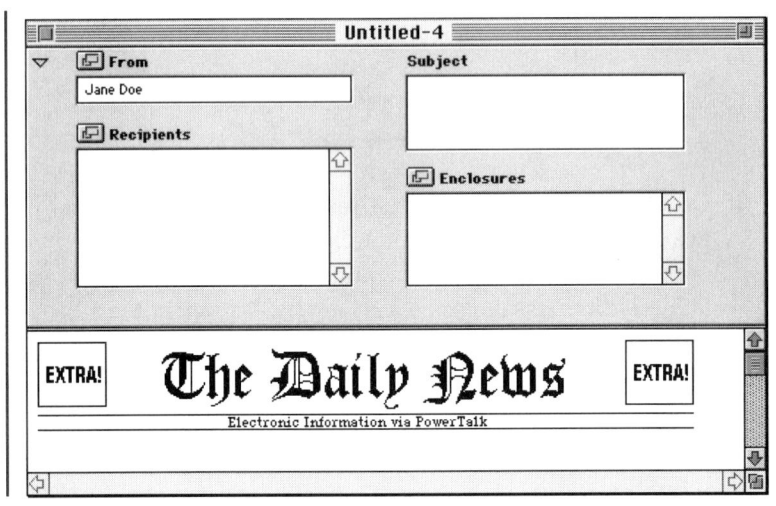

FIGURE 13.15
The "Hot News" letterhead

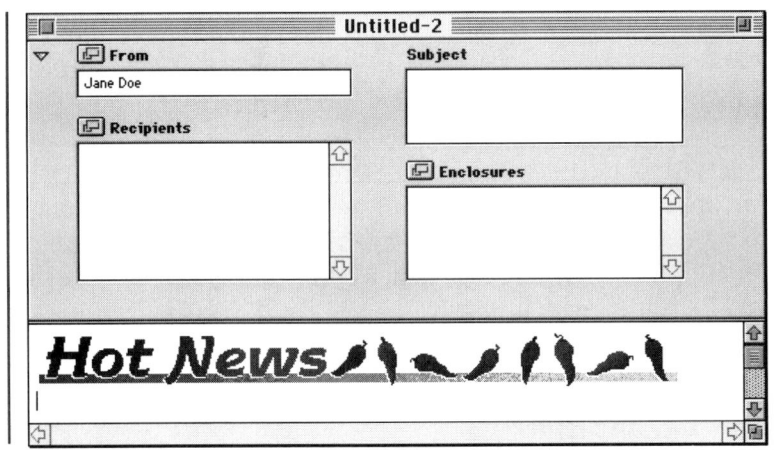

BY THE WAY! Letterheads are stored in the AppleMail Letterheads folder in the Preferences folder, inside the System folder. Unfortunately, you don't have any choice as to where to put them.

CHAPTER 13: System 7 Pro: Sending and Receiving Messages with PowerTalk   311

AppleMail designates one letterhead as the "default" letterhead that is used whenever you open a new AppleMail document. Unless you indicate otherwise, AppleMail uses the blank letterhead (an empty document with no graphics).

Letterheads are opened and managed with the Letterhead dialog box. To work with a letterhead, choose **Letterheads** from the File menu or press ⌘-L. The Letterheads dialog box appears (Figure 13.16). As you can see, the default letterhead has a diamond to the left of its name.

FIGURE 13.16
The Letterheads dialog box

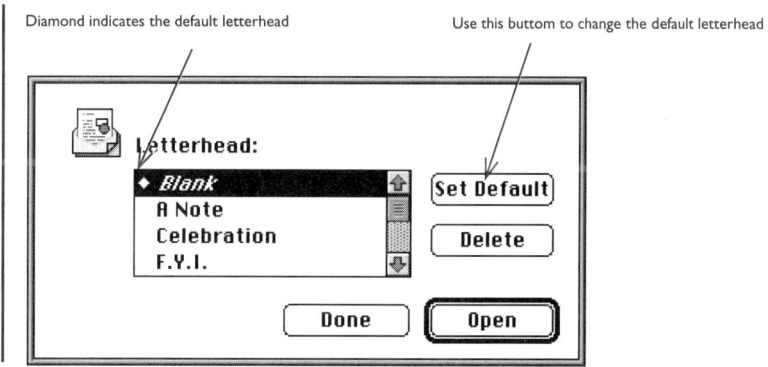

There are three things you can do from the Letterheads dialog box:

- Change the default letterhead: To change the default letterhead, highlight the name of the letterhead you want as the default and click the **Set Default** button.

- Delete a letterhead: To delete a letterhead, highlight the name of the letterhead you want to delete and click the **Delete** button.

- Open a copy of a letterhead as a new AppleMail document: To open a copy of a letterhead as a new AppleMail document, double-click on the name of the letterhead. AppleMail opens it as an untitled document.

You aren't necessarily restricted to the letterheads that come with AppleMail; you can create and save your own. To create a new letterhead:

1. Format a blank AppleMail document the way you want it to appear, including any graphics you want to paste in. (Keep in mind that storing a letterhead includes everything in the mailer as well as in the document portion.)

2. Choose **Save As Letterhead** from the File menu. The dialog box in Figure 13.17 appears.

FIGURE 13.17
Saving a new letterhead

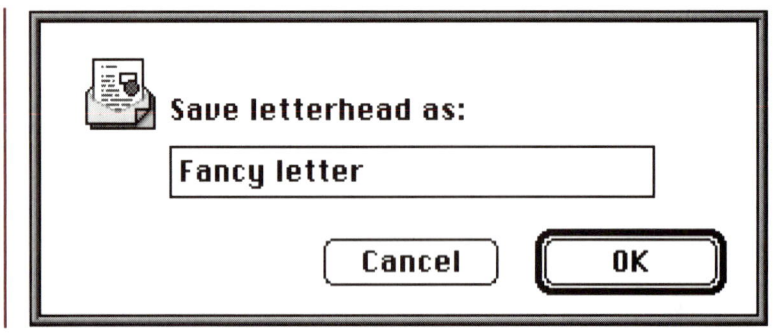

Save letterhead as:

Fancy letter

Cancel   OK

3. Enter a name for the letterhead.

4. Click **OK** or press the **Enter** button. The new letterhead is stored in the AppleMail Letterheads folder. (Remember that you can't choose where letterheads are stored.)

AppleMail Print Options

Like any other application program, you can use AppleMail to print the documents you create. (You can also print messages you receive via PowerTalk.) The Print dialog box, however, contains two new options: Print Mailer and Print Footer (see Figure 13.18).

FIGURE 13.18
The AppleMail Print dialog box

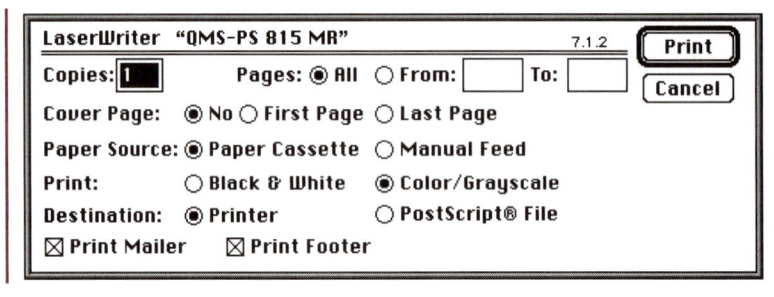

LaserWriter "QMS-PS 815 MR"   7.1.2   Print

Copies: 1   Pages: ◉ All ○ From: To: Cancel
Cover Page: ◉ No ○ First Page ○ Last Page
Paper Source: ◉ Paper Cassette ○ Manual Feed
Print: ○ Black & White   ◉ Color/Grayscale
Destination: ◉ Printer   ○ PostScript® File
☒ Print Mailer   ☒ Print Footer

The Print Mailer check box controls whether AppleMail produces a cover sheet for your mail. Should you leave it checked, the cover sheet will include all the information from the mailer, including the sender, the recipients, the subject, and the file names of any enclosures. If the Print Footer check box is checked, AppleMail prints a footer at the bottom of each document page that includes a page number, the sender, and the subject.

CHAPTER 13: System 7 Pro: Sending and Receiving Messages with PowerTalk **313**

The Mailer and Application Programs

As you know, application program developers can integrate the mailer into their programs to make it easier for you to send documents as electronic mail. For example, the word processor WordPerfect places a "mailer" button in its button bar. Clicking the button displays the mailer at the top of the current document (see Figure 13.19). Notice that it looks exactly like it does when it is a part of AppleMail, although there is no Mail menu in the menu bar.

FIGURE 13.19
A WordPerfect document with the integrated mailer

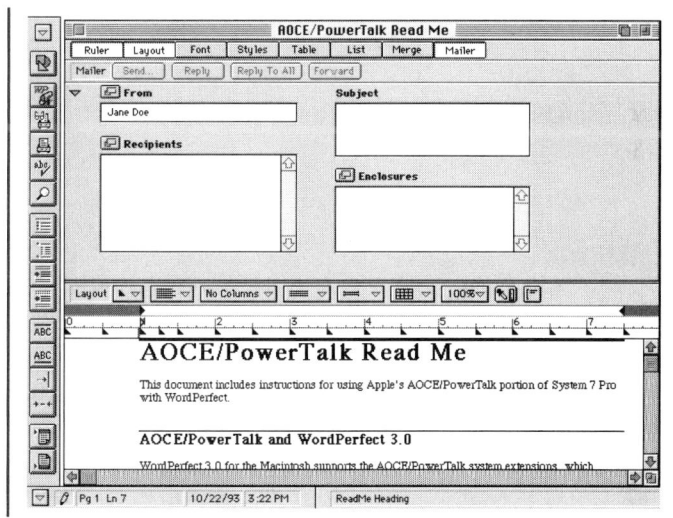

To send a document:

1. Create a document using any of WordPerfect's features.
2. Click the **Mailer** button to display the mailer.
3. Choose recipients and enter a subject.
4. Click the **Send** button at the far right of the lower ribbon menu. The Send dialog box appears. In this case, the Send As pop-up menu includes WordPerfect 3.0 as a possible format, along with AppleMail and snapshot.
5. Choose the format in which the document should be sent. To send more than one format, click the **Multiple Formats** check box. The available for-

mats turn into a set of check boxes (see Figure 13.20). Click the formats you want to use.

FIGURE 13.20
Sending a document in multiple formats

Send document "AOCE/PowerTalk Read Me"		Send
Send as: ☐ AppleMail	☐ Sign Letter	Cancel
☐ Snapshot	Priority: ○ High	
☒ WordPerfect 3.0	● Normal	
	○ Low	
☒ Multiple Formats		

6. Click the **Send** button or press **Enter**.

USING THE MAILBOX

The Mailbox is a holding area for incoming mail (the *In Tray*) and for outgoing mail (the *Out Tray*). Although the Mailbox icon appears on the Desktop, the mail inside it is stored on your startup disk. Nonetheless, you can't move the Mailbox off the Desktop.

> **BY THE WAY!** Because the contents of the Mailbox are stored on your startup disk, the space on your startup disk can disappear very quickly. PowerTalk doesn't give you any choice about where mail is stored, but you can use PowerRules, an add-on program from Beyond, Inc., to create alternative mailboxes. PowerRules is discussed later in this chapter.

The maximum number of messages that can be in your Mailbox is determined by an entry in the Mailbox's Get Info box (Figure 13.21). Although PowerTalk recommends allowing 400 letters, you can restrict the number of messages (and also the maximum amount of disk space consumed by mail) by entering a lower number. When the maximum number of messages is reached, PowerTalk deletes the oldest messages to make room for new ones.

CHAPTER 13: System 7 Pro: Sending and Receiving Messages with PowerTalk **315**

FIGURE 13.21
The Mailbox Get Info box

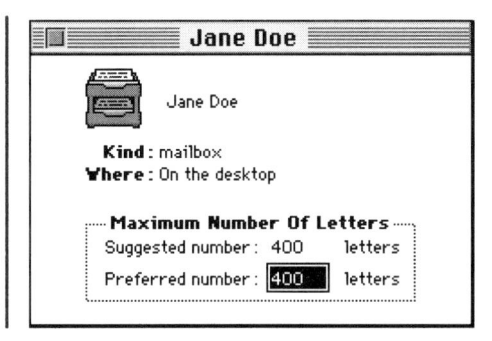

To work with the Mailbox, double-click on its icon. The In Tray opens and a Mailbox menu appears in the Finder's menu bar (Figure 13.22). The first time you open the Mailbox, you will probably want to configure your Mailbox environment by setting some preferences. To do so, choose the **Preferences** option from the Mailbox menu.

FIGURE 13.22
The Mailbox menu

As you can see in Figure 13.23, the Mailbox Preferences dialog box has four sections. The top section determines the order in which incoming mail is presented in the In Tray. If the "Show most recent first" box is checked, mail will appear in reverse chronological order. The second check box in the top section determines whether you will allow visitor mailboxes so other users can check their mail from your Macintosh. (Visitor mailboxes are discussed later in this chapter.)

The second section of the Mailbox Preferences dialog box governs the behavior of your Macintosh when new mail arrives. You can display an alert like that in Figure 13.24 (check the **"Display alert"** box), show a flashing Mailbox icon on top of the menu as in Figure 13.25 (check the **"Blink icon in menu bar"** box), and/or play a sound (check the **"Play this sound"** box and select a sound from the pop-up menu).

FIGURE 13.23
Setting Mailbox preferences

FIGURE 13.24
An alert announcing the arrival of new mail

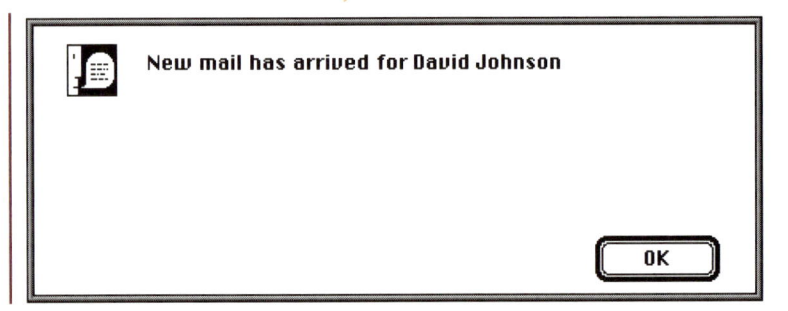

FIGURE 13.25
A flashing Mailbox icon announcing the arrival of new mail

The third section of the dialog box places controls on how long items remain in the Out Tray. By default, items are removed after 14 days. This includes items that have been sent and those that PowerTalk has been unable to send because the Macintosh to which the message should be sent hasn't been available. The fourth section of the dialog box concerns *tags*, classifications that you can attach to incoming mail. You will find out more about tags shortly.

CHAPTER 13: System 7 Pro: Sending and Receiving Messages with PowerTalk   **317**

WORKING WITH THE OUT TRAY

When you open the Mailbox, only the In Tray is displayed. To see the Out Tray, choose **Out Tray** from the Mailbox menu; the Out Tray appears in its own window (Figure 13.26). The Finder's View menu changes so that it can control the order in which items appear (Figure 13.27). Like any Finder window, you can change the sort order of the window's contents either by choosing the order from the View menu or by clicking on a column header in the window itself.

FIGURE 13.26
The Out Tray

Subject	Date Sent	Status	Mail Connection
Brochure (1st draft)	10/23/93, 4:40 PM	sending	Direct AppleTalk Mail
Another paper for you to re...	10/23/93, 4:39 PM	waiting	Direct AppleTalk Mail
Meeting schedule	10/23/93, 4:15 PM	done	Direct AppleTalk Mail
Memo to John	10/23/93, 4:07 PM	waiting	Direct AppleTalk Mail

Out Tray for Jane Doe — 4 items

FIGURE 13.27
The Out Tray View menu

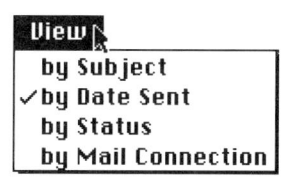

View
   by Subject
 ✓ by Date Sent
   by Status
   by Mail Connection

A message in the Out Tray has a status that indicates what PowerTalk has done or will do with the message. As you can see in Figure 13.26, this status has one of three values:

- sending: PowerTalk is currently sending the message.

- waiting: PowerTalk is doing nothing with the message and is waiting for instructions about what should be done with it. A waiting message might be a message that you sent while you were off-line (not connected to a network). It might also be a message for a Macintosh that currently isn't available on the network.

- done: PowerTalk has finished with the message. A "done" status means that PowerTalk has sent the message over the network or that PowerTalk has tried so many times to send the message that it has given up. Keep in mind that "done" doesn't necessarily mean that a message has been delivered to its intended recipient. In particular, when a message is intended for a user who has an account on a PowerShare server, "done" means that the message has reached a PowerShare server; it doesn't mean that it actually reached its recipient.

You can delete a message in the Out Tray at any time by dragging its icon from the Out Tray window to the trash. However, delete messages don't stay in the trash like other items; they are deleted immediately. You will therefore be asked to confirm a deletion from the Out Tray (Figure 13.28).

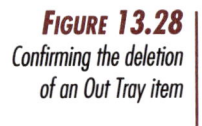

FIGURE 13.28
Confirming the deletion of an Out Tray item

> ⚠ The Out Tray item "Letterhead" cannot be left in the trash and will be deleted immediately. It will not be sent if it hasn't already been delivered.
>
> Do you want to delete it now?
>
> [Cancel] [[OK]]

WORKING WITH THE IN TRAY

The In Tray is a repository for messages that other people send to you. As you can see in Figure 13.29, the messages first appear in descending order by date. A message with a check mark to its left has been read. To change the order in which the messages are sorted, either choose or sort order from the View menu (Figure 13.30) or click a column heading in the In Tray window.

FIGURE 13.29
The In Tray

	Subject	Sender	Date Sent	Location	Priority
	Tomorrow's meeting	David Johnson	10/23/93, 5:49 PM	local	normal
	Weekend ball game	John Smith	10/23/93, 4:40 PM	local	high
✓	Three customers	Denise Jones	10/23/93, 3:12 PM	local	normal

In Tray for Jane Doe — 3 items

FIGURE 13.30
The In Tray View menu

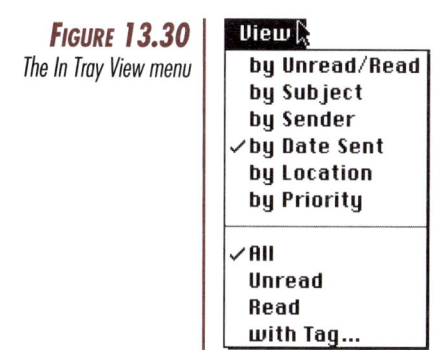

```
View
  by Unread/Read
  by Subject
  by Sender
✓ by Date Sent
  by Location
  by Priority

✓ All
  Unread
  Read
  with Tag...
```

The In Tray shows you the subject, sender, date the message was sent as well as the message's location and priority. The location of the item takes one of two values: local or remote. A "local" message is stored on your Macintosh's hard disk; a "remote" message is stored on a PowerShare server.

A message can be read, copied, or deleted:

- To read a message, double-click on the message's icon in the In Tray. The Macintosh operating system checks the message's creator string and opens the message with the application that created it. If you don't have the application that created the message, you can drag the message's icon over the icon of some other application program that *can* open the message.

- To copy a message, drag its icon from the In Tray to wherever you want to copy it.

- To dispose of a message in the In Tray, drag its icon to the trash. Unlike Out Tray items, In Tray items behave like other Finder objects in the trash: Messages stay in the trash until you empty it.

USING TAGS TO FILTER MAIL

If you receive a lot of mail, it can be difficult to sort through all the messages. *Tags* let you classify and group mail to make it easier to process. Each piece of mail can be assigned up to eight tags. Once you have placed tags on your mail, you can display only those messages that have been assigned a given tag.

ASSIGNING TAGS

To assign a tag to a mail item:

1. Highlight the item in the In Tray.
2. Choose **Tag** from the Mailbox menu. The Tag dialog box appears (see Figure 13.31).

FIGURE 13.31
Entering or choosing a tag for an In Tray item

3. Enter a tag of up to 32 characters or choose an existing tag from the pop-up menu.
4. Click the **Add** button or press **Enter**.

If you want to see which tags you have assigned to a given piece of mail, open the In Tray and display the Get Info box for the piece of mail. As you can see in Figure 13.32, the Get Info box from the In Tray looks somewhat different from the same document's Desktop Get Info box. In particular, the Get Info box displayed from the In Tray includes the message's tags.

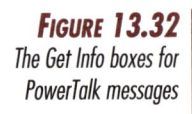

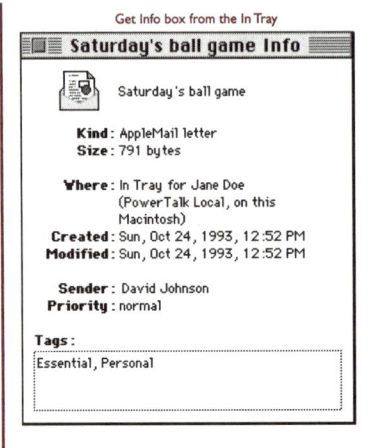

FIGURE 13.32
The Get Info boxes for PowerTalk messages

REMOVING TAGS

To remove a tag from an item:

1. Highlight the item from which you want to remove a tag.
2. Choose **Tag** from the Mailbox menu. The Tag dialog box (Figure 13.31) appears again.
3. Enter the tag or choose it from the pop-up menu.
4. Click the **Remove** button. Note that this removes the tag from the specific mail item but doesn't remove the tag from the list of tags.

FILTERING MAIL WITH TAGS

To filter your mail by tags:

1. Open the In Tray.
2. Choose **With Tag** from the View menu. The View with Tag dialog box appears (Figure 13.33).

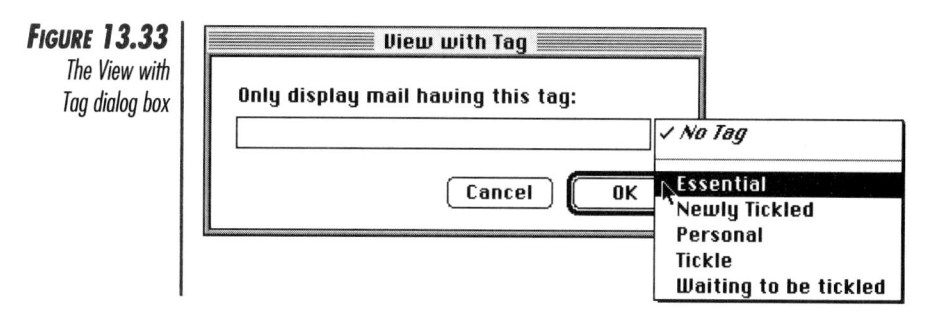

FIGURE 13.33
The View with Tag dialog box

3. Enter the tag by which you want to filter mail or choose the tag from the pop-up menu.
4. Click the **OK** button or press **Enter**. The In Tray changes to show you only those messages that have the selected tag, as in Figure 13.34.

FIGURE 13.34
The In Tray displaying messages with a specified tag

Maintaining the Tag List

As you have just seen, you can add tags to your tag list from the Tag dialog box. However, to delete a tag from the list you must return to the Mailbox Preferences dialog box. To perform the delete:

1. Open the Mailbox Preferences dialog box (Figure 13.23).
2. Click the **Edit** button in the Tags List section of the dialog box. The dialog box in Figure 13.35 appears.

Figure 13.35
Deleting a tag from the Tag List

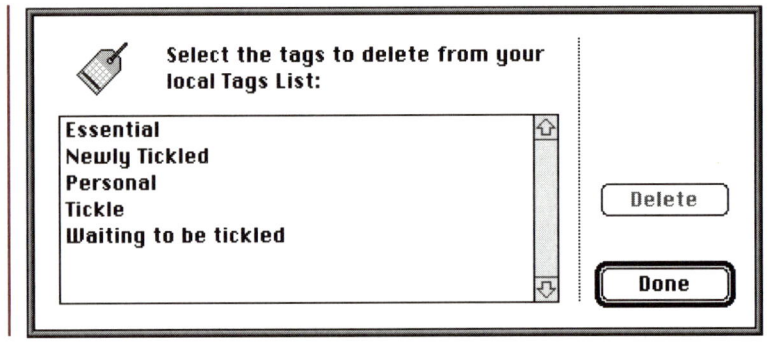

3. Highlight the tag you want to delete.
4. Click the **Delete** button.
5. Repeat steps 3 and 4 for each tag you want to delete.
6. Click the **Done** button or press **Enter**.

The Mailer and Incoming Mail

When you open a message that has been sent to you, there are several things you can do with that message:

- Read the message and discard it.
- Reply to the message.
- Forward the message to another person.

CHAPTER 13: System 7 Pro: Sending and Receiving Messages with PowerTalk   **323**

You read a message with the application that created it or some other compatible program. Replying to and forwarding messages is handled by the mailer. (If the message was a document sent by dragging it onto an information card rather than with the mailer, you won't be able to reply to it or forward it using the following procedures; they require the mailer.)

REPLYING TO MAIL

To reply to a message you have received:

1. Open the message.
2. Display the mailer.
3. Choose **Reply** from the Mail menu or press ⌘-**R**. The Reply To dialog box appears (Figure 13.36).

FIGURE 13.36
Replying to a message

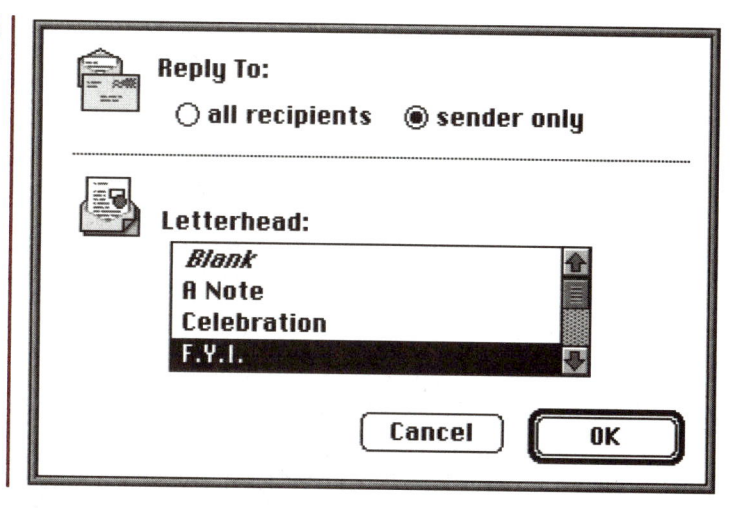

Reply To:
○ all recipients   ● sender only

Letterhead:
Blank
A Note
Celebration
F.Y.I.

[Cancel]   [OK]

BY THE WAY! If you are using the mailer from within an application other than AppleMail, you may not have a Mail menu. For example, if you look back at Figure 13.19 you can see that WordPerfect places **Reply** and **Forward** buttons in a button bar. Consult the documentation that comes with your application for the specific location of mail handling commands.

4. Click the **all recipients** radio button to send the reply to everyone who received the original message. Click the **sender only** radio button to reply to only the sender of the message.

5. Choose a letterhead to use when creating your reply.

6. Click the **OK** button or press **Enter**. The mailer opens the selected letterhead and fills in your name as the sender and the chosen recipient(s). The subject defaults to the subject of the original message preceded by "Re>".

7. Compose and send the message as if you were originating a message.

FORWARDING MAIL

Forwarded mail is sent unmodified to one or more additional recipients. To forward a message:

1. Open the message.

2. Display the mailer.

3. Choose **Forward** from the Mail menu. A second mail header appears on top of the original mail header. Click on the dog-eared lower left corner to switch between the two (see Figure 13.37). PowerTalk fills in your name in the Forwarded by box and precedes the subject of the original message with "Fwd>".

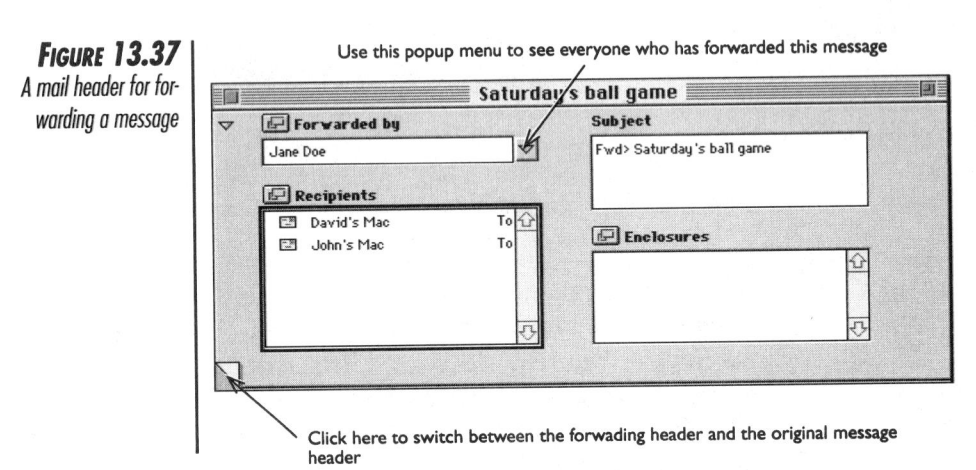

FIGURE 13.37
A mail header for forwarding a message

4. Choose recipients for the forwarded message.
5. Make any changes you want to the content of the message.
6. Choose **Send** from the Mail menu or press ⌘-**M**. The message is forwarded to all recipients.

USING POWERTALK OFF-LINE

Although you can only transmit mail when your Macintosh is connected to a network, you can prepare mail when you are off-line (not connected to a network) or when the PowerShare server to which a message will be sent isn't available. Mail waiting to be sent at a later time is placed in your Out Tray and stays there until you explicitly give the command to send it.

By default, PowerTalk attempts to send a message as soon as you issue the **Send** command. Although PowerTalk handles the situation of an unavailable recipient without a problem, if you know that you aren't connected to a network, then there's no point in even trying. You can handle the situation with the Special menu's **I'm At** command, which lets you choose which PowerTalk connections to activate.

The I'm At dialog box lets you create four sets of connection configurations (at work, at home, on the road, and off-line). If you are off-line (Figure 13.38), PowerTalk disconnects the mailbox; all messages you create are placed in the Out Tray to wait until you are reconnected. For each of the other three locations, choose which PowerTalk services are available (for example, see Figure 13.39). Messages for available services are sent immediately; messages for unavailable services are placed in the Out Tray.

FIGURE 13.38
Telling PowerTalk that you are working off-line

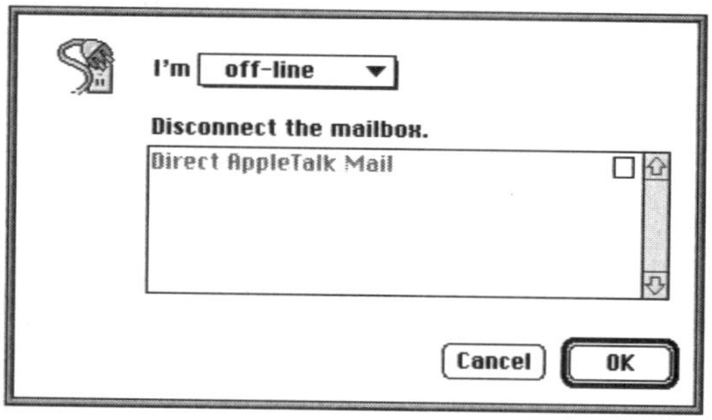

FIGURE 13.39
Choosing which services to use

	In Tray for Jane Doe			
3 items				
✓ Subject	Sender	Date Sent	Location	Priority
Tomorrow's meeting	David Johnson	10/23/93, 5:49 PM	local	normal
Weekend ball game	John Smith	10/23/93, 4:40 PM	local	high
✓ Three customers	Denise Jones	10/23/93, 3:12 PM	local	normal

When you are connected to the network or when the required PowerShare server is available again, you can go ahead and send any waiting messages in the Out Tray. To do so, open the Out Tray and choose **Send Now** from the Mailbox menu.

SETTING UP FOR GUEST USERS

As you have read, a guest user is someone you allow to use your Macintosh to check his or her electronic mail on a PowerShare server. A visitor must log on to your computer each time he or she wants to use it, creating a visitor's mailbox. You may have many visitor's mailboxes on the Desktop at any time. However, they are deleted when you restart your computer.

The first step in setting up for a guest user is to check the "**Allow visitor's mailbox**" check box in the Mailbox Preferences dialog box (Figure 13.23). Once you have done so, a new option appears in the Finder's Special menu: **Visitor's Mailbox**. From then on, any user who wants to use your Macintosh to check mail can do so.

To create a visitor's mailbox, the guest user must do the following:

1. Choose **Visitor's Mailbox** from the Special menu. The dialog box in Figure 13.40 appears.

2. Choose the PowerShare service on which you want to check mail from the pop-up menu.

3. Enter your user name and password.

4. Click the **OK** button or press **Enter**. PowerTalk creates a visitor's mailbox on the Desktop:

David Johnson

FIGURE 13.40
Setting up a visitor's mailbox

Notice that the visitor's mailbox has only one tray—an In Tray. That is because it can be used only to check mail, not to send it.

Customizing PowerTalk with PowerRules

PowerRules is add-on software from Beyond, Inc. that provides functions not currently present in PowerTalk. In particular, it lets you create alternate mailboxes that can be stored anywhere you choose and enhances filtering by tags by letting you use complex logical conditions for choosing which messages to display. PowerRules also tightly integrates AppleScript and PowerTalk, providing a way to use scripts to process incoming mail.

The power behind PowerRules is a special kind of program called an *agent*. An agent is a program that runs in the background to intercept Apple Events and run scripts that transmit Apple Events to other programs. The PowerRules agent works with AppleScript scripts (the PowerRules) that govern how incoming mail should be handled.

BY THE WAY! As AppleScript becomes more widespread throughout the Macintosh installed base, you will find that more software relies on agents.

The primary way in which you configure PowerRules is through MailMinders, a group of four "clerks" that handle mail based on rules that you write. Three of the

328 NAVIGATING SYSTEM 7: Understanding The Macintosh Operating System

MailMinders clerks—Letter Clerk, Travel Clerk, and Tag Clerk—are available from the MailMinders application (Figure 13.41). Rules associated with the Letter Clerk are triggered when new mail arrives. The Travel Clerk provides similar rules that are triggered on specific dates and times.

FIGURE 13.41
The MailMinders Letter Clerk summary window

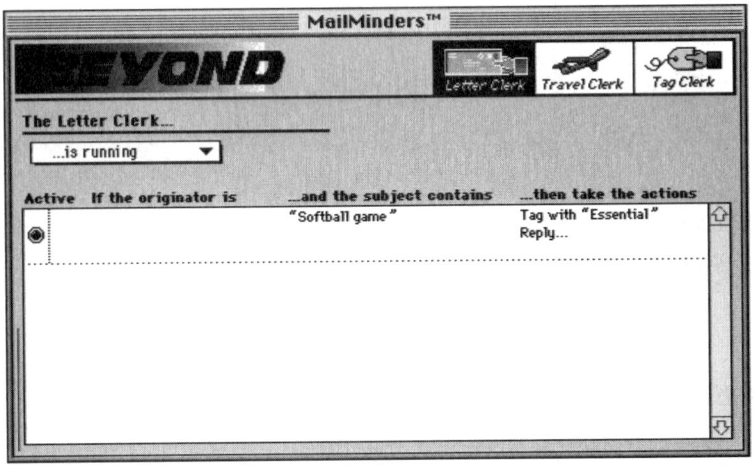

Creating Letter and Travel Clerk rules is as easy as recording an AppleScript script. As you can see in Figure 13.42, you "fill in the blanks" to specify the action you want PowerRules to take when the rule is triggered.

FIGURE 13.42
Creating a Letter or Travel Clerk rule

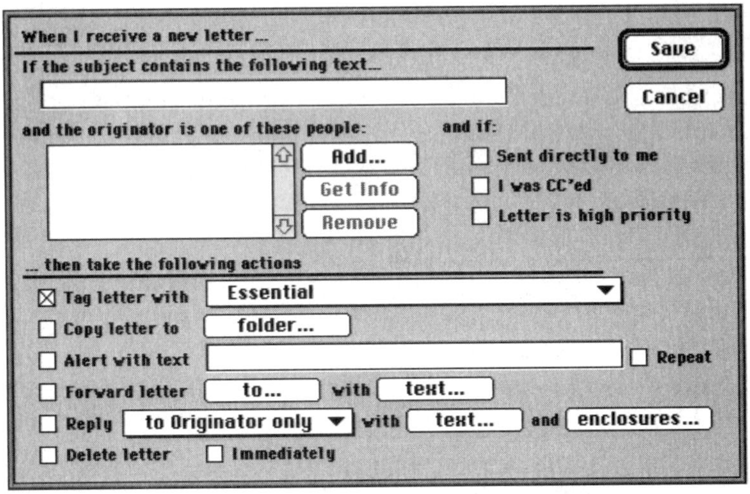

CHAPTER 13: System 7 Pro: Sending and Receiving Messages with PowerTalk   **329**

The Tag Clerk takes actions based on the tags attached to mail. Its rules can be triggered at system startup or shutdown or at some other date and time you specify. As you can see in Figure 13.43, Tag Clerk rules are designed to make sure that letters don't stay in your Mailbox indefinitely.

FIGURE 13.43
Creating a Tag Clerk rule

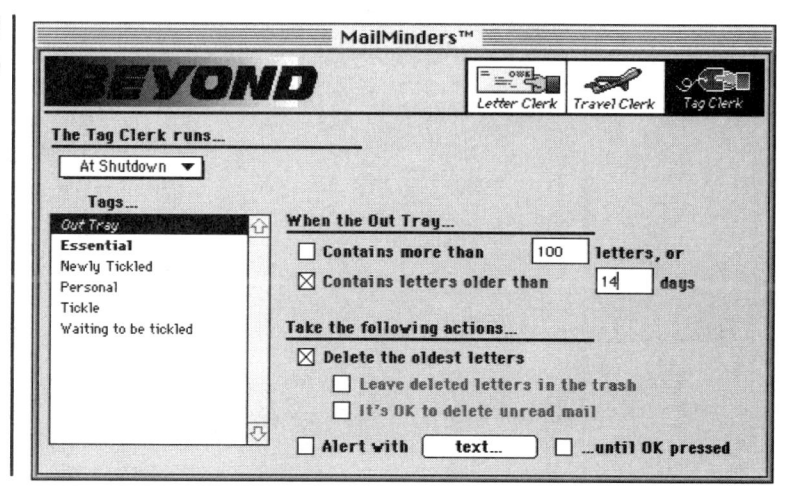

The fourth MailMinder—AutoTickle—has its own application. AutoTickle lets you set "alarms" on mail messages so that you are reminded of the contents of the messages or some other event. AutoTickle rules are created using the dialog box in Figure 13.44. Once a rule is created, you tickle the mail by dragging it onto the AutoTickle program icon. Then, when the date and time specified in the rule is reached, AutoTickle puts the mail into your MailBox as unread (new) mail. It also displays an alert containing the text you entered into the "with text" box when you created the rule.

If the mail processing provided by the MailMinders isn't flexible enough for you, there is another way to write PowerRules: the PowerRules Editor. The Editor provides a generic canvas for specifying mail handling criteria (see Figure 13.45). The actions taken when the IF criteria are met are expressed in AppleScript, although you don't need to be an AppleScript programmer to select actions. PowerRules provides a Quick Reference facility from which you can copy the necessary language elements. You don't necessarily need to be able to program, but some knowledge of programming logic is certainly helpful.

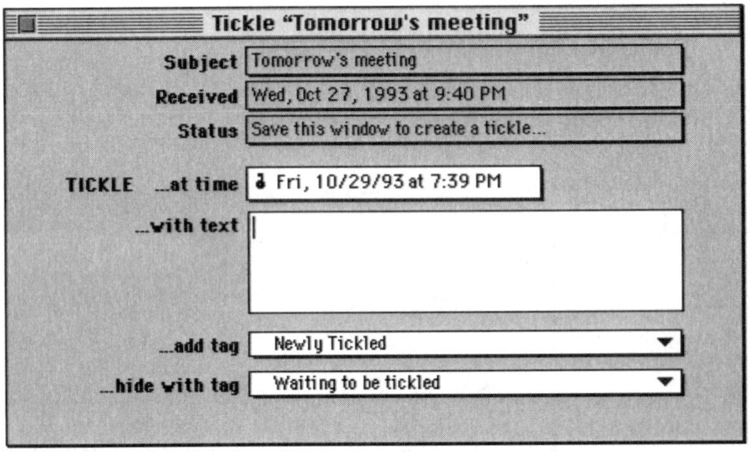

FIGURE 13.44
Creating an
AutoTickle rule

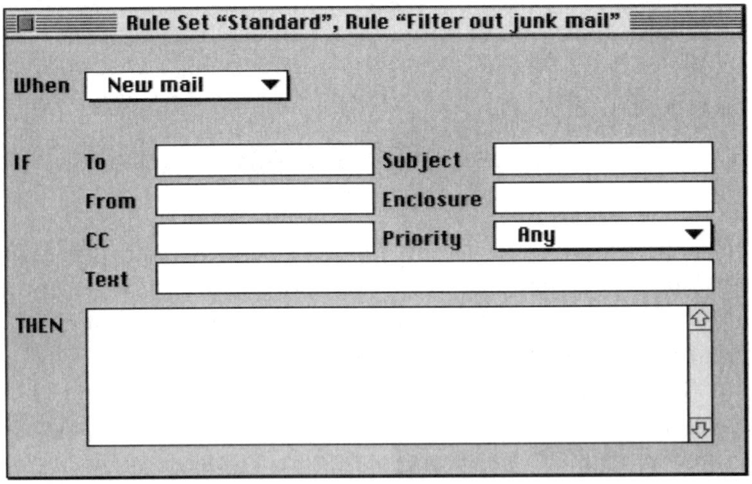

FIGURE 13.45
The PowerRules Editor

How flexible can a PowerRules rule be? The answer is "very." One of the sample rules provided with the PowerRules package is triggered when a Microsoft Excel spreadsheet containing an expense report arrives in a user's MailBox. The rule checks a specific cell that contains the total expenses on the worksheet. If the value is greater than 1,000, the mail is forwarded to another user who needs to handle the expense report. If the value is less than or equal to 1,000, the mail is left for the recipient to handle.

Document Security

Traditional paper mail has several advantages over electronic mail. First, you can sign a document to indicate that it came from you. If necessary, you can even get your signature notarized. Second, unless an expert forger has been at work, it's relatively easy to tell if the contents of a document have been altered. Finally, you can seal the document inside an opaque envelope to protect its contents from prying eyes while it is traveling from your location to its destination. However, because an electronic document is nothing more than a collection of bits, there's no way to sign it or to verify that no bits have been altered. There is also intrinsically no such thing as an "electronic envelope" to protect your document from being read by an unauthorized person. This means that documents sent electronically are more of a security risk than paper documents.

An effective electronic document transfer system must therefore have some way to provide security for the documents it handles. PowerTalk does this in two ways. First, it lets you add a *digital signature* to a document so that the recipient can verify that the message came from you (*authentication*). The digital signature includes a 128-bit summary of a document created by passing the entire document through a formula known as a *hashing algorithm*. This particular hashing algorithm (MD5) works very quickly. The recipient's Macintosh recomputes the summary from the document when the document is received. If the recomputed summary doesn't match the summary sent with the document, then the document has been altered during transmission.

Making a document unintelligible to unauthorized users relies on a process known as *encryption*. There are several standard encryption methods used in the computing industry in the United States, most notably the *Data Encryption Standard* (DES) and *public key encryption*. However, the United States government considers data encryption a matter of national security; software that uses DES is rarely given an export license. Because Apple wants to be able to use PowerTalk throughout the world, PowerTalk does not use DES to encrypt messages from sender to receiver. It does, however, use a proprietary encryption process (RC4) to encrypt messages as they travel from one PowerShare server to another. (It is relatively easy to get an export license for RC4.) This encryption is transparent to the user and occurs regardless of whether a digital signature has been added to a document. As you will see in the following section, public key encryption is used as part of PowerTalk's authentication process.

PowerTalk Encryption

To understand what is happening when you attach a digital signature to a message, you first need to know something about encryption methods. There are two general types of encryption schemes: secret key and public key.

A secret key encryption scheme such as DES or RC4 uses a single key to both encrypt and decrypt a message. The major problem with using a secret key lies in key management. The sender must give the secret key to the recipient so the recipient can decrypt the message. However, the secrecy of that key can be comprised while the key is in transmit from sender to recipient. In addition, if the recipient gets messages from many senders, he or she must keep secret a separate key for each sender.

Public key encryption—developed in 1977 by Rivest, Shamir, and Adelman (now RSA Data Security Inc.)—solves the problem of key management by providing two keys, one to encrypt a message and one to decrypt a message. The encryption key is made public; anyone can encrypt a message for a given recipient. The decryption key, however, is kept secret. Because the decryption key is never sent anywhere, it is far less likely to be comprised than the key from a single-key system.

Public key encryption does have one major disadvantage: It is very slow. Therefore, most encryption systems combine secret and public key encryption. Typically, a secret key encryption method is used to encrypt the contents of the message. Then, the secret key is encrypted using public key encryption and attached to the message. In this way, the secret key can travel safely with the message and the recipient doesn't have to manage any secret keys.

PowerTalk uses public key encryption in two ways. First, it encrypts the document summary (that 128-byte summary of the message that validates that a message hasn't been altered during transmission) with public key encryption using the sender's private key. It then appends the sender's public key to the package so that the summary can be decrypted when it is received. If this seems a bit backwards (encrypting with the private key and decrypting with the public key), don't worry. As it so happens, the mathematical formula behind public key encryption ensures that you are able to encrypt with either key and then decrypt with the other.

The mathematics security of any encryption scheme lies in how hard it is for an unauthorized person to deduce a secret key. Public key encryption relies on the difficulty of factoring a very large number that is the product of two large prime numbers. Here's how it works:

1. Pick two prime numbers, *p* and *q*. Although *p* and *q* are usually very large, for purposes of this example we'll use *p* = 3 and *q* = 5, just to keep the quantities small.

2. Multiple *p* and *q*, producing *n*. In our example, *n* = 15.

3. Pick a third prime number, *e*, that is greater than *p* or *q* but less than *n* to be the encryption key. For this example, we'll use *e* = 11.

4. Compute the private "decryption" key, *d*, according to the formula:

e *d mod *(p-1)* * *(q-1)* = *1*

This means that the quantity *e* * *d* divided by *(p-1)* * *(q-1)* must return a remainder of 1. Substituting the known quantities, the formula becomes:

11 * *d* mod *8* = *1*

Therefore, *d* = 3 (*11* * *3* =*33*; *33/8* = *4* with a remainder of *1*).

At this point, you make *e* and *n* public; these two values constitute the public key. Someone who wants to send you a message needs them both. To encrypt a character, the sender uses the formula

P^e mod *n* = *C*

where *P* is the binary value a portion of the unencrypted (plain text) message and *C* is the encrypted data (cyphertext). For example, if the plain text value we want to encrypt is 15, then:

12^{11} mod *15* = *743008370688* mod *15* = *3*

The *3* is then transmitted in place of the *12*.

To decrypt the message, the recipient uses a formula which is the mathematical inverse:

C^d mod *n* = *P*

For the example we have been using, the decryption is:

3^3 mod *15* = *27* mod *15* = *12*

The decryption accurately returns the encrypted data. Keep in mind that whichever key you use to encrypt a message (*e* or *d*), you must use the other key to decrypt it.

Remember that the security of this entire scheme rests with the inability of someone to factor *n* into the two prime numbers from which it was generated. Because public key encryption uses very large prime numbers that generate an even larger *r*, very few organizations have the computing power to reasonably factor *r*. Public key encryption is generally considered to be more secure than any other available encryption method.

Signing a Message

To sign a message, you use an approved signer file. (Getting an approved signer file is discussed later in this chapter.) This file, which contains both your public and private keys, has an icon consisting of a hand holding a pen:

Jane Doe Signer

The way in which you attach a digital signature to a file depends on whether you are working on the Desktop or with the mailer (either as part of AppleMail or as part of an application program).

If you are working on the Desktop, do the following to sign a file:

1. Drag the file you want to sign onto the approved signer file. The dialog box in Figure 13.46 appears.

Figure 13.46
Identifying your signer

Signing as "Jane Doe."

DigiSign Identification Code:

••••••••

[Cancel] [OK]

CHAPTER 13: System 7 Pro: Sending and Receiving Messages with PowerTalk 335

2. Enter your DigiSign Identification Code. (You create this code when you request an approved signer file.)

3. Click the **OK** button or press **Enter**. PowerTalk computes the 128-byte message summary, encrypts it, and attaches both the summary and your public key to the message.

> **BY THE WAY!** Don't unlock or attempt to modify a file after you've signed it. Anything you do will invalidate the message summary.

When you are working from within an application program, you can sign a document from the Send dialog box. To do so:

1. Create your document.

2. Fill in the required parts of the mailer.

3. Issue the **Send** command.

4. When the Send dialog box appears, click the Sign Letter check box (look back at Figure 13.13). PowerTalk looks for an approved signer file and displays the signer name in the Signer ID dialog box (Figure 13.47).

FIGURE 13.47
Signing a document from within an application

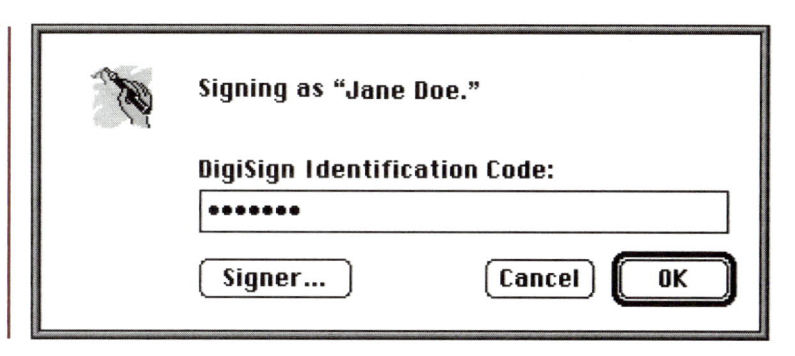

5. If PowerTalk has located the wrong signer, click the **Signer** button. Use the Open File dialog box that appears to identify the correct signer file.

6. Enter your DigiSign identification code.

7. Click the **OK** button or press **Enter**. PowerTalk computes the 128-byte message summary, encrypts it, and attaches both the summary and your public key to the message.

VALIDATING A RECEIVED MESSAGE

Validating a received message takes place from the document's Get Info box. To verify:

1. Open the document's Get Info box. As you can see in Figure 13.48, the Get Info box has a button to the right of its Comments box.

FIGURE 13.48
Validating a signature from the Get Info dialog box

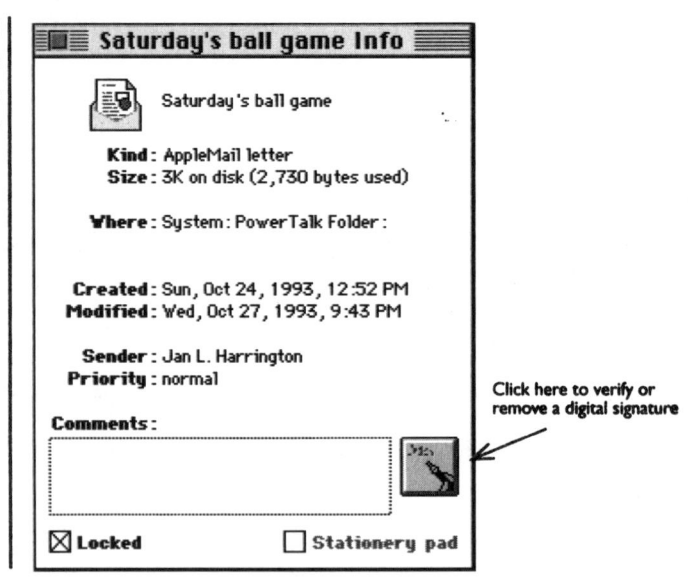

2. Click the button to the right of the Comments box. The dialog box in Figure 13.49 appears.

3. Click the **Verify** button or press **Enter**. PowerTalk performs the signature verification, displaying its progress as it works (Figure 13.50).

Assuming the validation is successful, PowerTalk lets you know who signed the file (see Figure 13.51).

FIGURE 13.49
Choosing validation options

FIGURE 13.50
Monitoring the process of signature validation

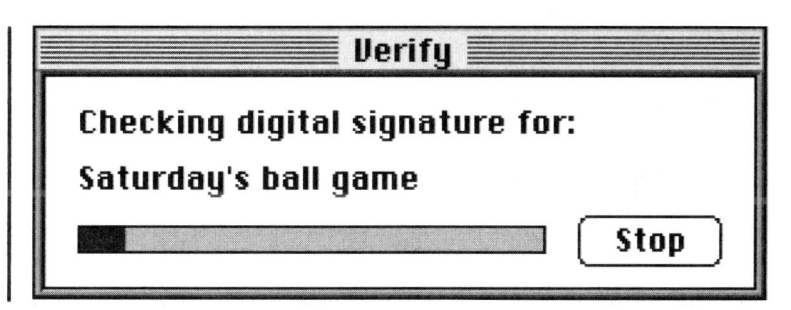

FIGURE 13.51
Verified signer information

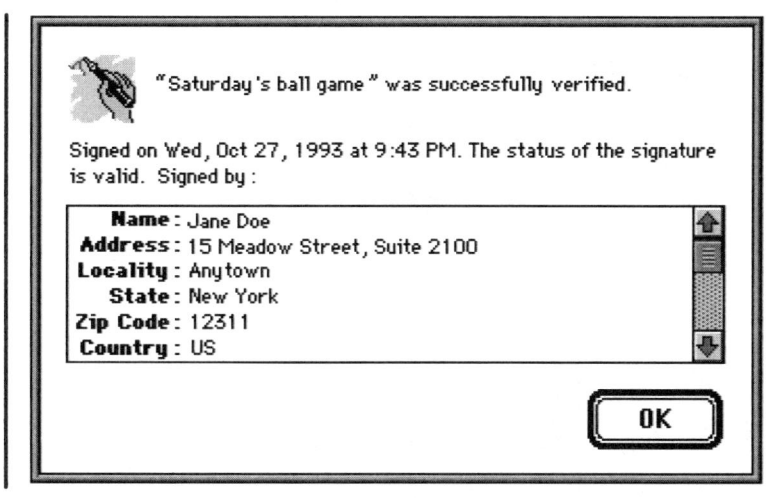

To remove the validation from a file, check the **Remove** button in the dialog box in Figure 13.49.

Getting an Approved Signer

Before you can attach a digital signature to a message, you must have a set of keys to use when signing. You may get your keys from your system administrator. You can also send for a set of keys from RSA, using the DigiSign Utility application that installs with PowerTalk. The process involves using DigiSign Utility to create a signer request, getting the request notarized, sending the request to RSA, and then applying the approval file you receive to the original request document.

Generating an Approval Request

To generate an approval request file and an unapproved signer file:

1. Launch the DigiSign Utility program. (It can be found in the PowerTalk Folder on your startup disk.)

2. Click the mouse pointer to make the title dialog box disappear.

3. Choose **New Request** from the File menu or press ⌘-N. The Signer Request dialog box appears (Figure 13.52).

FIGURE 13.52
Entering data for a signer request form

4. Enter the name and address you want on the signer request form.

5. Choose the country in which the address is located.

CHAPTER 13: System 7 Pro: Sending and Receiving Messages with PowerTalk **339**

6. Enter an identification phrase in the Phrase box.

7. Click the **Postal Address** button and make any changes necessary to the address to which you want the signer approval file sent (see Figure 13.53). Click the **OK** button or press **Enter**.

FIGURE 13.53
Entering a mailing address for a signer approval form

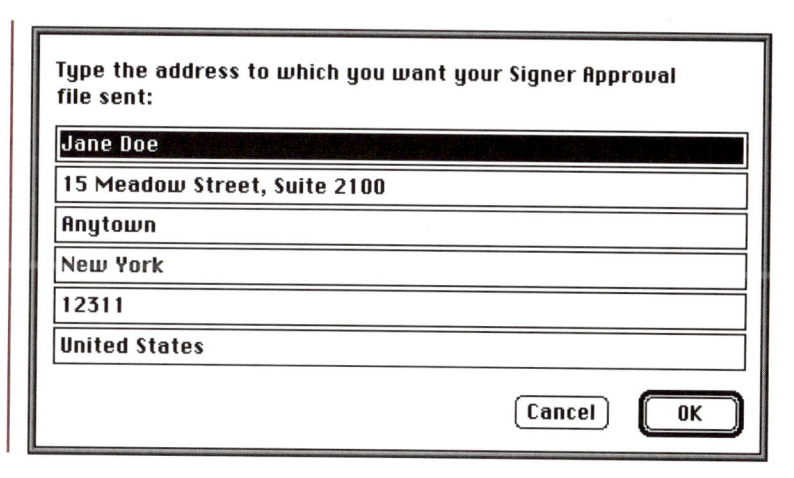

> Type the address to which you want your Signer Approval file sent:
>
> Jane Doe
> 15 Meadow Street, Suite 2100
> Anytown
> New York
> 12311
> United States
>
> [Cancel] [OK]

8. Click the **OK** button in the Signer Request dialog box or press **Enter**. An identification code dialog box appears.

9. Enter the identification code that you will use each time you want to access your signer. As you can see in Figure 13.54, the code must be at least six characters long.

FIGURE 13.54
Entering a signer identification code

> Type a DigiSign Identification Code which will be required each time you use your Signer. This code must be at least 6 characters.
>
> ••••••
>
> To make sure you typed your DigiSign Identification Code correctly, type it again.
>
> ••••••
>
> [Cancel] [OK]

340   NAVIGATING SYSTEM 7: Understanding The Macintosh Operating System

> **BY THE WAY!**
>
> The security of your signer relies on the secrecy of your DigiSign Identification Code. Therefore, make the code something that is easy for you to remember, but hard for someone else to guess. Two short, unrelated words with a punctuation mark between them (for example, foot!car) usually works well.

10. Click the **OK** button or press **Enter**. A Save File dialog box appears.

11. Choose a location for the signer and signer request files. Click the **Save** button or press **Enter**. DigiSign begins creating the files (Figure 13.55). When it has finished, DigiSign displays the Signer Approval Request Form and a dialog box (Figure 13.56).

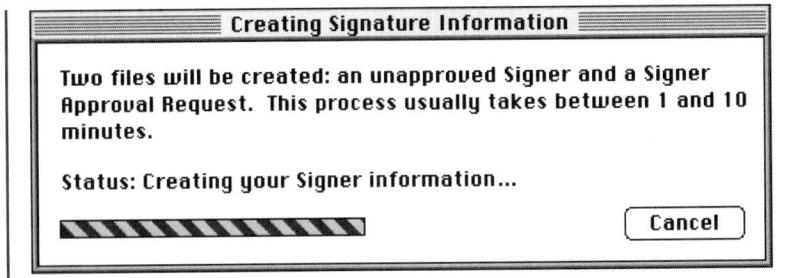

FIGURE 13.55
Creating the signer and signer approval request files

> **Creating Signature Information**
>
> Two files will be created: an unapproved Signer and a Signer Approval Request. This process usually takes between 1 and 10 minutes.
>
> Status: Creating your Signer information...
>
> [Cancel]

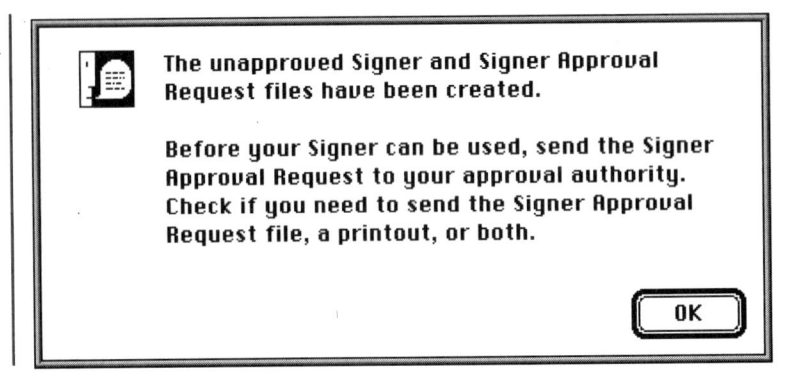

FIGURE 13.56
Confirming creation of the signer request files

> The unapproved Signer and Signer Approval Request files have been created.
>
> Before your Signer can be used, send the Signer Approval Request to your approval authority. Check if you need to send the Signer Approval Request file, a printout, or both.
>
> [OK]

12. Click the **OK** button or press **Enter** to dismiss the dialog box. The Signer Approval Request Form is left on the screen (Figure 13.57).

FIGURE 13.57
A Signer Approval Request Form

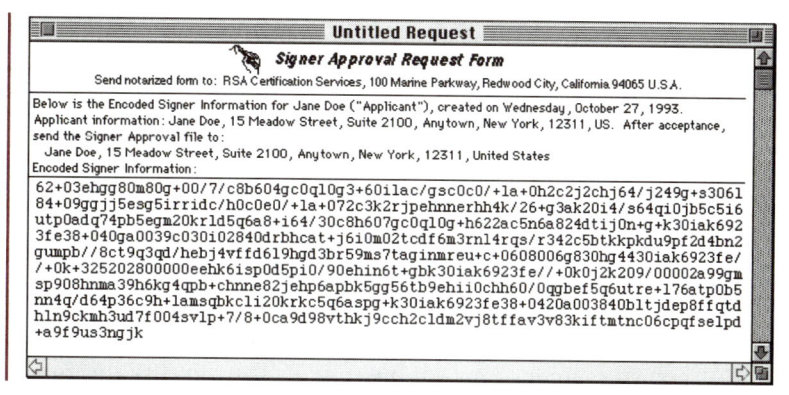

```
                        Untitled Request
                    Signer Approval Request Form
        Send notarized form to: RSA Certification Services, 100 Marine Parkway, Redwood City, California 94065 U.S.A.
Below is the Encoded Signer Information for Jane Doe ("Applicant"), created on Wednesday, October 27, 1993.
Applicant information: Jane Doe, 15 Meadow Street, Suite 2100, Anytown, New York, 12311, US. After acceptance,
send the Signer Approval file to:
    Jane Doe, 15 Meadow Street, Suite 2100, Anytown, New York, 12311, United States
Encoded Signer Information:
62+03ehgg80m80g+00/7/c8b604gc0ql0g3+60ilac/gsc0c0/+1a+0h2c2j2chj64/j249g+s3061
84+09ggjj5esg5irridc/h0c0e0/+1a+072c3k2rjpehnnerhh4k/26+g3ak20i4/s64qi0jb5c5i6
utp0adq74pb5egm20krld5q6a8+i64/30c8h607gc0ql0g+h622ac5n6a824dtij0n+g+k30iak692
3fe38+040ga0039c030i02840drbhcat+j6i0m02tcdf6m3rnl4rqs/r342c5btkkpkdu9pf2d4bn2
gumpb//8ct9q3qd/hebj4vffd619hgd3br59ms7taginmreu+c+0608006g830hg4430iak6923fe/
/+0k+325202800000eehk6isp0d5pi0/90ehin6t+gbk30iak6923fe//+0k0j2k209/00002a99gm
sp908hnma39h6kg4qpb+chnne82jehp6apbk5gg56tb9ehii0chh60/0qgbef5q6utre+l76atp0b5
nn4q/d64p36c9h+lamsqbkcli20krkc5q6aspg+k30iak6923fe38+0420a003840bltjdep8ffqtd
hln9ckmh3ud7f004svlp+7/8+0ca9d98vthkj9cch2cldm2vj8tffav3v83kiftmtnc06cpqfselpd
+a9f9us3ngjk
```

13. Turn on your printer and printer the Signer Approval Request Form.
14. Save the Signer Approval Request Form.
15. Quit the DigiSign Utility.

At this point you have an unapproved file on disk with an icon that shows a hand with a pen beside it:

Jane Doe Signer

You also have a document file that contains the Signer Approval Request Form that you saved in step 14 above.

Transmitting the Signer Approval Request

Turning the Signer Approval Request Form into an approval file that you can use to transform your unapproved signer into an approved signer means leaving your computer for a bit:

1. Take the form to a notary public along with three different forms of identification. One must have a photo on it; only one can be a major credit card. Get the form notarized.
2. Send the form to RSA, using the address at the top of the form. Include the green coupon that was included with your System 7 Pro upgrade package. If

you printed your form on a printer with less the 300-dpi resolution or if the form takes up more than one printed page, include a disk with the Signer Approval Request file on it.

Once it's all in the mail, sit back and wait.

Transforming an Unapproved Signer File into an Approved Signer File

When you receive your signer approval file from RSA, you can apply it to your unapproved signer file to turn it into an approved signer file. To do so:

1. Copy the signer approval file to your startup disk. In most cases, you'll want to put it in the PowerTalk Folder along with your unapproved signer file.

2. Make a copy of your unapproved signer file. This provides a backup copy in case something should go wrong during the approval process (for example, a power outage).

3. Double-click on the unapproved signer file. This launches the DigiSign Utility and opens the unapproved signer file. Because the signer is unapproved, the DigiSign Utility displays the warning in Figure 13.58.

FIGURE 13.58
A warning about an unapproved signer file

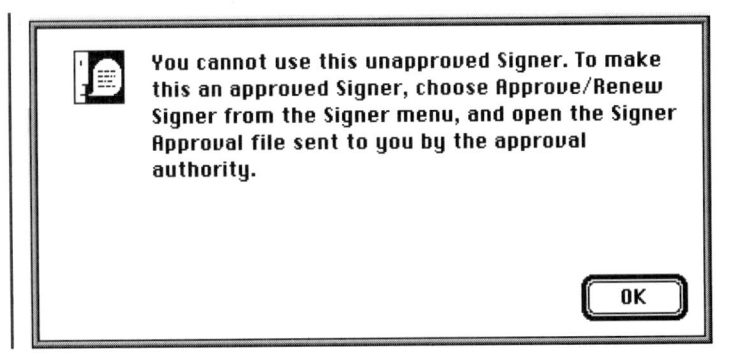

> You cannot use this unapproved Signer. To make this an approved Signer, choose Approve/Renew Signer from the Signer menu, and open the Signer Approval file sent to you by the approval authority.
>
> [OK]

4. Click **OK** or press **Enter** to dismiss the dialog box. A window for your unapproved signer can be seen (Figure 13.59).

5. Choose **Approve/Remove Signer** from the Signer menu. An Open File dialog box appears.

6. Locate the signer approval file and open it. The DigiSign Utility applies the approval.

CHAPTER 13: System 7 Pro: Sending and Receiving Messages with PowerTalk   **343**

Two things happen after the approval is applied. First, your signer file's icon changes to the approved signer file icon (the hand holding a pen that you saw earlier in this chapter). Second, the DigiSign Utility signer window changes to display information about your approved signer (see Figure 13.60).

FIGURE 13.59
An unapproved signer window

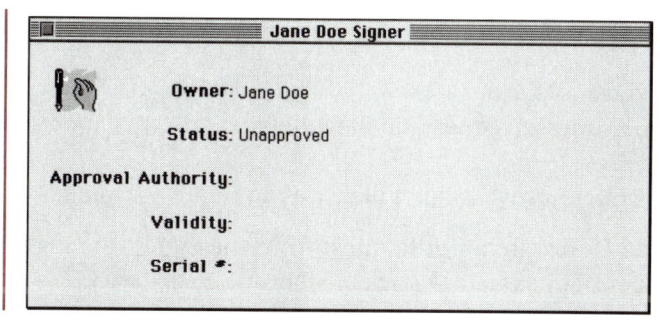

> **Jane Doe Signer**
> **Owner:** Jane Doe
> **Status:** Unapproved
> **Approval Authority:**
> **Validity:**
> **Serial #:**

FIGURE 13.60
Approved signer information

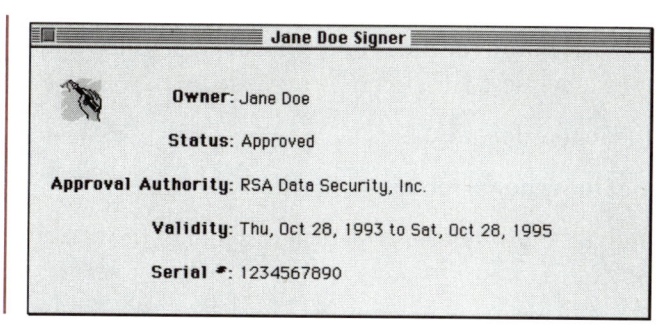

> **Jane Doe Signer**
> **Owner:** Jane Doe
> **Status:** Approved
> **Approval Authority:** RSA Data Security, Inc.
> **Validity:** Thu, Oct 28, 1993 to Sat, Oct 28, 1995
> **Serial #:** 1234567890

MAINTAINING AN APPROVED SIGNER

As you may have noticed in Figure 13.60, an approved signer is good for two years. A month or so before your signer expires, you will need to generate a renewal request. In addition, you should change your DigiSign Identification Code regularly (at least every three months) to protect it. You can do both of these things with the DigiSign Utility.

> **BY THE WAY!** When you open the DigiSign Utility by double-clicking on an approved signer file, you will see a dialog box containing help information. To stop the dialog box from appearing, choose **Preferences** from the File menu. Remove the check from the "Display assistance" check box (Figure 13.61)

FIGURE 13.61
The DigiSign Utility Preferences dialog box

> **Preferences:**
>
> ☒ Display assistance dialog when a Signer is opened
>
> [OK]

Generating a Renewal Request

To generate a renewal request, do the following:

1. Open your approved signer file with the DigiSign Utility.
2. Choose **Create Renewal Request** from the Signer menu. The Postal Address dialog box appears (look back at Figure 13.53).
3. Enter the address to which you want the renewal mailed.
4. Click the **OK** button or press **Enter**. The DigiSign Utility creates and displays the renewal request.
5. Save the renewal request file.
6. Print out the renewal request.
7. Send it to RSA (or whoever issued your signer approval).

BY THE WAY! Although there is a voucher in the System 7 Pro package for a free approved signer, there may be a fee for renewing the signer. Check with RSA or whoever issued your signer approval before sending in your renewal request.

Changing Your DigiSign Identification Code

As you have read, it's a good idea to change your DigiSign Identification Code regularly. Doing so will help keep your signer secure. To change the ID code:

1. Open your approved signer file with the DigiSign Utility.
2. Choose **Change DigiSign ID Code** from the Signer menu. The dialog box in Figure 13.62 appears.

FIGURE 13.62
Changing the DigiSign Identification Code

[Dialog: Type your old DigiSign Identification Code. / Type a new DigiSign Identification Code twice to ensure accuracy. This code must be at least 6 characters. / Cancel / OK]

3. Enter your current DigiSign Identification Code.
4. Enter your new DigiSign Identification Code twice.
5. Click the **OK** button or press **Enter**.

> **BY THE WAY!** If the security of your signer is compromised, call RSA or whoever issued your approved signer. Ask them to revoke your signer. Then you can submit a request for a new signer. You should also tell everyone with whom you exchange messages that your signer has been revoked. Give them your signer's serial number so they can check messages they receive after the date the signer was revoked for messages that weren't sent by you.

Appendix A
Product List

This book discusses a significant number of utilities and add-on programs that enhance the Macintosh operating system. Each program has been tested to ensure that it is compatible with System 7.1; most are also compatible with System 7 Pro. Please keep in mind, however, that mention in this book does not constitute an endorsement of a product. It's up to you to decide which software is right for your particular situation and which software is compatible with your particular collection of INITs.

Some of the products listed here are shareware. (Those marked with an asterisk are on the disk that comes with this book.) You can obtain them from user groups or on-line services such as CompuServe or America Online. If you choose to continue using shareware after you have tried it for 30 days, you should send the author the requested shareware fee. Registering your shareware also usually gets you a copy of the most recent version as well as complete documentation.

Other products are free products provided by commercial software developers. You can use and distribute these programs without cost. However, they cannot be resold; copyright remains with the developer. All freeware and shareware programs have been so designated.

The final group of products are commercial. Before deciding to purchase a commercial utility, consider looking for published reviews of the product and/or talking to other users. If you don't know anyone who is using a product in which you are interested, try reaching people over an on-line service such as CompuServe or America Online.

AccessPC
Insignia Solutions, Inc.
526 Clyde Avenue
Mountain View, CA 94043
Voice: (800) 848-7677
Fax: (415) 964-5434

Adobe Type Manager
Adobe Systems Inc.
1585 Charleston Road
P.O. Box 7900
Mountain View, CA 94039-7900
Voice: (800) 833-6687
Fax info request line: (408) 986-6587
(free with a $7.95 shipping and handling fee when ordered direct from Adobe; offer includes the Adobe Garamond font)

Adobe Type Reunion
Adobe Systems Inc.
1585 Charleston Road
P.O. Box 7900
Mountain View, CA 94039-7900
Voice: (800) 833-6687

After Dark
Berkeley Systems, Inc.
2095 Rose Street
Berkeley, CA 94709
Voice: (510) 540-5535
Fax: (510) 540-5115

Apple File Exchange
Apple Computer Inc.
20525 Mariani Avenue
Cupertino, CA 95014-6299
Main switchboard: (408) 996-1010
Customer support: (800) SOS-APPL

AppleScript Language Guide
Apple Computer Inc.
available from:

APDA
P.O. Box 319
Buffalo, NY 14207-0319
Voice: (800) 282-2732
Fax: (716) 871-6511
(part of the AppleScript Software Development ToolKit)

At Ease
Apple Computer Inc.
20525 Mariani Avenue
Cupertino, CA 95014-6299
Main switchboard: (408) 996-1010
Customer support: (800) SOS-APPL

*Attributes
John A. Schlack
824 Rhoads Avenue
Jenkintown, PA 19046
($10 shareware fee)

AutoDoubler
Fifth Generation Systems, Inc.
10049 N. Reiger Road
Baton Rouge, LA 70809-4562
Voice: (800) 225-2775
Fax: (504) 295-3268

Before Dark
Logical Solutions, Inc.
2124 University Ave. #102
Saint Paul, MN 55114
Voice: (612) 659-2495
Fax: (612) 659-2498

Capture
Maintstay
5311-B Derry Ave.
Agoura Hills, CA 91301
Voice: (818) 991-6540

*CatFinder
Keith Turner

ShadeTree Programming
P.O. Box 27
New Hill, NC 27562
($25 shareware fee)

Compact Pro
Cyclos Software
P.O. Box 31417
San Francisco, CA 94131
Voice: (415) 821-1448
($25 shareware fee)

Conflict Catcher
Casady & Greene, Inc.
22734 Portola Drive
Salinas, CA 93908-1119
Voice: (408) 484-9228

CopyDoubler
Fifth Generation Systems, Inc.
10049 N. Reiger Road
Baton Rouge, LA 70809-4562
Voice: (800) 225-2775
Fax: (504) 295-3268

CryptoMatic
Kent•Marsh Ltd.
Kent•Marsh Building
3260 Sul Ross
Houston, TX 77098
Voice: (713) 522-LOCK
Fax: (713) 522-8965

Desktape
Optima Technology
17526 Von Karman
Irvine, CA 92714
Voice: (714) 476-0515
Fax: (714) 476-0613
AppleLink: OTPIMA

Disinfectant
John Norstad
Northwestern University
(free; download from information services or obtain from a user group)

Easy Access
Apple Computer
20525 Mariani Avenue
Cupertino, CA 95014-6299
Main switchboard: (408) 996-1010
Customer support: (800) SOS-APPL

*Extension Manager
Apple Computer
20525 Mariani Avenue
Cupertino, CA 95014-6299
Main switchboard: (408) 996-1010
Customer support: (800) SOS-APPL

FileGuard
ASD Software, Inc.
4650 Arrow Hwy., E-6
Montclair, CA 91763
Voice: (909) 624-2594
Fax: (909) 624-9574

FolderBOLT
Kent•Marsh Ltd.
Kent•Marsh Building
3260 Sul Ross
Houston, TX 77098
Voice: (713) 522-LOCK
Fax: (713) 522-8965

Font Harmony
Fifth Generation Systems
10049 N. Reiger Road
Baton Rouge, LA 70809
Voice: (800) 873-4384
Fax: (504) 295-3268

Freedom of Press Classic
ColorAge Inc.
900 Technology Park Drive

Billerica, MA 01821
Voice: (508) 667-8585
Fax: (508) 667-8821

HAM
Inline Design
308 Main Street
Lakeview, CT 06039-1204
Voice: (800) 453-7671

Icon 7
Inline Design
308 Main Street
Lakeville, CT 06039-1204
Voice: (800) 453-7671

INITPicker 3
Inline Design
308 Main Street
Lakeville, CT 06039-1204
Voice: (800) 453-7671

KeyFonts
SoftKey Software Products, Inc.
201 Broadway
Cambridge, MA 02139
Voice: (617) 374-1450
Fax: (617) 577-7903

Macintosh PC Exchange
Apple Computer
20525 Mariani Avenue
Cupertino, CA 95014-6299
Main switchboard: (408) 996-1010
Customer support: (800) SOS-APPL

Maxima
Connectix
2655 Campus Drive
San Mateo, CA 94403-2520
Voice: (800) 950-5880
Fax: (415) 571-5195

Mode32
Connectix
2655 Campus Drive
San Mateo, CA 94403-2520
Voice: (800) 950-5880
Fax: (415) 571-5195

NightWatch II
Kent•Marsh Ltd.
Kent•Marsh Building
3260 Sul Ross
Houston, TX 77098
Voice: (713) 522-LOCK
Fax: (713) 522-8965

Norton Utilities
Symantec Corp.
10201 Torre Ave.
Cupertino, CA 95014-9854
Voice: (800) 441-7234
Fax: (408) 255-3344

Now Up To Date
Now Software
319 N.W. Washington St.
Portland, OR 97204
Voice: (800) 237-3611

Now Utilities
Now Software
319 N.W. Washington St.
Portland, OR 97204
Voice: (800) 237-3611

*OneClick
Rich Christianson
909 1/2 New York Avenue
Alamogordo, NM 88310
($7.50 shareware fee)

PowerRules
Beyond, Inc.

17 New England Executive Park
Burlington, MA 01803
Voice: (617) 229-0006
Fax: (617) 229-1114

QuicKeys
CE Software
P.O. Box 65580
West Des Moines, Iowa 50265
Voice: (515) 221-1801

ResEdit
Apple Computer Inc.
20525 Mariani Avenue
Cupertino, CA 95014-6299
Main switchboard: (408) 996-1010
Customer support: (800) SOS-APPL
(free; download from on-line information services)

Retrospect
Dantz Development Corp.
1400 Shattuck Ave., Suite 1
Berkeley, CA 94709
Voice: (415) 849-0293
Fax: (415) 849-1708

SoundMaster
Bruce Tomlin
15801 Chase Hill Blvd., Ste. 109
San Antonio, TX 78256
($20 shareware fee)

SpeedyFinder 7
Victor Tan
42 Waratah Avenue
Randwick, NSW, 2031
AUSTRALIA
($20US shareware fee)

Startup Manager
Now Software

319 N.W. Washington St.
Portland, OR 97204
Voice: (800) 237-3611

StuffIt Deluxe and Stuffit Expander
Aladdin Systems, Inc.
165 Westridge Drive
Watsonville, CA 95076
Voice: (408) 761-6200
Fax: (408) 761-6206

Suitcase
Fifth Generation Systems, Inc.
10049 N. Reiger Road
Baton Rouge, LA 70809-4562
Voice: (800) 225-2775
Fax: (504) 295-3268

SuperLaserSpool
Fifth Generation Systems
10049 N. Reiger Road
Baton Rouge, LA 70809
Voice: (800) 873-4384
Fax: (504) 295-3268

*Symbionts
B. Kevin Hardman
c/o Nivek Research
108 Kramer Court
Cary, NC, 27511
(shareware: $20 single user; $15 per machine (2–16 users; $250 unlimited site license)

TechTool
MicroMat Computer Systems
7075 Redwood Blvd.
Novato, CA 94945
Voice: (415) 898-6227
Fax: (415) 897-3901
(free; download from on-line serivces)

Virtual
Connectix Corp.
2655 Campus Drive
San Mateo, CA 94403-2520
Voice: (800) 950-5880
Fax: (415) 571-5195

Glossary

10 BaseT: A type of cable used to create an Ethernet network. 10 BaseT looks like heavy telephone cable with a large telephone jack on either end. When used to support AppleTalk, 10 Base T networks must use a star configuration.

32-bit clean: Software that runs without problems under 32-bit addressing.

32-bit dirty: Software that cannot run under 32-bit addressing but instead requires 24-bit addresses.

Access Code: The password that unlocks a PowerTalk Key Chain, providing access to all PowerTalk services.

Address bus: Part of the electronic pathway that connects the components of a computer. It carries addresses from one part of the computer to another.

Address space: The total range of main memory addresses that a computer can access. A computer's address space consists of numbered bytes, beginning with zero.

Address: The location of a byte in main memory.

Agent: A background program that accepts Apple Events and handles them by running an AppleScript script to handle the event.

Alias: A pointer to a file or folder. Launching or opening the alias acts on the original file or folder.

Allocation block: The smallest amount of disk space that can be added to a file at one time.

AOCE: The abbreviation for *Apple Open Collaboration Environment*.

Apple Event: A special type of event used to for interapplication communication. Apple Events are usually directed between programs, including the Finder and application programs such as word processors and spreadsheets.

Apple Open Collaboration Environment: A suite of system software designed to support data communications and collaboration across a network. The first parts of the Apple Open Collaboration environment include PowerTalk and PowerShare, which add electronic mail capabilities to the Macintosh Desktop.

Apple Sound Chip: An integrated circuit that generates sound.

AppleMail: An application program that provides electronic mail capabilities using PowerTalk.

AppleScript: A programming language that is used to write scripts that recognize and handle Apple Events.

AppleShare: System software that manages a server in a client/server AppleTalk network.

Applet: An AppleScript script that has been saved as a double-clickable application.

AppleTalk: A set of network protocols that govern the exchange of messages over a Macintosh network.

Application menu: The menu at the far right edge of the System 7 menu bar that lists all running applications.

ASC: The abbreviation for *Apple Sound Chip*.

Ascender: A character that rises above the x-height of a font, such as "h" or "d."

Authentication: Verifying that a message that has been transmitted electronically does indeed come from the source indicated in the message.

Background process: A program that continues to execute without user intervention while the user is working with another program.

Balloon Help: A feature of System 7 that, when implemented by an application, displays balloons filled with help text as the user passes the mouse pointer over objects in the application's environment.

Balloon Help menu: The second menu from the right edge of the System 7 menu bar that controls whether Balloon Help is active.

Binary point: In a binary number, the separator between the whole number portion of the number and the fractional portion of the number.

Binary: The base 2 numbering system, used to number and represent just about everything inside a computer.

Bit: A binary digit; 0 or 1.

Boot blocks: The initial blocks on a disk from which a Macintosh can start up. Disks without a system folder have zeros in their boot blocks.

Bridge: A piece of hardware that can be used to connect two smaller AppleTalk networks into a larger network.

Byte: Eight bits; the unit with which main memory is measured; enough storage space for a single character.

Catalog file: A directory on a hard disk that keeps track of the hierarchical structure of files and folders.

Catalog: A collection of information cards and networked hardware that are accessible via PowerTalk.

Catalogs icon: A Desktop object that stores shared PowerTalk user catalogs.

CDEV: A control panel device.

Client/server: A network architecture in which one or more computers are designated as central repositories for shared files (servers). Users (clients) access the shared files over a network.

Clump: The amount of space (one or more allocation blocks) added to a file each time an application program needs more file space.

Command interpreter: System software used by operating systems without graphic user interfaces that accepts a typed command and interprets what the command is asking the operating system to do.

Command-driven user interface: An operating system without a graphic user interface that requires typed commands for communication between the user and the operating system.

Context switch: The change that occurs when one program gives up control of the CPU so that another program can run.

Copy-back cache: A data caching scheme in which changes to data are made to the cache but not necessarily to main memory. The changed data are written to main memory when the data must be swapped out of the cache to make room for different data.

Crash: An unrecoverable system error that prevents a program from continuing to execute, usually identified by the appearance of the Macintosh bomb box.

Creator: A four-character string that identifies the application that created a file.

Data bus: A portion of the electronic pathway that connects the parts of a computer. The data bus carries data from one component to another.

Data cache: A small amount of high-speed memory inside a CPU, used to hold data most likely to be used next.

Data Encryption Standard: A single-key encryption method accepted as a U.S. standard.

DES: The abbreviation for *Data Encryption Standard*.

Descender: A character in a font that descends below the baseline, such as "y" or "g."

Desktop file: A set of files that store resources such as icons and comments used by files on a disk volume.

Device driver: System software that acts as a translator between application programs and external devices such as monitors, printers, and disk drives.

Device-independent I/O: Input and output operations that are performed in exactly the same way, regardless of the type of hardware involved in the operation. The Macintosh provides device-independent I/O.

Digital signature: Electronic identification attached to a document that is going to be transmitted over a network to verify that the document does come from the source indicated in the document.

Disk interleave: The order in which the sectors on a disk track are filled.

Download (a font): Transfer a font from a hard disk to a printer.

Downloadable font: A PostScript font that is designed to be sent to a PostScript-compatible printer.

Drag and drop: Initiating actions by dragging an item over the icon of an object that you want to handle the item dragged on it. For example, you can open a document file by dragging it over the application with which you want to open it.

Droplet: An AppleScript script that has been saved so that it works by dragging objects on top of it.

Edition container: A file that holds a published edition.

Edition: A portion of a document that has been published so that it can be subscribed to by another document.

Enabler: A system extension that adds functions to the basic operating system. In most cases, system enablers tailor the Macintosh operating system for specific models of Macintosh.

Enclosure: Any file sent along with an electronic mail message.

Encryption: Changing the content of a file so that it is unintelligible to anyone without the access rights to decrypt it.

Ethernet: A type of network over which AppleTalk protocols can run.

Event queue: A waiting list of events that the Macintosh operating system and/or application programs must handle.

Event: Something that happens in the Macintosh environment, such as pulling down a menu or clicking the mouse button.

Event-driven: A program that detects and takes actions based on events.

Extent: A term that is synonymous with *allocation block;* the smallest amount of space that can be allocated to a file at any one time.

Extents overflow file: A disk directory file used when the disk Catalog is full to hold information about the hierarchy of files and folders on a disk.

File system: The hierarchy of files and folders on a single disk volume.

FKEY: A small program that performs a single action and quits. FKEYs were widely used before the introduction of keyboard macro packages. Therefore, existing FKEYs are often quite old and generally incompatible with System 7.

Font suitcase: A file that holds bitmapped or TrueType fonts.

Font: To a typographer, a single typeface in a single style and size; to a Macintosh user, a single typeface.

Forced quit: An action, initiated by pressing 1-Shift-Esc, that forces an application program to quit, hopefully without affecting other programs that are running. A forced quit is useful if an application crashes or hangs.

Foreground process: The program with which the user is currently interacting.

Fragmentation: The breaking up of storage (either main memory or disk space) into small, discontinuous chunks.

G: An abbreviation for *gigabyte*.

Garbage collection: The act of coalescing available blocks of storage (either in main memory or on disk) into a single large block to eliminate fragmentation.

Gb: An abbreviation for *gigabyte*.

Gigabyte: A little over a billion bytes (exactly 2^{30}, or 1,073,741,824).

Handler: A section of an AppleScript script designed to respond to a single Apple Event.

Hang: A program error in which the program appears to freeze.

Hexadecimal: The base 16 numbering system, used primarily as a shorthand for binary.

Hierarchical File System: The file system used on Macintosh external storage devices, which maintains a hierarchy of nested folders and files.

Hub: The center of a star network, used with 10 BaseT Ethernet configurations.

In Tray: The portion of a PowerTalk Mailbox in which received messages are placed.

Information card: A Finder object, usually stored in a PowerTalk catalog, that contains information about someone with whom you exchange electronic messages.

INIT: A program that loads into main memory during the system startup process. INITs can be control panel devices, device drivers, or system extensions.

INIT conflict: A problem that occurs when the presence of INITs in main memory interferes with the operating of application programs or other INITs.

Integer: A whole number; a number without a fractional portion.

Interrupt: An action that occurs when an external device such as a disk drive interrupts the normal processing of the CPU so that the CPU can take care of the external device.

Interval timer: An internal CPU clock that keeps track of how long a given process has been executing in the CPU.

K: An abbreviation for *kilobyte*.

Kernel: The portion of an operating system that provides basic services; the portion of the operating system that is always resident in main memory.

Key Chain: A PowerTalk security device that lets you unlock all PowerTalk services with a single Access Code.

Keyboard macro: A small program that is invoked by pressing a combination of keys. A keyboard macro performs its function and then quits.

Kilobyte: A bit more than 1,000 bytes (exactly 2^{10}, or 1,024).

Label: A category to which a file or folder can be assigned. The Macintosh operating system provides eight labels that can be associated with colors on Macintoshes that support color.

Letterhead: A special type of stationery document designed for use with the PowerTalk Mailer.

Line: A single circuit in a bus.

LocalTalk: A type of cabling over which AppleTalk network protocols can run.

Logic board: A computer's main circuit board, usually containing the CPU, main memory, and the system bus along with other integrated circuits.

Logical block: A unit of 512 bytes of disk storage; the smallest amount of storage that can be allocated on a disk; all or part of an allocation block.

M: An abbreviation for *megabyte*.

Macintosh File System: The hierarchical organization of files and folders used by the Macintosh operating system to organize the contents of a disk.

Mailer: A part of PowerTalk that attaches sender, recipients, subjects, and enclosures to an electronic mail message. The mailer can be used as part of AppleMail, a stand-alone application, or can be integrated into an application program.

Major switch: A context switch in which a background process becomes the new foreground process and the current foreground process becomes a background process.

Master directory block: A disk block that contains housekeeping information about a disk volume, such as its name, the number of files and directories in the volume, and the location of the volume's Catalog file.

Mb: An abbreviation for *megabyte*.

Mbyte: An abbreviation for *megabyte*.

MDB: An abbreviation for master directory block.

Meg: An abbreviation for megabyte.

Megabyte: Approximately 1 million bytes (exactly 2^{20}, or 1,048,576, bytes)

Memory-mapped I/O: Input and output operations that are performed like reads from and writes to memory, regardless of the type of hardware device.

Menu-driven user interface: A user interface with which a user interacts by making choices from menus, either with a pointing device such as a mouse, the arrow keys, or special key combinations.

Minor switch: A context switch in which one background process relinquishes control of the CPU to another background process.

Modeless dialog box: A dialog box that can be moved around the screen; a dialog box that can remain on the screen while the user performs other actions.

Mounted: The state of a disk volume when its icon appears on the Desktop. Only mounted volumes are available for use.

Multi-user operating system: An operating system that supports simultaneous use of the same computer by more than one user.

Operating system: A group of programs that manages the computer and its hardware.

Out Tray: A portion of the PowerTalk Mailbox that contains messages waiting to be sent.

Outline font: A font whose characters are specified by the outlines of the shapes of the characters.

Page: The unit of memory that a virtual memory system swaps between virtual storage on disk and real storage in RAM.

Page frame: A block of physical RAM into which a page of virtual memory can be placed.

Paged memory management unit: A memory management unit designed to handle virtual memory.

Page-description language: A computer language used to describe the content of a printed page to a printer.

Parameter RAM: Battery-backed RAM that contains startup and configuration information for a Macintosh, including the current date and time and the startup disk.

Partition: A section of a hard disk that is mounted on the Desktop as a disk volume.

Patch: Computer program code that is applied to an existing program to fix a problem.

Pathname: The sequence of folders through which the operating system must navigate to locate a file.

Peer-to-peer: A type of network configuration in which any Macintosh can temporarily act as a server and any Macintosh can temporarily act as a client.

PhoneNet: Network cabling that uses standard telephone lines to carry AppleTalk network signals.

PMMU: The abbreviation for paged *memory management unit.*

PostScript: A page-description language developed by Adobe Corp.

PowerTalk service: A general destination to which PowerTalk messages can been sent. Services can be Direct AppleTalk (peer-to-peer message transfer), Direct Dialup Mail (message transfer through a modem), or PowerShare. Multiple PowerShare services—one for each PowerShare server to which a user has access—are possible.

Print Monitor: The application that manages background printing.

Print queue: A group of files waiting to be printed.

Protocol: Specifications for data communications behavior. AppleTalk, for example, is a set of protocols.

Public-key encryption: A two-key cryptographic system in which a public key is used to encrypt a message and a private key is used to decrypt a message. Public-key encryption can also be used to authenticate that a message came from the source indicated in the message.

Publish: Make a portion of a document available for subscription by another document.

Quantum: The amount of time a process has control of the CPU before it must relinquish the CPU to give another process a change to run.

RAM disk: A portion of RAM set aside to act as a disk drive.

RAM partition: The portion of RAM in which a process runs.

Real address space: In a virtual memory system, the physical address range of physical RAM.

Recordable: A program from which an AppleScript script can be recorded.

Resource: The specification of an element of the Macintosh user interface such as a window, menu, or menu item.

Round robin scheduling: A type of preemptive process scheduling in which a process that gives up control of the CPU is placed at the end of a process queue. The process at the head of the queue is given control of the CPU.

Router: A device to connect two local area networks. Routers usually connect networks of different types (for example, LocalTalk and Ethernet). However, today bridges and routers provide much the same functions.

Run-only script: An AppleScript script that can be executed but not viewed or edited.

Screen saver: A program that places a moving image on the screen after a specified period of system inactivity to keep the image on the monitor from burning in.

Scriptable: A program that can respond to Apple Events.

Sector: A pie-shaped section of a disk surface.

Server: A computer on a local area network dedicated as a centralized repository of shared files.

Single-user operating system: An operating system designed to support only one user at a time.

Snapshot: A PowerTalk mail format; a bitmapped image of the contents of a file.

Spool file: A file stored on disk waiting to be printed.

Spool queue: A collection of spool files.

Spooling: Saving a spool file to disk so that the file can be placed in the spool queue.

Star controller: A piece of network hardware that sits at the center of a star network and acts to direct messages from sender to recipient.

Star: A network configuration in which all nodes are connected to a central device (a hub or star controller).

Startup monitor: The monitor on which the Finder's menu bar appears.

Subscribe: Import a published edition into a document.

Suitcase: A special type of folder into which a collection of bitmapped or True Type fonts can be placed.

Suite: The collection of Apple Events to which an application responds.

System beep: The sound made by the Macintosh speaker to alert the user to a variety of conditions.

System software: Software designed to manage a computer rather than perform useful work for the user.

Tag: A classification applied to a PowerTalk message.

Token Ring: A type of local area network in which all nodes are connected to a single network cable with connected ends.

Track: A circular section of a disk drive.

Transceiver: A device that connects a node to an Ethernet network.

Typeface: A style of type, such as Times, Helvetica, or Garamond.

User interface: The way in which a user interacts with computer programs, including the operating system.

Utility: An add-on program that adds functions to an operating system.

VIB: The abbreviation for *volume information block*.

Video RAM: RAM dedicated to storing the bitmapped image of a Macintosh monitor.

Virtual address space: The total range of addresses provided by a virtual memory scheme.

Virtual memory: A scheme to extend the range of RAM addresses available to a computer by using hard disk space as simulated RAM.

Volume bit map: A disk directory file that indicates which blocks in a disk volume are in use and which blocks are available.

Volume information block: Another term for a master directory block.

Volume: A hard disk partition or any type of removable media that mounts on the Macintosh Desktop as a separate disk icon.

VRAM: The abbreviation for *video RAM*.

Word: The number of bits that a computer typically handles as a unit. The Macintosh has a 32-bit word size.

Write-back cache: A caching scheme in which changes to data in a data cache are written both to the data cache and to main memory.

Write-through cache: Another term for a *write-back cache*.

X- height: The height of the letter "x" in a font.

Zone: A group of nodes in an AppleTalk network that are connected directly without the intervention of a bridge or a router.

INDEX

A

About This Macintosh, 159
AccessPC, 250–251
Address bus, 149
Address (in main memory), 148
Address (PowerTalk), 282–284, 306–307
Address space, 148, 164–165
Adobe Type Manager, 180–181
Adobe Type Reunion, 192–193
After Dark, 74–75
Agents (AppleScript), 327–330
Alarm Clock control panel, 44–45
Alarm clock software, 45–46
Alert sound, 53
Aliases, 23, 97–100
Allocation blocks (on a disk), 107, 108
AOCE, 267
AppDisk, 173

Apple File Exchange, 246
 Menu, 23
Apple Menu Items folder, 18–19
Apple Open Collaboration Environment, 267
AppleEvents
   Definition of, 7
   Identifying support for, 258
   Suites, 256–257
AppleMail
   Adding enclosures, 307–308
   And application programs, 313–314
   Changing sender, 302–303
   Choosing recipients, 303–307
   Entering subject, 307
   Forwarding mail, 324–325
   Letterheads, 309–312
   Parts of, 301–302
   Printing, 312
   Replying to mail, 323–324
   Sending letters, 308–309
AppleScript
   Agents, 327–330
   And PowerTalk, 327–330
   AppleEvents for, 256–258
   Definition of, 7
   Droplets, 263
   Environment for, 253
   Handlers, 263
   Recording scripts, 258–260
   Run-only scripts, 260–261
   Running scripts, 261–262
   Saving scripts, 260–261
   System extensions for, 256
   Writing scripts, 262–265
AppleShare
   Logging on, 242–244
   Using for file sharing, 234

AppleTalk
    Activating, 59
    Configuration, 220–222
Application menu, 29
Application programs
    AppleEvent suites for, 256–257
    Crashes, 140–144
    Enabling linking for, 238–239
    Get Info, 91
    Hangs, 140–144
    Launching, 127–130
    Recordable, 258
    Setting memory size for, 159–161
    Switching, 133–134
Ascenders, 176
At Ease, 37–39
Attributes, 116–117
AutoDoubler, 119–120

B

Background printing, 134–140
Background processes, *see* Process management
Backup (of a disk), 120–122
Base 16, 151
Base 2, 146–147
Balloon Help, 35–37
Balloon Help menu, 30
Before Dark, 48
Binary number system, 146–147
Bitmapped fonts, 176–178
Blinking rate, 46
Blocks (on a disk), 107–112
Bomb box, 140–141
Boot blocks (on a disk), 109
Bus, 148–150
Byte, 146–148

C

Cache Switch control panel, 144
Caches, 143–144, 168–170
Capture, 63
Catalog file (on a disk), 111–112
Catalogs (PowerTalk)
    AppleTalk, 282, 295–296
    Personal, 282, 284–285, 293–295,
        304–305
    Icon, 268–269
    PowerShare, 282, 296, 304
    Searching, 296–298, 305–306
CatFinder, 89–90
CDEVs, *see* Control panels
CD-ROM, 80
Centrises, 151–154
Chooser, 58–60, 234–235
Clean install, 26–29
Clipboard file, 19–20
CloseView, 33–35
Clumps (on a disk), 107
Color control panel, 57
Colors, 51–52
Command-driven user interface, 4–5
Command interpreter, 4
Compact Pro, 119
Compression (of disks), 119–120
Compression (of files), 117–119
Conflict Catcher, 206
Context switching, *see* Process management
Control panels, 23–25, 196–197
Control panels, *see also* names of specific control panels
Control Panels folder, 20
Cooperative multitasking, *see* Multitasking
Copy-back cache, 143–144
CopyDoubler, 93
Copying (files and folders), 92–94

Crash
    And CPU caches, 143–144
    Definition of, 140
    Recovering from, 141–143
Crash Barrier, 142–143
Creator (of a file), 127–128, 129–130
CryptoMatic, 69–71
Cursor blinking rate, 46
Cycle stealing, 124

D

Data bus, 149
Data cache, 143–144
Date, 42–43
Date & Time control panel, 48–51
Date formats, 48–51
Debugger, 141
Descenders, 176
Desk accessories
    Adapting for use under System 7, 197–198
    Definition of, 18–19, 197
DeskTape, 79
Desktop, 77–79
Desktop file, 109, 112–113
Desktop pattern, 46–48
DeskTop Valet, 95–96
Device drivers, 7, 150–151
Device drivers, *see also* Printer drivers
Dialog boxes, modeless, 41
Dictionaries, 258
Digital signatures, 331, 334–345
Directories, 82, 102
Disinfectant, 73
Disk cache
    Choosing size for, 169
    Operation of, 168–169
    Setting size of, 169–170

Disks
    Backing up, 120–122
    Blocks, 107–112
    Cataloging contents of, 89–90
    Compressing, 119–120
    Ejecting, 80–81
    Erasing, 106
    Formatting, 105–106
    Fragmentation, 114–115
    Interleave, 106
    Mounting, 78, 82
    Printing directories of, 102
    Rebuilding Desktop file, 113
    Renaming, 94–95
    Unmounting, 80–81
    Viewing contents of, 84–90
    Volumes, 79, 82
Disks, *see also* CD-ROM, Floppy disks, Hard disks, SyQuest drives, RAM disks
Disk management, 7
Document linking, 127–130
Double-click speed, 55–56
Downloadable fonts, 179
Drag and drop, 128–129

E

Easy Access, 32–33, 251
Edit menu, 30–31
Editions, *see* Publish and subscribe
Electronic mail, *see* PowerTalk
Encryption, 331, 332–334
Erasing (a disk), 106
Ethernet, 222–224
Events, 5
Events, *see also* AppleEvents
Exchanging files with MS DOS PCs, *see* MS DOS
Extensions, 196
Extensions folder, 20

Extensions Manager
  Accessing during system startup, 204
  Disabling INITs, 203
  Enabling INITs, 204
  Installing, 203
  Sets, 204–205
Extents overflow file (on a disk), 111–112

F

File exchange, *see* MS DOS
File format translation, 251–252
File menu, 30–31
File sharing
  Groups, 229–232
  Monitoring, 241–242
  Mounting remote volumes, 234–237
  Naming the computer, 227–228
  Stopping, 239–241
  Turning on, 228–229
  Unmounting remote volumes, 237
  Users, 229–232
  Volume permissions, 232–233
File systems, 82–83, 92
File translation, 251–252
FileGuard, 67–68
Files
  Aliases for, 97–100
  Compressing, 117–119
  Copying, 92–94
  Creators, 127–128, 129–130
  Finding, 100–102
  Get Info window, 91
  Icons for, 102–104
  Invisible, 115–117
  Labels for, 96–97
  Opening, 130–131, 132–133
  Renaming, 94–95

Recovering deleted, 106
Saving, 131–133
Types, 127–128, 129–130
Finder, 16, 29–31
Finder Shortcuts, 36
Finding (folders and files), 100–102
FKEYs, 198
Floppy disks, 112, 245–251
FolderBolt, 69–71
Folders
    Aliases for, 97–100
    Copying, 92–94
    Definition of, 82
    Finding, 100–102
    Get Info window, 90
    Icons for, 102–104
    Labels for, 96–97
    Renaming, 94–95
    Viewing contents of, 88–90
Font Harmony, 192–193
Font menu, 191–193
Fonts
    Bitmapped, 176–178
    Definition of, 175
    Display of, 180–181
    Downloading, 179
    Harmonizing, 191–193
    Installing, 186–187
    Measuring, 176
    Obtaining, 185–186
    Organizing, 189–191
    PostScript, 178–182
    Removing, 187–188
    Suitcases, 177–178, 188–189
    TrueType, 183–184
Fonts folder, 21–22
Forced quit, 141
Foreground processes, *see* Process management

Formatting (disks), 104–105
Fragmentation
    Disk, 114–115
    Main memory, 157–158
Freedom of Press, 182

G

Garbage collection, 158
General Controls control panel, 42–48
Get Info, 90–92
Gigabyte, 147–148
Groups, 229–232

H

HAM, 23–26
Hang
    And CPU caches, 143–144
    Definition of, 140
    Recovering from, 141-143
Hard disks, 79–80, 107
Harmonizing fonts, 191–193
Help menu, *see* Balloon Help menu
Hexadecimal, 151
Hiding windows, 133–134
Hierarchical File System, 82
Hub, 223

I

Icon 7, 104
Icon views, 84, 85, 86–87
Icons (file and folder), 102–104
In Tray
    Definition of, 314
    Using, 318–319
INIT conflicts

Definition of, 200
Diagnosing, 201–207
Information cards
    Group, 292–293
    User, 282–294
INITPicker 3, 206–207
INITs
    Deciding how many to use, 198–199
    Deciding which to use, 208–209
    Definition of, 195
    Loading, 199–200
    Viewing RAM requirements, 200–201
Installation, 26–29
Interleave (of a disk), 106
Interprocess communication, 6
Interrupt, 125
Interval timer, 125
Invisible files, 115–117

K

Key Chain (PowerTalk)
    Changing access code, 278
    Locking, 277
    Operation of, 270–271
    Unlocking, 277
    Window, 279
Key repeat rate, 55
Keyboard control panel, 55
Keyboard layout, 55
Keyboard macros, 63–65

L

Label menu, 30, 97
Labels, 30, 96–97, 98
Labels control panel, 97, 98
LaserWriter Font Utility, 179

Launching applications, 127–130
Letterheads (PowerTalk), 309–312
Lines (in a bus), 149
Linking, *see* Program linking
List views, 84–90
LocalTalk, 221–222
Logic board, 14
Logical blocks (on a disk), 107, 108

M

Mac486, 245
Macintosh File System, 82
Macintosh Classic, 155–156, 166
Macintosh II, 151–154, 167
Macintosh LC, 155–156, 167
Macintosh LC II, 155–156
Macintosh LC III, 151–154
Macintosh PC Exchange, 247–249
Macintosh Plus, 166
Macintosh SE, 166
Macros, 63–65
Mac386, 246
Mailbox (PowerTalk)
   Get Info, 314–315
   Icon, 268–269
   In Tray, 318–319
   Out Tray, 317–318
Mailbox menu, 315
Mailbox Preferences, 315–316
Mailer, *see* AppleMail
Major switch, *see* Process management
Map control panel, 60–62
Master directory block (on a disk), 109–111
Maxima, 172–173
Megabyte, 147–148
Memory, *see* Memory management
Memory control panel, 162, 167–168, 169–170, 171–172

Memory management
   Allocation, 150–156, 159
   And the system bus, 148–150
   Definition of, 5–6
   Fragmentation, 157–158
   Garbage collection, 158
   Measuring, 146–148
   Partitions, 156–157
   Problems with insufficient, 160–161
   Setting application size, 159–161
   Virtual memory, 164–168
Memory-mapped I/O, 150
Menu blinking rate, 46
Menus
   hierarchical, 23–26
Menus, *see also* names of specific menus
Minor switch, *see* Process management
Mode32, 149, 162–163
Monitors
   Protecting the screen, 74–75
   Setting colors, 51–52
   Setting shades of gray, 51–52
   Setting startup, 51–52
Monitors control panel, 51–52
Mounting disks, 78
Mouse control panel, 55–56
Mouse pointer speed, 55–56
MS DOS
   And AOCE, 267
   Floppy disks, 245–251
   Opening files, 251
   Sharable items, 244–245
   Translating file formats, 251–252
MultiFinder, 17
Multiprocessing, definition of, 6
Multiprogramming, definition of, 3, 6
Multitasking
   Cooperative, 6, 126–127

INDEX **377**

    Definition of, 3, 123–124
    Preemptive, 6, 124–126
Multi-user operating system, 8–9, 125

N

Networks
    AppleShare, 242–244
    AppleTalk, 220–222
    Client/server, 226–227, 242–244, 271–273
    Components of, 220
    Ethernet, 222–224
    File sharing
        Groups, 229–232
        Monitoring, 241–242
        Mounting remote volumes, 234–237
        Naming the computer, 227–228
        Stopping, 239–241
        Turning on, 228–229
        Unmounting remote volumes, 237
        Users, 229–232
        Volume permissions, 232–233
    Peer-to-peer, 8, 226–227, 274–275
    Program linking, 237–239, 241
    Zones, 224–226
NightWatch II, 69–71
Norton Utilities, 106, 114
Note Pad file, 22
Now Up-to-Date, 45–46
Now Utilities, 23–26, 132–133, 205–206
NowMenus, 23–26
Number display format, 56
Numbers control panel, 56

O

OneClick, 129–130
Opening files, 130–131, 132–133

Operating systems (general concepts)
   Definition of, 1
   Functions of, 3–4
   History, 2–3
   Multi-user, 8–9
   Serial-batch, 2–3
   Single-user, 8
Out Tray
   Definition of, 314
   Off-line use of, 325–326
   Using, 317–318

P

Page-description language, 178
Page frames, 164–165
Paged memory management unit, 164, 167
Pages, 164–165
Parameter RAM, 42
Partition (of RAM), 156–158
Pathname, 83
Peer-to-peer networking, *see* Networking
PhoneNet, 221–222
PlainTalk, 65
PMMU, 164, 167
Points, 176
PostScript, 178
PostScript fonts, 178–182
PowerBook 100, 166
PowerBooks, 170–172
PowerRules, 327–330
PowerShare, *see* PowerTalk
PowerTalk
   Access control, 275–278
   Addresses, 282–284
   Catalogs, 268–269, 284–285, 293–298, 304–305
   Definition of, 14

Direct Dialup Mail, 279, 283
Electronic mail
  Attaching digital signature, 334–336
  Enclosures, 307–308
  Letters, 200, 308–309
  Mailer, 301–314, 323–325
  Tags, 319–322, 327–330
  Validating digital signature, 336–337
Files for, 267–269
Getting an approved signer, 338–345
Guest users, 326–327
Information cards
  Definition of, 282
  Group, 292–293
  User, 284–292
Key Chain, 270–271, 275–278
Mailbox, 268–269, 314–325
Off-line use, 325–326
Peer-to-peer (AppleTalk)
  Addresses for, 282–283
  Catalogs for, 282, 295–296
  Setting up for, 274–275
PowerShare server
  Addresses for, 282–283
  Catalogs for, 282, 296
  Setting up for, 271–273
Scripts for, 327–330
Security, 331–345
Sending files and folders, 299–300, 307–308
Services
  Adding, 280–281
  Removing, 281
  Types of, 278–280
Setting up, 269–275
PowerTalk Setup control panel, 275–276
Preemptive multitasking, *see* Multitasking
Preferences folder, 22

Print queue
   Definition of, 135
   Removing files from, 137–138
Print queue, *see also* PrintMonitor
Printer drivers, 58–60
Printers, choosing, 58–60
Printing
   Background
      Canceling, 137
      Operation of, 134–135
      Scheduling, 138–139
      Turning on, 135–136
   PostScript to non-PostScript device, 182
   To a PostScript file, 180
PrintMonitor, 136–140
PrintMonitor Documents folder, 22, 135
Process, definition of, 6
Process management
   Background processes, 124, 134–140
   Context switching, 124
   Definition of, 6–7
   Foreground processes, 124
   Major switch, 124, 133–134
   Minor switch, 124
Processes, *see* Process management
Program linking
   Enabling applications, 238–239
   Enabling users, 239
   Stopping, 241
   Turning on, 238
Public key encryption, *see* Encryption
Publish and subscribe
   Definition of, 7
   Editions
      Definition of, 211
      Missing, 216
   Edition containers, 211, 217
   Operation of, 211–212

Publishing
    Creating edition, 212–213
    Setting update options, 213–214
Subscribing
    Linking to an edition, 214–215
    Setting update options, 215–216

Q

Quadras, 151–154
Quantum, 125
QuicKeys, 63–65
QuickTime, 255

R

RAM allocation, 151–156
RAM disks
    Advantages of, 170–171
    Disadvantages of, 170–171
    Operation of, 170–171
    Using, 171–172, 172–173
Real address space, 164–165
Rebuilding (Desktop file), 113
Recovering (deleted files), 106
Renaming (disks, files, folders), 92–94
Reminder, 45–46
ResEdit, 116–116
Resources, 17
Retrospect, 122
ROM, contents of, 14–15
Round robin scheduling, 125

S

Saving files, 131–133
Scrapbook, 57
Screen savers, 74–75

Screen shots, 62–63
ScriptEditor, 258–261
Scripts, *see* AppleScript
Sectors (on a disk), 105–106
Security
    Definition of, 8, 66
    PowerTalk, 331–345
    Using passwords, 66–71
    Virus protection, 72–74
Serial-batch operating systems, 2–3
Shades of gray, 51–52
Sharing Setup control panel, 228–229
Showing windows, 133–134
Shutdown command, 110
Signer files, *see* Digital signatures
Single-user operating system, 8
SoftPC, 245
Sound control panel, 53–54
SoundMaster, 54–55
Special menu, 30–31
Speech recognition, 65
Speed Disk, 114
SpeedyFinder 7, 37, 95, 99–100, 112, 129
Spool queue, *see* Print queue
Spool files, 135
Spooling, 134–135
Startup Items folder, 22, 30
Startup Manager, 205–206
Startup monitor, 51–52
Startup screen, 52
Startup volume, 81–82
Sticky Keys, 32–33
Stuffit, 118–119
Subscribe, *see* Publish and subscribe
Suitcase, 189–191, 198
Suitcases, 177–178, 188–189
SuperBoomerang, 132–133
Switching applications, 133–134

Symbionts, 200–201
SyQuest drives, 80–81, 89
System beep, 53
System bus, 148–150
System date, 42–43
System Enablers, 20–21
System extensions, *see* Extensions
System file, 17
System folder
    Contents of, 16–25
    Role in system startup, 15–16
System 7
    Hardware configuration for, 11
    Hardware updates, 13–14
    Installation, 26–29
    Languages, 12
System 7 Pro
    Definition of, 14
    Installing, 254
    Time zones for, 50
System 7 Pro, *see also* AppleScript, PowerTalk, QuickTime
System shutdown, 110–111
System software, definition of, 2
System startup, 15–16
System time, 42–43

T

Tags (electronic mail)
    Assigning, 320
    Definition of, 319
    Maintaining list of, 322
    Removing, 321
    Scripts for, 327–330
    Using as mail filters, 321
Tape drives, 79
Tape management, 7
Task, definition of, 6

Tasks, *see* Process management
TechTool, 113
10 BaseT, 223
Text highlighting color, 57
3D Folders, 104
Thick Ethernet, 222
Thin Ethernet, 222
32-bit addressing, 162–163
32-bit clean, 149–150
32-bit dirty, 149–150
Time, 42–43
Time formats, 48–51
Time sharing, definition of, 3
Time zone, 50
Tracks (on a disk), 105–106
Transceiver, 224
Trash
   Emptying, 93–94
   Get Info, 93–94
   Unmounting disks, 80
TrueType fonts, 183–184
Type (of a file), 127–128, 129–130
Type 1 fonts, 178
Type 3 fonts, 178
Typefaces, 175

U

User & Groups control panel, 229–230
User interface
   Command-driven, 4–5
   Definition of, 4
   Enlarging, 33–35
   Simplifying, 32–33, 37–39
   Menu-driven, 5
Users, 229–232, 239
Utilities, definition of, 2

V

View menu, 30–31
Views control panel, 85–88
Views (of disk contents), 84–90
Virtual, 168
Virtual address space, 164–165
Virtual memory
    Advantages of, 166
    And specific Macintosh models, 166–167
    Disadvantages of, 166
    Operation of, 164–165
    Starting, 167–168
Volume bit map (of a disk), 111
Volumes, 79, 82, 107–112
Volumes, *see also* Startup volume
Virtual, 154
Viruses, 72–74

W

Window border color, 57
Windows
    Hiding, 133–134
    Showing, 133–134
Word (as unit of data), 148
Write-back cache, 143–144
Write-through cache, 143–144

X

X-height, 176

Z

Zones, 224–226

Disk Instructions

The disk accompanying this book contains six utility programs for System 7. They have been compressed into a self-extracting archive with Compact Pro.

To install and decompress the programs:

1. Make sure you have at least 1Mb of free disk space on a hard disk or removable disk cartridge (for example, a SyQuest drive). (The decompressed files will also fit on a high-density floppy disk, but if you have only one floppy drive, installing onto a high-density floppy will require a lot of disk swaps.)
2. Insert the disk into a floppy drive.
3. Double click on the "Sample programs.sea" icon. A Save File dialog box appears.
4. Choose the disk volume and folder on which you want to store the decompressed files.
5. Click the **Extract** button. The files will be automatically decompressed and copied to the chosen location. When it is finished decompressing, you will be returned to the Finder.

Each of the six utility programs on the disk is stored in its own folder, along with instructions for installing and using the utility. The instruction files are text files that can be opened with a word processor or a text editor (for example, TeachText).

To read an instruction file, drag its icon over the program you want to open it. Because these text files have been created with a variety of word processors, double-clicking on a file's icon won't work if you don't have the specific program with which the file was created. The excception to the above is CatFinder. To read CatFinder's instructions, simply double-click on the documentation file's icon; it will open in its own reader.